The Connected Iron Age

The Connected Iron Age

INTERREGIONAL NETWORKS IN THE EASTERN MEDITERRANEAN, 900–600 BCE

Edited by Jonathan M. Hall
and James F. Osborne

The University of Chicago Press CHICAGO AND LONDON

The University of Chicago Press, Chicago 60637
The University of Chicago Press, Ltd., London

Published 2022
Printed in the United States of America

31 30 29 28 27 26 25 24 23 22   1 2 3 4 5

ISBN-13: 978-0-226-81904-4 (cloth)
ISBN-13: 978-0-226-81905-1 (e-book)
DOI: https://doi.org/10.7208/chicago/9780226819051.001.0001

Library of Congress Cataloging-in-Publication Data
Names: Hall, Jonathan M., editor. | Osborne, James F., editor.
Title: The connected Iron Age : interregional networks in the eastern Mediterranean, 900–600 BCE / edited by Jonathan M. Hall and James F. Osborne.
Other titles: Interregional networks in the eastern Mediterranean, 900–600 BCE
Description: Chicago ; London : The University of Chicago Press, 2022. | Papers from a conference held at the University of Chicago's Franke Institute for the Humanities in January 2018. | Includes bibliographical references.
Identifiers: LCCN 2021054320 | ISBN 9780226819044 (cloth) | ISBN 9780226819051 (ebook)
Subjects: LCSH: Iron age—Middle East—Congresses. | Middle East—History—To 622—Congresses. | Middle East—Ethnic Relations—History—To 1500—Congresses. | Middle East—Commerce—History—To 1500—Congresses. | Middle East—Antiquities—Congresses.
Classification: LCC GN780.32.N4 C66 2022 | DDC 939.4—dc23/eng/20211112
LC record available at https://lccn.loc.gov/2021054320

♾ This paper meets the requirements of ANSI/NISO Z39.48-1992 (Permanence of Paper).

Contents

Figures

Preface

The chapters in this volume originated in a conference that was held at the University of Chicago's Franke Institute for the Humanities in January 2018. The conference was made possible through the generosity of the Loeb Classical Library Foundation and the Franke Institute and Oriental Institute at the University of Chicago. We are also grateful for the support and assistance that was provided by faculty and graduate students in the Departments of Classics, History, and Near Eastern Languages and Civilizations.

Of the eleven papers originally delivered at the conference, revised versions of eight are included in this volume. Regrettably, we were unable to include the contributions by Lin Foxhall, Hermann Genz, and Ömür Harmanşah, although we did solicit additional chapters from John Papadopoulos and Michael Dietler, both of whom made substantive contributions to the conference, and a desire to extend the coverage of the contributions to include Egypt led to a chapter being commissioned from Brian Muhs. We would like to thank all those who participated in the conference that set the stage for the current volume. We are especially indebted to the anonymous peer reviewers, whose detailed and valuable comments improved the volume immensely.

We would like to express our gratitude to our colleagues at the University of Chicago Press, Rebecca Brutus, Jenni Fry, and Adrienne Meyers, and to John Donohue at Westchester Publishing Services. As always, Susan Bielstein has been a constant source of encouragement and support.

Transliterations of Greek names follow the conventions in the English version of Brill's New Pauly Online.

✷ CHAPTER 1 ✷

Interregional Interaction in the Eastern Mediterranean during the Iron Age

JAMES F. OSBORNE AND JONATHAN M. HALL

The Mediterranean Sea has been the focus of the Western scholarly tradition for generations. This is particularly true for classicists, of course, for the obvious reason that their subject matter is located squarely within it. For scholars of the Near East, the Mediterranean occupies a less concrete space—a critical part of larger geopolitical interactions at specific moments, yet nevertheless a region that is for the most part bracketed and set aside in favor of inland dynamics and the great river systems of Egypt and Mesopotamia. Mesopotamian sources, after all, referred to the Mediterranean as the Upper Sea and considered it one of the conceptual borders of their knowable world—a body of water that, once reached, signified their world conquests complete.[1] By the time of the Roman Empire this had changed and the Mediterranean for the first time became not just a geographical phenomenon but also a political one, unified under a single formation that controlled its entire perimeter. But if its geographical unity has never really been in doubt, and its political unification clearly achieved by the Romans, far more ambiguous is the Mediterranean's status as a distinct cultural unit.[2] Even subdividing the pre-Roman Mediterranean into smaller regions such as "east" and "west," it is unclear whether neighboring contemporary cultures shared common values that cut across their differences or even whether they participated in shared economic enterprises.

This volume on cultural and economic connectivity in the eastern Mediterranean during the early first millennium BCE assumes that interregional connections are an indisputable aspect of the archaeological, historical, and iconographic record of this time and place. This much, at least, is likely something on which everyone can agree. But from here the critical next step is interpretation and explanation, and at this point scholarly paths diverge rapidly. By way of introduction, this chapter describes the nature of the problem of Iron Age cultural connections as well as the various models and theoretical approaches that have been deployed to explain them. Interregional connections in the eastern Mediterranean during the early first millennium have been subjected to nearly the entire gamut of approaches adopted by archaeologists from broader currents in social theory in the second half of the twentieth century. Indeed, one could use the topic as a single case to explore the intellectual trajectory of the discipline. To the extent that multiple explanations compete with one another inconclusively, it follows that our evidence is not sufficient to accommodate a single explanatory model by way of resolution. Our primary argument here is that rather than see this overview of the state of the field as a cause for pessimism, we should turn the lack of scholarly consistency to our interpretive advantage—by recognizing, in other words, that the absence of a convincing overarching narrative is not a problem in need of solving, but rather the very nature of the beast. This is not intended to be mere academic sleight of hand, but instead a frank assessment that if the data are complicated and ambiguous, it is logical and necessary that our explanations be likewise. One way to present the necessary nuance is to do what this volume attempts—namely, to offer a collection of papers that provides texture to these debates by exploring new methods, theoretical approaches, and geographical regions that have not been treated in previous work.

That the Mediterranean and its subregions ought to be considered a unified cultural phenomenon at all is a notion we owe predominantly to Fernand Braudel, whose magisterial work *The Mediterranean and the Mediterranean World in the Age of Philip II* established the scholarly agenda on the Mediterranean for half a century.[3] One of the most famous passages to this effect comes from the preface to the English translation of the second edition, written over twenty years after the original 1949 publication:

> Two truths have remained unchallenged. The first is the unity and coherence of the Mediterranean region. I retain the firm conviction that the Turkish Mediterranean lived and breathed with the same rhythms as the Christian, that the whole sea shared a common destiny . . . with identical problems and general trends if not identical consequences. And the second is the greatness of the Mediterranean, which lasted well after the age of Columbus and Vasco da Gama, until the dawn of the seventeenth century or even later.[4]

It is the first of Braudel's "truths," the Mediterranean's putative fundamental unity, that has received the most sustained criticism. Scholars such as the anthropologist Michael Herzfeld have referred to this assessment of pan-Mediterranean phenomena, for example, an alleged system of honor and shame in every Mediterranean region, as "Mediterraneanism." Coined on the model of Edward Said's *Orientalism*, Mediterraneanism is an ethnocentric romanticizing of reality and an attitude that serves the cultural and political interests of the northern European and North American actors who use it even while it becomes a self-defeating component of the identity of Mediterranean countries themselves.[5]

Although Braudel's emphasis on geographical features and the *longue durée* implied that he felt this unified Mediterranean cultural identity was more or less timeless, his analysis of the medium- and short-term timescales, or conjunctures and events, was nevertheless restricted to the early modern period. The extension of Mediterranean unity into antiquity appeared several decades later with the publication of Peregrine Horden and Nicholas Purcell's equally ambitious *The Corrupting Sea: A Study of Mediterranean History*.[6] Perhaps as a result of its historical approach the book has been less explicitly treated by Iron Age archaeology concerned with interregional connections but, given its emphasis on Mediterranean connectivity, it is worth summarizing its central claims here.[7] For Horden and Purcell, the region's distinctive unity derives from a combination of the Mediterranean's unambiguously easy seaborne communications and its highly fragmented microregional topography.[8] Their approach is thus at once both macroscopic and highly local, emphasizing connections between an almost infinite number of locations.

The feature that ties together the Mediterranean's ever-shifting microregions is its natural disposition for connectivity: here too Horden and Purcell argue that more important than transhistorical routes established by the environment are the necessities for connectivity demanded by specific historical circumstances.[9] Indeed, despite our cartographic habit of drawing ribbons over terrain and sea lanes to mark the overarching routes that connect places across the Mediterranean (and elsewhere), the authors argue that zooming in on individual journeys, especially those of small-scale cabotage, reveals something more akin to Brownian motion—the stochastic movement of particles bouncing around in an infinite array of possibilities that are offered by the expanse of the sea and the multitude of ports on the perimeter. Such short-distance journeys made by small boats at much higher frequencies than the large-scale shipping lines of institutionalized commerce may have had a far greater impact on connectivity than their relative archaeological invisibility would imply. And, in order to make their claim that it is this connectivity that converts the plurality of disparate Mediterranean microregions into a unified whole, Horden and Purcell quote Claude Lévi-Strauss: "It is not the resemblances, but the differences, which resemble each other."[10]

If Horden and Purcell sought to extend the time depth of Braudel's unitary vision to roughly 1000 BCE, they never attempted to isolate its origins. That task was left to another monumental work, Cyprian Broodbank's volume *The Making of the Middle Sea.*[11] It really is a history of the Mediterranean from the beginning, stretching all the way back to 1.8 million years ago and dealing, at least initially, with geological episodes such as the Messinian Salinity Crisis and the Tethys Ocean. Broodbank is less explicit than Horden and Purcell about his theoretical and methodological assumptions, though it is clear that he understands the primary variables driving social change to be economic ones. It is also apparent that Broodbank recognizes the Mediterranean's distinctive unity as a phenomenon in no need of defense or justification. On the contrary, what he intends to do is seek its origin and chronological trajectory. To the question "Whence Mediterranean unity?," Broodbank's answer is that it developed and expanded slowly over time, with certain moments causing especially transformative developments toward cultural and economic networks.

One particularly significant episode was the Early Bronze Age, or what he calls the "long third millennium," during which large-scale societies first expanded in the region and long-range sea travel first blossomed with new maritime technologies.[12] But the most significant moment of all, the one where he suggests the Mediterranean can first be justifiably treated as a single unified phenomenon, is the early first millennium BCE—the period under consideration in this volume. By the tenth and ninth centuries, the northern half of the Mediterranean is for Broodbank squarely within a single maritime network; the southern half followed shortly thereafter in the eighth century with the revolutionary expansion of the Phoenicians.[13] Yet, despite Broodbank's assertion that the existence of labels for the sea during the early first millennium (Assyria's Upper Sea or sixth-century Greece's "our sea") indicates an ancient recognition of Mediterranean unity, it is doubtful whether this is anything more than a geographical phenomenon.[14]

Connectivity in the Eastern Mediterranean

The chapters in this volume are devoted primarily to connections during the early first millennium BCE across the eastern Mediterranean—

roughly the Aegean to northern Mesopotamia. The archaeological lines of evidence for this connectivity can be sketched briefly. In the tenth and ninth centuries, the Neo-Assyrian Empire had begun to expand out of northern Mesopotamia while the Syro-Anatolian kingdoms of southern Turkey and northern Syria had coalesced into a stable city-state system. Together these polities were part and parcel of a larger regional dynamic, influencing one another artistically and architecturally, and indeed sharing enough cultural traits that Ömür Harmanşah has referred to this time and place, including Urartu in eastern Anatolia, as a commonly shared cultural koine.[15] But even in this early period connections farther afield are apparent. The site of Lefkandi on the large Greek island of Euboea, for example, is well known for the many Near Eastern products discovered in graves dating to the early first millennium, one of which was a cremation burial that included Cypriot or Levantine balance weights and an heirloom north Syrian cylinder seal.[16] By the mid- to late ninth century, unambiguously Greek pottery, especially the ubiquitous Euboean pendent semicircle *skyphos,* appears on the Levantine coast at sites like Al Mina.[17] At the same time, settlers from the Phoenician city of Tyre decisively expanded at least to the city of Citium on Cyprus and substantial Phoenician finds are now found as far away as Huelva, west of the Straits of Gibraltar.[18] Meanwhile, isolated fragments of decorated orthostats from the Phrygian capital of Gordion point to tantalizing connections with the Syro-Anatolian world, as does the Phrygian-style decoration on the dress of King Warpalawa on the slightly later Neo-Hittite relief at Ivriz.[19]

The eighth century BCE appears to be a genuine tipping point in the volume of interregional connections, with the earlier steady drip of interactions turning into a constant stream. By the end of the century the Neo-Assyrian Empire had conquered almost the entirety of the ancient Near East, extending briefly even into Egypt a few decades later. The Assyrian capital cities are thus, by far, the most productive source of Syro-Anatolian and Phoenician objects, which were absconded with as booty during over two centuries of conquest. Phoenician settlements continue to expand westward, as do newly founded Greek settlements. And the material unearthed by archaeologists increases in volume significantly. Ornate eastern-style bronze shields appear across Crete—including one excavated from Eleutherna, where it was found sealing a ninth-century Geometric cinerary pithos alongside Late Geometric vessels from approximately 730 BCE.[20] Similarly, the monumental tombs at Salamis on Cyprus contained many luxury and nonluxury items very likely manufactured elsewhere.[21]

Indeed, such luxury items are common across the Near East and Aegean but materially they fall into two large categories: bronzes and ivories. Intriguingly, the same class of object might be found in both media, such as the horse frontlets found in ivory in the terrace building from the Early Phrygian Destruction Level at Gordion but in bronze at the Near Eastern site of Tell Tayinat and the Greek sanctuary of Hera on the island of Samos; likewise, the ivory horse blinkers also excavated at Gordion parallel bronze examples from the sanctuary of Apollo at Eretria.[22] Other items are necessarily restricted to bronze, like the enormous bronze cauldrons and their attachments that are found from Etruria to Urartu, or the bronze sheeting decorated in Near Eastern style with the repoussé technique found in a well at Olympia, the largest collection of such material found anywhere.[23]

But this highly selective overview of the archaeological evidence for connectivity during the early first millennium brings us immediately to some of the significant challenges that this evidence presents for interpretation. First and foremost is the lack of contemporary documentation explicitly concerned with the matter. There are no excavated archives of tablets like those from the Old Assyrian colony period detailing even indirectly the mechanisms of trade. Assyrian royal inscriptions describe tribute and booty from their conquered victims in Syro-Anatolia, but barely mention economic relations with Phrygia, Cyprus, or the Aegean, none of which offer pertinent texts of their own from dated archaeological contexts. The historical sources that do contribute to the question of interregional activity in the early first millennium, referenced in several of the chapters in this volume, are often later than the period they describe (or have controversial and unclear dating) and are generally restricted to the Greek world.

There are also, however, interpretive challenges with the archaeological record itself. First, the geographical distribution of material is hardly even across the eastern Mediterranean and the Near East. We have already noted, for example, the disproportionate volumes of non-Assyrian luxury items in the palaces of Assyria—something that is, at least, eminently explicable in terms of the political dynamics of the day. But how should we account for the sheer density of Near Eastern materials in the west? Why are Near Eastern bronzes and ivories found so frequently in mainland Greece, Euboea, and the Dodecanese islands but not really on the intervening Cycladic islands? And why is all of this Near Eastern material in the Aegean not paralleled by accompanying Greek luxury goods in the Near East? Instead, the only Greek material culture that finds its way to eastern shores consists of ceramics—especially the pendent semicircle *skyphos*, attested at sites such as Tell Tayinat and Al Mina.[24] These almost certainly do not represent the same investiture of time, energy, and resources as do decorated and inscribed bronze horse frontlets. One way around this problem is to reject it as a problem at all. Tamar Hodos (chapter 10 in this volume), for example, has argued that Greek pottery was a highly valued commodity in Iron Age Syria and southeastern Anatolia.[25] In any case, this evidentiary imbalance has resulted in a parallel imbalance in our scholarship: the frequency and quality of Near Eastern goods in the west coupled with the scarcity and modesty of Greek goods in the east has meant that classicists are more likely to engage with these issues than are Near Eastern scholars, for whom the subject of east–west exchange can more easily remain unnoticed.

Second, there is often a chronological indeterminacy at play in that the final resting places of many artifacts appear to be deposits dated decades or even centuries after the objects' creation. Austen Henry Layard found twelve bronze cauldrons and 120 bronze bowls, several inscribed in Aramaic, in Room AB of Ashurnasirpal II's Northwest Palace at Nimrud.[26] All of these likely date to the ninth or eighth century, but the palace was not destroyed until 612 BCE, rendering precise dating impossible. Again, in this case the objects' means of deposition remains comparatively uncomplicated—compared, that is, to similar objects' findspots in the west. Some bronzes are found in burial contexts, providing a reasonably secure date: examples include a bowl from Athens's Kerameikos cemetery in a burial dating to the early ninth century or the monumental tombs from Salamis. But the most famous of all bronzes found in Greek sanctuary sites were excavated from disturbed or mixed contexts, usually wells. For example, the eighth- to seventh-century bronze reliefs from Olympia were found in a well near the stadium. Their original forms had been refashioned to suit three korai statues in the early sixth century, while the well itself would not be closed to further votive deposits until the early fifth century.[27] The previously cited horse trappings from Eretria and Samos have similarly problematic contexts.[28] Indeed, the only thing that provides these horse trappings with their ninth-century date is the Aramaic inscription of Hazael present on the Samos frontlet.

One final challenge that requires mentioning is the continually accumulating evidence for interaction in the form of new ivories, bronzes, lyre player seals, and so on that are found every year, even though we know so little about the actual economic, technological, or political mechanics that transported these objects around the Mediterranean. An obvious place to look would be the sea floor, where shipwrecks could, in theory, inform us about maritime routes and cargo. Yet for the early first millennium BCE the sea floor is frustratingly bare.[29] Following the well-known Late Bronze Age wrecks of Uluburun and Gelidonya and a newly discovered one near Kumluca, we have precious few from the Iron Age.[30] Two mid-eighth-century Phoenician wrecks found off the coast of southern Israel by Robert Ballard and Lawrence Stager are exceptional in this regard.[31] Yet the slow increase in wrecks, some only newly discovered, commences only in the mid- to late seventh century, the end of the period this volume considers.[32] It is most curious that hundreds of shipwrecks are attested a few hundred years later, yet during the early first millennium, when at least some of the interactions evidenced above must have taken place by sea, the total number of wrecks can be counted on a single hand. Perhaps one answer lies in reducing our conception of the scale of the venture—both macroscopically, in the sense of the total amount of exchange that took place, and microscopically, in the sense of small ships going short distances for small-scale economic purposes, thus reducing the likelihood of wreckage.[33]

It is not enough to catalog archaeologically traceable instances of exchange; we also want to understand the agency behind such interactions. Here too a range of diverse scenarios has been offered to explain how objects ended up where they did.[34] In the case of Aegean sanctuaries, for example, it has been argued that imported objects were brought from the Near East by itinerant easterners—either traders, as argued by Günter Kopcke, or Walter Burkert's religious specialists.[35] But another possibility is that they were brought there by Greeks: Mervyn Popham and Irene Lemos have hypothesized Euboean warrior-traders while Sarah Morris (chapter 5) has proposed that such objects were taken, redistributed, and eventually deposited by Greek soldiers after a raid abroad.[36] As Jan Paul Crielaard aptly states,

> In the end, almost every piece or class of votive has provided its own, singular explanation for its presence in a Greek sanctuary, leaving us with . . . a motley crowd of victorious Cypriots and Cretan Kouretes at Delphi, Kimmerian invaders at Samos and Ephesus, [and] Thracian warrior-pilgrims and their wives undertaking long journeys from the interior of Thrace to the prominent Greek sanctuaries.[37]

But where Crielaard implies this multitude of contradictory but apparently equally plausible historical scenarios to be a problem that would be eliminated if only we could find additional evidence or the right theoretical tool, we are more inclined to see it as accurately indicative of the social context of the eastern Mediterranean during the early first millennium. This was a highly decentralized socioeconomic environment populated by agents who were largely autonomous and able to travel and trade freely only in the most general sense. The Neo-Assyrian Empire comes close to providing a political formation whose agency might explain the whole system—the empire has been argued to have directly inspired the Phoenician expansion, for example, although the recently discovered early Phoenician material from Huelva on the southwest coast of the Iberian Peninsula appears to reject this proposal—but even a maximalist position on the agency of the empire cannot include all of the interactions that we see.[38]

Population Movements

Thus far, most of the interactions we have been considering were relatively informal and involved individuals or small groups. However, literary sources, and especially Greek authors, were in no doubt that the eastern Mediterranean witnessed significant mass movements of populations at the start of what we know as the Early Iron Age: Ionian Greeks from the Greek mainland to the Anatolian coastline or Dorians from northern Greece to the Peloponnese and the islands of the southern Aegean;[39] Cimmerians from the Transcaucasian region to Asia Minor;[40] or Briges from western Macedonia to Phrygia.[41] Yet the archaeological quest to find the material reflex of these transplanted populations has proved to be frustratingly elusive. Finds of Protogeometric pottery in the coastal settlements of Asia Minor could conceivably lend some support to the tradition concerning the Ionian migration but there are also clear signs of material continuity across the Bronze Age/Iron Age transition while some sites, such as Miletus, appear to have been settled by Mycenaean Greeks already in the Late Bronze Age.[42] As for the Dorians, a succession of artifacts and cultural forms once thought diagnostic of an intrusive population have now emerged as already present in the Mycenaean world or first attested in regions that later identified as Ionian rather than Dorian.[43] Were these movements literary fictions?

The notion that whole ethnic groups should be identifiable in the material cultural record was a basic tenet of the culture-historical approach pioneered by Gordon Childe. For Childe, an archaeological "culture" (i.e., "a plurality of well-defined diagnostic types that are repeatedly and exclusively associated with one another") should be "the material expression of what today would be called a people."[44] Yet, from the 1950s, the seemingly self-evident relationship between people and things began to be challenged by "processualist" archaeologists, who were more inclined to seek explanation in long-term economic and environmental factors. Susan and Andrew Sherratt, for example, charted the economic patterns present in the region in the early first millennium BCE, noting that economic trade was now, unlike in the Bronze Age, taking place more or less independently of the state; that the rise of ironworking was not only significant technologically but also socially transformative; and that the foundation of settlements far afield from cultural homelands was motivated by an economic appetite for raw materials, especially metals.[45] These forces expanded over time until they formed a genuine world-system by the sixth century.[46] As for social collectivities, David Clarke saw no a priori reason why archaeological patterns should equate with ethnic groups.[47] Others even began to question the validity of archaeological cultures themselves.[48]

This theoretical volte-face is especially evident in discussions of archaeological style. Traditionally, stylistic similarities within classes of objects were taken to serve as an index of social interaction; conversely, stylistic changes and discontinuities were attributed to invasions or migrations. Style was, in other words, viewed as a passive trace element—the unconscious, unintended residue of behavior.[49] It was also regarded as a supplementary, information-bearing element, distinct from an artifact's function. In 1977, however, James Sackett argued that style inheres in function, since it represents a choice of a few or just one among a range of equally viable ("isochrestic") options, all of which are dictated by the technological traditions in which its users have been enculturated.[50] It is this notion that informs Marian Feldman's definition of style in her contribution to this volume (chapter 4) as "ways of doing things," as well as Sarah Morris's caution that shared practices may be more important than individual objects in illustrating connectivity. Furthermore, ethnographic fieldwork has made it abundantly clear that style may also play a more active or "iconological" role, employed to target individuals beyond the immediate scope of the household or residence group and to communicate notions of social and cultural distinction.[51]

Yet there clearly was considerable mobility at the end of the Late Bronze Age. The destruction of the Mycenaean palaces circa 1200 BCE, the abandonment of entire regions such as Laconia, and the appearance, during the succeeding Late Helladic IIIC phase, of new "refugee" sites such as Lefkandi on Euboea, Perati in eastern Attica, or Kavousi Vronda on Crete testify to unsettled conditions and new patterns of settlement.[52] Similarly, although the dialectal similarities that link the Peloponnese with Crete and the Dodecanese, or Attica with Euboea, the Cyclades, and Ionia *could* be explained as a consequence of sustained contact rather than linguistic inheritance, there really is no other way of explaining the close affiliation between the Cypriot and the Arcadian dialects than to assume a significant movement of population eastward from the central Peloponnese.[53] Similar phenomena are attested across Anatolia, northern Syria, and the Levant, including shifting settlement patterns, new language distributions such as Hieroglyphic Luwian's spread south of the Taurus Mountains, and the presence of foreign material culture such as Aegean-style pottery, all accompanied by direct and indirect textual references to new populations.[54] The reason for the mismatch between the material evidence and the literary traditions concerning migrations is explained by closer analysis of the latter, which reveals them to be cumulative amalgams of diverse discourses, some of them mutually contradictory, that served the function of chartering social and ethnic affiliations in later historical periods.[55] In other words, the narratives related to migrations are best seen as ordered and rationalized representations of a reality that was far messier with a view to justifying social conditions in the present rather than preserving the memory of a past for its own sake.

The same goes for the later movements that brought Greek speakers to the coasts of South Italy and Sicily and, eventually southern France, Spain, northern Africa, the Sea of Marmara, and the Black Sea. Modern scholarship tends to distinguish between the migrations that are supposed to have taken place at the end of the Bronze Age and what is conventionally—if a little misleadingly—termed "colonization" in the last third of the eighth century, but ancient authors such as Thucydides (1.12.4) made no such distinction.[56] In fact, as in the case of migration traditions, the narratives that recount these new overseas Greek settlements were often written several centuries after the events they purport to describe and they are sometimes just as internally contradictory.[57] As with the migration traditions, "colonial" foundation stories seek to reconcile and adjudicate between competing narratives, constructing a tidy "official" account that is more concerned with articulating a corporate identity in the present than in transmitting historical realia.

This is not, of course, to cast doubt on the fact that Greek speakers really did set out from the mainland to establish new settlements abroad. The attestation of a Euboean script on inscribed pieces of pottery from the hypogeum of Methone in Macedonia would seemingly confirm Plutarch's notice (*Moralia* 293a–b) that Methone had been founded by Eretria, but there are also indications for influence from the alphabets of Boeotia, Argos, Ithaca, Crete, and Attica.[58] Furthermore, imported Corinthian wares are found among the earliest material assemblages at most colonial sites, whether or not they claimed to be Corinthian foundations, while ceramics attributed to an Achaean koine are found not only in those Italian cities that adduced Achaean origins but also at sites in eastern and southeastern Sicily, which did not.[59]

Projecting Ethnicity

One pitfall that arises from the existence of literary documentation is the tendency to "ethnicize" material assemblages. One can hardly discuss models of east–west interaction without mentioning the work of Sir John Boardman, whose volume *The Greeks Overseas,* first published in 1964, represented the standard reference on the topic for decades.[60] In some respects, at least, Boardman's work can be situated within the culture-historical tradition: the presence of Greek pottery in a settlement indicates the existence of resident Greeks. This is an assumption that has consistently underlain Boardman's copious writings on the earliest levels of Al Mina, for example, which he believes to be one of the first Greek colonies.[61] According to this logic, changes in the archaeological record from the ninth to the seventh centuries are the result of a migration of Greeks outward from the Aegean and Phoenicians away from the Levant. In the case of the Greeks, however, this "ethnicization" of material culture can lead to a curious double standard that becomes apparent when we consider the so-called Orientalizing movement.

Toward the end of the eighth century, the artifacts and cultural forms—including literary idioms and myths—of the Aegean basin begin to reveal patent influences from the Near East.[62] Imported North Syrian bronze cauldrons were swiftly imitated and modified by craftspeople in the Aegean; mythical beasts of Near Eastern origin, such as griffins, chimeras, and tritons together with motifs such as palmettes and lotuses begin to grace Greek—and especially Corinthian—pottery; the so-called Daedalic style of seventh-century Greek sculpture owes many of its characteristics to North Syrian models while metronomic analysis of Greek kouroi reveals their derivation from Egyptian prototypes.[63] We find a similar phenomenon in South Italy and Sicily and, a little later, Sardinia and Iberia, where indigenous practices and cultural forms begin to demonstrate clear influences from the Aegean basin. Yet, while it is commonly stated that the cultural traditions of the west were Helleniz*ed* (a passive verb), the term used to define cultural borrowing in the Aegean is Orientaliz*ing* (an active participle). This Hellenocentric point of view derives from the belief that the Greeks—unlike the populations of the Levant or central Mediterranean—were more active and discerning consumers of the cultural traditions of others. As Boardman puts it, "the Greeks chose, adapted and assimilated until they produced a material culture which was wholly Greek, despite all the superficial inspiration which the east provided."[64]

Most recent writing on the topic of overseas settlements is likely to cite a variety of inspirations drawn from anthropology and social theory of the late twentieth century. Taking inspiration from North American French colonial history, Irad Malkin argues that early Greek settlements abroad, such as Pithecussae and Cumae in Italy, were characterized not by the simple adoption of Greek culture by local Italic and Etruscan elites in a process of acculturation, but rather by the adaptation of Greek cultural expressions into new traits that were mutually intelligible to all parties.[65] Indeed, further or renewed investigations at sites such as Pithecussae or Sicilian Naxos have revealed that the earliest contexts for these interactions were far more complex than a simple colonialist model would suggest.[66]

Similarly, postcolonialist scholarship led Joanna Luke and Tamar Hodos to counter Boardman's assumption of Greek priority in east–west interaction with an examination of the role of Anatolian and Levantine actors in the relationship.[67] By the early 1990s it had become apparent that Levantine material culture arrived in Euboea before Euboean ceramics appeared in the Levant, indicating that Near Easterners had at least as much agency in early first millennium Mediterranean interactions as did the Greeks, and may even have precipitated it.[68] More thorough examination of the admittedly limited available material culture from Al Mina, for example, shows many local archaeological traits including previously unpublished locally produced pottery, while a new reading of Tiglath-pileser III's Iran Stele suggests that in fact the site belonged squarely within the orbit of a local Syro-Anatolian kingdom—likely Patina, with its capital at Tell Tayinat.[69] With such insights it becomes apparent that the relationship was as much easterners looking west as vice versa. Likewise, the art historians Marian Feldman and Ann Gunter (chapter 8) have turned to a number of recent anthropological and sociological concepts such as collective memory, agency and practice, and the social life of gift-given objects to explain why such interactions may have taken place among craft specialists, especially in the Assyrian imperial political context.[70]

Nor should we necessarily conceive of these interactions as taking place between preconstituted ethnic categories. Malkin has actually suggested that the emergence of an overarching Hellenic identity was the consequence of—rather than prerequisite for—Mediterranean-wide connectivity.[71] Drawing explicitly on network theory, Malkin posits that the connectivity established between multiple nodes created a multidirectional, decentralized network that facilitated information flow, ultimately creating a "small Greek world." The intensity of certain flows gave rise to clustered bundles, or regional networks (e.g., the connections between Rhodes, Phaselis, Gela, and Acragas), but a small number of random ties between distant nodes (e.g., itinerant professionals) created "shortcuts" that offered connectivity across the entire network.

To be sure, Malkin's model is open to certain objections. From a methodological point of view, the results are practically guaranteed at the outset because his nodes are selected on the basis of their being Greek maritime cities; the connections that he traces between these nodes are thus hardly surprising. Instead, it would perhaps have been more illuminating to focus on ethnically neutral categories of material to see what patterns emerged.[72] Furthermore, as Michael Dietler notes in chapter 11 of this volume, Malkin's approach is functionalist in that it attributes agency to a system that determines group and individual behavior; the networks that he "discovers" are ultimately more descriptive than explanatory. Perhaps it is for reasons like these that the contributors to this volume have generally eschewed network approaches as a means to explain their particular case studies, despite recent calls to consider network theory a powerful tool for illuminating maritime connectivity in the Mediterranean in all time periods.[73] At the same time, however, Malkin does propose a scenario that is worth considering in more detail. In discussing the construction of a "Phocaean" network in the western Mediterranean during the sixth century, he suggests that a massive influx of Phocaean refugees circa 545 BCE, culminating in the Battle of Alalia five years later, disrupted the existing equilibrium, resulting in a "fracturing" into Greek, Phoenician, and Etruscan "spheres of influence."[74] This would seem to lend weight to Dietler's caution that connectivity does not necessarily lead to greater cultural fusion or uniformity. Dietler offers the example of the Olympic Games, where shared norms, conventions, and practices actually contributed to reifying civic and cultural boundaries. Along similar lines, it would be interesting to examine the extent to which shared social practices such as drinking, feasting, and burial that brought together different ethnic groups (as described by Sarah Morris in this volume) actually contributed to the construction and maintenance of ethnic boundaries.

Emic and Etic Approaches

We have mentioned above the scholarly tendency to talk in terms of, for example, "Greek" pottery and architecture or "Phoenician" bowls. This is fine so long as we remember that it is a convention—a type of shorthand for describing artifacts whose form, style, and manner of manufacture have antecedents in the Aegean basin or the Levant, respectively. But we should never forget that this is *our* convention. One way of introducing conceptual clarity would be to examine these issues through the lens of the emic versus etic dichotomy, terms originally borrowed by anthropologists from the field of linguistics.[75] An "emic" viewpoint denotes the subjective perception of the insider, "etic" the supposedly more detached analysis of the outsider.[76] Ancient historians and archaeologists are, however, at a disadvantage compared with anthropologists, who can at least interrogate their subjects. As Carlo Ginzburg explains, historians typically "start from etic questions, which are inevitably anachronistic or ethnocentric, but can, if duly reworked, open up the possibility to rescue from the actors some emic answers."[77] In his chapter, Michael Dietler doubts whether archaeological evidence by itself could ever yield emic understandings of ancient social worlds. This is not to deny that material culture can be used actively and self-consciously to communicate an emic perspective but rather to question whether there are any criteria by which we can recognize the expression of that perspective. One thing, however, that distinguishes the archaeology of the eastern Mediterranean from world archaeology more generally is precisely the existence of self-conscious textual documentation—an emic viewpoint provided, of course, that we keep in mind all the interpretive problems noted above.

The case of the Phoenicians is illuminating in this respect. Actors named as Phoenicians appear in Greek literature as early as the Homeric epics, where they are portrayed as skilled craftspeople and merchants. Nevertheless, Irene Winter has argued that "the Phoenicians of the *Iliad* and *Odyssey* must be seen as neither historical nor ethnographic entities, but rather as well-crafted literary tropes," Rebecca Martin questions whether a distinct Phoenician culture predates the sixth century, and Josephine Quinn dismisses them altogether as an invention of the Greeks.[78] Conversely, in her contribution to this volume, Carolina López-Ruiz (chapter 2) argues strongly for the existence of a population that shared a language, a pantheon, an iconography, and specific crafts and industries that largely map onto networks that are described as Phoenician by Greek authors. What they lacked—and this is critical—was a literature, or at least literature that has survived from this period. The ethnonym "Phoenician" is, as López-Ruiz admits, a coinage of Greek speakers; we do not know whether they gave a collective name to themselves or, if they did, what it was. The term, then, is etic even if it is a contemporary etic viewpoint rather than a modern imposition. Nevertheless, López-Ruiz goes further and suggests that Greek etic characterizations of the Phoenicians were, in fact, informed by Phoenician emic self-representations. This is not at all impossible: after all, Greeks are Hellenes, no less today than when the Romans first gave them this name, while Germans, Allemands, Tedeschi, and Deutsche are not recognizably different groups. Along similar lines, it is at least possible that the etic description in an Assyrian text of an undergarment as "Phrygian" (discussed by Ann Gunter in chapter 8) is itself predicated on an emic promotion of a certain sort of dress as having an ethnic salience.

Themes of the Present Volume

A few significant aspects of Iron Age Mediterranean connectivity have not yet been sufficiently explored or recognized and might provide, if not conclusive answers to how and why all of this took place, at least productive avenues of insight. These themes provide the orientation around which the chapters contained in this volume are structured. The first is that Horden and Purcell's metaphor of Brownian motion in the eastern Mediterranean is at least as appealing an explanatory mechanism of interregional interaction as imperial processes in Syro-Anatolia and northern Mesopotamia. Any single narrative is incapable of encompassing the sheer diversity of evidence for Iron Age connectivity in the region. This is not because of a postmodernism-inspired skepticism of metanarratives in general; it simply seems implausible that one model will be empirically able to incorporate all of the material we already have at hand. One might even suggest that the only unifying feature that is inherent to Iron Age connectivity is its complexity and uniqueness. It is partly for this reason that in her chapter Tamar Hodos argues for a globalization model as a productive way to describe what was held in common across the Mediterranean in the early first millennium BCE even while remaining faithful to the large degree of variability.

Second, although the emphasis on human agency and the concomitant reluctance to appear environmentally deterministic (a characteristic of scholarship since the 1990s) was a necessary and important intellectual development, accounts of Iron Age Mediterranean connectivity have not paid sufficient attention to geographical and ecological considerations. For example, an illustration from Broodbank's *Making of the Middle Sea* shows relative indentation around the coast of the Mediterranean by dividing the coastal zone into cells and shading them according to how many surrounding cells also contain coastal elements.[79] Darkly shaded parts of the Mediterranean coast are therefore areas with a greater amount of coastline in the form of bays and harbors, suggesting regions where maritime activity is well suited to the coastal topography. That the Aegean is so densely shaded is no surprise, with Euboea, the Cyclades, and the Dodecanese standing out especially. But other locations are equally intriguing given what we know of the early first millennium—especially the zone of eastern Cyprus occupied by Citium, with its well-attested Phoenician connections, and the northeast corner of the Mediterranean where the trading hub of Al Mina is located.

In some cases, then, it seems unavoidable that the environment played a partially determining role in connectivity. In these instances, considering the relationship of local environmental forces to local human dynamics—what Horden and Purcell term microecologies—might prove helpful. One methodological avenue that has so far seen only limited application in the question of Iron Age interregional relations, but that might help relate specific geographical settings to exchange networks, is the application of geochemical analyses to the objects we treat as proxies of exchange. These techniques can be a powerful complement to the stylistic properties that typically guide our attributions of place.[80] For example, neutron activation analysis and X-ray fluorescence have demonstrated that a subset of Cypriot White Painted and Bichrome vessels in coastal Turkey was, in fact, produced locally despite being macroscopically identical to vessels genuinely imported from Cyprus. This provides high-resolution geographical information that hints at a much greater diversity and complexity of ceramic production and movement than traditional typological attributes provide alone.[81] In the present volume, Susan Sherratt (chapter 6) presents an argument for how cultural factors together with the restricting geography of the Dardanelles and the Bosporus conspired to block Greek settlements from the Black Sea until significantly later than was the case in the central Mediterranean.

Third, and closely related, we have perhaps devoted too much attention to the exchange of luxury goods and not enough on connectivity wrought by small-scale, irregular, quotidian, short-distance transfer. This one is harder to adjust for, since we can only analyze the data that we have and, as noted above, we mostly lack the shipping evidence that would provide precisely this type of information until the late seventh century. But it is significant that when they do appear at the very end of the period under consideration here, several of these shipwrecks contain evidence for olive and grape transport, not prestige items: examples include the eighth-century *Tanit* and *Elissa* shipwrecks with their dozens of torpedo amphora.[82] Back on land, geochemical sourcing of artifacts and comparisons with existing large archival geochemical datasets will also be able to point us in this direction, as will high-resolution surface surveys of archaeological landscapes that are as interested in rural dynamics as in the well-known urban centers.[83] As Marian Feldman argues in her contribution, however, an important distinction is not whether the material under examination is luxurious or mundane but rather how goods of all kinds are examined. Indeed, she proposes that close study of elite items like "Phoenician" metal bowls and their resistance to stylistic typologies challenges our tendency to "ethnicize" such materials (see the discussion above).

Fourth, we would do well to expand our geographical ambit from the usual suspects of the Levant, Cyprus, the Aegean, and to a lesser extent Italy—regions that are indeed explored in the present volume by Sarah Morris and by John Papadopoulos (chapter 7)—to encompass areas where evidence for connectivity seems sparser or less direct, but in fact may simply be less often investigated with these questions in mind.[84] Here one thinks of central Anatolia in particular, which clearly had economic and cultural relationships with both western Anatolia and the Aegean as well as Syro-Anatolia and northern Mesopotamia, as Ann Gunter demonstrates in her chapter in this volume. Likewise, explicit scholarly engagement with Egypt's role in eastern Mediterranean connectivity at this time is infrequent, even though the hallmark of Phoenician material culture is its allegedly Egyptianizing motifs. By exploring the economic relations between Egypt and Phoenicia throughout the Mediterranean, Brian Muhs (chapter 9) does much to bring the critically important Egyptian material into the conversation on Iron Age connectivity, while Susan Sherratt draws our attention to the often-neglected Black Sea. Likewise, the networks of connections do not at all end at the coastline or at the Assyrian capital cities on the Tigris, but rather spread their lines of communication very far inland and to related shores. This putative tension between hinterland insularity and coastline connectivity is robustly challenged by Catherine Kearns (chapter 3), who argues that a strict dichotomy in Iron Age Cyprus between connected coastal urban centers and isolated rural settlements is theoretically and empirically unfounded.

These four themes are considered directly and indirectly throughout this volume. Emerging frequently in the pages that follow is a productive tension between so-called top-down and bottom-up approaches to Mediterranean objects and cultures—a tension that manifests in two ways. On the one hand are those advocating for studying more closely the non-elite places, people, and things that have been neglected by previous generations of scholarship too focused on precious goods and mythical narratives. On the other are authors who propose taking the level of analysis down from metanarratives of cultural trajectories and into fine-grained analyses of objects—elite or otherwise—that have the potential to rebuild narrative structures from the ground floor. Combined with the themes just outlined, such perspectives cumulatively point toward dynamic new directions in the study of Mediterranean Iron Age interregional interaction.

Notes

1. E.g., the statement of Sargon of Akkad (ca. 2334–2284 BCE) that "To Sargon, lord of the land, the god Enlil gave no rival. The god Enlil gave to him the Upper Sea and the Lower Sea, so that from the Lower Sea to the Upper Sea, citizens of Agade held the governorships of the land." Douglas R. Frayne, *The Royal Inscriptions of Mesopotamia: Early Periods*, vol. 2, *Sargonic and Gutean Periods* (Toronto: University of Toronto Press, 1993), inscription E2.1.1.1, lines 67–85. See also Keiko Yamada, "'From the Upper Sea to the Lower Sea': The Development of the Names of Seas in the Assyrian Royal Inscriptions," *Orient* 40 (2005): 31–55.

2. The geographical unity of the Mediterranean is simply the coincidence of plate tectonics, of course. See Alastair Ruffell, "Geological Evolution of the Mediterranean Basin," in *The Mediterranean: Environment and Society*, ed. Russell King, Lindsay Proudfoot, and Bernard Smith (London: Arnold, 1997), 12–29.

3. Fernand Braudel, *The Mediterranean and the Mediterranean World in the Age of Philip II*, trans. Siân Reynolds, 3 vols. (New York: Harper and Row, 1972 [1966]).

4. Braudel, *Mediterranean and the Mediterranean World*, 14.

5. Michael Herzfeld, "'As in Your Own House': Hospitality, Ethnography, and the Stereotype of Mediterranean Society," in *Honor and Shame and the Unity of the Mediterranean*, ed. David D. Gilmore (Washington, DC: American Anthropological Association, 1987), 75–89; Herzfeld, "Practical Mediterraneanism: Excuses for Everything, from Epistemology to Eating," in *Rethinking the Mediterranean*, ed. William V. Harris (Oxford: Oxford University Press, 2005), 45–63; Edward W. Said, *Orientalism* (New York: Pantheon Books, 1978); and Ian Morris, "Mediterraneanization," *Mediterranean Historical Review* 18, no. 2 (2003): 30–55.

6. Peregrine Horden and Nicholas Purcell, *The Corrupting Sea: A Study of Mediterranean History* (Malden, MA: Blackwell, 2000).

7. See, e.g., papers in Cavan Concannon and Lindsey A. Mazurek, eds., *Across the Corrupting Sea: Post-Braudelian Approaches to the Ancient Eastern Mediterranean* (Abingdon, UK: Routledge, 2016); William V. Harris, ed., *Rethinking the Mediterranean* (Oxford: Oxford University Press, 2005); and Peter N. Miller, ed., *The Sea: Thalassography and Historiography* (Ann Arbor: University of Michigan Press, 2013).

8. Horden and Purcell, *Corrupting Sea*, 5.

9. Horden and Purcell, *Corrupting Sea*, 124, 130.

10. Horden and Purcell, *Corrupting Sea*, 51, 53; Claude Lévi-Strauss, *Totemism*, trans. Rodney Needham (Boston: Beacon Press, 1963), 77. Braudel was friends with Lévi-Strauss and considered his historical work on extremely long-term processes to be parallel with structuralism's emphasis on deep-seated, immutable structures. Braudel also took methodological inspiration from Lévi-Strauss, including the

quantification of cultural phenomena and interdisciplinary ambitions. See Fernand Braudel, "History and the Social Sciences: The *Longue Durée*," *Review (Fernand Braudel Center)* 32, no. 2 (2009): 171–203; and Immanuel Wallerstein, "Braudel on the *Longue Durée*: Problems of Conceptual Translation," *Review (Fernand Braudel Center)* 32, no. 2 (2009): 155–70.

11. Cyprian Broodbank, *The Making of the Middle Sea: A History of the Mediterranean from the Beginning to the Emergence of the Classical World* (Oxford: Oxford University Press, 2013).

12. Broodbank, *Making of the Middle Sea*, 292.

13. Broodbank, *Making of the Middle Sea*, 445–584.

14. Broodbank, *Making of the Middle Sea*, 20.

15. Irene J. Winter, "Art as Evidence for Interaction: Relations between the Assyrian Empire and North Syria," in *Mesopotamien und Seine Nachbarn: Politische und kulturelle Wechselbeziehungen im alten Vorderasien vom 4. bis 1. Jahrtausend v. Chr*, ed. Hans Jörg Nissen and Johannes Renger (Berlin: Rheimer, 1982), 355–82; and Ömür Harmanşah, *Cities and the Shaping of Memory in the Ancient Near East* (Cambridge: Cambridge University Press, 2013), 26.

16. Irene S. Lemos, *The Protogeometric Aegean: The Archaeology of the Late Eleventh and Tenth Centuries BC* (Oxford: Oxford University Press, 2002); Mervyn R. Popham and Irene S. Lemos, "A Euboean Warrior Trader," *Oxford Journal of Archaeology* 14 (1995): 151–57; and John H. Kroll, "Early Iron Age Balance Weights at Lefkandi, Euboea," *Oxford Journal of Archaeology* 27, no. 1 (2008): 37–48.

17. Rosalinde Kearsley, *The Pendent Semi-Circle Skyphos: A Study of Its Development and Chronology and an Examination of It as Evidence for Euboean Activity at Al Mina* (London: Institute of Classical Studies, University of London, 1989); and Joanna Luke, *Ports of Trade, Al Mina and Geometric Greek Pottery in the Levant* (Oxford: Archaeopress, 2003).

18. F. González de Canales Cerisola, L. Serrano Pichardo, and Llompart Gómez, "The Pre-Colonial Phoenician Emporium of Huelva ca. 900–770 BC," *Bulletin Antieke Beschaving* 81 (2004): 13–29.

19. G. Kenneth Sams, "Sculpted Orthostates at Gordion," in *Anatolia and the Ancient Near East: Studies in Honor of Tahsin Özgüç*, ed. Kutlu Emre, Barthel Hrouda, Machteld Mellink, and Nimet Özgüç (Ankara: Türk Tarih Kurumu Basımevi, 1989), 447–54.

20. Nicholas Chr. Stampolidis, "Near Eastern Imports and Imagery on Crete during the Early Iron Age," in *Assyria to Iberia at the Dawn of the Classical Age*, ed. Joan Aruz, Sarah B. Graff, and Yelena Rakic (New York: Metropolitan Museum of Art, 2014), 288–89.

21. Vassos Karageorghis, *Excavations in the Necropolis of Salamis*, vol. 1, *Salamis* 3 (Nicosia: Department of Antiquities of the Republic of Cyprus, 1967); Karageorghis, *Excavations in the Necropolis of Salamis*, vol. 3, *Salamis* 5 (Nicosia: Department of Antiquities of the Republic of Cyprus, 1973).

22. Rodney S. Young, "The 1961 Campaign at Gordion," *American Journal of Archaeology* 66, no. 2 (1962): 166–67, figs. 24 and 25; Helene J. Kantor, "Oriental Institute Museum Notes, No. 13. A Bronze Plaque with Relief Decoration from Tell Tainat," *Journal of Near Eastern Studies* 21 (1962), 93–117; H. Kyrieleis and W. Röllig, "Ein altorientalischer Pferdeschmuck aus dem Heraion von Samos," *Mitteilungen des Deutschen Archäologischen Instituts, Athenische Abteiling* 103 (1988): 37–75,

pls. 9–15; A. Charbonnet, "Le Dieu Aux Lions d'Eretrie," *Annali del Dipartimento di Studi del Mondo Classico e del Mediterraneo Antico, Sezione di Archeologia e Storia Antica* 8 (1986): 117–56, pls. 33–41.

23. Joan Aruz and Jean-François De Lapérouse, "Cauldrons," in *Assyria to Iberia at the Dawn of the Classical Age*, ed. Joan Aruz, Sarah B. Graff, and Yelena Rakic (New York: Metropolitan Museum of Art, 2014), 272–81; and Brigitte Borell and Dessa Rittig, *Orientalische und griechische Bronzereliefs aus Olympia: Der Fundkomplex aus Brunnen 17* (Berlin: Walter de Gruyter, 1998).

24. John Boardman, "Al Mina and History," *Oxford Journal of Archaeology* 9 (1990): 169–90, table 1.

25. Tamar Hodos, *Local Responses to Colonization in the Iron Age Mediterranean* (London: Routledge, 2006), 59–64.

26. Austen H. Layard, *The Monuments of Nineveh from Drawings Made on the Spot* (London: J. Murray, 1849); and Layard, *Discoveries in the Ruins of Nineveh and Babylon; with Travels in Armenia, Kurdistan and the Desert: Being the Result of a Second Expedition Undertaken for the Trustees of the British Museum* (London: J. Murray, 1853).

27. Borell and Rittig, *Griechische Bronzereliefs*; and Eleanor Guralnick, "A Group of Near Eastern Bronzes from Olympia," *American Journal of Archaeology* 108, no. 2 (2004): 187–222.

28. Kyrieleis and Röllig, "Altorientalischer Pferdeschmuck"; Konstantinos Kourouniotes, "Anaskaphē Eretrias," *Praktika tēs en Athēnais Archaiologikēs Hetaireias* (1910): 267–69; and Ulf Jantzen, *Ägyptische und orientalische Bronzen aus dem Heraion von Samos: Samos VIII* (Bonn: Deutsches Archäologisches Institut, 1972).

29. Anthony J. Parker, *Ancient Shipwrecks of the Mediterranean and the Roman Provinces* (Oxford: British Archaeological Reports, 1992); Andrew Wilson, "Developments in Mediterranean Shipping and Maritime Trade from the Hellenistic Period to AD 1000," in *Maritime Archaeology and Ancient Trade in the Mediterranean*, ed. Damian Robinson and Andrew Wilson (Oxford: School of Archaeology, University of Oxford, 2011), 33–59.

30. For the recent discovery near Kumluca, see Hakan Öniz, "A New Bronze Age Shipwreck with Ingots in the West of Antalya: Preliminary Results," *Palestine Exploration Quarterly* 151, no. 1 (2019): 3–14; and Öniz, "Antalya-Kumluca Bronze Age Shipwreck 2019 Studies: First Analyses," *Palestine Exploration Quarterly* 151, no. 3–4 (2019): 172–83.

31. Robert D. Ballard et al., "Iron Age Shipwrecks in Deep Water off Ashkelon, Israel," *American Journal of Archaeology* 106, no. 2 (2002): 151–68.

32. Elizabeth S. Greene, Justin Leidwanger, and Harun A. Özdaş, "Two Early Archaic Shipwrecks at Kekova Adası and Kepçe Burnu, Turkey," *International Journal of Nautical Archaeology* 40, no. 1 (2011): 60–68; Greene, Leidwanger, and Özdaş, "Expanding Contacts and Collapsing Distances in Early Cypro-Archaic Trade: Three Case Studies of Shipwrecks off the Turkish Coast," in *The Transport Amphorae and Trade of Cyprus*, ed. Mark L. Lawall and John Lund (Aarhus: Aarhus University Press, 2013), 21–34; Iván Negueruela, "Hacia la comprensión de la construcción naval fenicia segun el Barco 'Mazzarón-2' del siglo VII A.C.," in *La navegación fenicia: Technologia naval y derroteros; Encuentro entre marinos, arqueólogos historiadores*, ed. Victoria Peña, Carlos G. Wagner, and Alfredo Mederos (Madrid: Centro de Estudios Fenicios y Punicos, 2004), 227–78; and Mark E. Polzer and

Juan Pinedo Reyes, "Bajo de la Campana 2009 Phoenician Shipwreck Excavation," *Institute of Nautical Archaeology Annual* 3 (2009): 3–14.

33. See, for example, Thomas F. Tartaron, "Geography Matters: Defining Maritime Small Worlds of the Aegean Bronze Age," in *Maritime Networks in the Ancient Mediterranean World*, ed. J. Leidwanger and C. Knappett (Cambridge: Cambridge University Press, 2018), 61–92.

34. Jan-Paul Crielaard, "Powerful Things in Motion: A Biographical Approach to Eastern Elite Goods in Greek Santuaries," in *Sanctuaries and the Power of Consumption: Networking and the Formation of Elites in the Archaic Western Mediterranean World: Proceedings of the International Conference in Innsbruck, 20th–23rd March 2012*, ed. Erich Kistler, Birgit Öhlinger, Martin Mohr, and Matthias Hoernes (Wiesbaden: Harrassowitz Verlag, 2015), 351–72.

35. Günter Kopcke, "What Role for Phoenicians?," in *Greece between East and West: 10th–8th Centuries BC*, ed. Günter Kopcke and Isabelle Tokumaru (Mainz: Philipp von Zabern, 1992), 103–13; and Walter Burkert, *The Orientalizing Revolution: Near Eastern Influence on Greek Culture in the Early Archaic Age*, trans. Margaret E. Pinder and Walter Burkert (Cambridge, MA: Harvard University Press, 1992).

36. Popham and Lemos, "Euboean Warrior Trader"; and Sarah P. Morris, "The View from East Greece: Miletus, Samos and Ephesus," in *Debating Orientalization: Multidisciplinary Approaches to Change in the Ancient Mediterranean*, ed. Corinna Riva and Nicholas C. Vella (London: Equinox, 2006), 73–74; and see Morris, chapter 5 in this volume.

37. Crielaard, "Powerful Things," 352.

38. Susan Frankenstein, "The Phoenicians in the Far West: A Function of Neo-Assyrian Imperialism," in *Power and Propaganda: A Symposium on Ancient Empires*, ed. Mogens Trolle Larsen (Copenhagen: Akademisk Forlag, 1979), 263–94; and González de Canales, Pichardo, and Gómez, "Phoenician Emporium."

39. Mimnermus fr. 9 West; Herodotus 1.56, 143.2, 145; 9.26–27, 97; Pherecydes 3 *FGrH* 155; Hellanicus 4 *FGrH* 101; Thucydides 1.12.3; 7.57.2; Diodorus 4.57–8; Strabo 8.1.2, 7.1–4; and Pausanias 7.1.2–4.

40. Herodotus 1.6, 16; 4.11–13; and Strabo 1.3.21; 3.2.12; 11.2.5.

41. Herodotus 7.73; see also Papadopoulos, chapter 7 in this volume.

42. Wolf-Dietrich Niemeier, "The Mycenaeans in Western Anatolia and the Problem of the Origins of the Sea Peoples," in *Mediterranean Peoples in Transition, Thirteenth to Early Tenth Centuries BCE*, ed. Symour Gitin, Amihai Mazar, and Ephraim Stern (Jerusalem: Israel Exploration Society, 1998), 17–65, esp. 20–21; Irene Lemos, "The Migrations to the West Coast of Asia Minor: Tradition and Archaeology," in *Frühes Ionien: Eine Bestandsaufnahme*, ed. Justus Cobet et al. (Mainz: von Zabern, 2007), 713–27; and Naoíse Mac Sweeney, "Separating Fact from Fiction in the Ionian Migration," *Hesperia* 86, no. 3 (2017): 379–421, esp. 387–94.

43. James T. Hooker, "New Reflexions on the Dorian Invasion," *Klio* 61 (1979): 353–60; Annie Schnapp-Gourbeillon, "Le mythe dorien," *Annali, Istituto Universitario Orientale, Dipartimento di Studi del Mondo Classico e del Mediterraneo: Sezione di archeologia e storia antica* 1 (1979): 1–11; Schnapp-Gourbeillon, "L'invasion dorienne a-t-elle eu lieu?," in *La Grèce ancienne*, ed. Claude Mossé (Paris: Editions du Seuil, 1986), 43–57; Jacques Vanschoonwinkel, *L'Égée et la Méditerranée orientale à la fin du IIe millénaire: Temoignages archéologiques et sources écrites* (Louvain-la Neuve:

Département d'archéologie et d'histoire d'art, Collège Erasmus, 1991), 119, 184–85, 191–92, 234, 239; Jonathan M. Hall, *Ethnic Identity in Greek Antiquity* (Cambridge: Cambridge University Press, 1997), 114–28; and Hall, *Hellenicity: Between Ethnicity and Culture* (Chicago: University of Chicago Press, 2002), 73–82.

44. Gordon Childe, *The Danube in Prehistory* (Oxford: Clarendon Press, 1929), v–vi; cf. Childe, *Piecing Together the Past* (London: Routledge and Kegan Paul, 1956), 123; Stephen Shennan, "Introduction," in *Archaeological Approaches to Cultural Identity*, ed. Stephen Shennan (London: Routledge, 1989), 5–14; and Siân Jones, *The Archaeology of Ethnicity: Constructing Identities in the Past and Present* (London: Routledge, 1997), 17–18.

45. Susan Sherratt and Andrew Sherratt, "The Growth of the Mediterranean Economy in the Early First Millennium BC," *World Archaeology* 24, no. 3 (1993): 361–78.

46. Sherratt and Sherratt, "Mediterranean Economy," 374.

47. David Clarke, *Analytical Archaeology*, 2nd ed. (New York: Academic Press, 1979), 365.

48. Gordon Willey and Philip Phillips, *Method and Theory in American Archaeology* (Chicago: University of Chicago Press, 1958), 49; Lewis Binford, "Archaeological Systematics and the Study of Culture Process," *American Antiquity* 31 (1965): 203–10; Colin Renfrew, *Approaches to Social Archaeology* (Edinburgh: Edinburgh University Press, 1984), 34; and Jones, *Archaeology of Ethnicity*, 108–9.

49. Michael Shanks and Christopher Tilley, *Reconstructing Archaeology: Theory and Practice* (Cambridge: Cambridge University Press, 1987), 138–41.

50. James Sackett, "The Meaning of Style in Archaeology," *American Antiquity* 42 (1977): 369–80; "Style and Ethnicity in Archaeology: The Case for Isochrestism," in *The Uses of Style in Archaeology*, ed. Margaret Conkey and Christine Hastorf (Cambridge: Cambridge University Press, 1990), 32–43.

51. H. Martin Wobst, "Stylistic Behaviour and Information Exchange," *University of Michigan, Museum of Anthropology: Anthropological Papers* 61 (1977), 317–42; Polly Wiessner, "Style and Social Information in Kalahari San Projectile Points," *American Antiquity* 49 (1983): 253–76; Michael Shanks and Christopher Tilley, *Social Theory and Archaeology* (Cambridge: Polity Press, 1987), 85; Shennan, "Introduction," 16; and Margaret Conkey, "Experimenting with Style in Archaeology: Some Historical and Theoretical Issues," in Conkey and Hasdorf, *Uses of Style in Archaeology*, 5–17.

52. Catherine Morgan, "The Early Iron Age," in *A Companion to Archaic Greece*, ed. Kurt A. Raaflaub and Hans van Wees (Chichester: Wiley-Blackwell, 2009), 43–63; and Jonathan M. Hall, *A History of the Archaic Greek World, ca. 1200–479 BCE*, 2nd ed. (Chichester: Wiley-Blackwell, 2014), 59–66.

53. Antonio López Eire, "El retorno de los Heraclidas," *Zephyrus* 28–29 (1978): 287–97; Maria Pilar Fernández Alvarez, *El Argolico occidental y oriental en las inscripciones de los siglos VII, VI y V a.C.* (Salamanca: Universidad de Salamanca, 1981); and Hall, *Ethnic Identity*, 162–70.

54. See, e.g., James F. Osborne, *The Syro-Anatolian City-States: An Iron Age Culture* (Oxford: Oxford University Press, 2021), 30–68; and Assaf Yasur-Landau, *The Philistines and Aegean Migration at the End of the Late Bronze Age* (New York: Cambridge University Press, 2010). For an overview of archaeological and historical

evidence of demographic changes across the Late Bronze/Iron Age transition in all parts of the eastern Mediterranean, see Bernard A. Knapp and Sturt W. Manning, "Crisis in Context: The End of the Late Bronze Age in the Eastern Mediterranean," *American Journal of Archaeology* 120, no. 1: 99–149.

55. Hall, *Ethnic Identity*, 56–65; Hall, *Hellenicity*, 82–89; Naoíse Mac Sweeney, *Foundation Myths and Politics in Ancient Ionia* (Cambridge: Cambridge University Press, 2013); Mac Sweeney, "Separating Fact from Fiction," 401–12.

56. A. John Graham, *Colony and Mother City in Ancient Greece* (Manchester: Manchester University Press, 1983), 2; and Irad Malkin, *Religion and Colonization in Ancient Greece* (Leiden: Brill, 1987), 4. For a critique of the term "colonization," see Robin Osborne, "Early Greek Colonization? The Nature of Greek Settlement in the West," in *Archaic Greece: New Approaches and New Evidence*, ed. Nick Fisher and Hans van Wees (London: Duckworth, 1998), 251–69; and Anthony M. Snodgrass, "'Lesser Breeds': The History of a False Analogy," in *Ancient Colonizations: Analogy, Similarity, and Difference*, ed. Henry Hurst and Sara Owen (London: Duckworth, 2005), 45–58.

57. Jonathan M. Hall, "Foundation Stories," in *Greek Colonisation: An Account of Greek Colonies and Other Settlements Overseas*, vol. 2, ed. Gocha Tsetskhladze (Leiden: Brill, 2008), 383–426.

58. Manthos Bessios, Yiannis Tzifopoulos, and Antonis Kotsonas, *Μεθώνη Πιερίας 1: Επιγραφές, χαράγματα και εμπορικά σύμβολα στη γεωμετρική και αρχαϊκή κεραμική από το Υπόγειο της Μεθώνης Πιερίας στη Μακεδονία* (Thessaloniki: Ministry of Education, Instruction, and Religion: Center for the Greek Language, 2012).

59. John Boardman, *The Greeks Overseas: Their Early Colonies and Trade*, 4th ed. (London: Thames and Hudson, 1999), 163, 170–71, 173, 176, 184; and John Papadopoulos, "Magna Achaea: Akhaian Late Geometric and Archaic Pottery in South Italy and Sicily," *Hesperia* 70 (2001), 373–460.

60. Boardman, *Greeks Overseas*.

61. John Boardman, "Greek Potters at Al Mina?," *Anatolian Studies* 9 (1959): 163–69; Boardman, "Al Mina and Greek Chronology," *Journal of Hellenic Studies* 85 (1965): 5–15; Boardman, "Al Mina: The Study of a Site," *Ancient West and East* 2 (2002): 315–31; Boardman, "The Excavated History of Al Mina," in *Ancient Greeks West and East*, ed. Gocha Tsetskhladze (Leiden: Brill, 1999), 135–62; and Boardman, "Al Mina and History."

62. Burkert, *Orientalizing Revolution*; Sarah P. Morris, *Daidalos and the Origins of Greek Art* (Princeton, NJ: Princeton University Press, 1992); Martin L. West, *The East Face of Helicon: West Asiatic Elements in Greek Poetry and Myth* (Oxford: Clarendon Press, 1997); and Carolina López-Ruiz, *When the Gods Were Born: Greek Cosmogonies and the Near East* (Cambridge, MA: Harvard University Press, 2010).

63. Oscar Muscarella, "Greek and Oriental Cauldron Attachments: A Review," in Kopcke and Tokumaru, *Greece between East and West*, 16–45; Andrew Stewart, *Greek Sculpture: An Exploration*, vol. 1 (New Haven, CT: Yale University Press, 1990), 106; and Eleanor Guralnick, "The Egyptian-Greek Connection in the 8th to 6th Centuries BC: An Overview," in *Greeks and Barbarians: Essays on the Interactions between Greeks and Non-Greeks in Antiquity and the Consequences for Eurocentrism*, ed. John E. Coleman and Clark A. Walz (Bethesda, MD: CDL Press, 1997), 127–54.

64. Boardman, *Greeks Overseas*, 199–200. See also Hall, *Hellenicity*, 106–7.

65. Irad Malkin, "A Colonial Middle Ground: Greek, Etruscan, and Local Elites in the Bay of Naples," in *The Archaeology of Colonialism*, ed. Claire L. Lyons and John K. Papadopoulos (Los Angeles: Getty Research Institute, 2002), 151–81.

66. Roald F. Docter, "Pottery, Graves and Ritual I: Phoenicians of the First Generation in Pithekoussai," in *La ceramica fenicia di Sardegna: dati, problematiche, confronti*, ed. Piero Bartoloni and Lorenza Campanella (Rome: Consiglio Nazionale delle Richerche, 2000), 135–49; and Maria Costanza Lentini, "Le origini di Naxos. Nuovi dati sulla fondazione," in *Contexts of Early Colonization*, ed. Lieve Donnellan, Valentino Nizzo, and Gert-Jan Burgers (Rome: Palombi, 2016), 311–21.

67. Luke, *Ports of Trade*; and Hodos, *Responses to Colonization*. See also Peter Van Dommelen, "Colonial Constructs: Colonialism and Archaeology in the Mediterranean," *World Archaeology* 28, no. 3 (1997): 305–23.

68. Morris, *Daidalos*, 124–49.

69. Gunnar Lehmann, "Al Mina and the East: A Report on Research in Progress," in *The Greeks in the East*, ed. Alexandra Villing (London: British Museum, 2005), 61–92; and Ran Zadok, "Geographical and Onomastic Remarks," *Nouvelles Assyriologiques Brèves et Utilitaires* 1 (1996): 11–13.

70. Marian H. Feldman, *Communities of Style: Portable Luxury Arts, Identity and Collective Memory in the Iron Age Levant* (Chicago: University of Chicago Press, 2014); Ann C. Gunter, *Greek Art and the Orient* (Cambridge: Cambridge University Press, 2009); and Crielaard, "Powerful Things."

71. Irad Malkin, *A Small Greek World: Networks in the Ancient Mediterranean* (Oxford: Oxford University Press, 2011). For a critique, see Jonathan M. Hall, "Quanto c'è di 'greco' nella 'colonizzazione greca'?," in *Conceptualizing Early Colonisation*, ed. Lieve Donnellan, Valentino Nizzo, and Gert-Jan Bergers (Brussels: Belgian Institute at Rome, 2016), 51–59.

72. See, e.g., Lieve Donnellan, "A Networked View on 'Euboaean' Colonisation," in Donnellan, Nizzo, and Bergers, *Conceptualizing Early Colonisation*, 149–66.

73. Justin Leidwanger et al., "A Manifesto for the Study of Ancient Mediterranean Maritime Networks," *Antiquity Project Gallery* 88, no. 342 (2014), http://journal.antiquity.ac.uk/projgall/leidwanger342.

74. Malkin, *Small Greek World*, 143–69.

75. Kenneth L. Pike, *Language in Relation to a Unified Theory of the Structure of Human Behavior*, 2nd ed. (The Hague: Mouton, 1967).

76. Whether or not one can ever truly arrive at an authentic emic viewpoint and whether etic viewpoints are ultimately little more than the emic stances of Western observers are philosophical questions that need not detract from the analytical utility of the model.

77. Carlo Ginzburg, "On Dichotomies," *HAU: Journal of Ethnographic Theory* 7, no. 2 (2017): 139–42, at 139.

78. Irene Winter, "Homer's Phoenicians: History, Ethnography, or Literary Trope?," in *The Ages of Homer: A Tribute to Emily Townsend Vermeule*, ed. Jane B. Carter and Sarah P. Morris (Austin: University of Texas Press, 1995), 247–71, at 258; Rebecca S. Martin, *The Art of Contact: Comparative Approaches to Greek and Phoenician Art* (Philadelphia: University of Pennsylvania Press, 2017); and Josephine C. Quinn, *In Search of the Phoenicians* (Princeton, NJ: Princeton University Press, 2018).

79. Broodbank, *Making of the Middle Sea*, fig. 2.9.

80. See Feldman, chapter 4 in this volume.

81. Steven Karacic and James F. Osborne, "Eastern Mediterranean Economic Exchange during the Iron Age: Portable X-ray Fluorescence and Neutron Activation Analysis of Cypriot-Style Pottery in the Amuq Valley, Turkey," *PLoS One* 11, no. 11 (2016), https://doi.org/10.1371/journal.pone.0166399.

82. Greene, Leidwanger, and Özdaş, "Archaic Shipwrecks"; Greene, Leidwanger, and Özdaş, "Expanding Contacts"; and Ballard et al., "Iron Age Shipwrecks." One of the late seventh-century shipwrecks that *did* produce a number of exotic luxury objects intended for an elite clientele is the Bajo de la Campana wreck off the southeast coast of Spain, whose hold included fifty-four elephant tusks (at least nine of which bear Phoenician inscriptions), carved ivories, ostrich eggs, alabaster jars, and bronze furniture pieces, among many other important items and raw materials; Mark E. Polzer, "The Bajo de la Campana Shipwreck and Colonial Trade in Phoenician Spain," in *Assyria to Iberia at the Dawn of the Classical Age*, ed. Joan Aruz, Sarah B. Graff, and Yelena Rakic (New York: Metropolitan Museum of Art, 2014), 230–42.

83. See Kearns, chapter 3 in this volume.

84. Gunter, *Greek Art and the Orient*, 9–10.

✵ CHAPTER 2 ✵

Phoenicians and the Iron Age Mediterranean

A Response to Phoenicoskepticism

CAROLINA LÓPEZ-RUIZ

(In memory of Brigitte W. Treumann, 1938–2020)

Wandering by lone sea-breakers,
And sitting by desolate streams;
World-losers and world-forsakers,
On whom the pale moon gleams:
Yet we are the movers and shakers,
Of the world forever it seems.[1]

The Dead End of Skepticism

"In the 1980s Sabatino Moscati created the Phoenicians." So starts the creation myth of Phoenician studies. After the field passed through its Archaic and Classical periods, it is now in a Late Skeptical, revisionist mood. It has recently been argued that the catalog of the famous 1988 Venice exhibit, *I Fenici*, was an act of reification, which cemented our view of the Phoenicians and their material culture.[2] It is true that the exhibit and Moscati's work inevitably shaped our view of the material culture associated with the Phoenicians, but he was not a true demiurge, single-handedly creating a subject. Moscati was making a niche for what he took to be a homeless and growing body of material. He was also expanding our view of the Phoenicians' world from the Phoenician mainland to the other end of the Mediterranean, a framework as broad and complex as their commercial and colonial networks.[3] We are still dealing with the same problems as the founding father. The field of Phoenician studies remains scattered and fragmented, with few institutional or publishing homes. Moreover, Moscati already worried about the gap between those infected by Phoenicomania and those who denied that

Phoenicians existed. He hoped to stimulate more discussion and pointed out that, were he to ask the same questions about the Etruscans, a more dynamic debate would have ensued in his native Italy.[4]

The academic gap persists, if most scholarship falls somewhere in between those tendencies or does not engage head on with the problem. Despite increasing data and more conscientious postcolonial study of non-Greco-Roman, underrepresented groups, the Phoenicians are subject to ongoing deconstruction. The special treatment they receive, in my view, can be understood only through their tense relationship with classical scholarship: The Phoenicians, including their infamous Carthaginian heirs, are peripherally part of the discipline of classics but fall outside the construction of western tradition; they are trapped between Near Eastern studies and classical literature and history; they are present in the Greco-Roman corpus but are often treated as an intruding element, complicating the narrative of Greek exceptionalism. The ethnonym "Phoenician" is regularly placed in quotation marks, and it is not difficult to find in recent scholarship statements that confuse the convention with the referent, implying or explicitly stating that the Phoenicians never existed, or that we can talk about Phoenicians only from the sixth century BCE onward.

Written from the perspective of a classicist and Roman historian, Josephine Quinn's book *In Search of the Phoenicians* proposes that "the 'Phoenicians' never actually existed." Ironically, the formidable quantity of evidence that Quinn herself and other historians assemble in an effort to dismantle the alleged Phoenician construct highlights the importance of this culture, which even Phoenicoskeptics see as coalescing around "cities, family, colonial ties, and religious practices."[5] It may well be that we need to take the minimalist interpretation as partly rhetorical—that is, as an exercise we can apply to any ancient source, archaeological or literary, and to all scholarly categories and terms. This might also include the Greeks, who provide the inevitable backdrop for discussions of Phoenicians. Rhetorical deconstruction, however, exacts a higher price from noncanonical peoples, especially when we confuse our critical analysis of a scholarly concept with the denial of the agency or existence of the people to whom the concept refers. In Quinn's words, "the term 'Phoenician' itself is a Greek invention, and there is no good evidence . . . that these Phoenicians saw themselves, or acted, in collective terms above the level of the city or . . . simply the family."[6] Going beyond mere skepticism, this denialist stance leaves the Phoenicians defenseless as well as voiceless, since their own literature was lost (through a series of choices, we might add, that were complicit in Hellenocentrism and, later, Eurocentrism).

To access them we must fall back on the views of Greeks and Romans. The skeptical view not only questions the classical sources' accuracy and objectivity, as historians should, but goes too far by invalidating them as useful sources for the voiceless Phoenicians. This places the Phoenicians in a circular trap from which they cannot escape. By contrast, no amount of critique will persuade scholars that the Greeks and Romans "never existed."

Rebecca Martin's recent assessment of the relationship between Greek and Phoenician art is more constructive.[7] But her own disciplinary focus (art history), chronological coverage (the Classical period), and geographical constraints (mainland Phoenicia) leave us with a narrow treatment of the Phoenicians of the Early Iron Age and the Phoenician world at large. Her focus on Phoenician and Greek art in the Classical period makes an excellent case for the independence of Phoenician artistic expression and for their collective cultural or even ethnic identity, loosely understood; she even invokes "Phoenicianism," to mirror "Hellenism." This was subordinated to city-based identities, just as Greek identity was. Although Martin admits that "it is quite possible a collective Phoenician identity existed at some point in the Iron Age, even if we lack much evidence to support it,"[8] her view of this earlier phase is somewhat teleological, looking towards the period when we have more records. Hence, it is driven by arguments from silence, concluding that "Greeks and Phoenicians are useful fictions for the enterprise of writing Mediterranean art history, that of the Greeks from around the beginning of the first millennium BCE, that of the Phoenicians perhaps only from about five hundred years later."[9] On the one hand, she highlights the bias created by Hellenocentric perspectives and ideas of Greek exceptionalism but, when it comes to the earlier part of the millennium, Martin downgrades the Phoenicians (who never enjoyed such exceptionalism) from historical entities to "phantoms," a word also used by Quinn and at least John Boardman before them.[10] This ignores the fact that our sources for both Greeks and Phoenicians in the Iron Age are sketchy, arguably more so for the Greeks, since the Phoenicians' shared language and script are attested as early as the turn of the first millennium BCE (see below).

In the minimalist view, however, a distinct Phoenician culture emerges from a vacuum around the sixth century BCE, around the same time that the rise of "Panhellenism" is often placed. It is then that we can safely trace historically some instances of "collective 'Phoenician' action." But this is largely because, as for the Greeks, we know more about Phoenician states during the Persian period and later, both from internal and external sources.[11] Martin's brilliant analysis of Phoenician coins, inscriptions, and religious monuments from this later period reveals idiosyncrasies and signs of Phoenician identity even as their culture adjusted to the broader cultural frameworks (Persian, Hellenistic).[12] In my view, this interpretive approach could be applied productively to Phoenician materials of the previous period, and would help the field move beyond a focus on fine arts such as ivories and metal bowls and embrace all aspects of Phoenician culture, to reconstruct it from the bottom up. As matters stand, Iron Age Phoenician art tends to be seen as eclectic (i.e., lacking its own personality), if not altogether nonexistent.[13] Once more, the Phoenicians are seen as historical agents only when others see them as such. They are trapped in Greek referentiality, and they are granted "Phoenicianism" only as a parallel to "Hellenism" and within a periodization driven by a Greek historical framework. Here I propose that we should be looking earlier and beyond Greece and the Phoenician homeland to find Phoenician culture and collective agency, and that this view is essential to explaining the interconnected Iron Age.[14]

The Case for the Phoenicians

Keeping up with the surge of Phoenician-related studies requires flexibility, including an eye for archaeological reports from the Levant to Portugal and cross-cultural studies of Phoenician–local relations in several areas.[15] It also requires that we free ourselves from the constraints of the monodisciplinary perspective (whether archaeological or art-historical), and that we look beyond the stagnant Phoenician–Greek debate.

Does our Greek-derived label "Phoenician" point to a people who retained their ethnic or cultural coherence through all this complexity? The evidence strongly suggests that it did.[16] To reason according to categories used routinely by ancient historians, they unquestionably shared a distinct language and script with only slight variations[17] (its unity is straightforward, despite the fact that some nonlinguists and epigraphists have called it "difficult" and dialectal);[18] they shared a mutually identifiable pantheon with city-specific variations in emphasis and epithets of the same gods;[19] and they constructed lasting colonial relations, articulated through shared mythologies, as we can see in the foundation stories of Tyre, Carthage, and Gadir, as well as common cults (Baal Hammon, Ashtart, Melqart),[20] and rituals (funerary customs, types of amulets and symbols, the *tophet* ritual).[21] Already in antiquity, Phoenicians were associated with specific types of iconography, crafts, and industries, whose archaeological survival largely maps onto Phoenician networks.[22] But the success and resilience of those networks by necessity depended on the success of shared myths, which underpin institutions, identities, and even economic agendas among all diasporic groups; these are curated through both discursive and visual means, as Taco Terpstra has recently emphasized regarding Phoenician trade.[23] But even so, for many today, the Phoenicians do not pass the test of our idea of *ethnos*, or even of a group bound by cultural identity. The "fabled seafarers" of the Iron Age, as they are sometimes called, are to some nothing but a historical mirage, perhaps a useful fiction planted by the Greeks from Homer on, elaborated by later literature, and then taken up by modern scholarly and national discourses.[24]

What does it take, then, to be worthy of a collective name more comfortably accepted in scholarship? Two main concerns seem to drive the waves of skepticism. The first issue is the lack of a Phoenician political unit, a "state" encompassing the cities identified historically as "Phoenician." Not until Roman times was Phoenicia an administrative unit, and even then its borders were not fixed.[25] In discussions of Phoenician identity, concern about the lack of a central political unit is often aired without acknowledging that most ancient peoples, whose names (frequently also externally defined) are not regularly placed within quotation marks, also did not form single, unified political entities. Greeks and Etruscans,[26] for instance, were organized in independent city-states in a similar way as the Phoenicians, sometimes acting in alliances, sometimes fighting among themselves, yet bound by cultural and ethnic ties that set them aside vis-à-vis their other collectives. Likewise, just as for the Phoenician polities, most of their city-states were not unified as a single state until the Roman Empire engulfed them. Moreover, stating that Phoenicians would have largely identified themselves with their city is hardly an argument against a shared Phoenician identity, as this is the case with other contemporary societies. Regarding the Greeks, for instance, the scholarly narrative stresses how fierce civic loyalties coexisted within a loose ethnic framework with fuzzy edges.[27] But this complexity is not taken to the extreme of debunking Greek identity or culture in its entirety.

"But," the denialist will say, "they never called themselves Phoenicians," or indeed by any other well-attested name. There is some textual evidence of the use of the emic term "Canaanites" (*kana'anym*) for Northwest Semites, a term possibly connected to purple color or trade (see below);[28] the evidence, coming from North African sources and the New Testament, is for the moment meager, but still significant.[29] In any case, by the time we have more written sources stemming from the Phoenician region (written in Greek), from Hellenistic times on, they have readily accepted the Greek referent *Phoinix* (see more below).[30] Not surprisingly, we do not have anything of the sort attested for the Early Iron Age. At the same time, we have to admit that virtually nothing written by individuals from the Phoenician cities or the diaspora wherein they might have reflected upon their own collective ontology survives in the epigraphic or literary records. The Phoenicians are not alone in lacking a robust textual documentation of their own culture. Cultural autoethnographies from outside the privileged and selective corpus of Greek and Roman texts have been lost, and the Greco-Roman ones were passed down as educational and historical artifacts in Byzantium and the medieval west. But we know there was a Phoenician literature. Scraps of papyri with Phoenician script, clay seals with papyrus impression, and the Greek word for papyrus roll (*biblíon*, after the Phoenician center, Byblos) hint at a lost legacy largely written on perishable media. Moreover, works by Phoenicians-Carthaginians are mentioned in many literary genres, especially historiography, travel accounts, agricultural treatises, philosophy, archival documents, cosmogony, and mythology. References to these works and the few fragments we have are transmitted by Greek and Roman authors, sometimes quoting Phoenician authors who wrote in Greek. Even as late as Hellenistic or Roman times some Phoenician speakers are thought to have worked in both languages.[31]

Thus, the Phoenician voice is with a few exceptions confined to the thousands of inscriptions in Phoenician-Punic language, scattered throughout the Mediterranean, which are mostly brief and formulaic and limited to a few genres (funerary, votive, commercial). These are not useful testimonies from which to reconstruct a cultural history as they do not convey group self-reflection. But then again, how would Greek culture look if we had only Greek funerary and votive epigraphy? We would see a strong tribal, religious, and civic identity, rarely a Panhellenic one—exactly what we see in Phoenician epigraphs, which name the city and the family.[32]

Given the state of the written evidence, therefore, reconstructing a Phoenician culture based on emic accounts is not an option. Only in Roman times do we find something of the sort in the work of Philo of Byblos, who is often discredited because of his date.[33] But this is no reason to build an argument from silence.[34] In the absence of the sort of expansive literary evidence available for the study of ancient Greeks, our second-best resource would be external accounts that consistently treat them as a single, more or less coherent people, despite their division into city-states. Those accounts are indeed present in Assyrian, Hebrew, Greek, and Roman sources. These accounts are often dismissed as evidence of a unified Phoenician culture because the Phoenicians they describe are not uniformly or consistently located on the Phoenician mainland, because they are often vaguely "associated with the sea," or because they are not shown as sharing a coherent "Phoenician character, culture, or society."[35] However, these objections themselves are vague and do not only pertain to the Phoenicians for this period. We would not be able to identify any ancient culture, people, or ethnic group if we consistently demanded such precision in the sources. In fact, the ontology of the exonym is significant: Phoenicians in Greek and Latin texts (Gr. *Phoinikes*, Lat. *Punici*) are not defined geographically precisely because their encounters with the Greeks often took place outside the Phoenician city-states, especially at sea. This means that the name indicated a people, not a place. What is more, when one city, Tyre, established colonies and a commercial empire in the west, it was the general ethnic name that followed them there, not only the name of the metropolis. Clearly, the Greeks and Romans knew a Phoenician when they saw one.

Nevertheless, this image is vulnerable because it is inevitably bound up with literary representations. Irene Winter captured the classics-centered viewpoint in her highly influential piece "Homer's Phoenicians," when she wrote: "Homer's Phoenicians do not represent the world of the Phoenicians; rather, they present a masterful literary construct, at once produced by and working *to* produce the broader social, political, economic, and symbolic fabric of the early state in Archaic Greece."[36] This often-cited idea (or similar ones) captures the "utilitarian" attitude toward "others" in Greek literature (most famously the Persians),[37] but the tautology is evident: everything in Homer is literary.

The literary or ideological use of a thing does not, however, refute that thing's historical existence. We would be paralyzed by this principle if we applied it consistently: it would prevent us from conducting any historical inquiry. Granted, there are contexts and research questions for which the application of ethnic categories such as Greek or Phoenician is not useful or relevant. And our sources about other peoples' ethnicities are sometimes more revealing about our source's own culture than about its subject matter. This is not the problem I am addressing here. The problem is that skeptics frame the appearance of Phoenicians in our sources not just as representation or even (re)construction, but as invention, a subtle shift in categories for which theorists of the 1970s and 1980s were taken to task.[38] Are Phoenician denialists willing to accept the full epistemological implications of that position? This would require them to conclude that, in the case of the Phoenicians, the Greeks and Romans engaged for centuries in a massive and sustained act of arbitrary ethnic labeling, the likes of which they did for no other people whom they named and whose existence is assured: Egyptians, Persians, Thracians, and so on. The denialist position probably only wants to flirt with the language of representation and deconstruction, but not follow it through to its logical conclusion.

An affirmative view of the Phoenicians is, by contrast, relatively easy to state: If the Greeks had not invented a name for them, we would have had to do it ourselves. Given the archaeological advances of the last century, our postcolonial and postmonumental approach, and our post–fine-arts orientation, even *without* the Greek and Latin evidence, we would inevitably have had to devise an equivalent concept that encompassed Phoenician culture from the Iron Age into the later historical periods, and from the Levant to Iberia. Based on the clear consistencies among Phoenician communities in language and writing, religion, art, and other characteristics mentioned throughout this chapter, we would end up mapping our (re)constructed Phoenicians, by and large, onto the Greek and Roman category, which maintained a surprising degree of coherence in sources from Homer to imperial times. At a minimum, we can understand the category of Phoenician as a flexible external ethnonym used by Greeks when more specific pointers (Sidonians, Tyrians, Carthaginians, etc.) were not necessary or relevant.[39]

Not "Just" Levantines

A common "Phoenicianness" appears in other aspects of the historical record. We know of alliances among Phoenician cities in different periods and of their collective and distinctive treatment as subjects by Assyrians and others.[40] There was an undeniable sense of kinship between metropolitan Phoenicians and the colonial foundations, which is asserted, for example, as a reason not to join Persian expeditions against Phoenician cities in North Africa.[41] I already mentioned the religious and symbolic links among Tyre, Carthage, and Gadir. These were articulated through foundation stories and the cults of Melqart and Ashtart, as well as through shared ritual landscapes. The *tophet* sanctuaries (found in Carthage, Sardinia, Sicily, and Malta) also demonstrate a shared sense of identity among the Phoenicians of the central Mediterranean, seemingly under Carthage's influence, thus denoting a regional identity.[42] But the *molk* ritual and its gods harkened back to the motherland's mythologies and rituals (whether those were modified or even reinvented in the west) so the *tophet* may have become a marker of both regional differentiation and Phoenician pride, perhaps a way to present the Carthaginians as "more Tyrian than the Tyrians," so to speak.[43]

Indexes of Phoenician distinctiveness vis-à-vis other groups (e.g., Greeks, Persians, Judaeans) abound in Greek and Roman texts too. The coherence and consistency with which these texts refer to Phoenicians should be taken seriously. We cannot say that the ancient sources meant anything by the collective term "Phoenicians" other than the people defined by the traits listed earlier. Nor is it really the case that they used the name vaguely to generalize about eastern maritime merchants.[44] Israelites, Syrians, and Iberian groups, who were all in close contact with Phoenicians, are called neither *Phoinikes* by the Greeks nor *Punici* (the Latin equivalent). From Homer and Herodotus to Strabo and Josephus, the Phoenicians are identified with a string of cities in Lebanon and their diaspora.[45] For example, when Herodotus speaks about Phoenicians he uses either that term or specific civic names (Sidonians, etc.). However, he uses "Syrian" for other Northwest Semitic groups, such as "Syrians from Palestine," referring possibly to the Judaeans.[46] Instead of elaborating an ethnography of the Phoenicians, the historian showcases them from the start of his narrative as familiar agents in a story of historical, technological, and cultural change.[47]

It is impossible to know when these Tyrians, Sidonians, Byblians, and others became aware that others were referring to them collectively as Phoenicians. Surely it became evident in their interactions during centuries of contact with Greek sailors, mercenaries, merchants, and neighbors in the Iron Age. By the fourth century BCE, Greeks and Phoenicians had been bound up in contact and exchange for so long that, as Corinne Bonnet has shown, our emphasis on the Hellenization of Phoenicia becomes problematic.[48] Certain evidence for a self-aware Phoenician identity comes at the end of the fifth century BCE: when the Carthaginians first started to mint coins in Sicily, they chose the palm tree, or *phoinix*, to mark the currency.[49] From that point on, the symbol spread in Phoenician supraregional networks[50] from the Levant to Carthage and from Sicily to Iberia. The palm tree is a recurrent theme in the friezes of Orientalizing metallic bowls, although ascription of these to Phoenician artisanship and trade is the subject of recent debate.[51] Was the name derived from this old Levantine symbol, which the Greeks identified with their most frequent Levantine interlocutors? Did the association between the *Phoinikes* and purple color and dye come first? The question finds a dead end as *phoinix* appears to mean both red/crimson and palm tree already in Mycenaean records, and the word may not even be Greek or Indo-European.[52] Whatever the case, it is tempting to take this iconic use of the palm by Carthage and other Phoenician-Punic polities as nonverbal projections of the Greek stereotype for their collective identity.

Ironically, despite the fact that their own literature is lost, the Phoenicians were the torchbearers of literacy and alphabetic writing, salvaging and repurposing the Canaanite innovation of the alphabet. The study of comparative literatures suggests that some of the genres attested much later in fragments of Phoenician literature were cultivated in the area in parallel with the type of literature that emerges in Israel around the turn of the millennium: archival records, hymns, cosmogonic myths, and historical narratives. This rich Bronze Age literature cannot have found its only expression in the Hebrew Bible.[53] The works of Andrew George, Martin West, Walter Burkert, and others have postulated Phoenician and Aramaic literatures as likely vectors for the transmission of Canaanite and Mesopotamian literary tropes and genres.[54]

The lack of extant Phoenician literature is unfortunate for our efforts to reconstruct connectivity, especially in the early centuries of the first millennium BCE that concern this volume. It is in the eighth and seventh centuries BCE especially that we see the spread of Near Eastern models throughout the Mediterranean. With the exception of Greece, where we can also study these adaptations in the preserved epic poems, we are mostly confined to material culture and the so-called Orientalizing artistic wave. Notwithstanding the unpopularity of the term, which some art historians have used to label the entire "period," we must still understand the interactions behind the phenomenon, and for this we really cannot do without the Phoenicians. This volume exemplifies the range of approaches one can take to the evidence of cultural contact in this period. Especially relevant are the difficulties and risks in identifying the groups behind the demand and supply ends, of matching styles with cultures, let alone ethnicities.[55]

As Marian Feldman has shown,[56] challenges remain in our efforts to understand how or why the *style* of the luxury items often identified with Phoenicians (such as metal bowls and ivories) was adopted by Levantine communities and beyond. She finds the Phoenician association unsatisfactory and analyzes this type of art as part of a broader Levantine artistic community. The study of elite art indeed shows that a Levantine style spread precisely at this time and in tandem with a Phoenician economic and cultural boom in the Levant and colonial expansion in the Mediterranean. The style built on recognizable Assyrian, Egyptian, and Canaanite elements, but was otherwise distinct from those highly formulaic styles proper.[57] As Feldman shows, producers of this Levantine style actively promoted the Late Bronze Age and Canaanite artistic heritage, showing that continuities with that past were important for Levantine Iron Age communities at large.[58] The Phoenicians were in an excellent position to transmit such continuities; their position is nowhere more evident than in their leading role in developing and spreading their writing culture, to which I return below.

Phoenician language and script functioned as a marker of cultural prestige in the Iron Age Mediterranean. The script was adapted to write other languages, such as Hebrew, Aramaic, Greek (whence Etruscan), Tartessic in Iberia, and Phrygian, but it was also used for formal Phoenician inscriptions set in the broader Levant (e.g., in Cilicia).[59] We can try to disassociate this phenomenon from Phoenician culture and see the script (or the art, or the pottery) as vaguely Levantine, because it was used outside Phoenicia.[60] Or we can highlight the international desire for things Phoenician and connect this to their economic dynamism and cultural prestige. The notion of "Levantine networks" may be sufficient or useful for the study of particular objects, if we want to avoid specific identifications or we are highlighting regional or areal features. But replacing the Phoenician category with that of the greater Levant as a geocultural entity does not constitute much scholarly progress.[61] The Levant is simply not equivalent to the Phoenician realm in geographical, cultural, or historical terms. The label confuses the whole for the part and deprives us of a more specific subcategory that was functional since antiquity. In order to understand Iron Age networks, we need both specificity and macrolevel types of analysis, which requires dealing with the Phoenicians, despite the problems that accompany their study.

Mediterranean Models

We have good models for the study of networks and connectivity that surpass national or political boundaries and the structures imposed by historical periodicity. Peregrine Horden and Nicholas Purcell's *The Corrupting Sea* revived a *longue durée*, pan-Mediterranean perspective previously applied by Fernand Braudel to the European medieval and early modern period.[62] Nevertheless, in these histories *of* the Mediterranean (not only *in* it), it is easy to lose sight of who is doing what, when, and why. The approach is loyal to its focus on environmental conditions, which account for Mediterranean fragmentation and connectivity, the two key concepts-in-tension *The Corrupting Sea* explores. The authors' explicit interest in "general ecological principles" and "unintended patterns of behavior,"[63] together with their diachronic approach (from the Archaic period to Roman and medieval times), does not help identify concrete trends and agents. And when it comes to the Iron Age, Greek colonization and Greek literature are the authors' default resource, producing surprising omissions regarding Phoenician networks at key places.[64]

Cyprian Broodbank extended a similar approach further back in time in his *The Making of the Middle Sea*,[65] surveying the threads of development and interconnectivity from deep prehistory until the early first millennium BCE. This work places much needed emphasis on human innovation as a factor behind historical and environmental change. Even when his monumental survey is not about the Phoenicians, this group stands out as a main force in connecting the Iron Age Mediterranean, in a process that triggered the important transformations discussed throughout this volume. Phoenician settlements and networks emerge time and again as the torchbearers of innovation and continuity, thriving in commerce, arts, and writing, untouched by (even benefiting from) the rearrangement of powers at the dawn of the Iron Age Levant. As Broodbank shows, around 1200 BCE, new connections, forged for the first time, "created the maritime preconditions necessary for regular pan-Mediterranean travel. 'Phoenician' trade, which hides a multiplicity of participants beyond Tyre and the central Levant, was the most instantaneous result."[66]

Broodbank's work warns us against the teleological perspectives found in most histories of the region. Instead, he challenges us to see the Iron Age not as "the forerunner of the Classical world," but as the culmination of developments long in the making.[67] The transition from the Bronze to the Iron Age, therefore, is crucial to this first-millennium scenario, the key being in legacies and transitions, not in "origins."[68] Although our "movers and shakers" remain somewhat diluted, framed by quotes and scattered among Broodbank's "multiplicity of participants," his survey invites us to consider particular groups' innovation and initiative, going sometimes along with, and sometimes against, broader inertias.

Indeed, literary sources and the most recent archaeological evidence from the western Mediterranean (especially Gadir and Carthage) suggest a deliberate program of expansion led by the city of Tyre and not a desperate and shapeless migration forced by Assyrian oppression, as was long assumed.[69] Following earlier trade and ephemeral posts, urban foundations started in the late ninth century BCE as bases of trade and industry (mining, fisheries, salt pans) established at strategic nodal points in southern Iberia's Atlantic and Mediterranean shores, in North Africa (from Lixus in the Atlantic to Carthage in Tunisia), in the central Mediterranean (Malta, Sicily, Pithecussae), the Aegean (Crete, Perachora), and Cyprus.[70] As much as we may be inclined to hedge around the collective name, we cannot overestimate the historical agency of Phoenicians in this story of unprecedented connectivity.

Orientalization: Messy Problem or Interpretive Opportunity?

Materials traditionally classified as "Orientalizing" (inflected by Near Eastern traits), found all over the Mediterranean, have focused attention on specific locally bound contexts and prompted scholars to engage with ideas of hybridity and consumption-driven adaptations.[71] As Tamar Hodos proposes in chapter 10 of this volume, the phenomenon is akin to a cultural and economic globalization. Indeed, Orientalizing transformations in the eighth and seventh centuries BCE are a matter of choice, not an inevitable imposition, and they produced different results in different places. The phenomenon is at once local and global. Hodos had already shown in her study of colonial encounters of Greeks and (more marginally) of Phoenicians with local communities in Syria, Sicily, and Libya, that the type of hybridization we see as Orientalization sometimes does not happen at all, even in areas where contact lasted for centuries, such as in the North African hinterlands.[72]

The Orientalizing phenomenon, therefore, captures the "amazingly complicated and unique" nature of our data in this period, as James Osborne and Jonathan Hall put it in their introduction to this volume's topic (see chapter 1). I agree with their call to search for ways to turn this messiness into an interpretive opportunity. One such avenue is to investigate how the geographical parameters of Orientalizing art and Phoenician activity overlap.[73] Here we run into a series of methodological and disciplinary problems: the field of Iron Age archaeology is fragmented, and works that deal with Orientalizing materials are usually limited to one geographical area;[74] they often focus on one type of material, with a disproportionate focus on luxury items;[75] and, generally, more attention falls on Greek materials and colonial networks, with Phoenicians entering the scene only marginally.[76] To be fair, Tamar Hodos and others have opened up important conversations about pockets of Greek and Phoenician artisans living among others in noncolonial contexts, such as in North Syrian enclaves.[77] To give another example, Nikos Stampolidis and Antonis Kotsonas have proposed that burials at Iron Age Eleutherna, on Crete, belong to Phoenicians.[78] But the traditional general tenet in classical archaeology maintains that where there are no Phoenician colonies there are no Phoenicians, while where there are Greek materials there is intense cultural influence by Greeks. This approach is perhaps best exemplified by John Boardman's *The Greeks Overseas* and a subsequent school of study especially focused on Euboean archaeology.[79]

It seems that scholarship has therefore reached an important inflection point. Perhaps we can yield to the apparent confusion and postulate that the Orientalizing movement is not a real, meaningful phenomenon but a chaotic splash of capricious adaptations from random Near Eastern models, in which case we *cannot* go beyond site-by-site study. Alternatively, we can see the phenomenon as a widespread and persistent (if not uniform) cultural wave, which happens to overlap in chronological and geographical terms with Phoenician cultural contact.

The challenge is to find a way to make these two concepts, the Orientalizing material culture and the Phoenician expansion, articulate in meaningful ways without becoming paralyzed by the recognition that we are working with historical constructs and heuristic models. I have already outlined the case for moving past the alleged reification of the Phoenicians. What about Orientalizing, that gross reification of the Orient? The nuanced study of the style or the manufacture of Orientalizing artifacts, which is often the focus of art historians, offers limited answers to limited questions. As Robin Osborne has pointed out, if we focus solely on the agency of objects, we only "replace the agency, and obscure the responsibility, of human actors."[80] Despite the problems of the vague "Orientalizing" category, and since it is not likely to disappear, our best option is to refresh our relationship with it. I argue that the vague category "Orientalizing" conveys a meaningful factor in the dynamics of those contacts: the admiration and appropriation (on the local side) and the projection and marketing (on the Phoenician side) of a desirable image that was itself usefully vague and malleable. While the notion of Orientalizing may not be useful for isolating the origins of specific features, it is useful in a different way, specifically in understanding the global context of the exchange itself. In the case of the Iron Age Mediterranean, the so-called Orientalizing phenomenon was the most tangible manifestation of increasing interconnectedness among emerging proto-urban societies, who now had within their reach the opportunity to join international markets and project to their neighbors a new image of sophistication, technological advancement, and progress. This was a global international culture of sorts (on a Mediterranean scale), as Hodos proposes.[81]

In my view, a particular group of Levantines known since antiquity as Phoenicians were most involved in the creation of a cultural package or "kit" that could be marketed, sold, and consumed as a Near Eastern ("Oriental") and Near Eastern–inflected culture. This kit was customizable on demand and boosted by the perception of prestige stemming from the eastern polities and empires.[82] After all, branding and stereotyping are not the exclusive property of modernity, and they are not always negative. Orientalist polemic (e.g., exoticism, effeminacy, and tyranny) drive Greek and Roman constructs of the east, but ancient Orientalisms had nothing to do with western colonial worldviews, and have to be extracted from a bigger mixed bag of perceptions of Near Eastern peoples. This was far from homogeneous: it included admiration, imitation, praise, and a long history of relations reflected also in mythological narratives and historical developments.

In the Iron Age, the Phoenicians are the ones who most extensively benefited from the spread of this sort of globalization articulated through Near Eastern motifs that represented royalty, prestige, sophistication, remote antiquity, memory, knowledge, and technology. Their posts from east to west thrived precisely because of their ability to provide what their local markets coveted, to channel the needs of a growing urban network across the Mediterranean (and beyond) toward what they could trade. Their commercial network reached west into the Atlantic, east into Mesopotamia, and south into the African trade routes, which positioned them well to selectively mold and exploit local perceptions of the international, the prestigious, and the sophisticated. These overlapped considerably with what we classify as Near Eastern. While we may discard the term "Oriental" when it is used in opposition to a reified "West," in this Iron Age context it refers to the prestige of the ancient cultures of the Near East in the eyes of Mediterranean cultures.

Modern efforts to locate the origins of the different eastern models of local Orientalizing artifacts (e.g., Assyrian, Egyptian, Anatolian) distract us from the general meaning and history of this eclecticism. The Canaanites of the Phoenician coastland had appropriated artistic and cultural traits from the major Near Eastern civilizations since the Bronze Age. What is more, this eclecticism formed part of what was perceived and projected as Phoenician. Looking at the other side, the recipient indigenous peoples who developed Orientalizing cultures, including the Greeks, did not necessarily distinguish among (or care about) the diverse roots of the new cultural artifacts that accompanied the Phoenician mercantile-colonial expansion. What mattered was the relevance of this package for their own advancement, the way it allowed them to position themselves ahead of the curve, and how they could customize it to suit their habits and tastes.

In other words, the Phoenicians capitalized on forces developing in the Mediterranean since the dawn of the Iron Age. Their exploration and search for resources involved not only the ones usually cited (metals, good harbors, wood) but also productive land, despite the repeated stereotype that the Phoenicians were not interested in inland routes or agriculture, always in contrast to the Greeks.[83] They were met by eager local societies on the path to urbanization who benefited from adding new elements to their mechanisms of internal stratification and identity projection vis-à-vis their own neighbors.

Compared to other Iron Age groups of the western Mediterranean, the Phoenicians are much better documented and established than their native partners in Iberia, Sardinia, or North Africa.[84] A westward vantage point highlights methodological differences among groups of scholars studying the same period: while classical and eastern Mediterranean art historians tend to focus on the fine arts and high commerce that account for the circulation of luxury goods, western Mediterranean archaeologists follow more mundane traces of mobility and contact ("bottom-up," to adopt the language of other contributions to this volume). As already noted, for some cultures of this period, we have a much poorer set of tools than for the Phoenicians, such as for the protohistoric Iberian culture known as Tartessus.[85] Despite their unique, still-undeciphered language and script (the latter adapted from Phoenician) and their stunning Orientalizing culture (stimulated by contact with Phoenicians), the Tartessians remain even more voiceless, and also appear in western history thanks only to classical sources. Ironically, as a minor culture in a corner of Iberia, the Tartessians are almost invisible in the Phoenicians' shadow. For the skeptics on that side, the Phoenicians are the solid historical entity, while Tartessus is a modern scholarly construction, at most a Greek invention.[86] Skepticism here acquires a fractal aspect. We can deconstruct any individual culture that has not been privileged by Hellenocentric and Eurocentric models of history. What we risk, therefore, is to continue seeing the ancient Mediterranean through Greek and Roman lenses, reinforcing the biases of western scholarship and its institutionally supported, comfortable relationship with the past.

Conclusion

I have chosen to be the Phoenicians' advocate not because I think they were the *only* agents in this fascinating period of interconnectedness, but because *only* with their agency can we make sense of this first global Mediterranean in all its complexity. Phoenician culture exerted a tremendous gravitational pull on the peoples around them wherever they went. Their presence ties together phenomena we see at work in material and literary cultures. As we continue with our art-historical and archaeological investigations, it is important not to lose sight of this element, to avoid an unfair and unnecessary theoretical error of the first order. Of all the peoples without a voice in the interconnected Iron Age, whatever they called themselves and whoever they thought they were, the Phoenicians were recognized by Greeks and Romans as principal bringers of cultural change and technological advancement.

Notes

1. Arthur O'Shaughnessy's *Ode*, 1873 (*Music and Moonlight* [London: Chatto and Windus, 1874]). I thank the three anonymous readers and the editors Jonathan Hall and James Osborne for their feedback, and Anthony Kaldellis for many conversations about this topic. I dedicate this chapter with love to my late friend Brigitte Treumann (1938–2020), who wandered the Mediterranean following the Phoenician trail and whose research advanced our understanding of the Phoenician timber industry and trade (she received her PhD from the University of Chicago in 1997).

2. E.g., Nicholas Vella, "The Invention of the Phoenicians: On Object Definition, Decontextualization and Display," in *The Punic Mediterranean: Identities and Identification from Phoenician Settlement to Roman Rule*, ed. Josephine C. Quinn and Nicholas C. Vella (Cambridge: Cambridge University Press, 2014), 24–41; Nicholas Vella, "Birth and Prospects of a Discipline," in *The Oxford Handbook of the Phoenician and Punic Mediterranean*, ed. Carolina López-Ruiz and Brian Doak (Oxford: Oxford University Press, 2019), 23–35; and Josephine C. Quinn, *In Search of the Phoenicians* (Princeton, NJ: Princeton University Press, 2018), 22–26.

3. Sabatino Moscati, ed., *I Fenici* (Milan: Bompiani, 1988); also, by Moscati, "La questione fenicia," *Rendiconti dell'Accademia Nazionale dei Lincei* 8, no. 18 (1963): 483–506; *The World of the Phoenicians* (London: Weidenfeld and Nicolson, 1968); and *Problematica della Civiltà Fenicia* (Rome: CNR, 1974). See also Vella, "Birth and Prospects."

4. Moscati, *Problematica*, 8. Full statement in Vella, "Birth and Prospects," 23–35.

5. The monograph's chapter titles and subtitles include "Phantom Phoenicians," "Inventing the Phoenicians," and "Mythical Communities" (Quinn, *In Search*, 1, 16, 45).

6. Quinn, *In Search*, xviii. Cf. similar position in Fabio Porzia, "Review of Quinn, *In Search of the Phoenicians*," *American Journal of Archaeology* 123, no. 3 (July 2019), https://www.ajaonline.org/book-review/3893; Porzia, "'Imagine There's No Peoples': A Claim against the Identity Approach in Phoenician Studies through Comparison with the Israelite Field," *Rivista di Studi Fenici* 46 (2018): 11–27.

7. Rebecca S. Martin, *The Art of Contact: Comparative Approaches to Greek and Phoenician Art* (Philadelphia: University of Pennsylvania Press, 2017).

8. Martin, *Art of Contact*, 132; cf. 98: "The process by which Phoenician identity emerged certainly began in the Iron Age, and it is likely that the crucible of the Persian Wars helped shape it."

9. Martin, *Art of Contact*, 179; cf. 95: "We do not really know who they [the Phoenicians] were or *if* they were as a collective entity."

10. "Phantom Phoenicians" is Quinn's title for part 1 of *In Search*. See also John Boardman, "Al-Mina: Notes and Queries," *Ancient West and East* 4, no. 2 (2005): 278–91, esp. 284–86.

11. Martin, *Art of Contact*, 133–34.

12. Martin, *Art of Contact*, 97–131.

13. Martin, *Art of Contact*, 173.

14. I explore this subject in *Phoenicians and the Making of the Mediterranean* (Cambridge, MA: Harvard University Press, 2021).

15. See López-Ruiz and Doak, *Oxford Handbook*.

16. See a discussion of Phoenician identity in "The Resilience of a 'Non-People': The Case for a Reconstructed Phoenician Identity," in *Identities in Antiquity*, ed. V. Manolopoulou, J. Skinner, and C. Tsouparopoulou (forthcoming).

17. E.g., Maria Giulia Amadasi Guzzo, "The Language," and Madadh Richey, "Inscriptions," and "The Alphabet and Its Legacy," in López-Ruiz and Doak, *Oxford Handbook*, 199–221 and 222–40; and Christopher A. Rollston, *Writing and Literacy in the World of Ancient Israel: Epigraphic Evidence from the Iron Age* (Atlanta: SBL Press, 2010).

18. E.g., Martin, *Art of Contact*, 99; Quinn, *In Search*, 71; and cf. Barry B. Powell, *Homer and the Origin of the Greek Alphabet* (Cambridge: Cambridge University Press, 1991) 71, who groups it with the Cypriot and Linear B syllabaries.

19. Paolo Xella, "Religion," in López-Ruiz and Doak, *Oxford Handbook*, 273–92.

20. Manuel Álvarez Martí-Aguilar, "The Network of Melqart: Tyre, Gadir, Carthage and the Founding God," in *Warlords, War and Interstate Relations in the Ancient Mediterranean*, ed. Toni Ñaco and Fernando López-Sánchez (Boston: Brill 2017), 113–50.

21. E.g., Mireia López-Bertrán, "Funerary Ritual," in López-Ruiz and Doak, *Oxford Handbook*, 293–309; and coverage in Paolo Xella, ed., *The "Tophet" in the Phoenician Mediterranean (= SEL 29–30)* (Essedue: Verona, 2013).

22. E.g., on pottery: Hélène Sader, "The Northern Levant during the Iron Age I Period," in *The Oxford Handbook of the Archaeology of the Levant: c. 8000–332 BCE*, ed. Margreet Steiner and Ann Killebrew (Oxford: Oxford University Press, 2013), 607–23; María Eugenia Aubet, "Phoenicia during the Iron Age II Period," in Steiner and Killebrew, *Oxford Handbook*, 710–16; and Francisco J. Núñez Calvo, "Phoenicia," in *Beyond the Homeland: Markers in Phoenician Chronology*, ed. Claudia Sagona (Leuven: Peeters, 2008), 19–95. On art and crafts: Brian R. Doak, *Phoenician Aniconism in Its Mediterranean and Ancient Near Eastern Contexts* (Atlanta: SBL Press, 2015), 11–12, 41–44; Glen Markoe, "The Emergence of Phoenician Art," *BASOR* 279 (1990): 13–26; and Eric Gubel, "Art and Iconography," in López-Ruiz and Doak, *Oxford Handbook*, 349–69.

23. See Taco Terpstra, *Trade in the Ancient Mediterranean: Public Order and Public Institutions* (Princeton, NJ: Princeton University Press, 2019), 33–82. Cf. Irad Malkin, *A Small Greek World: Networks in the Ancient Mediterranean* (Oxford: Oxford University Press, 2011) for the Greek networks.

24. Quinn, *In Search*.

25. See Fergus Millar, *The Roman Near East: 31 BC–AD 337* (Cambridge, MA: Harvard University Press, 1993), 236–336; and Maurice Sartre, *The Middle East under Rome* (Cambridge, MA: Harvard University Press, 2005), 55–60.

26. On Greeks and Etruscans, see Martin, *Art of Contact*, 133, who admits the ancient Greeks did not constitute a national group "in any period," though the

implications of this parallel are lost in the overall deconstruction of the Phoenician category.

27. E.g., Jonathan M. Hall, *Hellenicity: Between Ethnicity and Culture* (Chicago: University of Chicago Press, 2002).

28. E.g., María Eugenia Aubet, *The Phoenicians and the West: Politics, Colonies, and Trade*, 2nd ed. (Cambridge: Cambridge University Press, 2001), 11.

29. For the problems, see Josephine C. Quinn et al., "Augustine's Canaanites," *Papers of the British School at Rome* 82 (2014): 175–97; and Quinn, *In Search*, 33–37. Cf. further discussion of the term and its connection to Phoenicians in López-Ruiz, "Resilience."

30. First attested in the Kerameikos bilingual funerary epigram, where the deceased, an Askelonite, says, "I left Phoenicia." For the inscription, see Olga Tribulato, "Phoenician Lions: The Funerary Stele of the Phoenician Shem/Antipatros," *Hesperia* 82 (2013): 459–86. For the use of "Phoinix" or related terms in Phoenician texts, see Edward Lipiński, *Itineraria Phoenicia* (Leuven: Peeters, 2004), 169–73.

31. Overview in Carolina López-Ruiz, "Phoenician Literature," in López-Ruiz and Doak, *Oxford Handbook*, 257–69; López-Ruiz, "'Not That Which Can Be Found Among the Greeks': Philo of Byblos and Phoenician Cultural Identity in the Roman East," *Religion in the Roman Empire* 3, no. 3 (2017): 366–92.

32. See a discussion of some Persian-period inscriptions in Martin, *Art of Contact*, 99–107.

33. López-Ruiz, "Not That Which Can Be Found."

34. See Anthony J. Frendo, "review of *In Search of the Phoenicians*, by Josephine C. Quinn," *Ancient History Bulletin* 8 (2018): 74–78.

35. E.g., Quinn, *In Search*, 49; and Martin, *Art of Contact*, 95.

36. Irene Winter, "Homer's Phoenicians: History, Ethnography, or Literary Trope? (A Perspective on Early Orientalism)," in *The Ages of Homer: A Tribute to Emily Townsend Vermeule*, ed. Jane Carter and Sarah Morris (Austin: University of Texas Press, 1995), 247–71, quote on 264.

37. For similar views, see Martin, *Art of Contact*, 98; Marian Feldman, *Communities of Style: Portable Luxury Arts, Identity, and Collective Memory in the Iron Age Levant* (Chicago: University of Chicago Press, 2014), 75; and Quinn, *In Search*, 49.

38. E.g., Noël Carroll, "Interpretation, History and Narrative," *The Monist* 73, no. 2 (1990): 134–66; and Peter Lamarque and Stein Haugom Olsen, *Truth, Fiction, and Literature: A Philosophical Perspective* (Oxford: Oxford University Press, 1997). About the notion of inventing the Phoenicians, cf. comments in Frendo, "Review," 77.

39. López-Ruiz, "Not That Which Can Be Found," 378.

40. Vadim Jigoulov, *The Social History of Achaemenid Phoenicia: Being a Phoenician, Negotiating Empires* (London: Equinox, 2010); Jigoulov, "Phoenicia under the Achaemenid Empire," in López-Ruiz and Doak, *Oxford Handbook*, 89–97; cf. Martin, *Art of Contact*, 96–135.

41. E.g., Herodotus 3.19; Diodorus Siculus 17.40.3, 20.14; Polybius 31.12.12; and other sources; see Martin, *Art of Contact*, 97; and Josette Elayi, *The History of Phoenicia* (Atlanta: Lockwood Press, 2018), 223–26.

42. Quinn, *In Search*, 91–112; Quinn, "The Cultures of the Tophet: Identification and Identity in the Phoenician Diaspora," in *Cultural Identity in the Ancient Mediterranean*, ed. Erich Gruen (Malibu, CA: Getty, 2011), 388–413; and Matthew

M. McCarty, "The Tophet and Infant Sacrifice," in López-Ruiz and Doak, *Oxford Handbook*, 311–25.

43. Dannu Hütwohl, "The Birth of Sacrifice: Ritualized Deities in Eastern Mediterranean Mythology" (PhD diss., Ohio State University, 2020), 342 (discussion on 336–43); for further discussion of the *tophet* and its background, see Xella, "Religion"; Xella, *"Tophet"*; and McCarty, "The Tophet."

44. References in Tamar Hodos, *Local Responses to Colonization in the Iron Age Mediterranean* (London: Routledge, 2006), 25; cf. Quinn, *In Search*, 49.

45. E.g., Herodotus 2.104.3. The parameters for the mainland Phoenicians outlined by pseudo-Scylax (fourth century BCE) are not off the mark, as an *ethnos* occupying the Syrian coast from the Orontes to Askelon (brought up by Quinn, *In Search*, 53); cf. Ann Killebrew, "Canaanite Roots, Proto-Phoenician, and the Early Phoenician Period: c. 1300–1000 BCE," and Helene Sader, "The Archaeology of Phoenician Cities," in López-Ruiz and Doak, *Oxford Handbook*, 125–38.

46. Herodotus 2.104.3.

47. Dannu Hütwohl, "Herodotus' Phoenicians: Mediators of Cultural Exchange in the Mediterranean," *Rivista di Studi Fenici* 48 (2020): 107–20.

48. Corinne Bonnet, *Les enfants de Cadmos: Le paysage religieux de la Phénicie hellénistique* (Paris: De Boccard, 2014); and Bonnet, "The Hellenistic Period and Hellenization in Phoenicia," in López-Ruiz and Doak, *Oxford Handbook*, 99–110.

49. Suzanne Frey-Kupper, "Coins and Their Use in the Punic Mediterranean: Case Studies from Carthage to Italy from the Fourth to the First Century BCE," in Quinn and Vella, *Punic Mediterranean*, 76–110, esp. 80–81.

50. See Frey-Kupper. "Coins and Their Use," 77, for the supraregional nature of Punic coinage.

51. See a discussion of the bowls in Feldman, chapter 4 in this volume.

52. R. S. Beekes, *Etymological Dictionary of Greek*, 2 vols. (Leiden: Brill, 2010); classical study in M. C. Astour, "The Origin of the Terms 'Canaanite,' 'Phoenician,' and 'Purple,'" *Journal of Near Eastern Studies* 24 (1965): 346–50.

53. E.g., Mark Smith, *The Early History of God: Yahweh and the Other Deities in Ancient Israel*, 2nd ed. (Grand Rapids, MI: Dove Booksellers, 2002).

54. E.g., Andrew George, "Gilgamesh and the Literary Traditions of Ancient Mesopotamia," in *The Babylonian World*, ed. Gwendolyn Leick (London: Routledge, 2007), esp. 458; Martin L. West, *The East Face of Helicon: West Asiatic Elements in Greek Poetry and Myth* (Oxford: Oxford University Press, 1997), 587–88, 629; Walter Burkert, *Babylon, Memphis, Persepolis: Eastern Contexts of Greek Culture* (Cambridge, MA: Harvard University Press, 2004), 47–48; Mary Bachvarova, *From Hittite to Homer: The Anatolian Background of Ancient Greek Epic* (Cambridge: Cambridge University Press, 2016), 299; see also Carolina López-Ruiz, "Greek and Near Eastern Mythology: A Story of Mediterranean Encounters," in *Approaches to Greek Myth*, 2nd rev. ed., ed. Lowell Edmunds (Baltimore: Johns Hopkins University Press, 2014), 154–99, and *Phoenicians and the Making*, 226–48, for the Phoenicians' "intangible legacies."

55. E.g., Feldman, *Communities*; Ann Gunter, *Greek Art and the Orient* (Cambridge: Cambridge University Press, 2009).

56. Feldman, *Communities*, and chapter 4 in this volume.

57. For Assyrian art especially, see Feldman, *Communities*, 108–9.

58. Feldman, *Communities*, 46–47, 64–65.

59. E.g., Richey, "Alphabet"; and Rollston, *Writing and Literacy*.

60. Feldman, *Communities*, 178.

61. Feldman, *Communities*, 3–4.

62. Fernand Braudel, *The Mediterranean and the Mediterranean World in the Age of Philip II* (in French, 1949; repr., London: Harper Collins, 1972); Peregrine Horden and Nicholas Purcell, *The Corrupting Sea: A Study of Mediterranean History* (Malden, MA: Blackwell, 2000); David Abulafia, *The Great Sea* (Oxford: Oxford University Press, 2011); for essays reacting to the approach, see W. V. Harris, ed., *Rethinking the Mediterranean* (Oxford: Oxford University Press, 2005).

63. Horden and Purcell, *Corrupting Sea*, 44.

64. For example, Carthage and Phoenicians are not mentioned in their discussion about ancient colonial networks in North Africa in Horden and Purcell, *Corrupting Sea*, 397–99.

65. Cyprian Broodbank, *The Making of the Middle Sea: A History of the Mediterranean from the Beginning to the Emergence of the Classical World* (Oxford: Oxford University Press, 2013).

66. Broodbank, *Making*, 602.

67. Broodbank, *Making*, 27, 535.

68. Broodbank, *Making*, 347–48.

69. Susan Frankenstein, "The Phoenicians in the Far West: A Function of Assyrian Imperialism," in *Power and Propaganda*, ed. Mogens Trolle Larsen (Copenhagen: Akademisk Verlag, 1979). The Assyrian-driven, peripheral view of the Phoenicians has been overcome by earlier evidence of Phoenician expansionism, e.g., María Eugenia Aubet, "Political and Economic Implications of the New Phoenician Chronologies," in Sagona, *Beyond the Homeland*, 179–91; Aubet, "Tyre and Its Colonial Expansion," in López-Ruiz and Doak, *Oxford Handbook*, 75–87.

70. E.g., Aubet, "Political and Economic Implications."

71. E.g., for Syria, see Hodos, *Local Responses*, esp. 7, 55–88; for Etruria, see Corinna Riva, "The Orientalizing Period in Etruria: Sophisticated Communities," in *Debating Orientalization: Multidisciplinary Approaches to Processes of Change in the Ancient Mediterranean*, ed. Corinna Riva and Nicholas C. Vella (London: Equinox, 2006), 110–34; for Sardinia, see Peter van Dommelen, "The Orientalizing Phenomenon: Hybridity and Material Culture in the Western Mediterranean," in Riva and Vella, *Debating Orientalization*, 135–52; for Iberia, see Sebastián Celestino and Carolina López-Ruiz, *Tartessos and the Phoenicians in Iberia* (Oxford: Oxford University Press, 2016), esp. 129–31, and chapters in Sebastián Celestino and Javier Jiménez Ávila, eds., *El Periodo Orientalizante*, 2 vols. (Mérida: CSIC, 2005).

72. Hodos, *Local Responses*, 184–88, 198–99; Hodos, *The Archaeology of the Mediterranean Iron Age: A Globalising World c. 1100–600 BCE* (Cambridge: Cambridge University Press, 2020), 203–4.

73. E.g., Eric Gubel, "Notes on the Phoenician Component of the Orientalizing Horizon," in Riva and Vella, *Debating Orientalization*, 85–93. See also López-Ruiz, *Phoenicians and the Making*, 84–89.

74. E.g., Riva and Vella, *Debating Orientalization*.

75. E.g., Feldman, *Communities*, 16–17; Gunter, *Greek Art*; and Martin, *Art of Contact*, 18–19, 178 for the Iron Age; however, she attempts to detach Phoenician art from traditional art taxonomies when she looks at later periods.

76. Hodos, *Local Responses*; Malkin, *Small Greek World*; and Denise Demetriou, *Negotiating Identity in the Ancient Mediterranean: The Archaic and Classical Greek Multiethnic Emporia* (Cambridge: Cambridge University Press, 2012).

77. E.g., Hodos, *Local Responses*, 185–86. See also examples throughout Hodos, *Archaeology of the Mediterranean Iron Age*, for previous scholarship on this more integrated model, long defended by Sarah Morris (e.g., *Daidalos and the Origins of Greek Art* [Princeton, NJ: Princeton University Press, 1992]) and others. See also López-Ruiz, *Phoenicians and the Making*, esp. 44–62, 67–70.

78. E.g., Nicholas Stampolidis and Antonis Kotsonas, ''Phoenicians in Crete,'' in *Ancient Greece from the Mycenaean Palaces to the Age of Homer*, ed. Sigrid Deger-Jalkotzy and Irene Lemos (Edinburgh: Edinburgh University Press, 2006), 337–60.

79. John Boardman, *The Greeks Overseas: Their Early Colonies and Trade*, 4th ed. (London: Thames and Hudson, 1999); see also Irene S. Lemos, *The Protogeometric Aegean: The Archaeology of the Late Eleventh and Tenth Centuries BC* (Oxford: Oxford University Press, 2002), 212–17 for a "Euboean Koine." In the same vein, see Robin Lane Fox, *Travelling Heroes in the Epic Age of Homer* (New York: Alfred A. Knopf, 2009). For this trend, see criticism in John K. Papadopoulos, "'Phantom Euboians:' A Decade On," in *Euboea and Athens: Proceedings of a Colloquium in Memory of Malcolm B. Wallace, Athens 26–27 June 2009*, ed. David W. Rupp and Jonathan E. Tomlinson (Toronto: Canadian Institute in Greece, 2011), 113–33.

80. See Robin Osborne, "W(h)ither Orientalization?," in Riva and Vella, *Debating Orientalization*, 153–58, quote on 156, as a useful convention with the necessary caveats.

81. Hodos, *Archaeology of the Mediterranean Iron Age*.

82. See López-Ruiz, *Phoenicians and the Making*, esp. 63–89.

83. See Brien Garnand, "Phoenicians and Greeks as Comparable Contemporary Migrant Groups," in *A Companion to Greeks across the Ancient World*, ed. Francesco De Angelis (Malden, MA: Blackwell, 2020), 139–72.

84. E.g., for Iberia, see essays in M. Dietler and C. López-Ruiz, eds., *Colonial Encounters in Ancient Iberia: Phoenician, Greek, and Indigenous Relations* (Chicago: University of Chicago Press, 2009); and cases discussed throughout Hodos's *Archaeology of the Mediterranean Iron Age*.

85. Celestino and López-Ruiz, *Tartessos*.

86. Discussed in Carolina López-Ruiz, "Reificar o no reificar? Fenicios, tartesios, y el problema de las identidades sin voz," in *Un viaje entre el Oriente y el Occidente del Mediterráneo: IX Congreso Internacional de Estudios Fenicios y Púnicos*, ed. S. Celestino and E. Rodríguez (Mérida: CSIC, 2020), 51–56.

✷ CHAPTER 3 ✷

Mediterranean Interconnections beyond the City

Rural Consumption and Trade in Archaic Cyprus

CATHERINE KEARNS

Cyprus has long played an important role in studies of Iron Age interconnections. Whether invoked via the presence of its ceramic wares in the spectacular tenth-century tombs at Lefkandi or among settlement debris in the Amuq valley,[1] Cyprus's Iron Age mercantilism appears self-explanatory: an island with valued copper and timber resources facing the proverbial east and west,[2] and clearly anchored in the increasingly important communication and trade routes of the eastern Mediterranean during the early first millennium BCE (figure 3.1).[3] The movement of Euboean pendent semicircle *skyphoi* across Cyprus to the Levantine coast, as James Osborne and Jonathan Hall mention in chapter 1, has proved one conspicuous example of the residues of this transregional interaction.[4] The site of the Iron Age political center of Amathus, on the south-central coast, features prominently as a stop on this line, with considerable amounts of Greek and Levantine pottery and their local imitations found in Cypro-Geometric (ca. 1050–750 BCE) and early Cypro-Archaic (ca. 750–600 BCE) tombs.[5]

How did the consumption of Euboean *skyphoi* and the mechanics of these trade interactions structure or generate Cypriot Iron Age society at sites like Amathus, and at different local and regional scales? This chapter questions how the island has featured in scholarship on Iron Age connections and offers an approach to studying possible consumption and interaction practices through small-scale social formations, drawn from the eastern edges of Amathus' territory. In the words of Nicolas Coldstream,[6] vessels like Euboean *skyphoi* "place Amathus firmly on the route from the Aegean to the Phoenician metropolis," but we rarely look beyond the acropolis, and particularly its elite tombs, to consider how

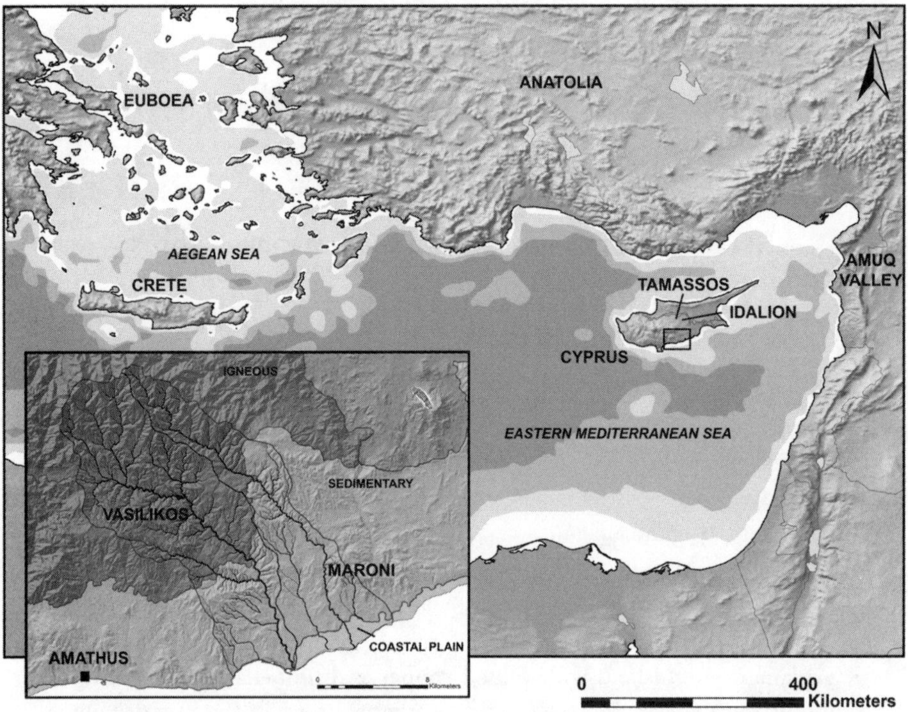

FIGURE 3.1 Map of Cyprus in its eastern Mediterranean context, with Vasilikos and Maroni valleys in detail. Created by author, data from Geological Survey Department of Cyprus.

consumption of imports worked among diverse territorial and socioeconomic groups. Connectivity, in other words, almost always means *urban* connectivity to the growing number of scholars applying the concept or questioning its interpretive limitations, particularly those related to scale, as Michael Dietler lays out in chapter 11 of this volume. How did people in rural contexts intersect at varying scales with forms of interregional, cross-Mediterranean trade? Scholars often treat Cyprus as a whole or, in recent years, have used versions of central place theory to frame heuristically the territories of the island's Iron Age kingdoms as a combination of coastal trading site, dependent agropastoral hinterland, and interior copper mines.[7] These arguments position the island's several harbors as critical conduits of goods and commodities, which then slowly permeated the hinterlands of royal subjects, if at all.[8]

In addition to a bias toward excavations at urban sites and necropolises, many scholars treat the surroundings of Cypriot towns and harbors as relatively nondescript, with the exception of extra-urban sanctuaries.[9] When imports do appear in hinterlands, usually in the form of scarce fragments found in archaeological surveys, archaeologists tend to use them to locate elites through prestige commodity vessels and infer a lack of access for non-elite, rural inhabitants constrained by subsistence economies.[10] My aim here is to complicate this picture by arguing that nonurban settlements were heterogeneous and their archaeological records sometimes contradict the explanations we impose that see culture "flowing inland."[11] While Cypriot traders clearly played significant roles in the movement of objects, materials, and people around the eastern Mediterranean, in this chapter I look instead at consumption and its connective capacities beyond the urban center.[12] I focus primarily on indexes of trade through ceramic vessels, acknowledging that exchange in perishable goods could very well have been occurring, but its traces remain frustratingly difficult to discern. As archaeologists, how might we interpret the agency of rural coastal or near-shore communities who, despite having the capacity to engage in maritime, interregional trade, appear not to have used or chosen to acquire ceramic imports?

I use the site of Amathus to foreground these questions of the spatial conditions of trade and the social spectrum of town and country integration, for two reasons. First, Amathus itself presents an interesting case of a regional town with a clearly strong signature of foreign exchange,[13] especially as a market for feasting accessories deposited in palatial and tomb contexts, but which ancient sources attest as an "indigenous" kingdom in distinction from other Cypriot centers with more recognizably Greek and Phoenician kings and populations (figure 3.2).[14] As a polity Amathus thus reveals evidence for outward-looking consumption practices as well as inward-looking local styles and non-Greek language and scripts, and the relationship of connections between its town harbor and rural populations invites more inquiry.[15] Second, while we know less about what may have distinguished urban and rural practices due to the bias in excavations toward urban contexts, survey evidence in the territories around Amathus, outside the city walls of Archaic and Classical date, provides rich information for exploring the kingdom's material practices during the eighth to fifth centuries BCE. Survey work around the acropolis of Amathus and in the Vasilikos and Maroni valleys to the east has revealed a range of smaller settlements, installations like canals or threshing floors, and diverse artifact scatters, and their development after the later ninth century seems tied to the political economy of the town.[16]

After a period of significant occupation during the Late Bronze Age (ca. 1700–1050 BCE), with at least two urban centers at Kalavasos-*Ayios*

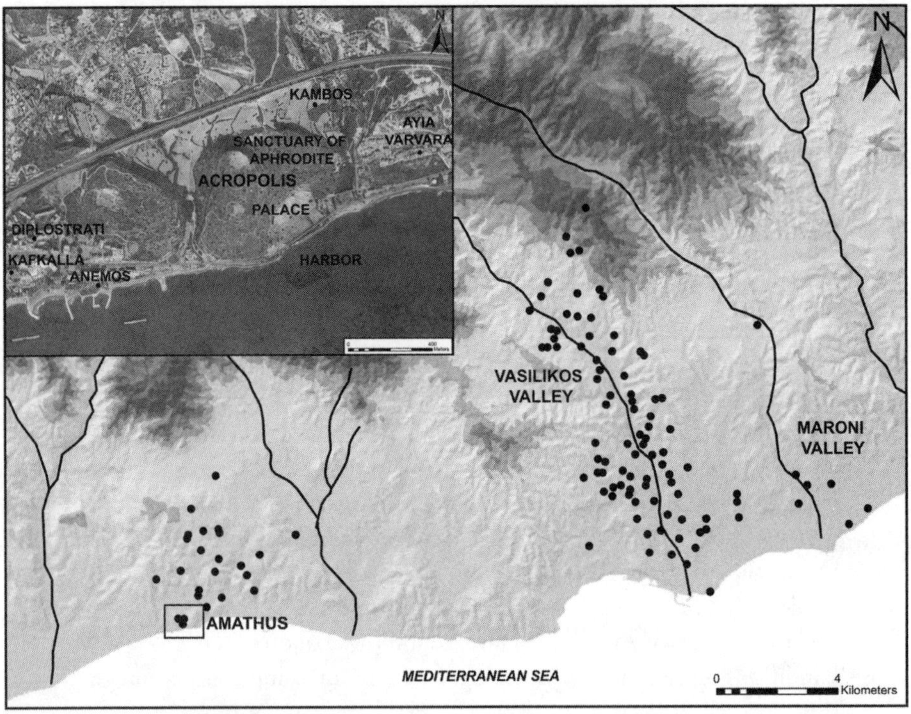

FIGURE 3.2 Map of Amathus showing acropolis and necropolises in inset, with Iron Age survey finds from Amathus and Vasilikos and Maroni valleys. Created by author, data from Geological Survey Department of Cyprus.

Dhimitrios and the Maroni complex, settlement evidence in these eastern valleys reappears only toward the end of the ninth century BCE, increasing in density during the eighth and seventh centuries and concurrent with the growth of the palatial, sanctuary, and mortuary complexes at Amathus.[17] The two watersheds also have, moreover, clear access to coastal trade, a considerably rich series of agricultural zones with evidence for water management,[18] and copper mines with radiocarbon dates that suggest activity starting from the eighth century BCE.[19] Most scholars situate the Iron Age settlements in the Vasilikos and Maroni region within the territory of Amathus, arguing that indications of villages were dependent on the town and its trade. If this region were a countryside or farther *chora* of Amathus, outside the four-kilometer range of daily farming commutes, its role within the wider fabrics of labor, production, and the mobilization of resources of Amathus are critical to understanding the town's mechanisms of interaction and settlement ecology, *sensu* Peregrine Horden and Nicholas Purcell.[20]

This chapter examines some of the local complexity on a town's margins from a bottom-up perspective, using evidence from survey archaeology. For these purposes, "bottom-up" connotes the term's conceptual origins in discussions of labor and power that advocate for the perspective of laborers outside of the monarchical center, in contrast to the ruling authorities (for a contrasting application of a "bottom-up" approach, see Marian Feldman, chapter 4 in this volume).[21] After a brief introduction to Iron Age Cyprus and current emphases on urban connectivity, I synthesize the available evidence for indications of trade in the Vasilikos and Maroni valleys, from potential signs of harbor activity to imports in local tombs. I conclude with a discussion on the scaled practices of material consumption among the diverse populations living outside the town. This case study highlights how existing top-down narratives of static or passive ruralism can misrepresent the complexities of Iron Age social and economic processes.

Iron Age Landscapes: Spatial Developments

A significant watershed in the history of Cyprus occurred after the ninth and eighth centuries BCE, when a network of apparently autonomous polities had fully established towns with various ties to, or discontinuities from, the political topography of the preceding Late Bronze Age. These polities, which scholarly consensus holds were ruled by kings (*basileis*) due to later epigraphical and written evidence, grew through regional economic development, engagement with maritime trade systems, and investment in resources like copper and agricultural or pastoral commodities.[22] Political institutions are poorly documented for this early period, but we do have some evidence that suggests the existence of a ruling elite with iconographic and later numismatic claims to authority. The so-called royal tombs at Salamis are often invoked as evidence for such elites around the eighth century BCE: Tomb 79, the most opulent, contained inlaid ivory furniture and bronzes manufactured in the Near East, numerous items made of precious metal artifacts, chariots, and sacrificed animals, among other offerings.[23] Perhaps less evocative of interregional prestige are the three dozen plain basket-handled amphorae and grinding or processing vessels of Cypriot manufacture also included in the tomb. These presumably held contents of regional agricultural production, such as one with a syllabic sign for olive oil, and their inclusion among grave goods could be interpreted as a conspicuous display of landed wealth and control over agricultural or industrial labor.[24] Similar feasting assemblages included in elite tombs across the island make it possible to argue for a developing set of values linked to semi-luxuries of arable and pastoral production, such as olive oil and wine, as Lin Foxhall has argued for contexts in Greece.[25]

Survey projects have documented a considerable rise in the number of settlements across the island during the later ninth, eighth, and seventh centuries BCE following a period of scarce evidence of occupations during the twelfth to tenth centuries BCE. In addition, the construction of monumental buildings and storerooms at central sites like Amathus and Idalium,[26] various scripts and languages,[27] and forms of burial, feasting, and ritual practice suggest novel social inequalities as well as political connections with foreign authorities accelerating during the seventh century. I have argued elsewhere that landownership and control over increasingly productive fields, in addition to rising population dynamics, generated social complexities outside of these centers that restructured settlement and economic networks.[28] Some of these new configurations of community adhered closely to the remnants of earlier prehistoric occupations, indicating some attention or investment in existing valued or productive places such as terraced hillslopes.[29] Other actors seem to have carved out novel mortuary or sacred landscapes apart from existing prehistoric remains that show potentially diverse claims of status and belonging. Evidence of these smaller settlements begins to weaken in many survey records during the Cypro-Classical period (ca. 500–300 BCE), suggesting that this Iron Age landscape activity endures for only a few centuries.

The Vasilikos and Maroni valleys pose an interesting problem for how to approach the links between Amathus and smaller settlements in the region, and how far to push the data to theorize how village settlements in this area were politically tied to the state or economically integrated in wider markets (figure 3.3). Methodologically, it can be quite difficult to "chase the Iron Age countryside" on Cyprus.[30] Two intensive survey projects conducted in the 1970s to 1990s and more recent pedestrian surveys in this region have focused mostly on prehistoric research questions, leaving their Iron Age finds largely unstudied.[31] Few Iron Age sites have been the focus of excavations in either valley, although evidence suggests that the Late Bronze Age urban complexes of Kalavasos-*Ayios Dhimitrios* and Maroni were reoccupied at different scales during the Archaic period.[32] There are thus problems with identifying Iron Age ceramic wares in this region because materials need to be compared to stratified se-

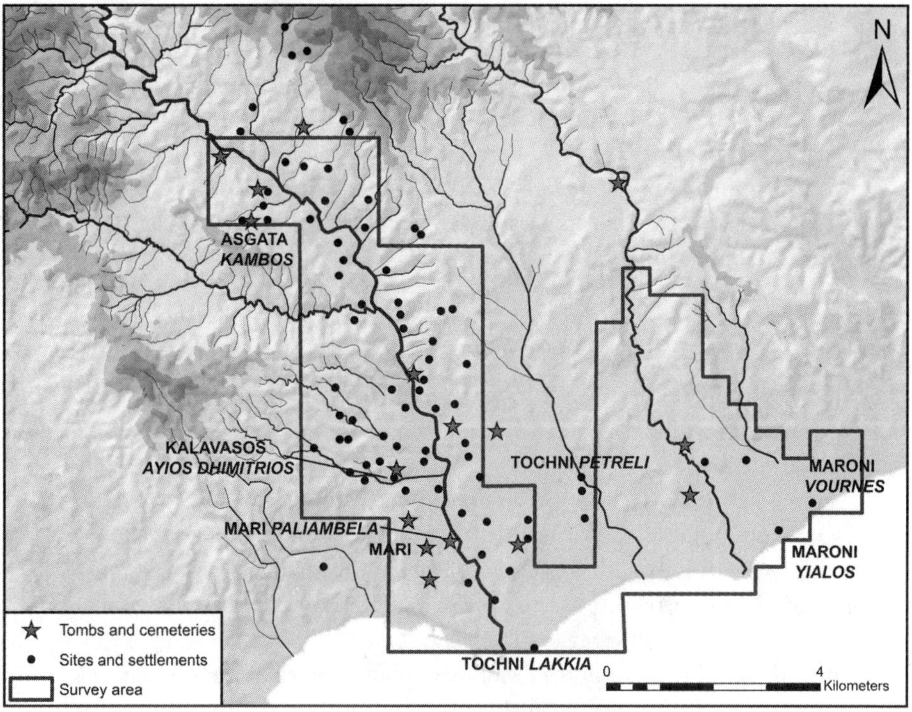

FIGURE 3.3 Map of Vasilikos and Maroni valleys with survey finds and sites mentioned in text. Created by author, data from Geological Survey Department of Cyprus.

quences at major sites like Amathus or Idalium.[33] Nevertheless, almost one hundred artifact scatters dating to the Cypro-Geometric and Archaic periods have been recovered in the two valleys and together with a number of rescue-excavated tombs, this evidence suggests that the region supported the growth of communities whose consumption patterns warrant further attention.

The Vasilikos and Maroni Watersheds

A review of the evidence for these Iron Age landscapes can frame an assessment of nonurban connectivity. In terms of harbors, the south-central coast east of Amathus has several recorded sites indicating Iron Age or later use.[34] Recent underwater surveys, geophysical investigations, and excavations at Tochni-*Lakkia*, near the mouth of the Vasilikos River, have revealed a multiperiod settlement with evidence for craft production as well as buildings with multiple occupation horizons, dating from the Late

Bronze Age through the Iron Age and with a probable later Roman presence.[35] The site is one of only a few documented in the region to preserve early Geometric evidence.[36] While anchors have not been found at *Lakkia* due to the heavily disturbed seabed, the frequency of imports suggests that trading activity occurred here, and it is plausible that the site served as a stopping point for traders traveling between Euboea and the Levant. Tochni-*Lakkia* thus seems a candidate for a coastal access point for the watershed following the abandonment of its Late Bronze Age centers, the closest at Kalavasos-*Ayios Dhimitrios*.[37]

No shipwrecks dating to this period have been found off the coast of Cyprus, but recently three shipwrecks discovered close to Turkey, dating to roughly the mid-seventh to early sixth centuries BCE, suggest indirectly what trade at Tochni-*Lakkia* may have looked like. The recovered cargoes contain a large percentage of basket-handled amphorae, locally sourced to Cyprus through composition analysis, indicating trade in rural commodities such as olive oil, grain, and wine.[38] The combination of Cypriot vessels with those of East Greek provenance points to a network from the Aegean to the eastern Mediterranean that operated between small and interregional scales of trade.[39] The three cargoes also included various numbers of *mortaria,* shallow open vessels with thick rims and walls that were probably used for grinding and that may imply a shipment of agricultural goods and processing equipment. These finds attest to the expansion of interregional market relationships beyond the exchange of luxury goods.[40]

A handful of tombs have been excavated that shed some light on local dynamics and connections to Amathusian burial practices. One of these, a rock-cut chamber tomb containing two adults and a child, from the middle of the modern village of Mari, revealed an overwhelming number of Amathusian ceramic vessels in common wares and shapes of the mid-eighth to seventh centuries BCE.[41] Only one import was included, a fragmentary jug of Levantine ware. While the tomb likely indicates a claim of status distinction, particularly in the inclusion of an iron sword and possible bronze weights, that distinction does not seem tied to the presentation of imported or conspicuously nonlocal vessels. Excavated tombs from the village of Maroni farther inland and outside the Neolithic site of Chirokitia follow this pattern, with few to no imports.[42] One potential Phoenician vessel, a hand-burnished jar from a tomb excavated in Maroni village, may more likely be a local copy.[43]

The two surveys conducted in the Vasilikos and Maroni valleys in the 1970s–1990s, the Vasilikos Valley Project and the Maroni Valley Archaeological Survey Project,[44] while difficult to compare due to their different sampling methodologies, shared a research design aimed at exposing prehistoric activity in addition to Late Bronze Age urbanism. For the Iron Age, analysis by Anna Georgiadou of both this survey material and survey data collected in 2016–17 has revealed significant, if preliminary, Iron Age patterns.[45] The fabrics, shapes, and assemblages are all clearly oriented toward production workshops at Amathus, sharing material properties and stylistic attributes with the nearby center, although it is difficult to confirm whether they were produced locally or supplied directly from Amathusian workshops. Spatial analysis of the collected diagnostics from forty-five of roughly eighty sites, however, indicates complex histories as compared to the immediate surroundings of Amathus.

Only a few pieces of imported ceramics out of hundreds of diagnostic fragments from earlier survey work can be confidently identified, including two Euboean vessel fragments—one a plate with semicircles similar to those found at Amathus and one the base of a *skyphos*.[46] The former comes from the apparent eighth-century reoccupation of the Bronze Age urban center of Kalavasos-*Ayios Dhimitrios*. The *skyphos*, on the other hand, was recovered in a small scatter on the edge of the survey grid at Tochni-*Petreli*, along a buried water channel linked to the Ayios Minas River of the Maroni valley.[47] Imitations of foreign shapes in the survey finds are even rarer, but include one fragment of a Greek-style *skyphos*, found within an area of looted tombs at the site of Mari-*Paliambela*, and produced with the signature traits of Amathusian workshops.[48] Far up the valley, about half a kilometer from the known ancient copper mines, ceramic scatters indicate several interrelated small settlements.[49] One fragment of a Levantine amphora was found here at a site called Asgata-*Kambos*, and has what appear to be signs incised on the neck before firing. Comparanda from Amathus remain enigmatic yet may reveal an administrative system connected to local, island-directed trade using or recycling vessels produced on the Levantine coast.[50]

Additional survey work conducted in 2016–17 has aimed to bring these differences into relief with more intensive study at targeted sites that show a range of Iron Age occupations and connections to trade routes and earlier Bronze Age settlements.[51] These surveys used a standard walking methodology and sampling of diagnostic ceramics, which allows for a comparative look at two Iron Age survey assemblages that suggest some patterns of change developing during the eighth and seventh centuries, further complicating the picture of insular ruralism. Although this admittedly coarse evidence comes from likely domestic or processing contexts that often lack clear indications of social consumption, the findings illustrate local contingencies that shaped access to traded goods in the valleys.

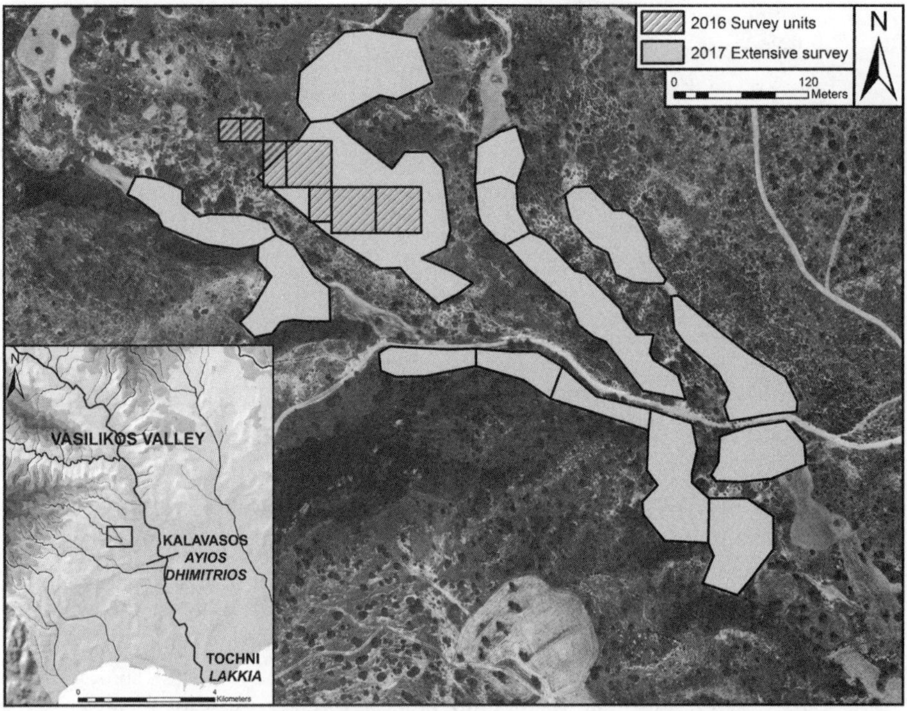

FIGURE 3.4 Position of Kalavasos-*Vounaritashi* in the mid-Vasilikos valley showing survey units. Satellite photograph, 2014. Created by author, data from Geological Survey Department of Cyprus.

Kalavasos-*Vounaritashi*, first identified in the 1970s as a multicomponent prehistoric site that included an isolated area with dense Archaic ceramics,[52] sits on a limestone terrace with gypsum outcrops overlooking side drainages of the Vasilikos River (figure 3.4). On the terrace, the Vasilikos Valley Project found enough material to suggest a series of settlements of prehistoric to Late Roman date, but the Archaic assemblage is relatively small, about a half hectare. In 2017 extensive surveys with walkers spaced ten meters apart revealed little to no material in the surrounding alluvial channels or fields, indicating that the site was likely confined to the flatter surface of the gypsum outcrop with deeper soil deposits. The ceramics recovered in the surface collections are largely plain cooking wares, storage vessels like pithoi or basket-handled amphorae, and grinding vessels like *mortaria* or stone basins, which indicate a domestic and perhaps agropastoral processing site of the later eighth to sixth centuries. A recent geophysical survey at the site, including magne-

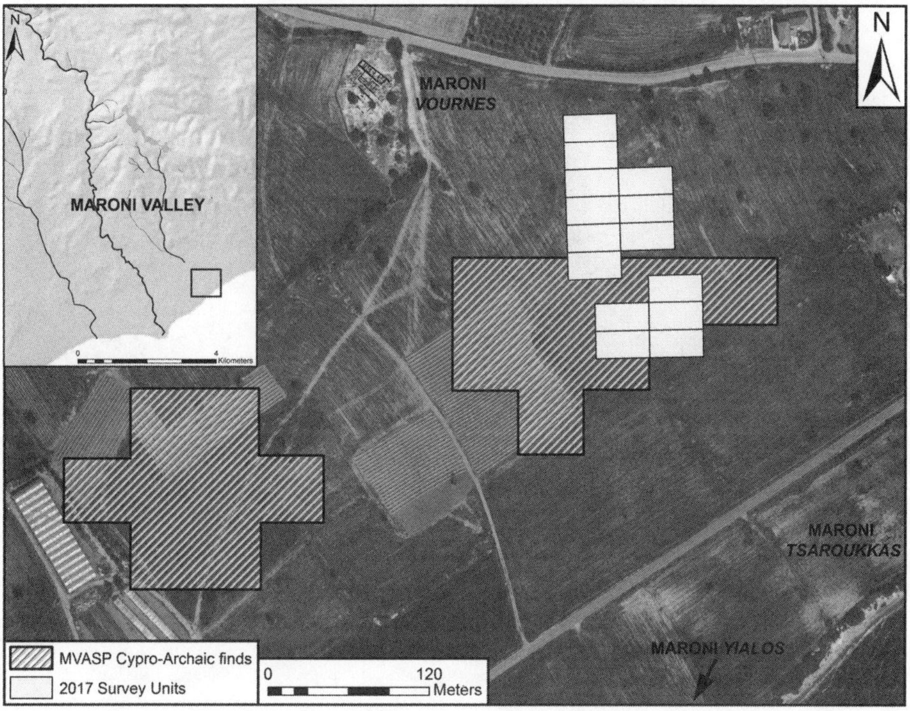

FIGURE 3.5 Position of Maroni-*Vournes* on littoral showing survey units. Satellite photograph, 2014. Created by author, data from Geological Survey Department of Cyprus.

tometry and ground-penetrating radar, also suggests a relatively discrete settlement with several buried walls.[53] Cross-channel walls in the two side drainages, while difficult to date without further archaeometric investigation, may imply long-term attention to alluvial soil management.[54] The small area of Archaic material is about half a kilometer from the Late Bronze Age center of Kalavasos-*Ayios Dhimitrios,* which is connected to the major east–west route across the valley.

In the Maroni Valley, survey work in the 1990s revealed a high concentration of Iron Age materials to the south and southeast of the Late Bronze Age site of Maroni-*Vournes* (figure 3.5).[55] Sitting on iron-rich soils of the coastal plain, and near a channel of the river, the urban complex at *Vournes* was abandoned in 1200 BCE with no reoccupation until the eighth century.[56] Excavations revealed a small sanctuary built within the monumental remains, in operation between the eighth and third centuries BCE and oriented to a male and female pair of deities associated with

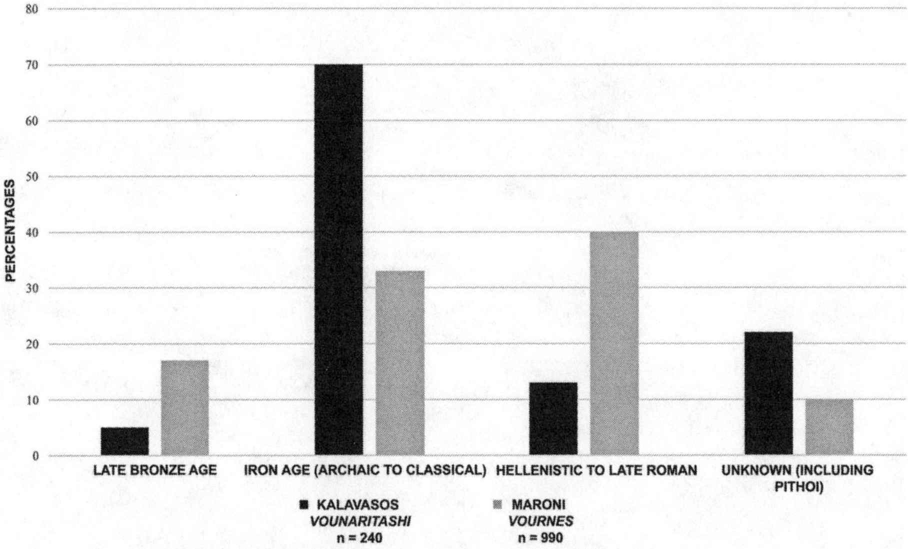

FIGURE 3.6 Chart detailing the percentages of known types of ceramic wares, in chronological categories, from (a) Kalavasos-*Vounaritashi* and (b) Maroni-*Vournes*. Data from author, Anna Georgiadou, and Agata Dobosz.

fertility.[57] Recent survey work has confirmed the Archaic presence, and geophysical survey has located several promising areas of potential buildings or installations.[58] The ceramics recovered through survey show similarly high numbers of coarse and utilitarian vessel fragments, including amphorae and pithoi, as well as diagnostic fine wares associated with the Late Bronze Age occupations. This area, now heavily engineered for the cultivation of citrus and wheat, sits between *Vournes* and the coast, where evidence of an anchorage at Maroni-*Tsaroukkas* indicates at least intermittent use as a distribution and production site from the Late Bronze Age to the Roman period.[59] A short distance to the west, Maroni-*Yialos* was also a late Archaic and Classical site with an associated anchorage.[60]

Preliminary analysis of the assemblages at Kalavasos-*Vounaritashi* and Maroni-*Vournes* confirms their differences in chronological span (figure 3.6). At *Vounaritashi*, the majority of diagnostic pieces (70 percent) are Iron Age and more specifically Cypro-Archaic to Classical in date, with smaller proportions of Late Bronze Age (5 percent) or Hellenistic to Late Roman (13 percent) pieces that may have eroded from other occupations on the plateau. No clear Cypro-Geometric pieces were identified, suggesting a beginning of activity by the early or mid-eighth century. At *Vournes*, the diachronic use of the Maroni littoral is much more evident, with comparable amounts of identifiable Late Bronze Age (17 percent), Iron Age (33 percent), and Hellenistic to Late Roman (40 percent) material present. One Iron Age figurine fragment of an upper torso with raised arms was found, likely associated with the nearby sanctuary, while the overwhelming signature of domestic and utilitarian ceramic fragments may suggest some settlement or processing activities in the area.[61]

In addition, this recent survey work has corroborated the trend seen in the local mortuary contexts for a small percentage of imported wares. Analysis by Agata Dobosz has confirmed the presence of transport amphorae from the Aegean that remain difficult to date precisely, but are indicative of forms from the later Archaic through Hellenistic and Roman periods. At *Vounaritashi*, the nine imported pieces make up only 4 percent of the total assemblage. Six are plain transport amphorae, as well as three cooking pot and jar fragments. The presence of nonlocal transport amphorae may indicate access to interregional markets. The lack of imported open vessels, such as plates or drinking cups, marks an absence of conspicuous feasting, or at least alternate modes of consumption that did not require imported styles. At *Vournes*, only 2 percent of the total diagnostic assemblage of 993 fragments were diagnostically confirmed as nonlocal, and none can confidently be dated to the Iron Age period. Transport amphorae also dominate this category, mostly of Hellenistic or later date from areas around northern Africa, the Syrian coast, and the Black Sea, as well as earlier Mycenaean cups and the ubiquitous Canaanite jar.

Discussion

What is especially striking about the scarce imports found in the Iron Age assemblages in these valleys is the comparatively rich evidence of interregional exchange, from the Levant to the Aegean and central Mediterranean, visible for the preceding Late Bronze Age and the subsequent Hellenistic to Late Roman sites in the area: How do we start to make sense of the divergent patterns of village practices of interaction or acquisition for the first millennium BCE?

While secure dates for an established Iron Age anchorage near Maroni-*Vournes* are lacking, the littoral attracted communities reinvesting in the area during the eighth century, following the abandonment of the Late Bronze Age complex and its associated sites and landscapes.[62] Evidently, these reoccupations were integrated within the remnants of the urban fabric of the site. Olive oil processing activities associated with the sanctuary may indicate the cultivation of olives for ritual needs in the surrounding fields, which equally afford lowland pasture.[63] Although the accessibility to presumed coastal trading points might warrant assumptions about the acquisition of conspicuous foreign goods, this accessibility appears not to have demarcated local consumption patterns of the Archaic period in ways that privileged the display of foreign or imported ceramic vessels. Rather than frame this as an argument about trade from the absence of imports, I suggest that these findings reveal how practices tied to the sanctuary at Maroni looked inward, perhaps geared toward attracting passersby on an east–west coastal road. Similar patterns of scarce imports have been interpreted for Cypro-Archaic ceramic finds at the rural sanctuary of Athienou-*Malloura*, in the central plain of the island,[64] as well as at the excavated nonurban settlement of Panayia Ematousa northwest of the center of Citium on the eastern coast.[65]

Further inland in the Vasilikos valley, some transport amphorae were making their way to Kalavasos-*Vounaritashi*, a small, seemingly work-related site with little direct connection to coastal networks. The low number of fine wares found here, aside from a discrete assemblage that may attest to nearby tombs, underscores the likelihood that nonlocal vessels were traded for their contents, not as conspicuous markers of status. The site's accessibility to different routes of distribution, however, which brought Levantine or Euboean vessels up the Vasilikos River to settlement areas like Asgata-*Kambos*, provides more indication of local markets and a wider entailment of economic integration than previously assumed.

Together the two survey collections may suggest what Dietler has called a "logic of indifference," or the practices by which inhabitants came to ignore, or refuse, opportunities for acquiring imported objects for appropriation as modes of consumption or use.[66] In cases like eastern Crete during the sixth and fifth centuries, similar patterns of low levels of imported vessels have alternatively revealed institutional practices of austerity and intentional limitations on sumptuary practices.[67] Without more fine-grained data collected through the excavation of Iron Age sites in the Vasilikos and Maroni region, it is difficult to contextualize these kinds of selective consumption in their smaller settlements. The extension of urban practices of feasting or conspicuous consumption into local contexts might have required special material participants, but the excavated mortuary evidence in this region does suggest that imported vessels were not the conduit through which an elite distinctiveness was sought, or alternatively, controlled or managed by some authoritative body. The iron swords, knives, and adzes recovered from tombs in this area, on the other hand, do suggest an achievable local performance of status or potentially warrior identity that could echo and dialogue with elite shared practices across the island, from the tombs at Salamis to those closer at Amathus, or farther afield, as Sarah Morris argues in chapter 5 of this volume.[68]

It does seem that the activities that brought agricultural producers to the coast become attenuated if we measure connectivity only by an index of imported ceramics.[69] In other words, conceptual problems arise if connectivity is merely understood as a static quality of a site or group and quantified in categories of objects, rather than a process with a politics of space, involving local actors and broader structural systems within distinct historical and ecological frameworks. Similar critiques of formalist attributes have become common when discussing the rise of the Archaic city and processes of urbanization.[70] To return to the Amathusian polity, we can see similar assumptions locating the concentration of trade among its urban elite, with a largely vacuous or "backwater" countryside.[71] In prevailing models of site hierarchies, where rurality is identified and measured in terms of site size, smaller settlements recorded through survey are typically viewed as simple, uniform nodes between copper-mining installations in the foothills and the port.[72] Undoubtedly, we have to imagine that Amathusian authorities had some level of control over the flows of goods coming through its port and into its broader territory. The evidence of diverse practices at *Vounaritashi* and *Vournes*, however, suggests that rural settlements may have been integrated in more complex ways with these politicoeconomic systems.

We should keep in mind that not all rural or small settlements map neatly onto non-elite status or a complete dependency on the conditions and modes of consumption shaping social change in towns.[73] Ethnographic studies drawn from twentieth-century villages offer some analogies, with the caveats that any heuristic insights are challenged by their capitalist contexts. Roger Just discovered in his study of the village of Spartokhori on the Greek island of Meganisi, for example, that rural communities with strong economic and social connections to metropolitan networks could still lack outward markers of "transplanted urbanity."[74] The ceramic assemblages from the Vasilikos valley, which indicate at least some "high-status" social groups with network connections to imported goods like iron swords, raise interesting possibilities for understanding the developments of polities and economic growth during the first millennium BCE.[75] On the one hand, the intensification and mobilization of agropastoral production in these valleys may indicate intentional strategies of the political class of Amathus, conditioned through more extensive kinship or group networks that integrated the produce of dependent sites like Kalavasos-*Vounaritashi* with feasting rituals of Amathusian elites. These lines of acquisition and the wealth that they afforded forged new social capital and authority at Amathus, chiefly displayed through rich burial offerings, while that wealth was potentially replicated by those in smaller settlements looking to gain status distinction. Although arguments from one sherd are superficial at best, the recovery of the Euboean plate fragment at the site of Kalavasos-*Ayios Dhimitrios* mentioned above hints at the potential orientation of local elite feasting toward Amathusian tastes.[76]

On the other hand, we can also surmise the existence of locally situated actors or groups with their own spheres of Mediterranean interconnection, whose ability to manage and control the production of semi-luxuries like olive oil created opportunities for independent networks and status differentiation, and a more malleable territorial relationship to Amathus.[77] Sites like Tochni-*Lakkia* or the Maroni littoral may, for example, align more with a model of significant smaller regional interaction that included items from foreign cargoes, yet whose logics of trade did not necessarily require oversight or supervision through the port at Amathus. These interpretations, while circumstantial without further investigation, highlight the underlying mediations of countryside dynamics that are elided when scholars gloss the rural as traditionally a sphere of occupation.

Conclusion

This chapter has aimed to challenge, or complicate, the idea that cities are inherently connected to the wider world and rural expanses unconnected, as if the practices of interconnection forged through economic or political strategies are a static, essential trait of urbanism. A comparative look at the smaller scale of two watersheds outside of an emerging Iron Age center, Amathus, exposes some of the social mechanisms at work beneath the economic ones, and helps fill in what Stefano Campana has recently described as an "emptyscape"—gaps in the archaeological record that extend between our prevailing attention to sites.[78] In turning our focus to the consumption practices of one productive landscape, the evidence hints at the agency of different groups during the eighth and seventh centuries and invites more inquiry into patterns of acquisition and material uptake.[79] I have argued that instead of treating the region as wholly reliant on the harbor at Amathus, we can question whether local actors conducted their own off-island trade but chose not to bring the imported vessels of urban appeal into their own social lives. In doing so, we can ask different questions of the material practices of these communities as more than the undifferentiated, local foil to elite commodity acquisition. Of course, surface survey necessarily skews our interpretive focus to studying ceramic fragments and can only go so far in recuperating the largely ephemeral traces of the movement of perishable goods and the exchange of materials like textiles or animal products. Future excavations at these and other sites in the Vasilikos and Maroni valleys intend to explore these questions.

The broader goals of this project are to address the dialectical relationships between urbanization and smaller settlements and the investment in new configurations of wealth, inequality, and social boundaries that cocreated Cypriot polities. Or more conceptually, in Michael Herzfeld's words, to "recover entities such as the village as valuable *topoi*" in archaeological research.[80] While any conclusions on the mechanics by which these settlements negotiated structures of power at Amathus remain tentative, this work prompts us to reassess how we often distort the places and spaces of connectivity outside of urban emporia, especially on islands. Attending to the complexities of rural island communities requires avoiding a priori assumptions that they were either economically determined to be outward looking and mercantilist, or isolated from the pressures of interregional contacts or sociopolitical demands.[81] Excavation work that provides more spatial and chronological resolution on the material culture and landed economies of these countryside settlements is thus crucial to understanding how these inhabitants perceived and engaged with urban practices, including as discriminating consumers with their own preoccupations and tastes.[82]

The methods of survey archaeology and landscape analysis, however, still provide important avenues for thinking about the triangulations of mobility, landscape, and networks of trade at scales that incorporate known centers and their surrounding heterogeneous populations. Countering the urban bias of Cypriot archaeology of the Iron Age requires such wider, diachronic perspectives.[83] The analytical messiness of survey data, and the patterns of inconsistency or ambiguity that they often reveal, can offer interpretive benefits to uncovering the dynamics of rural markets or production areas alongside urbanizing processes.

Our prevailing structural focus on the consumption of high-status objects obscures a more complicated picture of traded goods and multiscalar distribution networks circulating around the eastern Mediterranean.[84] The Vasilikos and Maroni watersheds offer evidence for targeted production in certain staples or semi-luxuries and access to trade routes, but whose emerging Iron Age communities were seemingly not including Greek or Levantine objects within local systems of value and meaning, despite significant politicoeconomic connections to the closest town. The evidence rather suggests other local markers of distinctiveness, especially choices in places for communal action, which helped condition new forms of settlement. In addition to moving beyond a reified idea of the city, or of top-down assumptions about foreign permeation of the countryside, this work reaffirms growing claims that interaction processes and patterning do not always manifest in the steady accumulation of goods or practices, and that their residues may be masked by consumption practices aimed at interiority rather than exteriority. Indeed, Iron Age Cyprus is a case in which various agents may have engaged with, and even shaped, some levels of interregional maritime exchange, but they also cultivated their own social boundaries.

Notes

1. Nicole Schreiber, *The Cypro-Phoenician Pottery of the Iron Age* (Leiden: Brill, 2003), 285; Steven Karacic and James F. Osborne, "Eastern Mediterranean Economic Exchange during the Iron Age: Portable X-Ray Fluorescence and Neutron Activation Analysis of Cypriot-Style Pottery in the Amuq Valley, Turkey," *PLoS One* 11, no. 1 (2016), https://doi.org/10.1371/journal.pone.0166399. On Cypriot imports at Lefkandi, see John Papadopoulos, chapter 7 in this volume. I wish to thank James Osborne and Jonathan Hall for organizing a productive conference and for providing editorial help, and all the participants who offered critical feedback. I thank Sturt Manning for his help with an earlier draft, Anna Georgiadou and Agata Dobosz for their expertise with the survey material, and the members of the Kalavasos and Maroni Built Environments Project. This fieldwork was funded in part through a Loeb Classical Library Fellowship and the Mellon Foundation. Any omissions or errors are solely my own.

2. Joseph G. Manning, *The Open Sea: The Economic Life of the Ancient Mediterranean World from the Iron Age to the Rise of Rome* (Princeton, NJ: Princeton University Press, 2018), 86.

3. Susan Sherratt and Andrew Sherratt, "The Growth of the Mediterranean Economy in the Early First Millennium BC," *World Archaeology* 24, no. 3 (1993): 361–78; A. Bernard Knapp, *Prehistoric and Protohistoric Cyprus: Identity, Insularity and Connectivity* (Oxford: Oxford University Press, 2008), 281–97; Nota Kourou, "Phoenicia, Cyprus and the Aegean in the Early Iron Age: J. N. Coldstream's Contribution and the Current State of Research," in *Cyprus and the Aegean in the Early Iron Age*, ed. Maria Iacovou (Nicosia: Bank of Cyprus Cultural Foundation, 2012), 37–38; and Cyprian Broodbank, *The Making of the Middle Sea: A History of the Mediterranean from the Beginning to the Emergence of the Classical World* (Oxford: Oxford University Press, 2013), 449–51, 487–88.

4. Irene S. Lemos and H. Hatcher, "Early Greek Vases in Cyprus: Euboean and Attic," *Oxford Journal of Archaeology* 10, no. 2 (1991); Nicolas Coldstream, *Light from Cyprus on the Greek "Dark Age"?* (Oxford: Leopard's Head Press, 1998); Coldstream, "Cypriot Taste in Early Greek Ceramic Imports," *Ancient West & East* 8 (2009): 22; Jan P. Crielaard, "Production, Circulation and Consumption of Early

Iron Age Greek Pottery (Eleventh to Seventh Centuries BC)," in *The Complex Past of Pottery: Production, Circulation and Consumption of Mycenaean and Greek Pottery (Sixteenth to Early Fifth Centuries BC)*, ed. Jan P. Crielaard, V. Stissi, and G. J. van Wijngaarden (Amsterdam: J. C. Gieben, 1999), 49–81; and Rosalinde Kearsley, *The Pendent Semi-Circle Skyphos: A Study of Its Development and Chronology and an Examination of It as Evidence for Euboean Activity at Al Mina* (London: University of London, Institute of Classical Studies).

5. Patricia Bikai, *The Phoenician Pottery of Cyprus* (Nicosia: A. G. Leventis Foundation, 1987), 70; and Nicolas Coldstream, "Greek Geometric and Archaic Imports from the Tombs of Amathus—II," *Report of the Department of Antiquities*, Cyprus (1995), 199.

6. Coldstream, *Light from Cyprus*, 6.

7. Maria Iacovou, "Site Size Estimates and the Diversity Factor in Late Cypriot Settlement Histories," *Bulletin of the American Schools of Oriental Research* 348 (2007): 18; Iacovou, "From Regional Gateway to Cypriot Kingdom: Copper Deposits and Copper Routes in the Chora of Paphos," in *Eastern Mediterranean Metallurgy and Metalwork in the Second Millennium BC*, ed. V. Kassianidou and G. Papasavvas (Oxford: Oxbow Books, 2012), 56–67; V. Kassiandou{~?~AQ: Should this be "Iacovou" instead?}, "Historically Elusive and Internally Fragile Island Polities: The Intricacies of Cyprus's Political Geography in the Iron Age," *Bulletin of the American Schools of Oriental Research* 370 (2013): 32; Anna Satraki, *Κύπριοι Βασιλείς από τον Κοσμάσο στο Νικοκρέοντα: Ηπολιτειακή οργάνωση της αρχαίας Κύπρου από την Ύστερη Εποχή του Χαλκού μέχρι το τέλος της Κυπροκλασικής περιόδου με βάση τα αρχαιολογικά δεδομένα* (Nicosia: University of Cyprus, 2012), 333–34; Vassiliki Kassianidou, "The Exploitation of the Landscape: Metal Resources and the Copper Trade during the Aof the Cypriot City-Kingdoms," *Bulletin of American Schools of Oriental Research* 370 (2013): 49–82.

8. Nicolas Coldstream, "The Geometric and Archaic Periods," in *Archaeology in Cyprus 1960–1985*, ed. V. Karageorghis (Nicosia: A. G. Leventis Foundation, 1985), 53; cf. P. Nicholas Kardulias, Derek B. Counts, and Michael K. Toumazou, "Research by Design: An Integrated Approach to Culture Contact in the Malloura Valley," in *Crossroads and Boundaries: The Archaeology of Past and Present in the Malloura Valley, Cyprus*, ed. M. K. Toumazou, P. N. Kardulias, and D. B. Counts (Boston: American Schools of Oriental Research, 2011), 1–12.

9. Sabine Fourrier, "Les territoires des royaumes Chypriotes archaïques: Une esquisse de géographie historique," *Cahiers du Centre d'Études Chypriotes* 32 (2002): 135–46; Fourrier, "Constructing the Peripheries: Extra-urban Sanctuaries and Peer-Polity Interaction in Iron Age Cyprus," *Bulletin of the American Schools of Oriental Research* 370 (2013): 103–22; and cf. Toumazou, Kardulias, and Counts, *Crossroads and Boundaries*.

10. See Vassos Karageorghis, *Two Cypriote Sanctuaries of the End of the Cypro-Archaic Period* (Rome: Consiglio nazionale della ricerche, 1977). For a comparison of outward-looking coastal sites and detached hinterlands in the Roman period, see also Jody Michael Gordon, "Insularity and Identity in Roman Cyprus: Connectivity, Complexity, and Cultural Change," in *Insularity and Identity in the Roman Mediterranean*, ed. Anna Kouremenos (Oxford: Oxbow Books, 2018), 31, 34.

11. See Kardulias, Counts, and Toumazou, "Research by Design," 6. On town–countryside complexities, see William Cronon, *Nature's Metropolis: Chicago and the*

Great West (New York: W. W. Norton, 1991); Carrie Hritz, "Urbanocentric Models and 'Rural Messiness': A Case Study in the Balikh River Valley, Syria," *American Journal of Archaeology* 117, no. 2 (2013): 141–61; Donald C. Haggis, "The Archaeology of Urbanization: Research Design and the Excavation of an Archaic Greek City on Crete," in *Classical Archaeology in Context: Theory and Practice in Excavation in the Greek World*, ed. Donald C. Haggis and Carla Antonaccio (Berlin: Walter de Gruyter), 219–58; Lin Foxhall and David Yoon, "Carving Out a Territory: Rhegion, Locri and the Households and Communities of the Classical Countryside," *World Archaeology* 48, no. 3 (2016): 431–48.

12. Paul R. Mullins, "The Archaeology of Consumption," *Annual Review of Anthropology* 40 (2011): 140; Lin Foxhall, "Small, Rural Farmstead Sites in Ancient Greece: A Material Culture Analysis," in *Chora und Polis*, ed. F. Kolb (Munich: Oldenbourg Wissenschaftverlag, 2004), 249–70; and Foxhall, "Village to City: Staples and Luxuries? Exchange Networks and Urbanization," in *Mediterranean Urbanization 800–600 BCE*, ed. Robin Osborne and Barry Cunliffe (Oxford: Oxford University Press, 2005), 233. See also Haggis, "Archaeology of Urbanization," 254–55.

13. Coldstream, "Cypriot Taste," 21–22.

14. Thierry Petit, "The First Palace of Amathus and the Cypriot Poleogenesis," in *The Royal Palace Institution in the First Millennium BC: Regional Development and Cultural Interchange between East and West*, ed. Inge Nielsen (Athens: Danish Institute at Athens, 2001), 53–75; Anna Georgiadou, "À propos de la production céramique chypro-géométrique d'Amathonte," *Cahiers du Centre d'Études Chypriotes* 41 (2011): 167–82; Sarah Janes, "Death and Burial in the Age of the Cypriot City-Kingdoms: Social Complexity Based on the Mortuary Evidence," *Bulletin of American Schools of Oriental Research* 370 (2013): 145–68; Antoine Hermary, "Amathus, Capital of the Kingdom and City-State," in *Lemesos: A History of Limassol in Cyprus from Antiquity to the Ottoman Conquest*, ed. A. Nicolaou-Konnari and C. Schabel (Newcastle upon Tyne: Cambridge Scholars Publishing, 2015), 1–15; and Thierry Petit, *La naissance des cités-royaumes Cypriotes* (Oxford: Archaeopress, 2019).

15. For the evidence of scripts, see Philippa Steele, *Syllabic Writing on Cyprus and Its Context* (Cambridge: Cambridge University Press, 2013), 99, 101, 105–21. On the "rustic" or "local" quality of Amathusian ceramics, see Einar Gjerstad, "Pottery Types: Cypro-Geometric to Cypro-Classical," *Opuscula Atheniensia* 3 (1960): 106; Einar Gjerstad, John Lindros, Erik Sjoqvist, and Alfred Westholm, *The Swedish Cyprus Expedition: Finds and Results of Excavations in Cyprus 1927–1931*, vol. 2 (Stockholm: The Swedish Cyprus Expedition, 1935), 434; Coldstream, "Greek Geometric," 200.

16. Catherine Petit, "Amathonte et son territoire à traverse les âges," in *Guide d'Amathonte*, ed. Pierre Aupert (Paris: École Française d'Athènes–Fondation A. G. Leventis, 1996), 173–82.

17. Maria Iacovou, "Amathous: An Early Iron Age Polity in Cyprus; The Chronology of Its Foundation," *Report of the Department of Antiquities, Cyprus* (2002): 101–22; T. Petit, *La naissance*.

18. Malcolm Wagstaff, "Agricultural Terraces: The Vasilikos Valley, Cyprus," in *Past and Present Soil Erosion: Archaeological and Geographical Perspectives*, ed. Malcolm Bell and John Boardman (Oxford: Oxbow Books, 1992), 155–61; Catherine Kearns, "Re-survey and Spatial Analysis of Landscape Developments during the First Millennium BCE on Cyprus," *Antiquity Project Gallery* 90, no. 353 (2016): 1–8.

19. Kassianidou, "Exploitation of the Landscape," 75, table 9.2.

20. Peregrine Horden and Nicholas Purcell, *The Corrupting Sea: A Study of Mediterranean History* (Malden, MA: Blackwell, 2000), 89–122. See also Haggis, "Archaeology of Urbanization," 254–55.

21. E.g., Marshall Sahlins, *Apologies to Thucydides: Understanding History as Culture and Vice Versa* (Chicago: University of Chicago Press, 2004), 139.

22. E.g., Iacovou, "Migrations"; Satraki, *Κύπριοι Βασιλείς*.

23. Vassos Karageorghis, *Salamis: Recent Discoveries in Cyprus* (New York: McGraw-Hill, 1969), 76–98; and Ann Gunter, *Greek Art and the Orient* (Cambridge: Cambridge University Press, 2009), 21–28.

24. Karageorghis, *Salamis*, 71, plate 24; Elizabeth S. Greene, Justin Leidwanger, and Harun Ozdas, "Expanding Contacts and Collapsing Distances in Early Cypro-Archaic Trade: Three Case Studies of Shipwrecks off the Turkish Coast," in *Transport Amphorae and Trade of Cyprus*, ed. M. L. Lawall and J. Lund (Aarhus: Aarhus University Press, 2013), 32; see also Karageorghis, *Salamis*, plate 35.

25. Lin Foxhall, *Olive Cultivation in Ancient Greece: Seeking the Ancient Economy* (Oxford: Oxford University Press, 2007), 17, 89–95.

26. Amathus: T. Petit, "First Palace"; Idalium: Maria Hadjicosti, "The Kingdom of Idalion in the Light of New Evidence," *Bulletin of the American Schools of Oriental Research* 308 (1997): 49–63.

27. Maria Iacovou, "The Cypriot Syllabary as a Royal Signature: The Political Context for the Syllabic Script in the Iron Age," in *Syllabic Writing on Cyprus and Its Context*, ed. Philippa Steele (Cambridge: Cambridge University Press, 2013), 133–52.

28. Catherine Kearns, "Mediterranean Archaeology and Environmental Histories in the Spotlight of the Anthropocene," *History Compass* 15, no. 10 (2017), https://doi.org/10.1111/hic3.12371; Kearns, "Discerning 'Favorable' Climates: Science, Survey Archaeology, and the Cypriot Iron Age," in *New Directions in Cypriot Archaeology*, ed. C. Kearns and S. W. Manning (Ithaca, NY: Cornell University Press, 2019), 266–94.

29. Kathy D. Morrison, "Capital-esque Landscapes: Long-Term Histories of Enduring Landscape Modifications," in *Landesque Capital: The Historical Ecology of Enduring Landscape Modifications*, ed. N. T. Hakansson and M. Widgren (Walnut Creek, CA: Left Coast Press, 2014), 49–74.

30. David Pettegrew, "Chasing the Classical Farmstead: Assessing the Formation and Signature of Rural Settlement in Greek Landscape Archaeology," *Journal of Mediterranean Archaeology* 14, no. 2 (2001): 189–209.

31. Sturt W. Manning, Diane L. Bolger, Andrea Swinton, and Matthew J. Ponting, "Maroni Valley Archaeological Survey Project: Preliminary Report on the 1990–1991 Seasons," *Report of the Department of Antiquities, Cyprus* (1994); Ian A. Todd, *Vasilikos Valley Project 9: The Field Survey of the Vasilikos Valley*, vol. 1 (Sävedalen: Paul Åströms Förlag, 2004).

32. Alison South, "Late Bronze Age Settlement Patterns in Southern Cyprus: The First Kingdoms?," *Cahiers du Centre d'Études Chypriotes* 32 (2002): 59–72; Anja Ulbrich, "Hellenistic Evidence from the Sanctuary at Maroni *Vournes*," *Keryx* 2 (2013): 31–62. Recent excavations at Kalavasos-Vounaritashi may indicate a later Archaic-Classical Building: Catherine Kearns and Anna Georgiadou, "Rural Complexities: Comparative Investigations at Small Iron Age Sites in South-Central Cyprus," *Journal of Field Archaeology* 46, no. 7 (2021): 461–79.

33. Sarah Janes and Kristina Winther-Jacobsen, "Iron Age Pottery," in *Landscape and Interaction: The Troodos Archaeological and Environmental Survey Project, Cyprus*. vol. 1, *Methodology, Analysis and Interpretation*, ed. Michael Given, A. Bernard Knapp, Jay Noller, Luke Sollars. and Vassiliki Kassianidou (London: Council for British Research in the Levant, 2013): 62–63.

34. Georgia M. Andreou and David Sewell, "Tochni-*Lakkia* Revealed: Reconsidering Settlement Patterns in the Vasilikos and Maroni Valleys, Cyprus," in *PoCA: Postgraduate Cypriot Archaeology 2012*, ed. Hartmut Matthäus et al. (Newcastle upon Tyne: Cambridge Scholars, 2015): 198–219.

35. Andreou and Sewell, "Tochni-*Lakkia* Revealed"; Georgia M. Andreou et al., "Integrated Methods for Understanding and Monitoring the Loss of Coastal Archaeological Sites: The Case of Tochni *Lakkia*, South-Central Cyprus," *Journal of Archaeological Science: Reports* 12 (2017): 197–208.

36. Todd, *Vasilikos Valley Project 9*, 133–34; Anna Georgiadou, "Geometric-Archaic," in *The Vasilikos Valley Project 10: The Field Survey of the Vasilikos Valley Vol II, Artefacts Recovered by the Field Survey*, ed. Ian Todd (Sävedalen: Åströms Förlag, 2016), 104.

37. South, "Late Bronze Age"; and Kevin D. Fisher, "Making the First Cities on Cyprus: Urbanism and Social Change in the Late Bronze Age," in *Making Ancient Cities: Space and Place in Early Urban Societies*, ed. A. Creekmore and K. D. Fisher (Cambridge: Cambridge University Press, 2014), 181–219.

38. Greene, Leidwanger, and Ozdas, "Expanding Contacts."

39. *Sensu* Ian Morris, "Mediterraneanization," *Mediterranean Historical Review* 18, no. 2 (2003): 30–55.

40. See Osborne and Hall, chapter 1 in this volume.

41. Maria Hadjicosti, "The Family Tomb of a Warrior of the Cypro-Archaic Period at Mari," *Report of the Department of Antiquities, Cyprus* (1997).

42. A. Christodoulou, "A Cypro-Archaic I Tomb-Group from Maroni," *Report of the Department of Antiquities, Cyprus* (1972); 156–60; Vassos Karageorghis, "Chronique des fouilles et découvertes archéologiques à Chypre en 1971," *Bulletin de Correspondence Hellénique* 96, no. 2 (1972): 1005–88; Karageorghis, "Chronique des fouilles et découvertes archéologiques à Chypre en 1977," *Bulletin de Correspondence Hellénique* 102, no. 2 (1978): 879–938; Karageorghis, "Chronique des fouilles et découvertes archéologiques à Chypre en 1983," *Bulletin de Correspondence Hellénique* 108, no. 2 (1984); 893–966; and Pavlos Flourentzos, "An Archaic Tomb from Khirokitia," *Report of the Department of Antiquities, Cyprus* (1985): 221–31.

43. Bikai, *Phoenician Pottery*, 18 no. 186.

44. Todd, *Vasilikos Valley Project 9*; Manning et al., "Maroni Valley."

45. Georgiadou, "Geometric-Archaic"; and Anna Georgiadou, "The Vasilikos Valley within the Amathusian Territory in the Iron Age: Settlement Patterns and Inequalities," in *Structures of Inequality on Bronze Age Cyprus: Studies in Honor of Alison K. South*, ed. L. Hulin, L. Crewe, and J. M. Webb (Uppsala: Astrom Editions, 2018): 155–68.

46. Georgiadou, "Geometric-Archaic," 103.

47. Todd, *Vasilikos Valley Project 9*, 140–41.

48. Georgiadou, "Geometric-Archaic," 106.

49. Todd, *Vasilikos Valley Project 9*, 30–32.

50. Georgiadou, "Geometric-Archaic," 103; Hermary, "Amathus, Capital," 18.

51. Kearns, "Re-survey and Spatial Analysis"; Kearns and Georgiadou, "Rural Complexities."

52. Archaic cermaics: Todd, *Vasilikos Valley Project* 9, 58–60; Ian A. Todd, *Vasilikos Valley Project 12: The Field Survey of the Vasilikos Valley*, vol. 3, *Human Settlement in the Vasilikos Valley* (Uppsala: Åströms Förlag, 2013), 100; Kearns and Georgiadou, "Rural Complexities."

53. Kearns, "Discerning 'Favorable' Climates," 284–85.

54. Wagstaff, "Agricultural Terraces."

55. David Sewell, personal communication.

56. Sturt W. Manning et al., "Becoming Urban: Investigating the Anatomy of the Late Bronze Age Complex, Maroni, Cyprus," *Journal of Mediterranean Archaeology* 27, no. 1 (2014): 3–32.

57. Ulbrich, "Hellenistic Evidence."

58. Manning et al., "Becoming Urban," 17–22.

59. Sturt W. Manning, David A. Sewell, and Ellen Herscher, "Late Cypriot I A Maritime Trade in Action: Underwater Survey at Maroni *Tsaroukkas* and the Contemporary East Mediterranean Trading System," *Annual of the British School at Athens* 97 (2002): 97–162.

60. Jane Johnson, *Maroni de Chypre* (Gothenburg: Paul Åströms Förlag, 1980), 6.

61. Kearns and Georgiadou, "Rural Complexities."

62. Manning et al., "Becoming Urban."

63. Ulbrich, "Hellenistic Evidence."

64. Fourrier, "Les territoires," 128–29.

65. Lone W. Sørensen, "Painted Iron Age Pottery," in *Panayia Ematousa I: A Rural Site in South-Eastern Cyprus*, ed. L. W. Sørensen and K. Winther Jacobsen (Athens: Danish Institute at Athens, 2006), 180.

66. Michael Dietler, *Archaeologies of Colonialism: Consumption, Entanglement, and Violence in Ancient Mediterranean France* (Berkeley: University of California Press, 2010), 57.

67. Thomas Brisart, "Isolation, Austerity and Fancy Pottery: Acquiring and Using Overseas Imported Fine Wares in 6th- and 5th-Century Eastern Crete," in *Cultural Practices and Material Culture in Archaic and Classical Crete*, ed. O. Pilz and G. Seelentag (Berlin: De Gruyter, 2014), 263–83.

68. Yiannis Hamilakis and Susan Sherratt, "Feasting and the Consuming Body in Bronze Age Crete and Early Iron Age Cyprus," in *Parallel Lives: Ancient Island Societies in Crete and Cyprus*, ed. G. Cadogan, M. Iacovou, K. Kopaka, and J. Whitley (Athens: British School at Athens, 2012), 195, 200–201; and Janes, "Death," fig. 9; for mobile warrior culture on Cyprus, see Sarah Morris, chapter 5 in this volume.

69. See also S. Murray, "Imported Objects as Proxy Data for Change in Greek Trade after the Mycenaean Collapse: A Multi-variate Quantitative Analysis," in *EUDAIMON: Studies in Honour of Jan Bouzek*, ed. P. Pavúk, V. Klontza-Jaklová, and A. Harding (Prague: Czech Institute of Egyptology, 2018), 71–91.

70. Horden and Purcell, *Corrupting Sea*, 89–110; Haggis, "Archaeology of Urbanization," 220–21.

71. Todd, *Vasilikos Valley Project* 12, 120.

72. See Hritz, "Urbanocentric Models."

73. Foxhall, "Small, Rural Farmstead Sites."

74. Roger Just, *A Greek Island Cosmos* (Santa Fe, NM: School of American Research Press, 2000), 18–28.

75. Georgiadou, "Geometric-Archaic," 105.

76. Georgiadou, "Geometric-Archaic," 104.

77. *Sensu* James F. Osborne, "Sovereignty and Territoriality in the City-State: A Case Study from the Amuq Valley, Turkey," *Journal of Anthropological Archaeology* 32, no. 4 (2013): 774–90.

78. Stefano Campana, "Emptyscapes: Filling an 'Empty' Mediterranean Landscape at Rusellae, Italy," *Antiquity* 91, no. 359 (2017): 1223–40.

79. Greene, Leidwanger, and Ozdas, "Expanding Contacts."

80. Michael Herzfeld, "The Village in the World and the World in the Village: Reflections on Ethnographic Epistemology," *Critique of Anthropology* 35, no. 3 (2015): 343.

81. Fourrier, "Les territoires," 130; on islands as isolated or integrated, see, e.g., Knapp, *Prehistoric and Protohistoric Cyprus*, 13–30.

82. Foxhall and Yoon, "Carving Out a Territory," 438.

83. Kardulias, Counts, and Toumazou, "Research by Design."

84. See, e.g., A. Bernard Knapp and Peter Van Dommelen, eds., *Material Connections: Mobility, Materiality, and Mediterranean Identities* (London: Routledge, 2010).

CHAPTER 4

Connectivity, Style, and Decorated Metal Bowls in the Iron Age Mediterranean

MARIAN H. FELDMAN

The title of this volume draws upon the pioneering scholarship of Peregrine Horden and Nicholas Purcell in *The Corrupting Sea* (2000) and Cyprian Broodbank's *The Making of the Middle Sea* (2013).[1] Horden and Purcell propose *connectivity*, along with a fragmented microecology, as a central concept defining the Mediterranean, and it is one of the prime legacies of their monumental work. Building directly on Horden and Purcell, Broodbank defines *connectivity* as a characteristic or "propensity" of the Mediterranean environment "that enables people to link the fragments, pool resources or relocate in bad times and seek gain abroad in good ones. . . . [It is] the common necessity of mobility for survival and prosperity in a Mediterranean theatre full of challenges and sudden openings."[2] For both Horden and Purcell, and for Broodbank as well, the Mediterranean landscape propels an infinite number of small-scale, local, "uneventful" happenings connected through multiple, flexible, and fluid relations.

How, then, does one study or even identify connectivity in the past? In periods with little or no textual evidence, the movement of material items constitutes a principal method for tracking mobility. And in order to determine that an item has moved, one has to be able to ascertain its place of origin as different from its find spot. Several methods for identifying a place of production have been developed in the absence of textual evidence. Traditionally, the main means by which this determination has been made is through style, and this remains a central approach despite recent advances in materials science analysis.[3] While materials analysis can yield important information regarding geochemical sourcing, especially in the case of ceramics, many preserved artifacts do not yield easily to these methods.[4] This is particularly so for a class of objects—decorated metal bowls—that have served as prime markers of mobility and connectivity across the Mediterranean and Near East during the Early Iron Age. Metals have proved especially complicated for geochemical sourcing due to questions of primary versus secondary manufacturing that might occur in very different locations, the recycling and mixing of metals over time, and difficulties in associating chemical fingerprints with specific sources.[5]

In light of the problems surrounding the analysis of metals, one might make the case to turn attention away from objects such as the decorated metal bowls, which have traditionally been a focus of studies of pan-Mediterranean connections. Along similar lines, Horden and Purcell and Broodbank call for scholars to concentrate more on small-scale trading and cabotage as significant vectors of connectivity, and they are certainly correct in shifting attention to these lesser pathways. Nonetheless, as scholars we still confront the need to bridge the gap between the fragmentary and laconic record of small-scale mobility and the evidence that does survive such as the metal bowls. Although the metal bowls might be dismissed as elite items, they too can be studied from bottom-up perspectives that include their extended *chaînes opératoires* and the multitude of peoples and places involved in their production, circulation, and use.

Because material sciences analyses provide reliable and useful results for only certain kinds of materials and has limitations associated with costs and accessibility of testing, stylistic analysis continues to be a central tool for studying connectivity. Yet *style*, as an intellectual construct, has generally not been assessed critically in discussions such as those by Horden and Purcell and Broodbank. Although these scholars do not engage critically with the concept of style, they nonetheless rely on it (especially Broodbank) in a traditional archaeological manner to attribute material culture to specific times and places. In general, these authors tend to accept the stylistic delineations of material culture proposed by earlier scholarship. Yet, in accepting these prior designations without question, they run the risk that their intellectual projects will be built on a house of cards. It is, therefore, worth examining how style is conceived and used within these studies, and how alternative approaches to style, such as a practice-oriented one, might complicate and enrich their theories of connectivity. After first describing the use in Mediterraneanist scholarship of a traditional culture-historical concept of style, this chapter reassesses style as a socially contingent practice. It then explores a case study of decorated metal bowls found across the Mediterranean and Near East during the Iron Age. The bowls have resisted stylistic classification, challenging our use of style to locate place or identity. I argue that the corpus of ostensibly elite decorated bowls, when analyzed through the lens of a practice-oriented notion of style exemplifies conceptions of Mediterraneanism propounded by Horden and Purcell and Broodbank: their technological associations despite geographical separation signal connectivity over large expanses of space, while their seemingly endless variation speaks to a concomitant fragmentation. Moreover, looking vertically through the *chaînes opératoires* of their production and horizontally at the web of technological connections and variations permits the visualization of social networks that belies any reductionist interpretation of these vessels simply as elite goods.

Style in The Corrupting Sea *and* The Making of the Middle Sea

Although neither Horden and Purcell nor Broodbank discuss style directly, we can infer assumptions they make from a close reading of the books. Horden and Purcell rarely mention style or even related terms such as types, cultural traits, or characteristics. They are primarily historians and heavily favor texts—as historical narratives (that is, as conveyers of information rather than as literary creations)—over material culture. Their emphasis focuses on places more than people, so when they do discuss something like *characteristics,* it is in relation to microregions, and they argue against traditional approaches that would seek to define such characteristics through an articulation of topographical or climatic features. Instead, they define a microregion's characteristics by means of its "changing interaction of human productive opportunities."[6] In their discussion of connectivity and the difficulties surrounding its documentation with respect to non-elite commerce, Horden and Purcell acknowledge both the usefulness and challenges of using stylistic attributions for ceramics. With respect to a particularly poorly documented period (the seventh and eighth centuries CE), they write: "Pottery, that unsurpassed aid to precision in other periods, seems either to have become stylistically quite crude, and thus chronologically indeterminate, or gradually to have given way to perishable container materials such as leather and wood—annoyingly for the archaeologist."[7] Statements such as this, and the authors' discussion of mobility of goods and people, in which they most closely engage with material artifacts rather than texts, suggest that they accept a traditional archaeological approach to style as a means of attributing a place and time of production to individual objects.[8]

Broodbank's book concentrates on periods when material remains assume a greater evidentiary weight; yet, despite the greater role of material culture in his argument, he follows a similarly uncritical use of style as diagnostic of the place and time of production. In discussing the rise of the complex political entities of Egypt and Mesopotamia in what he calls the "long" third millennium BCE, Broodbank states that "new kinds of elite culture and large-scale economy arose inextricably with them [Egypt and Mesopotamia], and these reveal much common ground despite separate origins and enduringly different stylistic 'looks.'"[9] These "enduringly different stylistic looks" do not receive further attention or definition; yet the phrase itself reveals certain assumptions Broodbank makes in his use of style. The "endurance" of these looks (to be understood perhaps as "unchanging-ness" or "constancy") conveys permanence, an effect that seems somehow to exist as its own epiphenomenal being and not as the product of human actions.[10] A separation of style from human action is also implied in the use of the term with reference to less elite forms of material culture, such as pottery. For example, discussing pottery found in Iberia and southern France during the third millennium BCE, Broodbank states, "The southern French sequence begins at coastal and riverine sites with 'international' beakers of the maritime type prevalent in Atlantic Europe, later replaced by *spreading local styles*."[11] How or why these styles might have spread remains unexplored.

Returning to Broodbank's comparison between Egyptian and Mesopotamian elite arts, that their stylistic looks are different from one another suggests cultural distinctiveness that can be circumscribed, defined, and delimited. It is unclear what the scare quotes around "looks" might be signaling; is it that "looks" might be deceiving in some way, because they are not really what they appear to be? Broodbank's assertion that the enduringly different stylistic looks relate to "separate origins," origins and style having closely intertwined intellectual histories, further demonstrates that his conceptualization of styles and cultures defined these as sealed entities with singular points of origins and straight lines of development. Such a notion of style is rooted in functionalist models, with little attention to human or social agency. In a similar way, Broodbank seems to accept a straightforward equation of style with a culturally defined group of people. For example, he concludes that, during the thirteenth century BCE in the southern Levant, Egyptianizing traits, for example, anthropoid clay coffins, "testify to the presence of Egyptians" in the southern Levant, despite the fact that these anthropoid coffins, while perhaps inspired by Egyptian examples, occur in burial assemblages of decidedly un-Egyptian type and represent a uniquely Levantine practice.[12]

From the few uses of the term "style" in *The Corrupting Sea* and *The Making of the Middle Sea*, we can infer that the authors of these texts accept traditional approaches to style, defining it as something inherent in an object that indexes where and when it was produced. Such a use of style has a long history in archaeology, intertwined with art-historical considerations of the concept. Most influential in archaeological scholarship is the culture-historical tradition that was dominant in the early twentieth century. Culture-historical studies seek to map formal aspects of manufactured objects onto geographical and temporal frameworks in order to define cultural entities in history.[13] V. Gordon Childe (1892–1957), one of the most prominent proponents of this approach, articulated a theory of culture as normative, the shared characteristics of a group of people evident in the material remains they produced—that is, the style inhering in the objects.[14] The approach has been foundational for archaeology, constructing regional and chronological classification systems that continue to scaffold the field today. It is this culture-historical approach, though not designated as such, that permits Broodbank, and to a lesser extent Horden and Purcell, to analyze patterns of mobility in the absence of (or in addition to) historical texts.

A Critique of Style

Yet such a concept of style, and of culture, is open to critique. Without entering into an extensive debate about the concept of culture—the focus in this chapter being on style—it has been acknowledged for some time that "cultures" are not monolithic, nor rigidly bounded.[15] If culture is not singular and homogeneous, then the one-to-one correspondence of style to culture must already be suspect. Furthermore, the concept of style that underlies the culture-historical model derives from an idealist art-historical tradition that views style as an ineffable expression of essential, interior spirit or cultural will, as I have discussed elsewhere.[16] For example, Rhys Carpenter's 1963 review of style in archaeology expresses an underlying notion of style as a psychological emanation and affirms a belief in "stylistic determinants" that can be transferred from one period to another.[17] His exemplar is John Beazley, whose "spectacular feat" of attributing painted pottery to specific hands and workshops draws directly on the art-historical tradition of discerning stylistic principles that transcend specific times and places.[18] In the culture-historical conception, style is accepted de facto as existing, indeed inhering, in the material properties of manufactured items. No explanation for its existence is considered, and the means by which style might come into existence are taken as self-evidently linked to psychological expressions of self-being.

However, already in the 1980s, archaeologists such as Michael Shanks and Christopher Tilley, Margaret Conkey, and Ian Hodder had begun to think seriously about style and its role in our reconstruction of the past, critiquing the notion of style as a passive reflection of identity, especially cultural identity.[19] With the acknowledgment that no culture or group is homogeneous, monolithic, or bounded, the post-processualists challenged an epiphenomenal view of style, instead arguing that it is the result of social and material, rather than individual and psychological, processes situated in particular human-material practices. Acknowledging the fluidity and flexibility of group identity should have radical implications for how we understand and use style, which can no longer be seen to have a one-to-one relationship with culture.[20] Yet these implications have not penetrated archaeological scholarship as thoroughly as one might have expected. Rather, "newer" postmodern understandings of fragmentation and fluid connectivity, such as described by Horden and Purcell and Broodbank, continue to be built on a historical framework derived from a culture-historical concept of style. While there is no doubt that the historical frameworks constructed using the culture-historical model of style have been integral to our field, the ultimate contradiction between these two conceptions of culture presents a somewhat terrifying challenge: If cultures are all heterogeneous, fluid, and in flux, how can similarities among material objects (i.e., style) be pinned down and associated with anything stable?

It seems, therefore, that a reassessment of the concept of style, and how this influences the role of style in assessing mobility, cultural interactions, and exchanges, should go hand in hand with other bottom-up approaches espoused by scholars such as Horden and Purcell and Broodbank. Conkey reflects upon how the very nature of objects changes within the new paradigm of culture as contested, temporal, and emergent; objects come to be seen as praxis (following Pierre Bourdieu)—not as reflective of social entities but as an active, constitutive element of social practice.[21] Style equates with ways of doing things: ways that have been taught, reinforced, and modified through choices that are made by human producers.[22]

I have argued elsewhere that in order to use style for interpretive purposes, we need to have a better understanding of where style comes from and what produces it.[23] I propose that contexts of learning and practice, highly social situations, shape and constrain the choices producers make, which in turn generate particular visual and physical characteristics that we identify as style. Style thus results from human actions in relation to physical properties of a given medium, in which the actions have become embodied in the human practitioner through a complex social dynamic involving practices learned through habitual senses and formal training. I therefore understand style to be socially contingent in ways that can powerfully affect the interpretive potential of stylistic analysis. On the one hand, close stylistic analysis will inform us about the past social actions and practices that produced the stylistic properties. Yet on the other hand, it is critical to have as full an understanding as possible of the past social context that produced the style in order to most accurately infer these practices from the style itself. This may sound like circular reasoning; however, I see the process instead as dialectical, moving back and forth between the stylistic analysis, its interpretive possibilities in the social realm, and any additional archaeological or textual evidence for the context of production.

One serious, potential ramification of a radical critique of style and culture is the complete undermining of the chronological and regional frameworks constructed by the culture-historical approach. However, I would argue that this is not the case—at least not wholesale. For instance, in Mesopotamia, during historically well-documented periods, we can say that material culture (from pottery through the so-called fine arts) often does exhibit stylistic patterning that can be mapped more or less onto temporal and geographical frames. Yet what we have learned is that we cannot assume that style (i.e., what we discern as formal variation) will always and only correlate with a singular (usually conceived of as ethnic or political) group identity.[24] Therefore, we must constantly interrogate these presumed or potential correlations.

Revisiting Connectivity and Style in the Iron Age

How then does this practice-oriented, socially contingent concept of style influence questions of connectivity as raised by Horden and Purcell or Broodbank? And how does it relate specifically to the question of the "connected" Iron Age? In placing connectivity front and center, these inquiries emphasize movement rather than fixity. However, movement in the distant (archaeological) past is never actually present in itself; it must be inferred from materials that are themselves not in movement when excavated and studied by modern scholars. In the absence of texts that document movement, connectivity has to be inferred through material objects, and these inferences often rest on analysis of formal variation patterning—that is, on stylistic analysis.

Yet the connectivity conceived by Horden and Purcell and Broodbank is more complex than simple arrows of movement from one geographical place to another. It is an all-encompassing feature (one might almost be tempted to call it a "mindset") that characterizes the Mediterranean as the Mediterranean per se.[25] It is what makes the Mediterranean distinctive.[26] If one takes this approach to connectivity—as something that is a defining characteristic and not as a process awaiting discovery through analysis—an alternate consideration of style might come into focus, which would align more closely to a practice-oriented concept of style. As part of this intellectual reorientation, the other defining characteristic of the Mediterranean, according to Horden and Purcell—the multiplicity of its microregions—also needs to be brought into the equation. These two characteristics appear at first glance to be contradictory: infinite fragmentation and complete interconnection. Yet what these authors argue for is the opposite, something more like a kaleidoscope,[27] which creates vistas of geometrically patterned (connected) colors out of the reflected images of many, individual, small pieces of colored glass. One might imagine (or deduce) that from fragmented microregions would emerge fluid, flexible, and changing social practices.

If, rather than arguing for connectivity because of distribution patterns of styles, one assumes connectivity existed, albeit to different degrees, as a defining characteristic of the Mediterranean, then one can assume that at least some people were moving around and interacting with one another, impacting ways of doing things. Who exactly was moving around, with whom they interacted, where and with what frequency, are all specifics that require close analysis in particular circumstances, and may elude precise definition for some times and places. One of the implications of thinking about style as social practice rather than linked in an essentialized manner to static, monolithic groups is that stylistic patterns ought to point to connections among people engaged in social activities with one another in numerous different ways and through a variety of different relationships.

This brings me to another key element in Horden and Purcell and Broodbank—the privileging of "low" commerce, what Horden and Purcell refer to as *cabotage* or *tramping*.[28] Horden and Purcell argue that the study of "high commerce" (generally prestigious and of great economic value) can actually "harm" attempts to study Mediterranean connectivity.[29] This is because, according to them, "the glamour" of high commerce may "detach" it from its "real social context."[30] Such a focus also overlooks noncommercial (irregular, arbitrary, or even illicit) exchanges. While Horden and Purcell make a persuasive case for the need not to neglect other forms of exchanges, I would argue that to assert a disconnect between high commerce and real social context ignores the complicated intertwining of all forms of exchange during any period of time.[31] Given that during the Iron Age our sources are fragmentary and full of gaps, we can and should investigate all possible forms of exchange, whether high or low.[32]

As one example of the complex entanglement of all objects within dispersed networks of exchange, we can consider the *chaînes opératoires* of the decorated metal bowls, expanding beyond the technical aspects of the decoration that are discussed later in this contribution. These ostensibly elite objects of high commerce nonetheless existed within complex networks of people and places that incorporated a range of different exchanges. The most common metal used in their production was bronze, an alloy of copper and usually tin. Copper deposits are found around the Near East and Mediterranean, with particularly important sources during the Iron Age in Faynan, Jordan, Timna on the Arabian Peninsula, and on Cyprus.[33] The source of tin has generated extensive debate with proposals for areas in central Asia, Turkey, the western Mediterranean, and as far away as Cornwall in England.[34] Silver and gold, used less but still with a certain frequency, could have come from sources in Egypt, Nubia, Turkey, the Aegean, or farther west as well as locations to the east.[35] Indeed, much maritime activity during the Iron Age has been attributed to the quest for metals, and the basic use of these metals points to complicated chains of interactions. Analysis of bronze bowls from Nimrud, to be discussed further below, determined relatively high percentages of tin, ranging from 8 percent to 13 percent, with an average of 10 percent, in contrast to other bronze from the site such as fibulae, hooks, arrowheads, and weights, which ranged from 4 percent to 9 percent tin.[36] This indicates both an access to amounts of tin that did not require skimping and a desire to produce a harder bronze alloy that results from higher tin contents.

Regardless of the sources, mining and processing of metal ores, smelting, and alloying all involved large numbers of people, many of whom were probably basic laborers along with those who controlled the skilled metallurgical knowledge and technologies necessary for extraction and refinement.[37] These metallurgical processes in turn relied on fuels, facilities, and tools, each of which involved additional groups of people to gather, build, or produce them. Thus, in addition to the crafters who shaped and decorated the bowls, an extensive network of individuals and exchange pathways existed in order for these items to come into being. Their material form surviving today points back to these entangled networks.

If we accept that exchanges of all levels influenced one another in various ways, then whatever evidence we have—be it of high or low commerce—needs to be included in our analyses. Indeed, for early periods such as the Iron Age, it may only be through close study of purportedly high commerce such as decorated metal bowls that evidence of low commerce can emerge (or be inferred). Thus, while we may not be able to access all aspects of connectivity, particularly at the "lower" end of more irregular, non-elite interactions, stylistic patterns should indicate networks of interaction, while the types of materials belonging to these stylistic groups can point to the participants in the social relationships. It is important not to confuse bottom-up approaches with the study of non-elite evidence and to keep the intellectual approach used distinct from that of the evidence being studied. That is to say, one can apply a top-down model to non-elite materials (for example, a world systems model that uses pottery for its main object of analysis) just as one can employ bottom-up approaches to elite materials, such as close readings and contextual analyses of a particular group of elite objects.[38]

The Case of Decorated Metal Bowls and Mediterraneanism

Having put forth a case for the relevance of both "high" and "low" commerce, their mutually constitutive intertwining, and the need to investigate whatever evidence we have for the Iron Age, I turn in this final section to a brief consideration of a corpus of decorated metal bowls (figure 4.1). The bowls have eluded consensus concerning their stylistic classification. As supremely mobile items found at sites throughout the Near East and Mediterranean, they align well with the Mediterraneanist connectivity proposed by Horden and Purcell and Broodbank despite their elite characterization. If we examine the bowls through the lens of a socially contingent, practice-oriented concept of style, and consider them with respect to Mediterranean connectivity, new perspectives regarding their place in Iron Age society emerge.

Metal bowls made of bronze, gold, and silver and figuratively decorated by repoussé and engraving have been found over a wide geographical area, from Iran to the western Mediterranean.[39] They have been dated from the tenth/ninth to the seventh century and are generally taken by scholars as a coherent corpus of objects, often referred to as "Phoenician." Whether these bowls should in fact be taken as a coherent corpus is not entirely clear, especially when outlier specimens are included, such as a gold bowl with unique decorative features reportedly found in the eighteenth century at Sant'Angelo Muxaro, Sicily, or a large bronze bowl from a late seventh/early sixth-century tomb in southwestern Iran that includes unusual, local, Iranian motifs.[40] Moreover, they share technical features with some metal bowls from this period that do not include figurative imagery.[41] Nonetheless, for the purposes of this case study, I concentrate on the core assemblage of figuratively decorated metal vessels, which when studied as a group, constitute an excellent sample for

FIGURE 4.1 Bronze bowl said to be from Idalium, Cyprus. Ninth–eighth century BCE. H. 4 cm, diameter 13.3 cm. Metropolitan Museum of Art 74.51.5700; The Cesnola Collection, Purchased by subscription, 1874–76.

investigations through the lens of what I call Mediterraneanism along the lines laid out by Horden and Purcell and Broodbank.

The bowls exhibit, on the one hand, great diversity and eclecticism, yet on the other hand, an acknowledged cohesion in their forms and decorations.[42] This difference-among-sameness and sameness-among-difference has generated considerable debate regarding their place(s) of production. They are often considered to be Phoenician in manufacture, especially those vessels that display a number of Egyptianizing elements, and studies have tended to focus on locating specific, regional production centers. While I disagree with the moniker of "Phoenician" to describe these bowls, and thus do not consider them relevant to a study of Phoenician art or culture,[43] they are an important corpus for thinking about connectivity in the Iron Age because of their shared features and wide geographical distribution. In addition, if we consider style not as the ineffable emanation of personal or cultural spirit or essence (in this instance, the Phoenicians), but instead as the physical and visual results of acquired ways of doing, we can approach these bowls from an entirely different perspective.

If style is generated from social practices of doing and making, a close analysis of specific techniques used to produce the vessels should allow us to retrace potential social networks of practice. It should be noted that the appearance of shared techniques on two different vessels does not necessarily signal a direct link between the producers of the two bowls; many of the techniques used to work these vessels are long-standing and well-established metalworking techniques. Yet tracing many different shared techniques, among other formal features, across a large number of objects provides at least a rough outline of networks of shared social practices, which in turn imply shared knowledge and know-how, even if at a remove.

The decorated metal bowl corpus offers an excellent set of objects with which to conduct such a study: they are relatively numerous in quantity, and traces of metalworking techniques are particularly visible on the finished works.[44] To conduct such a study for the corpus as a whole would constitute a major undertaking, requiring close physical examination of as many of the bowls as possible, which was not feasible for this short chapter. Here, in addition to general remarks regarding the metallurgical processes, I rely on studies that have focused on the technical aspects of smaller subsets of the metal bowls, in particular by Glenn Markoe and Francesca Onnis.[45] Markoe examines examples from Cyprus and Etruria, with some comparisons to bowls from elsewhere; Onnis considers bronze bowls from the Assyrian capital of Nimrud, studying a total of forty-two vessels from a major cache excavated there in the nineteenth century.

The technical production of the vessels forms a common feature linking these objects together and, as Onnis notes, the techniques employed were fundamental in generating the style that we see.[46] Most are made from hammered metal, using repoussé, chasing, embossing, and engraving to create the decoration.[47] Starting from a single bun- or disc-shaped piece of cast metal, the bowls were hammered from the exterior over a shaped stake or form (known as *raising* in metallurgical terminology) and display a number of different profiles.[48] There is some inconsistency in the scholarly usage of the technical terms, but generally, repoussé refers to the technique of using variously shaped tools to raise the metal surface from behind through punching and hammering, while chasing represents the reverse of repoussé, pushing the metal back from the front side.[49] Embossing is a form of repoussé in which punching tools raise the sheet metal from the back in specific shapes such as circles or squares, while engraving refers to the incision of lines onto the front side of the work by displacing the metal.[50] The repoussé relief on the bowls ranges from shallow (no more than 0.3 cm above the surface, found on most of the bowls from the broader Mediterranean contexts) to slightly higher (between 0.3 and 0.5 cm, seen on many of the Nimrud examples).[51] The small range in the height of the relief signals a common practice of low-relief work that extends across these bowls as a group and that contrasts with other metal vessels from this period that evince higher relief.[52]

Markoe's analysis of his corpus, which however excludes the Nimrud bowls, finds that they share several basic technical ways of decorating.[53] For example,

> the use of small rounded bosses to accentuate the ends of feathers, rosette petals, and the like . . . the use of the raised line to heighten the effect of the repoussé . . . [and] the "punctured dot" and the "punch-marked circle," both used interchangeably in border bands and in interior decoration. The former is produced by a sharp, pointed awl, the latter by a hollow, circular punch.[54]

Looking at smaller subsets, Markoe sees groups of specific, shared practices that occasionally cluster geographically. For example, he notes that the vessels found in Etruscan tombs at Praeneste and Cerveteri (Caere) in Italy, which he describes as "an exceptionally close-knit unit," exhibit numerous common technical practices, such as the use of simple geometric bosses to denote motifs such as heads, shields, and landscape elements.[55] Markoe likewise discerns a general process for producing most of the gold-plated silver bowls found on Cyprus, in which the entire interior was plated first, then outlines and ornaments were engraved on the inside before the repoussé relief was executed from the outside, followed by final details added through punching and incision.[56] Markoe concludes that the gold-plated Cypriot bowls share many technical features among themselves while being distinct from many of the other bowls, suggesting to him that a major metalworking atelier was located on Cyprus.[57]

At the same time, Markoe finds technical and stylistic features on some bowls discovered on Cyprus that differ from the other Cypriot bowls and instead exhibit connections with bowls from elsewhere. For example, his bowl Cy3 from Idalium on Cyprus is distinct within the Cypriot corpus (figures 4.1–4.3).[58] Made of bronze, the vessel has a depressed central rosette

FIGURE 4.2 Profile view of bronze bowl said to be from Idalium, Cyprus. Ninth–eighth century BCE. H. 4 cm, diameter 13.3 cm. Metropolitan Museum of Art 74.51.5700; The Cesnola Collection, Purchased by subscription, 1874–76.

FIGURE 4.3 Detail showing decorating techniques of bronze bowl said to be from Idalium, Cyprus. Ninth–eighth century BCE. H. 4 cm, diameter 13.3 cm. Metropolitan Museum of Art 74.51.5700; The Cesnola Collection, Purchased by subscription, 1874–76.

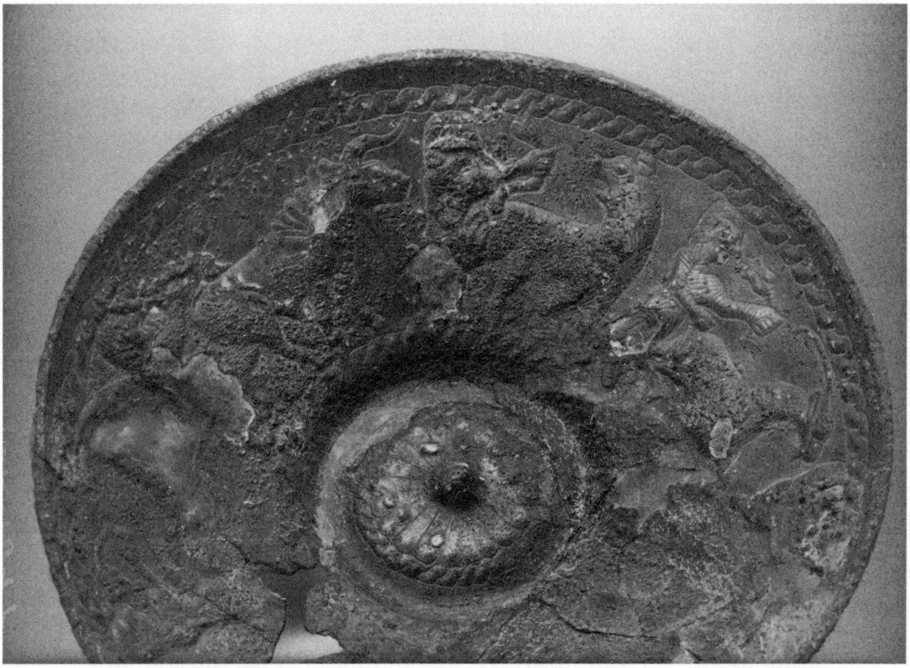

FIGURE 4.4 Bronze bowl from Grave 42, Kerameikos cemetery, Athens. Ninth century BCE. H. 4.8 cm, diameter 17 cm. Kerameikos Archaeological Museum, Athens, inv. no. M5. Image courtesy of the Deutsches Archäologisches Institut Athen, "KER 4847."

with a raised omphalos marking the center. A similar feature is present on a bronze bowl from the Kerameikos cemetery in Athens (Markoe G1) (figure 4.4).[59] Markoe notes that the bowls are two out of only three in his entire corpus taking the shape of footed vessels, and Cy3 and G1 both have a low cylindrical ring base.[60] Other "stylistic" features link Cy3 and G1, including the composition of a single large figural register surrounding the central rosette/omphalos and the method of rendering the engraved lines decorating the garments. A third bronze bowl displaying similar technical and stylistic features was excavated from a female burial in the Toumba cemetery at Lefkandi on Euboea, Greece (figure 4.5).[61] It too features a central rosette/omphalos surrounded by a single figurative register depicting figures in garments marked by engraved lines. According to Markoe's study of techniques, then, we can see a cluster of features that link together several bowls found on Cyprus, suggestive of an island-wide / island-bound network of shared practices. At the same time, technical

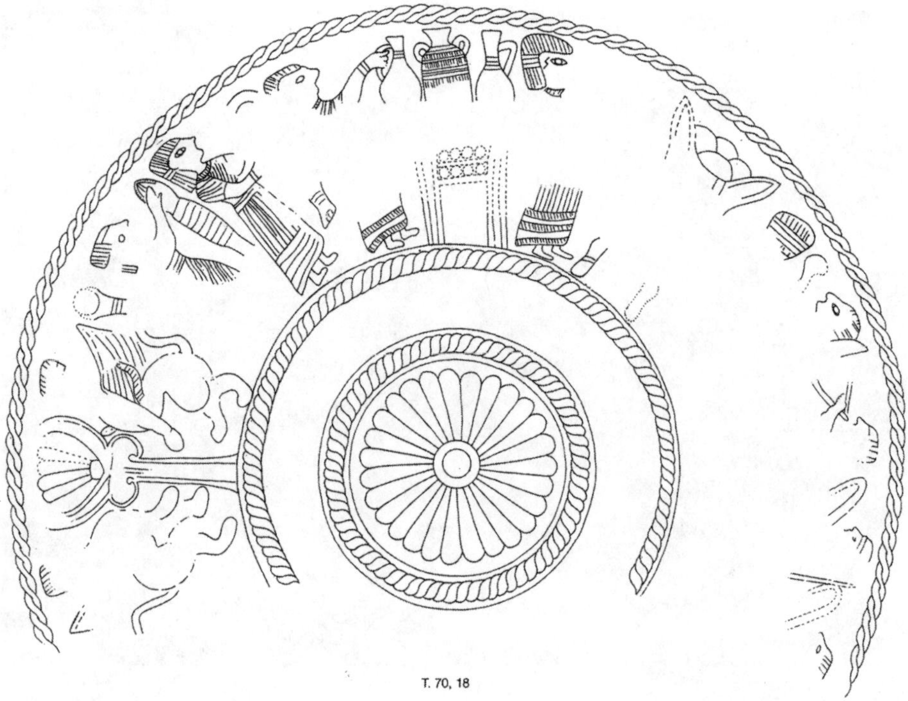

FIGURE 4.5 Line drawing of bronze bowl from Tomb 70, Toumba cemetery, Lefkandi. Ninth century BCE. H. 5.5 cm, diameter 15 cm. After Popham and Lemos, *Lefkandi* III, pl. 134: T.70,18. Reproduced with permission of the British School at Athens.

and stylistic features link vessels from sites in different regions, such as Idalium (Cyprus), Athens (Greece), and Lefkandi (Greece).

Onnis's work examines the manufacturing and decorating techniques visible on a cache of bronze bowls found at Nimrud that were excluded from Markoe's study.[62] The vessels were discovered during early excavations in the nineteenth century, housed together in a small storage room (AB) of the Northwest Palace. The bowls are assumed to be Levantine products (although their precise locations of manufacture continue to elude scholars),[63] which were acquired by the Assyrian king as either tribute or booty during campaigns in the west. It is unknown whether the group represents a single acquisition or was the result of a series of campaigns over time, but the bowls are assumed to derive from multiple different locales. Onnis sought correlations between vessel profile, decorating techniques, and prior groupings of the vessels based on imagery, in particular the groupings proposed by Richard Barnett.[64] Barnett divided the bowls into four main groups according to both decorative designs and characteristic features: the "bowls with central rosebud," the "marsh pattern" group, "swinging-handle bowls," and "star bowls." Acknowledging the difficulties in attributing the bowls to geographical locations of production, Barnett nevertheless used the styles and motifs found among his four groups, along with a few inscribed names, to suggest origins in the area of the northern and central Levant (which he refers to as north Syria and Aram) and Phoenicia.

Despite the variety of imagery, in her analysis Onnis found a relatively standard repertoire of decorating techniques across all the bowls, and she notes that some of the techniques were consistently combined. At the same time, she did not find any correlation between the shape of the vessel, its imagery and composition, and technical features.[65] The consistently shared ways of doing, along with some shared general principles of composition, led her to conclude that the group forms a single corpus that cannot be subdivided.[66] Yet the lack of clear correlations indicates a multiplicity of production locales. Accordingly, Onnis reconstructed an earlier, tightly knit Late Bronze Age tradition that fractured and became more locally diverse over the course of the Iron Age.[67] If the bowls derive from Assyrian campaigns in the Levantine region, as seems likely, their shared techniques in conjunction with their heterogeneous forms and visual elements suggest a complicated crafting network extending across the diverse polities of the region in which we might envision the frequent movement of crafters.[68]

It would take a much longer and more involved study than is possible here to try to trace the many connections among all the bowls, from Iran and Nimrud across the Mediterranean. Links might take the form of materials (gold, silver, bronze), vessel profile, size (diameter and depth), motifs (figural, vegetal, geometric), composition, and metalworking techniques. But even in the absence of such a systematic, large-scale study, the analyses of the two subsets discussed here demonstrate that, while certain features link bowls together across large geographical distances, at the same time, no assemblage of multiple features bundles together to form any specific, clearly demarcated group with the possible exception of some (but not all) the vessels found in Etruria. Extrapolating from the technical analyses to practices, there appear to have been extensive networks of shared metallurgical processes in which crafters engaged in similar techniques of production and execution of decoration that suggest similarly extensive networks of communication and exchange among the crafters.

At the same time, the diversity within these technical parameters indicates a degree of flexibility, experimentation, and deviation on the part of individual crafters that speaks against any centrally organized oversight of the production.

The problem of so-called Phoenician bowls, which have resisted attribution to specific geographical locales of manufacture, highlights the complicated way in which style has operated in studies of Mediterranean interconnections. However, taken together, the formal analysis of the bowls, a reconsideration of style as socially contingent and practice based, and the Mediterraneanism proposed by Horden and Purcell and Broodbank produce some new insights. If we dispense with the need to link style to a homogeneous, bounded cultural group (such as the Phoenicians) and instead study the bowls as part of Mediterranean connectivity, we can trace networks of shared practices that nonetheless permit what appears to be an infinite amount of variety.[69] In fact, these decorated metal bowls can stand as quintessential objects of Mediterranean fragmentation and connectivity during the Iron Age.

Nicholas Vella has proposed a similar way of thinking about the bowls' connectivity, focusing on the imagery itself rather than on style or technique.[70] Shifting his attention away from the question of production locales, Vella considers the bowls from the perspective of narratology, viewing the imagery depicted in the concentric registers as narratives of spatial knowledge associated with the sea. The metal bowls, according to Vella, encoded knowledge of connections between landscapes and practices. He calls them "boundary objects" that can mediate divergent viewpoints among the disparate groups inhabiting the various "worlds" of the Mediterranean. The complex subject matter depicted on the bowls—scenes that have been associated with cosmological implications among other meanings—may elude precise enumeration. However, Vella reads the imagery, including scenes of battle, hunt, and presumably mythological creatures drawn from a variety of cultural traditions, as privileging mobility, encounters, and social practices such as feasting and music. Vella further sees the reception of the bowls at sites across the Near East and Mediterranean as key to how they functioned to construct a "middle ground" among the disparate users. That is, the bowls acted to provide knowledge and commonality that helped bind together the different users through their shared encounters with these objects, which are nonetheless distinct and specific to each region, a notion that provides an intriguingly similar perspective on fragmentation and connectivity in the Mediterranean and complements the conclusions reached through the technical and stylistic analysis.

Conclusion

In the opening chapter to this volume, James Osborne and Jonathan Hall call attention to the interpretive possibilities afforded by the complicated and messy nature of the surviving data for the Iron Age. Such possibilities, however, must be grounded in methodological approaches that can sustain close critical analysis. Style has tended to be linked with elite arts, which Osborne and Hall also suggest should receive less of our attention, concentrating instead on overlooked non-elite materials. Yet it should be clear from the preceding discussion that style is a fundamental concept in archaeology as well as art history, and its uncritical use may result in inaccurate reconstructions of past social situations. When viewed through the lens of practice theory, style can take on an active role in interpretive approaches, providing agency to multiple actors in the past, whether elite or not. Moreover, elite materials are always entangled with multiple strata and spheres of society, and therefore, their study can (if so directed) provide important access to non-elite spheres that may be little documented in either the archaeological or written records. For example, for our metal bowls, we could consider crafting networks that may shed light on processes of training and craft organization. But we could also consider the procurement and initial working of the metals, the installations and tool kits needed to work the vessels, even the fuel sources for supplying the necessary heat and the smiths who produced the tools used to decorate the vessels.[71] These metal bowls were hardly items that existed in a vacuum of only elites. In other words, both elite and non-elite spheres can benefit from bottom-up analyses that start by looking closely at the small scale, which includes reassessing stylistic attributions and patterns.

The decorated metal bowls studied here offer one starting point for such a close, bottom-up analysis, as well as for a revised use of the concept of style. Looking carefully at technical ways of making and decorating the bowls—that is, the very building blocks of the visual and formal properties that produce what we call style—reveals no clearly delineated groups. Rather, networks of connections among and across the distribution patterns of the bowls articulate webs of connectivity, while distinctive features consistently appear, suggestive of fragmentation. When these technical and stylistic connections and distinctions are viewed through a lens of practice theory, in which they are understood to emerge from ways of doing that have been learned through various social situations, a picture of social connectivity (and fragmentation) can form alongside that of the bowls. Even without being able to pinpoint precise locales of production, such a study should reveal webs of greater or lesser degrees of connectivity, which might then be mapped onto similarly charted connective webs derived from other corpora of material culture. In this way, a truly kaleidoscopic picture of Mediterranean connectivity can be built—from the bottom up.

Notes

1. Peregrine Horden and Nicholas Purcell, *The Corrupting Sea: A Study of Mediterranean History* (Malden, MA: Blackwell, 2000); and Cyprian Broodbank, *The Making of the Middle Sea: A History of the Mediterranean from the Beginning to the Emergence of the Classical World* (Oxford: Oxford University Press, 2013). I would like to thank Jonathan Hall and James Osborne for including me in their stimulating workshop. I also thank the anonymous reviewers who provided feedback that made this contribution stronger, as well as the following individuals who offered advice and bibliographical suggestions: Michael Harrower, A. Bernard Knapp, Joseph Lehner, and Paige Paulsen.

2. Broodbank, *Making of the Middle Sea*, 19–20. Closely associated with the concept of connectivity is that of the *network* as a flexible mesh entangling people and things.

3. Richard Neer, "Connoisseurship and the Stakes of Style," *Critical Inquiry* 32 (2005): 1–26.

4. Sourcing materials through archaeometric techniques can identify geological origins in some cases, such as for obsidian and clays, and can illuminate important aspects of mobility as discussed by Osborne and Hall in the introduction to this volume, but also brings with it its own set of complications and interpretive issues, including the limited range of materials that can yield productive sourcing information and the question of whether the materials moved in their worked or unworked states. See, e.g., Ellery Frahm, "Evaluation of Archaeological Sourcing Techniques: Reconsidering and Re-Deriving Hughes' Four-Fold Assessment Scheme," *Geoarchaeology* 27 (2012): 166–74; A. M. Pollard et al., *Beyond Provenance: New Approaches to Interpreting the Chemistry of Archaeological Copper Alloys* (Leuven: Leuven University Press, 2018); and D. J. Killick, J. A. Stephens, and T. R. Fenn, "Geological Constraints on the Use of Lead Isotopes for Provenance in Archaeometallurgy," *Archaeometry* 62, Suppl. 1 (2020): 86–105.

5. See especially Pollard et al., *Beyond Provenance*, 187–91; and Ernst Pernicka, "Provenance Determination of Archaeological Metal Objects," in *Archaeometallurgy in Global Perspective: Methods and Syntheses*, ed. B. W. Roberts and C. P. Thornton (New York: Springer, 2014), 239–68. For specific analyses of the decorated metal bowls, see M. J. Hughes, J. R. S. Lang, M. N. Leese, and J. E. Curtis, "The Evidence of Scientific Analysis: A Case Study of the Nimrud Bowls," in *Bronzeworking Centres of Western Asia c. 1000–539 B.C.*, ed. J. Curtis (London: Kegan Paul International, 1988), 311–15; and Alessandra Giumlia-Mair, "Phoenician Metalwork: Composition and Techniques," in *Phoenician Bronzes in the Mediterranean*, ed. Javier Jiménez Ávila (Madrid: Real Academia de la Historia, 2015), 481–515.

6. E.g., Horden and Purcell, *Corrupting Sea*, 124.

7. Horden and Purcell, *Corrupting Sea*, 160.

8. For example, "Wandering potters who imitated the styles of their homeland have done much to complicate the typology of the ceramics which are our most abundant testimony to the Archaic Greek period" (Horden and Purcell, *Corrupting Sea*, 370).

9. Broodbank, *Making of the Middle Sea*, 276.

10. Constancy is a key element in Meyer Schapiro's influential 1953 definition of style: "By style is usually meant the constant form—and sometimes the constant elements, qualities, and expression—in the art of an individual or a group. The term is also applied to the whole activity of an individual or society, as in speaking of a 'life-style' or 'the style of a civilization.'" Meyer Schapiro, "Style," in *Theory and Philosophy of Art: Style, Artist, and Society; Selected Papers* (New York: George Braziller, 1994), 51–102. (Reprinted with changes from *Anthropology Today: An Encyclopedic Inventory*, ed. A. L. Kroeber [Chicago: University of Chicago Press, 1953], 287–312.)

11. Broodbank, *Making of the Middle Sea*, 334; emphasis added.

12. Broodbank, *Making of the Middle Sea*, 451. For the anthropoid coffins as a local Levantine practice, see Dana Douglas DePietro, "Piety, Practice, and Politics: Ritual and Agency in the Late Bronze Age Southern Levant" (PhD diss., University of California, Berkeley, 2012), 80–83.

13. Bruce G. Trigger, *A History of Archaeological Thought* (Cambridge: Cambridge University Press, 1989), 148–206.

14. V. Gordon Childe, *The Danube in Prehistory* (Oxford: Oxford University Press, 1929), v–vi. Much has been written with respect to the German culture-historical scholar, Gustaf Kossinna (1858–1931), whose work undergirded the racist ideology of Nazi Germany. See J. Laurence Hare, *Excavating Nations: Archaeology, Museums, and the German-Danish Borderlands* (Toronto: University of Toronto Press, 2015), 89–113; Siân Jones, *The Archaeology of Ethnicity: Constructing Identities in the Past and Present* (London: Routledge, 1997), 2–3; and Ulrich Veit, "Ethnic Concepts in German Prehistory: A Case Study on the Relationship between Cultural Identity and Archaeological Objectivity," in *Archaeological Approaches to Cultural Identity*, ed. S. J. Shennan (London: Routledge, 1989), 35–56.

15. See, e.g., Stephen Shennan, "Introduction: Archaeological Approaches to Cultural Identity," in Shennan, *Archaeological Approaches to Cultural Identity*, 11–13.

16. Marian H. Feldman, "Style as a Fragment of the Ancient World: A View from the Iron Age Levant and Assyria," in *The Tiny and the Fragmented: Miniature, Broken, or Otherwise Incomplete Objects in the Ancient World*, ed. S. Rebecca Martin and Stephanie Langin-Hooper (Oxford: Oxford University Press, 2018), 99–115.

17. Rhys Carpenter, "Archaeology," in James S. Ackerman and Rhys Carpenter, *Art and Archaeology* (Englewood Cliffs, NJ: Prentice Hall, 1963), 1–122, at 118.

18. Carpenter, "Archaeology," 117–18. See also Neer, "Connoisseurship," 20.

19. Michael Shanks and Christopher Tilley, *Re-Constructing Archaeology* (Cambridge: Cambridge University Press, 1987), 137–55; Margaret W. Conkey, Experimenting with Style in Archaeology: Some Historical and Theoretical Issues," in *The Uses of Style in Archaeology*, ed. Margaret Conkey and Christine Hastorf (Cambridge: Cambridge University Press, 1990), 5–17; and Ian Hodder, *Symbols in Action: Ethnoarchaeological Studies of Material Culture* (Cambridge: Cambridge University Press, 1982), 204–7.

20. Conkey, "Experimenting with Style," 12.

21. Conkey, "Experimenting with Style."

22. This concept has been explored in scholarship through the notion of technological style and the *chaîne opératoire*; see, with references to earlier literature, Heather M.-L. Miller, *Archaeological Approaches to Technology* (Amsterdam: Academic Press, Elsevier, 2007), 191–95. See also Michael Dietler and Ingrid Herbich, "*Habitus*, Techniques, Style: An Integrated Approach to the Social Understanding of Material Culture and Boundaries," in *The Archaeology of Social Boundaries*, ed. Miriam T. Stark (Washington, DC: Smithsonian Institution Press, 1998), 232–63.

23. Feldman, "Style as a Fragment."

24. As just one particularly clear example of a "style" (the Achaemenid royal court style) not correlating with the onset of Achaemenid political power, see Richard L. Zettler, "On the Chronological Range of Neo-Babylonian and Achaemenid Seals," *Journal of Near Eastern Studies* 38 (1979): 257–70.

25. Note Horden and Purcell's discussion of connectivity as analogous to shifting perceptions of one's environment (*Corrupting Sea*, 124).

26. This, at least, is how I understand their use of connectivity. See the critique of this very issue—that is, whether connectivity is preexisting or the end result—by Gadi Algazi, "Diversity Rules: Peregrine Horden and Nicholas Purcell's *The Corrupting Sea*," *Mediterranean Historical Review* 20, no. 2 (2005): 242, https://doi.org/10.1080/09518960500495172.

27. Purcell refers to the Mediterranean as "kaleidoscopic" in Nicholas Purcell, "Orientalizing: Five Historical Questions," in *Debating Orientalization: Multidisciplinary Approaches to Change in the Ancient Mediterranean*, ed. Corinna Riva and Nicholas C. Vella (London: Equinox, 2006), 26.

28. Horden and Purcell, *Corrupting Sea*, 140.

29. Horden and Purcell, *Corrupting Sea*, 144–46.

30. Horden and Purcell, *Corrupting Sea*, 144.

31. A point also championed by Horden and Purcell, *Corrupting Sea*, 365–72.

32. Horden and Purcell (*Corrupting Sea*, 160) acknowledge the problem that low-level connectivity is hard to document because of scanty evidence.

33. P. R. S. Moorey, *Ancient Mesopotamian Materials and Industries: The Archaeological Evidence* (Winona Lake, IN: Eisenbrauns, 1999), 242–78; Jack Ogden, "Metals," in *Ancient Egyptian Materials and Technology*, ed. Paul T. Nicholson and Ian Shaw (Cambridge: Cambridge University Press, 2000), 149–61; A. Bernard Knapp, *Prehistoric and Protohistoric Cyprus: Identity, Insularity and Connectivity* (Oxford: Oxford University Press, 2008), 133; Vasiliki Kassianidou, "Cypriot Copper for the Iron Age World of the Eastern Mediterranean," in *Structure, Measurement and Meaning: Studies on Prehistoric Cyprus in Honour of David Frankel*, ed. Jennifer M. Webb (Uppsala: Åströms Förlag, 2014), 261–71.

34. Moorey, *Ancient Mesopotamian Materials*, 297–301; K. Aslıhan Yener, *The Domestication of Metals: The Rise of Complex Metal Industries in Anatolia* (Leiden: Brill, 2000); K. Aslıhan Yener et al., "New Tin Mines and Production Sites near Kültepe in Turkey: A Third-Millennium BC Highland Production Model," *Antiquity* 89, no. 345 (June 2015): 596–612; Daniel Berger et al., "Isotope Systematics and Chemical Composition of Tin Ingots from Mochlos (Crete) and Other Late Bronze Age sites in the Eastern Mediterranean Sea: An Ultimate Key to Tin Prov-

enance?," *PLoS ONE* 14, no. 6 (2019): e0218326, https://doi.org/10.1371/journal.pone.0218326.

35. Moorey, *Ancient Mesopotamian Materials*, 217–40; Ogden, "Metals," 161–66.

36. Hughes et al., "Evidence of Scientific Analysis," 312–13.

37. Paul T. Craddock, *Early Metal Mining and Production* (Edinburgh: Edinburgh University Press, 1995); Miller, *Archaeological Approaches to Technology*, 144–66.

38. For an example of such a bottom-up approach, see the study of ivories from the Nimrud Town Wall Houses, Arslan Tash, and Til Barsip in Marian H. Feldman, *Communities of Style: Portable Luxury Arts, Identity, and Collective Memory in the Iron Age Levant* (Chicago: University of Chicago Press, 2014), 146–53.

39. For the primary study of these bowls, see Glenn Markoe, *Phoenician Bronze and Silver Bowls from Cyprus and the Mediterranean* (Berkeley: University of California Press, 1985). However, Markoe did not include a large set of bronze bowls excavated at Nimrud, which are housed in the British Museum where they are the object of ongoing study. See Richard D. Barnett, "Layard's Bronzes and Their Inscriptions," *Eretz Israel* 8 (1967): 1–7; Richard D. Barnett, "The Nimrud Bowls in the British Museum," *Rivista di Studi Fenici* 2 (1974): 11–34; and posted on the British Museum website, http://www.britishmuseum.org/research/research_projects/all_current_projects/the_nimrud_bowls.aspx; for a recent overview of "Phoenician" bowls, including those from Nimrud, with stylistic, typological, and iconographic analyses, see Martin Almagro-Gorbea, "Los cuencos decorados fenicios o 'Phoenician bowls,'" in Jiménez Ávila, *Phoenician Bronzes*, 57–90.

40. For the Sant'Angelo Muxaro bowl, see, Markoe, *Phoenician Bowls*, cat. no. Si1. For the so-called Arjan bowl, see, with earlier references, Javier Álvarez-Mon, *The Arjan Tomb: At the Crossroads of the Elamite and the Persian Empires* (Leuven: Peeters, 2010), 122–43.

41. There is, in fact, a sliding scale among figurative, vegetal, and geometric imagery, as well as entirely undecorated bowls that share the same forms as decorated vessels, further complicating the question of the coherence of this assemblage as a group. See, for example, a bronze bowl from a burial in Tragana in central Greece featuring only a raised central omphalos surrounded by rosette petals and a circular band with a herringbone design (*La Méditerranée des Phéniciens, de Tyr à Carthage*, exhibition catalog [Paris: Institut du Monde Arabe, 2007], cat. no. 177), or bronze bowls with central rosette decorations from tombs at Assur in Iraq such as one from Tomb 38: Arndt Haller, *Die Gräber und Grüfte von Assur* (Berlin: Verlag Gebr. Mann, 1954), 116, pl. 25d. See also the general discussion in Almagro-Gorbea, "Los cuencos decorados fenicios," 57–58.

42. Markoe, *Phoenician Bowls*, 1.

43. Marian H. Feldman, "Levantine Art in the 'Orientalizing' Period," in *The Oxford Handbook of the Phoenician and Punic Mediterranean*, ed. Carolina López-Ruiz and Brian Doak (Oxford: Oxford University Press, 2019), 371–84.

44. Markoe (*Phoenician Bowls*) catalogs at least fifty-six bowls with secure archaeological provenances (he also includes several bowls without provenances). The number of bowls from Nimrud is uncertain, but around fifty known decorated vessels have been published (*Phoenician Bowls*, 16). Several other decorated bowls have come to light since Markoe's 1985 volume, including the Arjan bowl in ancient Elam (Álvarez-Mon, *Arjan Tomb*, 122–43); a gold bowl found in one of the Queens'

Tombs under the Northwest Palace at Nimrud (with earlier references, see Dirk Wicke, Angela Busch, and Erika Fischer, "Die Goldschale der Iabâ—eine levantinische Antiquität," *Zeitschrift für Assyriologie* 100 [2010]: 109–41); and two bowls found in the Orthi Petra necropolis at Eleutherna, Crete (with references, see Joan Aruz, Sarah G. Graff, and Yelena Rakic, eds., *Assyria to Iberia at the Dawn of the Classical Age* [New York: Metropolitan Museum of Art, 2014], cat. nos. 155 and 158).

45. Markoe, *Phoenician Bowls*; Francesca Onnis, "The Nimrud Bowls: New Data from an Analysis of the Objects," *Iraq* 71 (2009): 139–50.

46. Onnis, "Nimrud Bowls," 143.

47. Markoe, *Phoenician Bowls*, 10. Onnis ("Nimrud Bowls," 141) notes two examples (BM N7 and N15) from her total sample of forty-two that are made by casting rather than hammering techniques.

48. Markoe, *Phoenician Bowls*, 10; Hughes et al., "Evidence of Scientific Analysis," 314; Miller, *Archaeological Approaches to Technology*, 163.

49. For a useful overview of metalworking techniques, including repoussé and chasing, see Oppi Untracht, *Metal Techniques for Craftsmen: A Basic Manual for Craftsmen on the Methods of Forming and Decorating Metals* (Garden City, NY: Doubleday, 1975), esp. 93–110.

50. Untracht, *Metal Techniques for Craftsmen*, 84–85, 111.

51. Markoe, *Phoenician Bowls*, 9.

52. Markoe, *Phoenician Bowls*, 9.

53. Markoe (*Phoenician Bowls*, 9–12) devotes a short chapter to "Technique," where he discusses the general techniques found across all the bowls in his catalog (discussed above), as well as some examples from specific subsets of bowls, in particular those from Cyprus and Etruria.

54. Markoe, *Phoenician Bowls*, 9–10.

55. Markoe, *Phoenician Bowls*, 11.

56. Markoe, *Phoenician Bowls*, 10. For recent technical notes on one of these Cypriot bowls, see Aruz, Graff, and Rakic, *Assyria to Iberia*, 160; for decorated metal bowls from Cyprus, see Christian Vonhoff, "Phoenician Bronzes in Cyprus," in Jiménez Ávila, *Phoenician Bronzes*, 269–94.

57. Markoe, *Phoenician Bowls*, 89. The comparative analysis he used to arrive at this conclusion focuses heavily on just a few of the bowls found on Cyprus (Cy1, Cy2, Cy4, Cy 6, Cy8, Cy11), masking the actual heterogeneity of the Cypriot corpus as a whole.

58. Metropolitan Museum of Art 74.51.5700. H. 4 cm, diameter 13.3 cm. The Cesnola Collection, purchased by subscription, 1874–76. Chronological differences may account in part for the differences between this bowl and the other Cypriot bowls, but does not negate the close connections it displays with bowls from outside of Cyprus.

59. Kerameikos Archaeological Museum, Athens, inv. no. M5. H. 4.8 cm, diameter 17 cm. Karl Kübler, *Kerameikos V: Die Nekropole des 10. bis 8. Jahrhunderts* (Berlin: Walter de Gruyter, 1954), pl. 162.

60. Markoe, *Phoenician Bowls*, 11. The third bowl is also from Cyprus (Cy10 from Curium; not reproduced in his catalog). It is, however, quite different in technique from Cy3 and G1, having a wide, flat rim decorated with regularly spaced, embossed "rivets" (https://www.metmuseum.org/art/collection/search/244495, accessed July 6, 2018).

61. H. 5.5 cm, diameter approx. 15 cm. Mervyn Popham, "An Engraved Near Eastern Bronze Bowl from Lefkandi," *Oxford Journal of Archaeology* 14, no. 1 (1995): 103–7; M. R. Popham and I. S. Lemos, *Lefkandi III: The Toumba Cemetery: The Excavations of 1981, 1984, 1986 and 1992–4*, Plates (Oxford: The British School at Athens, 1996), pls. 70:18, 134, 144, and 145. This bowl is not footed, having instead a hemispherical profile.

62. Nimrud served as the principal Assyrian capital from the reign of Ashurnasirpal II (883–859 BCE) until Sargon II (721–705 BCE) and afterward continued as a major administrative center until the fall of the empire at the end of the seventh century. For a general overview of the site, see Joan Oates and David Oates, *Nimrud: An Assyrian Imperial City Revealed* (London: British School of Archaeology in Iraq, 2001).

63. With earlier references, see Marian H. Feldman, "Metalwork," in Aruz, Graff, and Rakic, *From Assyria to Iberia*, 157–59.

64. Barnett notes, in 1974, that neither the techniques of producing nor the profiles of the Nimrud bowls have been analyzed despite the desirability of such a study (Barnett, "Nimrud Bowls in the British Museum," 18). Barnett's study itself focuses mainly on the designs, although he also takes into consideration the general morphology of the bowls.

65. Onnis, "Nimrud Bowls," 147.

66. Onnis, "Nimrud Bowls," 148.

67. Onnis, "Nimrud Bowls," 149.

68. A conclusion that I came to also in my study of the Levantine ivories; see Feldman, *Communities of Style*.

69. For a contradictory view on the Phoenicians and their scholarship, see López-Ruiz, chapter 2 in this volume.

70. Nicholas Vella, "'Phoenician' Metal Bowls: Boundary Objects in the Archaic Period," *Bollettino di Archeologia On Line* 1 (2010): 22–37.

71. For an overview of approaches to the technological stages of production, see Miller, *Archaeological Approaches to Technology*, esp. fig. 7.1.

CHAPTER 5

Close Encounters of the Lasting Kind

Greeks, Phoenicians, and Others in the Iron Age Mediterranean

SARAH P. MORRIS

What kind of models should we adopt for exploring the connected Early Iron Age in the Mediterranean? James Osborne and Jonathan Hall (chapter 1 in this volume) offer a stimulating review of the leading approaches (and their critics), from Fernand Braudel, who isolated the Mediterranean from its surrounding polities or empires as a unit of focused research, through Peregrine Horden and Purcell's principle of connectivity in *The Corrupting Sea*, which focused on microregions within this unity, to Cyprian Broodbank's *The Making of the Middle Sea*.[1] Broodbank's final chapter is titled "The End of the Beginning," signaled by what he calls the full "cultural Mediterraneanization" of the region, citing factors such as increased mobility, the spread of the alphabet, and convivial practices, all key factors in this chapter. This joins the scope of this volume (the Early Iron Age, once called the Axial Age) to the end of his project—much as Andrew and Susan Sherratt mark a new interactive era in the first millennium BCE.[2] Yet broad models are still needed to synthesize textual narratives with archaeological evidence in the successful reconstruction of protohistory. I will begin by reviewing three recently active approaches and setting forth my own methods.

Popular yet contested is the use of network analysis, mathematical modeling developed for mapping social relations within living populations, applied to long-distance interaction in the past.[3] This has been widely applied in the Mediterranean, including in the Early Iron Age, but may be more productive for ancient prosopography and social networks than with material culture.[4] Among successful examples of the latter, Christine Johnston applied to the eastern Mediterranean in the Late Bronze Age what Carl Knappett did for the Middle Bronze Age.[5]

Another overused model for analyzing interaction in the Mediterranean is the so-called middle ground, made famous in Richard White's 1991 study of a particular phase in Native American and European interaction in the Great Lakes region. Irad Malkin promoted its use in the western Mediterranean, where it is now widely applied to transcultural interaction and novel cultural forms (including at Selinus, where I have argued against it to understand an unusual fusion of Greek and Semitic rites).[6] It should be used with caution and full understanding of the complexities of the case study where it was developed, rather than merely as the latest term for hybrid cultural forms or overlapping cultures: it involved asymmetrical power relations and even deliberate misunderstandings in its original context, beyond colonialism and resistance.

A novel approach adopted by Catherine Pratt reframes Greek and Phoenician interaction on Crete in terms of "minor transnationalism," a concept developed for modern socioeconomic globalization and applied to contemporary societies and literatures.[7] Transnationalism is attractive to the study of the ancient Mediterranean for its focus on the locales of daily interaction and the rise of small-scale hybrid practices, as well as the role of "border-crossing agents." Its offshoot, minor transnationalism, acknowledges the role of nondominant populations in cross-cultural traffic and the creation of new cultural forms. This kind of model would satisfy concerns expressed by authors in this volume for a bottom-up approach to connectivity, by offering a method well suited to the recovery of the archaeological record. It is one that I prefer to the concept of globalization recommended by Tamar Hodos (chapter 10 in this volume).

My own approach applies Marian Feldman's use of "communities of style" to revisit some close encounters between Greeks, Phoenicians, and others in the Mediterranean, for shared ritual traditions lasting beyond initial contacts.[8] In addition, I emphasize new agents of interaction, mercenaries or mobile fighters, as potential "border-crossing agents" who may have settled or married in new locales, drawing on evidence from several sites in Crete to support this claim. Finally, I probe emerging new horizons in the north Aegean for both early encounters and lasting practices. Building on the work of Susan Sherratt (chapter 6 in this volume), I will edge past this book's time span to consider how expansionist powers (Assyria, Phrygia, Lydia, and Persia) harnessed existing mobile networks of connectivity among "Ionians." This involves a delicate balance of proxy data and historical sources, but has wider applications to other regions.

Inevitably, we view the map of the Early Iron Age Mediterranean under the rubric of colonization, which neatly organizes various movements into broad ethnic streams, often dominated by two primary actors,

"Greeks" and "Phoenicians." But "Phoenicians" identified themselves as Sidonians or Tyrians (as Greek poets did), not under a generic rubric, while Greek cities likewise colonized as Corinthians, Megarians, Laconians, and other polis identities.[9] Moreover, with the exception of Etruscan Italy, until recently there was limited consideration of crucial third parties, in particular the indigenous peoples of Sicily, Sardinia, Africa, and Iberia.[10] This neglect of local native populations has kept many Mediterranean encounter zones far from a modern, postcolonial perspective, and limited our purview to the trail of literate colonizers.[11]

The second framework that dominates classical scholarship on Greeks and Phoenicians is the quest for contacts that might have fostered the Greek adaptation of the Phoenician alphabet. This has encouraged a method I call the "smoking gun," by seeking locales where writing in both scripts is copresent, as if a single act of transliteration, complete with Semitic letter names in Greek, took place.[12] In this quest, we have chased Phoenicians where they appear in ancient sources (e.g., on Cythera or Thasos) in vain, while missing other zones of encounter only visible in excavations (Crete and the north Aegean). In my investigation, I try to transcend these two frameworks—colonization and alphabetization—to highlight the role of third parties such as mercenaries. I make this argument from the lasting effects wrought by these early encounters, as promised in my title.

Speaking Bowls: Shared Scripts, Shared Practices?

I will begin with Crete, the island that lay in the path of Phoenician expansion—midway between Cyprus and Sicily, or on the route from Tyre to Carthage—but was never formally settled by Levantine cities.[13] I continue to connect the early record of Near Eastern imports in Iron Age Crete to the expansion of Assyria, with the Phoenicians as their clients, in major traffic from the Levant to the west.[14] Crete is home to some of the richest discoveries of Orientalia (at Knossos, Kommos, Eleutherna, and the Idaean Cave), as well as arguably the earliest form of the Greek alphabet.[15] This would make Crete a prime locale for adaptation, both for its early letter forms and for ample evidence of interaction, in particular Knossos, in the center of the northern coast. Our "smoking gun" here would be the bronze hemispherical bowl from Tekke Tomb J at the North Cemetery, inscribed in Semitic letters that read "I am the cup of Shema son of La'amon."[16] The letters have been dated anywhere from 1200 BCE (Puech) to 1100 or 1000 (Cross) or 900 (Sass) BCE, at the latest, while the pottery found with two burials belongs to the Early Protogeometric (tenth century) and Middle Protogeometric (late ninth–early eighth); later still are the earliest alphabetic inscriptions in Greece, which appear only in the mid-eighth century. So if this is our smoking gun (i.e., the earliest Semitic inscription in a Greek context), its bullet took up to 250 years to meet its target (i.e., the earliest Greek letters, whose Cretan forms do not resemble the Semitic letters on the Tekke bowl). Presumably, no one needed a writing system, or not this one, until the eighth century, when a number of sites such as Pithecussae on the Bay of Naples and Eretria in Euboea produced graffiti in both Greek and Semitic (Aramaic, as well as Phoenician) writing systems.[17] This leaves the Tekke bowl as an "impressive unicum" in the archaeological record but a dead end for the history of the early alphabet.[18] Wherever Greeks first adapted Semitic letters for Greek use, in Archaic Crete, the word *poinikastas* identified a scribe (as public recorder and "rememberer"), with letters called *poinikeia*, and *poinikazein* was the verb to write (*SEG* XXVII, 631), as if letters and scribes were known, at least locally, as "Phoenician," even long after adaptation.[19]

A recent study of the early alphabet argues that literacy followed Phoenician maritime trade, presuming the existence of written contracts, now lost, based on Near Eastern precedents and classical documents, and linking these contracts to the absence of early Phoenician coinage to imagine a credit-based maritime economy.[20] This model revives an economic rather than cultural role for the *transmission* of the Semitic alphabet, yet cultural institutions and practices may still explain its *dissemination*. Significant is the habit of inscribing vessels as personal possessions, a custom Semitic in origin but modified in Greek contexts, first evident in this early tomb in Crete. For the Tekke bowl is the earliest in a series that Marian Feldman has eloquently termed "speaking bowls," in her study of sixteen inscribed bronze bowls found across Greek and Near Eastern interface zones.[21] While these metal bowls (whether "Phoenician" or otherwise Near Eastern) are inscribed with personal names of owners, their Greek counterparts in clay claim owners who are also poets and drinkers, often giving their vessel a first-person voice that makes it truly a "speaking bowl."[22] Following Marek Węcowski, it is more productive to focus on form and function of the earliest Greek inscriptions and their role in social circles and practices, rather than mapping their geographical distribution or chronological order.[23] Moreover, this approach brings study of the diffusion of the Semitic alphabet in line with new approaches to its origins and early uses in bottom-up "script communities," for personal and ritual purposes.[24] Inscribed bowls indicate shared drinking if not feasting practices, perhaps involving since their onset an association with warfare and ideology also borrowed from the Levant.[25] On Crete, communal drinking follows an idiosyncratic trajectory, entangled with the *syssitia* tradition and other shared feasting practices that include martial connections, to be examined further below.[26]

Connectivity in Death: Burial and Worship

Turning to a second, classical set of evidence from Cretan cemeteries, the exquisite jewelry buried beneath the floor in a ninth-century Tekke tomb at Knossos was once identified as the property and product of an Eastern craftsman, a notion now largely rejected.[27] Gail Hoffmann has cautioned against past arguments for separating Greek from foreign in the archaeological record, especially using imports to ascribe ethnic identity to individuals. She also revised John Boardman's identification of North Syrians burying themselves in Levantine style at Afrati, a site associated with the inscriptions naming *poinikastas* (scribe) and *mnamon* (reminder, rememberer?).[28] As someone who has long sought to identify foreigners, or their influence, in Cretan burials, I remain convinced that ritual practices in burial and worship indicate more lasting results of Iron Age connectivity than individual, imported objects. Building on Philip Schmitz's analysis of graves at Tyre with Egyptian mortuary beliefs and rites imported into the Phoenician world, I introduce a Cretan extension of his argument, by reaching out to the Greek island for Levantine ritual connections traced in both graves and shrines.[29]

What is more persuasive than tomb offerings for a Semitic presence in Crete is the use of Phoenician-type tomb markers, at both Eleutherna and Knossos, in the Early Iron Age. Two stone markers or *cippi* found on the surface at Eleutherna in 1985 must belong to the period of the cemetery's use (ninth to sixth centuries BCE).[30] A third, even earlier *cippus* was later excavated at Eleutherna; these discoveries helped archaeologists recognize two examples from the Knossos area, one used to seal a chamber tomb at Atsalenio in the late eighth century, and a second, more anthropomorphic one, from the North Cemetery dating to the seventh century.[31] All are of local limestone, thus made on Crete to mark the graves of individuals or families who chose a Phoenician burial custom, whatever their ethnic affiliation. These finds and their dates suggest a repeated practice, beyond a single foreign-style gravestone, in a family custom that disseminated nonlocal ritual beliefs and practices, perhaps through intermarriage.[32] Such choices are surely a more powerful index of foreign influence than imported (or locally made, in foreign style) jewelry and inscribed bronze vessels, which could merely reflect exchange with the Levantine coast and Cyprus, and elite local consumption of imports. This moves discussion beyond defining ethnic identity through artifacts, to admit the possible role of "hybrid go-betweens" or "minor transnationals" sharing practices, as important agents of connectivity.

I have argued elsewhere for a similar fusion of Near Eastern and Greek ritual practices at Selinus in western Sicily, a contact zone between Phoenicians, Sicilians, and Greek colonists. Here, an extra-urban complex of shrines with sacred texts and stone monuments seems to document a mixed community with a set of hybrid practices that defies classification.[33] Another locale where a few imports trace a palimpsest of encounters is the Cycladic island of Naxos, whose graves sheltered Cypriot imports such as gold relief plaques with goddess figures from the Late Bronze Age at Kamini, and a Cypriot Black and Red juglet of the Early Iron Age, buried with local handmade kantharoi, in an extraordinary inland necropolis (Tsikalario) of built-stone enclosures and megalithic monuments.[34] Other Aegean islands with mixed imports may indicate the intersection of Greek and Eastern trade routes, beyond Rhodes and its well-known repertoire of Greek and Phoenician(izing) products, without offering us textual sources to certify them.[35]

Soldiers of Fortune: Mercenaries in Motion?

The Phoenician *cippi* introduced above join other examples of stone funerary markers from Eleutherna, under excavation since 1985.[36] The scale of imports, their range of types, and the diversity and quality of burial goods here indicate far more than casual trade, be it consumption by aggressive and prosperous local elites or generations of Easterners (Cypriot, Phoenician, Levantine?) who settled in this valley. Beyond the rich variety of imports, we need to ask how are they used and what do they inspire in terms of innovative local shared practices?

I offer another local fusion in monumental, visible form rather than portable grave goods: the funerary structure of the seventh-century Building 4A, which rises over the early tombs at Orthi Petra. As reconstructed, it offers a square monument (3.6 × 3.5 m) of ashlar faces fronting rubble, open inside but devoid of any burials, with a niche in the façade resembling a false door, where Nikolaos Stampolidis has restored a *kore* figure found nearby (twin of the Auxerre maiden in the Louvre).[37] However, parts of a kouros were also found here, as well as ten limestone figures of warriors—originally restored on a pitched roof along the ridgepole but more recently as some kind of acroteria on a flat(ter?) roof.[38] Such a reconstruction borrows from the enigmatic Chania stone relief, which depicts a temple façade or city gate framing a female figure flanked by warriors defending the city against a charging chariot.[39] The figures found at Eleutherna bear stone tangs to fit into a stone base or the earth, but it is not at all clear where they once stood or whom they represented. (Stampolidis suggests the mythical Curetes.) Beyond architectural decoration, they recall individual funerary *stelai*, a Cretan specialty in use at Eleutherna, Archaic Prinias, and in Bronze Age predecessors from Armenoi. A tapering stone pillar set up at Eleutherna across from Building 4A in a square base, once at least four meters tall, enhances this notion of commemorating the dead with built-stone monuments, an idea that owes much to Iron Age north Syria. Without the kind of settlement evidence that survives in the western Mediterranean in the Early Iron Age (e.g., in Iberia), our focus on connectivity in the Aegean must rest on such evidence for hybrid ritual in burial.[40]

What emerges clearly in these examples in early Crete is the prominent figure of the warrior in art, in stone statues and in relief, which complements the value placed on weapons in burials, as well as in related scenes of warfare on bronze armor.[41] An eloquent example is the tomb group from the Pantanassa *tholos* in the Amari valley—a cremation burial of an adult male with finds akin to those from Lefkandi, including a bronze amphoroid krater of Cypriot type, used as an ash urn.[42] Dating to the eleventh century BCE, this import and its context link the burial to bronze kraters from Knossos and Euboea,[43] tracing an early wave of mobility following the Late Bronze Age collapse. His other grave goods include weapons such as iron knives, daggers, and bronze spears that appear in related tombs on Cyprus, at Lefkandi, and in other "weapon burials" of the transition from the Bronze Age to the Early Iron Age.[44] I propose that such assemblages, linked over two decades ago by Hector Catling to "heroes returned" from Eastern adventures, express and empower a military ethos and a warrior class as active social agents.[45]

I introduce this selection of evidence in order to emphasize the role of mobile warriors, not just traders and craftspeople, in the dissemination and reproduction of novel cultural traditions. Particularly in the period following disruptions throughout the eastern Mediterranean around and after 1200 BCE, scholars now identify displaced military personnel, released from service as mercenaries or in palace armies, who sought new environments, often abroad.[46] In the era between 1200 and 1000 BCE, we can imagine large numbers of displaced fighters resettling in new locales in the Aegean, including eastern Crete, where their graves are marked by widespread weapon types including, inevitably, the Naue II sword. In locales where this phenomenon was particularly intense (for example,

Achaea in the northwest Peloponnese), such warriors—whether native or newcomers—must have sustained memories of Bronze Age warfare that helped shape the epic tradition in Greek poetry.[47] The circulation of weapons as well as warriors across the Late Bronze Age eastern Mediterranean left a trail of military technology and related goods that outlasted 1200 BCE, as is now widely recognized.[48] During the twilight between the palatial era and one that forged new, Iron Age communities, military—including seafaring—skills may have sustained local resilience and vitality, along with the ideology of heroic warfare forged from memories (or fantasies?) of Bronze Age battles. New masters in the Near East and Egypt seeking to hire troops inaugurated the next era of warfare, when soldiers of fortune—mobile fighters—played a crucial role in human and cultural diffusion, by intermarriage with non-Greek partners, and in other interactions with a lasting influence on our archaeological and historical record.[49] While recent scholarship advises caution on the evidence for Greek hoplites in Near Eastern armies, I approach an earlier era, and in material evidence rather than texts.[50]

This scenario follows Roger Woodard's complex vision of the origins of the Greek alphabet, in which he assigns a key role to mercenaries who served in Assyrian armies, where they may have been exposed to Semitic writing systems that they then brought back to Cyprus.[51] Images of such warriors on Cypro-Phoenician bowls (figure 5.1) wear hoplite armor and fight near Assyrian fortress architecture, thus feeding Woodard's arguments for the kind of historical settings that spread a new writing system. While the new script soon disappeared from Cyprus itself, which continued to use its Bronze Age syllabic writing system, Woodard imagines it spreading among Greeks unfamiliar with writing, such as the other, non-Cypriot mercenaries serving the Assyrian king. This offers an ingenious way to bridge "returning heroes" of an earlier era (the eleventh–tenth centuries BCE?) with those whom Woodard imagines returning from imperial military service in the eighth and seventh centuries. Indeed, some of the earliest Semitic alphabetic inscriptions belong to mercenaries serving in Egypt, and the greatest concentration of early Cretan inscriptions appears on bronze armor—perhaps booty—from Afrati.[52] This scenario also anticipates their lasting contributions to Archaic Greek art, where the role of mercenaries and armorers in Egyptian service has recently been reconnected to the development of Greek figural sculpture, and to Eastern Mediterranean literature.[53] And such mechanisms of relocation and settlement would have involved intermarriage and the formation of new, "blended" or bilingual families—the most lasting form of connectivity to be imagined in this highly mobile, Iron Age Mediterranean.[54]

FIGURE 5.1 "Phoenician" silver bowl with battle scenes in relief, from Amathus, Cyprus. BM 123053. Courtesy of the Trustees of the British Museum. Diameter 19.5 cm, H. 5 cm.

These suggest some productive ways to look for social phenomena in archaeological contexts, beyond specific imports or their origins, as the most eloquent elements in the web of connectivity and in establishing lasting communities of practice and their products.

Returning to evidence from Crete, new roles for armed fighters are expressed not only in decorated armor and funerary art, but in sanctuary settings as well. This emerges on the south coast in the sanctuary at Kommos, which preserves a unique fusion of Near Eastern and Greek ritual practices.[55] First active in the tenth century BCE when it was frequented by Phoenician merchants, it indicates a far different form of investment by foreigners in local communities and practices, through cult rather than in burial. The design of Temple B (800–600 BCE), with its tri-pillar shrine, is widely accepted as Phoenician in inspiration, following the presence of imported Phoenician amphorae in the earlier Temple A. Levantine practices also prevail at this shrine in both choice of animal victim—the

"Phoenician" phase shows a conspicuous absence of pig bones, which resume in later "Greek" phases—and method of sacrifice: Kommos is one of the first Greek sanctuaries with evidence of the Israelite ritual of burning the tail (*osphys*) that was adopted into Greek practice.[56] As the focus of this cult, a possible trinity of Egyptian/izing deities was first identified in two figurines (Sekhmet and Nefertum, lacking only Ptah to make up a Theban trinity, perhaps a progenitor of Cretan divine triads at Gortyn and Drerus). Following Joseph Shaw's revised view of these figures as Semitic deities (Baal, Astarte, and Asherah?), Megan Daniels suggests they represent a Sidonian triad (Astarte, Eshmun, and Baal) linked to commercial activity at this harbor, frequented by Phoenicians on their way to the western Mediterranean. In particular, she emphasizes the military aspect of Astarte and her worship, and connects her "with the warrior aristocracy active at Knossos," explored in other Kommos finds.[57]

The shrine at Kommos also offers us a remarkable incised cup of the seventh century BCE with an unusual scene (figure 5.2). Of a type and ware at home in central Crete since the ninth century, and in a shape eventually enlarged to serve as a krater or mixing bowl at shared feasts, the very fabric and surface of this so-called coated cup vividly imitate dark and glossy metal, while its incised decoration echoes that on metal shapes.[58] The incised scene was first interpreted as the *prothesis* of a warrior, attended on the right by a hoplite, while on the left, the composition begins to show a runner, possibly associated with funeral games. Here is a bowl "speaking" through images rather than words, and offering us armed warriors, a funeral scene, and perhaps games in honor of the dead. In a new study of the Kommos cup, Antonis Kotsonas argues for a mythological interpretation of the scene as specific episodes of the Trojan War, rather than a generic epic or ritual scene as advanced in earlier studies and enhanced recently by Megan Daniels.[59] In either scenario, one can witness the fusion of Levantine metal bowls, decorated with friezes of battle (figure 5.1), hunting, and banqueting, or inscribed with personal names (chapter 7, figure 7.1), with emerging Greek ideologies of warfare and commemoration. These objects express the kind of ideology implied in warrior burials on Crete since the tenth century, but appear in sanctuary contexts as at Kommos, and may anticipate shared dining customs in *andreia*.[60] I am not the first to point out how such a warrior class might have "assisted the diffusion of cultural phenomena such as syncretism [and] the transmission of the alphabet."[61]

Evidence for Greek and Phoenician encounters in burials and shrines on the north and south coasts of Crete was more than a coastal phenomenon, thanks to the rich imports from the Idaean Cave, located high in

FIGURE 5.2 Cretan black cup with incised scene of footrace (funeral game?), from temple at Kommos, Crete; late seventh century BCE. H. 11 cm, max. diameter 13 cm, rim diameter 12 cm. Herakleion Archaeological Museum (Π 25787), Crete. Courtesy of Hellenic Ministry of Culture and Sports, Hellenic Organization of Cultural Resources Development (H.O.C.RE.D.). Photo author.

the mountains of western Crete. Osborne and Hall (chapter 1 in this volume) urge us to consider inland sites and not just coastal interactions, a strategy also successful in fieldwork on Cyprus by Catherine Kearns (chapter 3 in this volume), and indeed objects from the cave play a leading role in any consideration of Near Eastern connections, local military elites, and banqueting customs in Early Iron Age Crete, indicating their penetration much farther than the coast.[62]

Moreover, Crete is not the only Archaic locale where early, militarized associations are celebrated in ritual contexts. Miletus in coastal Asia Minor was settled, according to legend, by Ionians, who expelled or killed

Carians and established early sanctuaries at Melie and on Mount Mycale (Herodotus 1.142–48). Recent discoveries on Mycale have uncovered an early settlement at Çatallar Tepe with a seventh-century *naiskos* followed by an Archaic, tripartite temple, including what has been identified as a *lesche*, decorated with weapons but also full of drinking cups, wine sieves, and ivory plaques, possibly from furniture.[63] A pair of conjoined terracotta warrior figures belonged to the earlier shrine, echoing the image of martial solidarity promoted in the art and ritual of early Crete. Whether or not this complex was the ancient Panionion or an early Carian shrine, it clearly replicates the fusion of drinking and fighting communities in a zone of encounter between Greeks and Carians. In central Greece, the early sanctuary at Kalapodi in Phocis attracted votive weapons and at least one bronze relief bowl from North Syria, then battle scenes were painted on Archaic temple walls: fusing Oriental booty with warrior ideology?[64] Farther west, the Monte Prama statues of archers in limestone on Sardinia, famously identified as "entangled objects," mark a similar convergence of factors, where Phoenician exploration met local militarism and lent it monumental form in stone.[65]

New Horizons: The North Aegean

Here I turn our attention to the north Aegean, a newly revealed, important zone of encounters in the "connected" Iron Age, if not for the transmission of the alphabet, which I introduce on the basis of my collaborative fieldwork at Methone in Pieria with the Greek Ephorate of Antiquities of Pieria.[66] While northern Greece was associated in ancient sources with Phoenicians attracted to the metal ores of Thasos and the Pangaion (Herodotus 6.47), recent discoveries—transport amphorae, juglets, and even an inscription—reveal new Greek destinations for Phoenicians around the Thermaic Gulf.[67] Thanks to finds of early Greek and Phoenician amphorae, this region is home to "the oldest organized commercial network of the historic period,"[68] one that well predates, and may even have attracted, formal Greek colonization. An area rich in minerals, close to upland timber sources for a new age of shipbuilding, but also producing the first standardized container (the North Aegean amphora) for transporting commodities, the north Aegean offered coastal footholds from Thessaly to Thrace to entrepreneurs from the Near East and southern Greece in the early first millennium. Before Methone attracted an Eretrian colony circa 733/732 BCE (Plutarch *Quaestiones Graecae* 11), local manufacturing and exchange in the Early Iron Age were already active. Important early deposits have yielded both early Greek graffiti (figure 5.5), *and* Phoenician imports (figure 7.7), but no Semitic writing yet. Unlike Early Iron Age Crete, Methone is so far exposed not in cemeteries (beyond a single Euboean oenochoe at Melissia), but in its industrial quarters, with copious evidence for local manufacture in metal, ivory and bone, glass, and ceramics (figure 5.3).[69]

However, the richest deposits of these objects, which also produced the early inscribed vessels, are two deep pits filled in with copious materials; the first one discovered dates to the Late Geometric/Early Archaic period with nearly 200 examples of graffiti, including some that may be sympotic, and in verse. The second pit, excavated in 2015 to 2017, was filled in three deposits—largely with domestic debris that includes examples of Archaic Greek drinking cups with owners' names in graffiti (figure 5.4).[70] A late Archaic cup with letters preserving ΞΣΕΝΙ- (figure 5.5) may have been destined for "guests" or visitors; if not marking a personal name, these letters could be an explicit sign of entertaining strangers, within a community of practice marked by a variety of imports from around the Aegean.[71]

Thus Methone demonstrates, in one place, early environmental conditions to attract trade, a site with an indigenous population already trafficking in commodities, followed by Greek and Phoenician exploration that introduced early script use and its legacies. It offers lasting and widespread practices, far from the early bowl from Crete in space and time, perhaps acquired over generations of cohabitation and co-practices in drinking and feasting. This promising, expanding arena of Early Iron Age interaction and connectivity in the north Aegean also anticipates local developments in the Archaic and Classical periods. As argued by Susan Sherratt (chapter 6), Greek exploration of the Black Sea by coastal Ionians, especially Milesians, may reflect a trading alliance to supply landlocked Lydian overloads, or even earlier, the Phrygians. As Sherratt lays out, citing an important study by David Hill, exploration of northern regions by Ionians may reflect arrangements with their inland neighbors for "accessing the sea by proxy on behalf of Lydians," making Miletus more a partner or client for Anatolian overlords than an independent explorer and colonizer, as in classical sources.[72] Her arguments find support in Alexander Fantalkin's revision of the foundation of Naucratis in Egypt as a venture enabled by Lydian alliance with Miletus and Pharaonic relations in the late seventh century (Strabo 17.1.8), long before Amasis II invited Greeks to settle in the Egyptian delta (Herodotus 2.178).[73]

Following Sherratt's model, the exploitation of mineral (silver, gold, and copper) and timber resources in Thrace and Macedonia, by East Greek clients for Lydian and later Achaemenid interests, could have at-

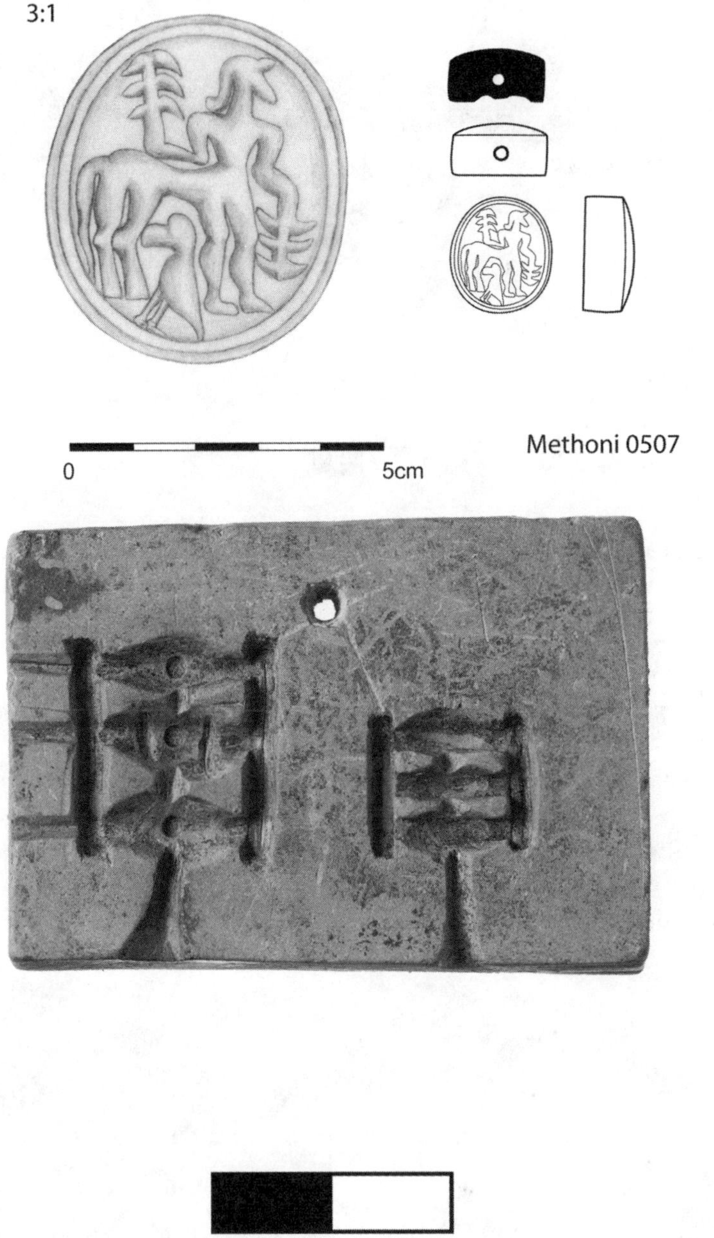

FIGURE 5.3 (a) Early Iron Age carved ivory seal, from the Hypogeion at Methone: centaur with branches. ΜΕΘ 0507. 1.6 × 1.5 cm. Bessios, *Πιερίδων Στέφανος*, 110. Drawing: Tina Ross. (b) Archaic stone mold (half) for metal jewelry, Methone: ΜΕΘ 8175. Found in Early Iron Age Archaic level below topsoil in Trench 2, 2017: Morris et al., "Methone 2014–2017," fig. 64d. Photo Jeffrey Vanderpool.

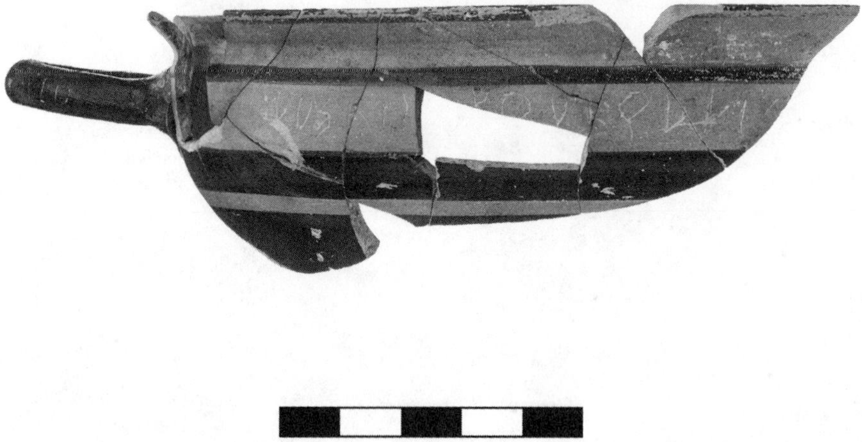

FIGURE 5.4 Archaic Attic cup from Methone (ΜΕΘ 8103), graffito owner's inscription: Λυσάν[δ]ρου ἐ φύλισ[χ - *vac*. From the Archaic level of Pit 46, Methone. H. 5.5 cm, rim diameter 18 cm. Morris et al., "Methone 2014–2017," figs. 58c, 65d. Photo Jeffrey Vanderpool.

FIGURE 5.5 Late or Subgeometric *skyphos* from Methone with incised inscription under handle: ΣΧΕΝΙ- (ΧΣΕΝΙ?). ΜΕΘ 2247. Bessios et al., *Μεθώνη Πιερίας* 1, 365–66, no. 22. H. 9.7 cm, rim diameter 13 cm, max. diameter 16 cm. Photo Orestes Kourakis.

tracted northern Greek colonies (for example, Abdera, founded by Teos) and accounted for the local dispersal of East Greek material culture. Evidence includes Clazomenian sarcophagi at Akanthos (Ierissos), Ionic marble temples at Neapolis (Kavala) and Therme (Thessaloniki), East Greek pottery at many coastal sites from Mount Olympus to the Hebrus River, and even Ionian and Carian graffiti.[74] Several striking new finds suggest the long reach of Persian influence in the sixth and fifth centuries, during a time of active Achaemenid engagement with the Argead dynasts of Macedonia and military activity in the north Aegean.[75] More significant is that northern Greek cities minted electrum and silver coinage earlier than Athens or Euboea, and did so on the Ionic (Milesian) standard, surely a legacy of their early entanglement in East Greek markets.[76] Such are the "lasting" encounters in my title, attested through indirect material evidence, that reflect the distant influence of Phrygian, Lydian and finally Achaemenid economic imperialism in a resource-rich area. And key players in these developments and their distribution were not just merchants and miners, sailors and settlers, but also mobile fighters engaged in imperial armies. Revealing their role involves looking beyond ancient sources and stylistic identification of artifacts to imagine the networks that activated traffic and the conjoined practices that linked communities across cultural boundaries.

Conclusion

As chapter 1 of this volume argues, a complex landscape of encounters may discourage the use of universal models of interaction that can be applied widely and consistently across the Iron Age Mediterranean. By introducing new microregions (the north Aegean) and vectors (mobile warriors) of mobility and a practice-based approach, I may fail to transcend Horden and Purcell's or Broodbank's models with a wider form of connectivity to embrace the Iron Age Mediterranean. Archaeologists focused on microregions lose opportunities to build on wider models, beyond defining border-crossing agents and their practices within wider networks that may be linked to imperial action. Some promising hybrid cultural forms may have remained locally unique or short-lived, and barely advance us beyond "glocalism." While studies thus confined in space dissolve wider connectivities, diachronic analyses (as pursued in this chapter) can be criticized for their "timelessness."[77] New settings in recent research or reanalysis in settings far from Eastern Mediterranean power centers (Iberia) may deliver some of the most transformative lessons about the reach of mobility and even the origins of the western alphabet. New regional studies that follow a diachronic, multiscalar approach to networks, focused on dynamics by tracking mobility, technology, and innovation, show great promise.[78] Beyond filling in details from microregions, we need to continue robust comparative work to reveal diachronic patterns of interaction that lend substance to the notion of connectivity.

Notes

1. Peregrine Horden and Nicholas Purcell, *The Corrupting Sea: A Study of Mediterranean History* (Malden, MA: Blackwell, 2000); and Cyprian Broodbank, *The Making of the Middle Sea: A History of the Mediterranean from the Beginning to the Emergence of the Classical World* (Oxford: Oxford University Press, 2013). Since the 2018 conference that inspired this volume, new contributions to the connected Iron Age Mediterranean include J. G. Manning, *The Open Sea: The Economic Life of the Ancient Mediterranean World from the Iron Age to the Rise of Rome* (Princeton, NJ: Princeton University Press, 2018); Saro Wallace, *Travellers in Time: Imagining Movement in the Ancient Aegean World* (Abingdon: Routledge, 2018); Lukasz Niesiołowski-Spanò and Marek Węcowski, eds., *Change, Continuity, and Connectivity: Northeastern Mediterranean at the Turn of the Bronze Age and in the Early Iron Age* (Wiesbaden: Harrassowitz, 2018); Tamar Hodos, *The Archaeology of the Mediterranean Iron Age: A Globalising World c. 1100–600 BCE* (Cambridge: Cambridge University Press, 2020); and Alex Knodell, *Societies in Transition in Early Greece: An Archaeological History* (Berkeley: University of California Press, 2021).

2. Andrew Sherratt and Susan Sherratt, "The Growth of the Mediterranean Economy in the Early First Millennium BC," *World Archaeology* 24, no. 3 (1993): 361–78.

3. Søren M. Sindbaek, "Northern Emporia and Maritime Networks: Modelling Past Communication Using Archaeological Network Analysis," in *Harbours and Maritime Networks as Complex Adaptive Systems*, ed. Johannes Preiser-Kapeller and Falko Daim (Mainz: RGZM, 2015), 105–17; Justin Leidwanger et al., "A Manifesto for the Study of Ancient Mediterranean Maritime Networks," *Antiquity* Project Gallery 88, no. 342 (2014), http://journal.antiquity.ac.uk/projgall/leidwanger342. For a cogent critique, see Dieter, chapter 11 in this volume.

4. Lieve Donnellan, "'Greek Colonization' and Mediterranean Networks: Patterns of Mobility and Interaction at Pithekoussai," *Journal of Greek Archaeology* 1 (2016): 109–48; Donnellan, "A Networked View on Euboean 'Colonisation,'" in *Conceptualising Early Colonisation*, ed. Lieve Donnellan, Valentino Nizzo, and Gert-Jan Burgers (Brussels: Institut Historique Belge de Rome), 149–66. On uses in ancient history, see Diane Harris Cline, "Six Degrees of Alexander: Social Network Analysis as a Tool for Ancient History," *Ancient History Bulletin* 26, nos. 1–2 (2012): 59–70; Cline, "Athens as a Small World," *Journal of Historical Network Research* 4 (2020): 36–56.

5. Christine L. Johnston, "Networks and Intermediaries: Ceramic Exchange Systems in the Late Bronze Age Mediterranean" (PhD diss., UCLA, 2016), https://escholarship.org/uc/item/5gz5b3hk; and Carl Knappett, ed., *Network Analysis in Archaeology: New Approaches to Regional Interaction* (Oxford: Oxford University Press, 2013).

6. Irad Malkin, "A Colonial Middle Ground: Greek, Etruscan, and Local Elites in the Bay of Naples," in *The Archaeology of Colonialism*, ed. Claire L. Lyons and John

K. Papadopoulos (Los Angeles: Getty Information Institute, 2001), 151–81; Malkin, *A Small Greek World: Networks in the Ancient Mediterranean* (Oxford: Oxford University Press, 2011), 45–48; Corinne Bonnet, "Greeks and Phoenicians in the Western Mediterranean," in *A Companion to Ethnicity in the Ancient Mediterranean*, ed. Jeremy McInerney (Chichester: Wiley-Blackwell, 2014), 330–40; Carla Antonaccio, "Networking the Middle Ground? The Greek Diaspora, Tenth to Fifth Century BC," *Archaeological Review from Cambridge* 28, no. 1 (2013): 237–51; and Sarah P. Morris, "Close Encounters in Sicily: Molech, Meilichios and Religious Convergence at Selinus," in *Religious Convergence in the Ancient Mediterranean*, ed. Sandra Blakely and Billie Jean Collins (Atlanta: Lockwood Press, 2019), 77–99.

7. Catherine E. Pratt, "Minor Transnationalism in the Prehistoric Aegean? The Case of the Phoenicians on Crete in the Early Iron Age," *Diaspora: A Journal of Transnational Studies* 18, no. 3 (2009): 305–35; cf. Jan Paul Crielaard, "Hybrid Go-Betweens: The Role of Individuals with Multiple Identities in Cross-Cultural Contacts in the Late Bronze Age and Iron Age Central and Eastern Mediterranean," in Niesiołowski-Spanò and Węcowski, *Change, Continuity, and Connectivity*, 196–220.

8. Marian Feldman, *Communities of Style: Portable Luxury Arts, Identity and Collective Memory in the Iron Age Levant* (Chicago: University of Chicago Press, 2014).

9. Brian Peckham distinguishes early Sidonian entrepreneurs from later colonizing Tyrians: "Phoenicians in Sardinia: Tyrians or Sidonians?" in *Sardinian and Aegean Chronology: Towards the Resolution of Relative and Absolute Dating in the Mediterranean*, ed. Miriam S. Balmuth and Robert H. Tykot (Oxford: Oxbow Books, 1999), 347–54. For recent critiques of "Phoenician" identity, see Josephine Crawley Quinn, *In Search of the Phoenicians* (Princeton, NJ: Princeton University Press, 2018); and S. Rebecca Martin, *The Art of Contact: Comparative Approaches to Greek and Phoenician Art* (Philadelphia: University of Pennsylvania Press, 2017). For a defense against "Phoenicoskepticism," see López-Ruiz, chapter 2 in this volume.

10. Tamar Hodos, *Local Responses to Colonization in the Iron Age Mediterranean* (London: Routledge, 2006); Michael Dietler and Carolina López-Ruiz, *Colonial Encounters in Ancient Iberia: Phoenician, Greek and Indigenous Relations* (Chicago: University of Chicago Press, 2009); and Michael Dietler, *Archaeologies of Colonialism: Consumption, Entanglement and Violence in Ancient Mediterranean France* (Berkeley: University of California Press, 2010), 50.

11. Meanwhile, Robin Osborne advises against using the term "colonization" at all: "Early Greek Colonisation? The Nature of Greek Settlement in the West," in *Archaic Greece: New Approaches and New Evidence*, ed. Nick Fisher and Hans van Wees (London: Duckworth, 1998), 251–70.

12. Roger Woodard, "*Phoinikeia Grammata*: An Alphabet for the Greek Language," in *A Companion to the Ancient Greek Language*, ed. Egbert Bakker (Malden, MA: Wiley-Blackwell, 2010), 41, describes seeking "a bit of Greek ingenuity situated within the context of a Phoenician social and commercial presence"; Giorgios Bourogiannis, "The Transmission of the Alphabet to the Aegean," in Niesiołowski-Spanò and Węcowski, *Change, Continuity, and Connectivity*, 235–57.

13. Nikolaos Stampolidis and Antonios Kotsonas, "Phoenicians in Crete," in *Ancient Greece: From the Mycenaean Palaces to the Age of Homer*, ed. Sigrid Deger-Jalkotzy and Irene S. Lemos (Edinburgh: Edinburgh University Press, 2006), 337–60.

14. Susan Frankenstein, "The Phoenicians in the Far West: A Function of Neo-Assyrian Imperialism," in *Power and Propaganda: A Symposium on Ancient Empires*,

ed. M. T. Larsen (Copenhagen: Akademisk, 1979), 263–94; Sarah P. Morris, *Daidalos and the Origins of Greek Art* (Princeton, NJ: Princeton University Press, 1992), 125–26; Giorgos Bourogiannis, "The Phoenician Presence in the Aegean during the Iron Age: Trade, Settlement, and Cultural Interaction," *Rivista di Studi Fenici* 46 (2018): 78; and Alexander Fantalkin, "Identity in the Making: Greeks in the Eastern Mediterranean during the Iron Age," in *Naukratis: Greek Diversity in Egypt; Studies on East Greek Pottery and Exchange in the Eastern Mediterranean*, ed. Alexandra Villing and Udo Schlotzhauer (London: British Museum, 2006), 199–208. Contra Christopher M. Monroe, "Marginalizing Civilization: The Phoenician Redefinition of Power ca. 1300–800 BC," in *Trade and Civilisation: Economic Networks and Cultural Theory, from Prehistory to the Early Modern Era*, ed. Kristian Kristiansen, Thomas Lindkvist, and Janken Myrdal (Cambridge: Cambridge University Press, 2018), 195–241.

15. Richard Janko, "From Gabii and Gordion to Eretria and Methone: The Rise of the Greek Alphabet," *Bulletin of the Institute of Classical Studies* 58, no. 1 (2015): 7; cf. Woodard, "*Phoinikeia Grammata*," 41.

16. See Papadopoulos, chapter 7 in this volume, figure 7.1.

17. Janko, "Greek Alphabet"; Jenny Strauss Clay, Irad Malkin, and Yannis Z. Tzifopoulos, eds., *Panhellenes at Methone: Graphê in Late Geometric and Proto-Archaic Methone, Macedonia (ca 700 BCE)* (Berlin: De Gruyter, 2017); John K. Papadopoulos, "The Early History of the Greek Alphabet: New Evidence from Eretria and Methone," *Antiquity* 90, no. 353 (2016): 1238–54; Papadopoulos, chapter 7 in this volume.

18. Nota Kourou, "Phoenician Presence in Early Iron Age Crete Reconsidered," in *Actas del IV Congreso Internacional de Estudios Fenicios y Púnicos: Cadiz, 2 al 6 de Octubre de 1995* (Cádiz: Servicio de Publicaciones, Universidad de Cádiz, 2000), 1068–81, esp. 1072.

19. Sarah P. Morris, "The View from East Greece: Miletus, Samos and Ephesus," in *Debating Orientalization: Multidisciplinary Approaches to Change in the Ancient Mediterranean*, ed. Corinna Riva and Nicholas Vella (London: Equinox, 2006), 79–80.

20. Eleutheria Pappa, "'You Give Me Letters instead of Money?' Commercial Transactions in the Near East and Western Mediterranean ca. 1100–600 BCE: Social Innovation and Institutional Inhibition of Phoenician Commerce," *Revista do Museu de Arqueologia e Etnologia* 28 (2017): 1–30; and Pappa, "The Poster Boys of Antiquity's 'Capitalism' Shunning Money? The Spread of the Alphabet in the Mediterranean as a Function of a Credit-Based, Maritime Trade," *Revista do Museu de Arqueologia e Etnologia* 33 (2019): 91–138.

21. Feldman, *Communities of Style*, 111–37.

22. Marek Węcowski, *The Rise of the Greek Aristocratic Banquet* (Oxford: Oxford University Press, 2014); and Adam Rabinowitz, "Drinkers, Hosts or Fighters? Masculine Identities in Pre-Classical Crete," in *Cultural Practices and Material Culture in Archaic and Classical Crete: Proceedings of the International Conference, Mainz, May 20–21, 2011*, ed. Oliver Pilz and Gunnar Seelentag (Berlin: De Gruyter, 2014), 91–119. On the origin of these bowls, see Nicolas Vella, "'Phoenician' Metal Bowls: Boundary Objects in the Archaic Period," *Bollettino di Archeologia* 1 (2010): 22–37; López-Ruiz, chapter 2 in this volume; and Feldman, chapter 4 in this volume.

23. Marek Węcowski, "Wine and the Early History of the Greek Alphabet," in Strauss Clay, Malkin, and Tzifopoulos, *Panhellenes at Methone*, 309–28.

24. Alice Mandell, "Rethinking the Study of Southern Levantine Iron Age Inscriptions: New Ways of Thinking about Old Problems," in *Formation, Organisation,*

and Development of Iron Age Societies: Proceedings of the Workshop held at the 10th ICAANE in Vienna, April 2016, ed. Alexander E. Sollee (Vienna: Austrian Academy of Sciences, 2020), 83–107.

25. A. J. Nijboer, "Banquet, *Marzeah*, *Symposion* and Symposium during the Iron Age: Disparity and Mimicry," in *Regionalism and Globalism in Antiquity: Exploring Their Limits*, ed. Franco de Angelis (Leuven: Peeters, 2013), 98; Kevin Solez, "Multicultural Banqueting in the Development of Archaic Greek Society: An Investigation into Modes of Intercultural Contact" (PhD diss., University of British Columbia, 2014), 77–83; but see S. Rebecca Martin, "Eastern Mediterranean Feasts: What Do We Really Know about the Marzeah?," in Niesiołowski-Spanò and Węcowski, *Change, Continuity, and Connectivity*, 294–307.

26. Antonis Kotsonas, "Ceramic Variability and Drinking Habits in Iron Age Crete," in *The "Dark Ages" Revisited: Acts of an International Symposium in Memory of William D. E. Coulson, University of Thessaly, Volos, 14–17 June 2007*, ed. A. Mazarakis Ainian (Volos: University of Thessaly, 2011), 899–911; James Whitley, "Citizenship and Commensality in Archaic Crete: Searching for the *Andreion*," in *Cretan Cities: Formation and Transformation*, ed. Florence Gaignerot-Driessen and Jan Driessen (Louvain: Presses Universitaires, 2014), 227–48; and Jesica Harrison Lewis, "The Warrior's Banquet: Syssitia in Ancient Crete" (MA thesis, North Carolina State University, 2015).

27. John Boardman, "The Khaniale Tekke Tombs, II," *British School of Archaeology at Athens* 62 (1967): 57–75; Gail Hoffmann, *Imports and Immigrants: Near Eastern Contacts with Iron Age Crete* (Ann Arbor: University of Michigan Press, 1997); and Antonis Kotsonas, "Wealth and Status in Iron Age Knossos," *Oxford Journal of Archaeology* 25, no. 2 (2006): 149–72.

28. John Boardman, "Orientalen auf Kreta," in *Dädalische Kunst auf Kreta im 7. Jahrhundert v. Chr* (Mainz: Von Zabern, 1970), 20–21; Morris, *Daidalos*, 160–61; contra Hoffmann, *Imports and Immigrants*, 165–72. Inscriptions: Whitley, "Citizenship and Commensality," 233–35, fig. 9.1; and Bourogiannis, "Transmission of the Alphabet," 237.

29. Philip Schmitz, "The Owl in Phoenician Mortuary Practice," *Journal of Ancient Near Eastern Religions* 9, no. 1 (2009): 51–85, esp. 60–61, connects terracotta owls in burials at Arkades and Knossos (and the Cretan myth of Glaucus) to Phoenician practices.

30. Nikolaos Stampolidis, "A Funerary Cippus at Eleutherna: Evidence of Phoenician Presence?," *Bulletin of the Institute of Classical Studies* 37 (1990): 99–106; Stampolidis, ed., *Eleutherna: Polis—Acropolis—Necropolis* (Athens: Museum of Cycladic Art, 2004), 238, catalog no. 257; Stampolidis, "On the Phoenician Presence in the Aegean," in *Ploes—Sea Routes—Interconnections in the Mediterranean 16th–6th c. BC: Proceedings of the International Symposium Held in Rethymnon, Crete, September 29th–October 2nd, 2002*, ed. Nikolaos Stampolidis and Vassos Karageorghis (Athens: University of Crete / A. G. Leventis Foundation, 2003), 217–32, esp. 221–26; and Nikolaos Stampolidis, *Ancient Eleutherna: West Sector* (Athens: Archaeological Receipts Fund, 2008), 133, 139–40, figs. 96–97.

31. Nota Kourou and Alexandra Karetsou, "An Enigmatic Stone from Knossos: A Reused Cippus?," in *Eastern Mediterranean: Cyprus, Dodecanese, Crete 16th c–6th c BC: Proceedings of the International Symposium, Rethymnon, 13–16 May 1997*, ed. Vassos Karageorghis and Nikolaos Stampolidis (Athens: University of Crete / A. G. Leventis Foundation, 1998), 243–55; Nota Kourou and Eva Grammatikaki,

"An Anthropomorphic Cippus from Knossos, Crete," in *Archäologische Studien in Kontaktzonen der antiken Welt*, ed. Renate Rolle, Karin Schmidt, and Raul Docter (Göttingen: Vandenhoeck und Rupprecht, 1998), 237–49; and Stampolidis and Kotsonas, "Phoenicians on Crete," 352–53. Socrates Koursoumis, "Η ανθρωπόμορφη στήλη από το βόρειο νεκροταφείο της Κνωσού. Μία διαφορετική προσέγγιση," in *Proceedings of the 10th International Cretological Congress (Chania, 8–10 October 2006)*, vol. A5, ed. Maria Andreaki-Vlassaki and Eleni Papadopoulou (Chania: Philological Association "Chrysostomou," 2011), 311–27, calls the anthropomorphic stone Roman (as Antonis Kotsonas reminded me).

32. Nicholas Coldstream, "Mixed Marriages at the Frontiers of the Early Greek World," *Oxford Journal of Archaeology* 12, no. 1 (1991): 89–107 (on Crete: 99–100); and Barry Powell, *Writing and the Origins of Greek Literature* (Cambridge: Cambridge University Press, 2002).

33. Morris, "Close Encounters in Sicily."

34. Xenia Charalambidou, "Ceramics, Cultural Interconnections and Influences on Naxos," in *ΤΕΡΨΙΣ: Studies in Mediterranean Archaeology in Honour of Nota Kourou*, ed. Vicky Vlachou and Anastasia Gadolou (Brussels: CReA Patrimoine, 2017), 379–83. See also Cypriot imports at the Yria sanctuary: Eva Simantoni-Bournia, "Un masque humain à Hyria de Naxos, nouveau témoignage de contacts chypriotes," *Bulletin de Correspondance Hellénique* 128–29 (2004–5): 119–32.

35. See Sherratt, chapter 6 in this volume; Frankenstein, "Phoenicians in the Far West" (on Rhodes, 275–76); Giorgios Bourogiannis, "Who Hides behind the Pots? A Reassessement of the Phoenician Presence in Early Iron Age Cos and Rhodes," *Ancient Near Eastern Studies* 50 (2013): 139–89.

36. Stampolidis, *Eleutherna*, 234–95; Stampolidis, *Ancient Eleutherna*, 104–62.

37. Nikolaos Stampolidis and Dimitris Koutsogiannis, "*Quaestiones Daedalicae*: Αποκατάσταση δύο μνημείων του 7ου αιώνα π. Χ. στην νεκρόπολη της ʹΟρθης Πέτρας' της αρχαίας Ελεύθερνας," in *Kreta in der geometrischen und archaischen Zeit*, ed. Wolf-Dietrich Niemeier, Oliver Pilz, and Ivonne Kaiser (Munich: Hirmer Verlag, 2013), 221–32. The restored monument resembles Egyptian tomb traditions of the "empty door"; its carved stone decoration recalls the tomb door (?) behind the effigy of the dead on the (Bronze Age) Hagia Triada sarcophagus.

38. Stampolidis, *Eleutherna*, 234–35, nos. 250–51; Stampolidis *Ancient Eleutherna*, 143–44, fig. 100; Stampolidis and Koutsogiannis, "*Quaestiones Daedalicae*," 223–25; Nikolaos Stampolidis, "Πρωτοαρχαϊκή πλαστική από την Ελεύθερνα της Κρήτης. Προκαταρκτική προσπάθεια μίας συνολικότερης προσέγγισης," in *Neue Funde archaischer Plastik aus griechischen Heiligtümern und Nekropolen: Internationales Symposium, Athens, 2–3 November 2007*, ed. Georgia Kokkorou-Alevras and Wolf-Dietrich Niemeier (Munich: Hirmer, 2012), 1–17.

39. Chania relief: Stampolidis, *Ancient Eleutherna*, 148–49, fig. 104; and Matteo D'Acunto, "The City Siege and the Lion: The Fortetsa Bronze Belt and Quiver between Near Eastern Models and Heroic Ideology," in Niemeier, Pilz, and Kaiser, *Kreta*, 471–87.

40. Ana Delgado and Meritxell Ferrer, "Cultural Contacts in Colonial Settings: The Construction of New Identities in Phoenician Settlements of the Western Mediterranean," *Stanford Journal of Archaeology* 5 (2007): 18–42.

41. I am grateful to Antonios Kotsonas for sharing his research on early Crete in advance of publication, including "Homer, the Archaeology of Crete, and the 'Tomb of Meriones' at Knossos," *Journal of Hellenic Studies* 138 (2018): 1–35.

42. Pantanassa tomb: Evi Tegou, "Θολωτός τάφος της πρώϊμης εποχής του Σιδήρου στην Παντανάσσα Αμαρίου Ν. Ρεθύμνης," in *Καύσεις στην Εποχή Χαλκού και την Πρώϊμη Εποχή Σιδήρου: Πρακτικά του Συμποσίου Ρόδος 29 Απριλίου—2 Μαίου 1999*, ed. Nikolaos Stampolidis (Athens: University of Crete and ΚΒʹ ΕΡΚΑ, 2001), 121–54; Stampolidis and Kotsonas, "Phoenicians in Crete," 340; and N. Kourou, "The Aegean and the Levant in the Early Iron Age: Recent Developments," in *Interconnections in the Eastern Mediterranean: Lebanon in the Bronze and Iron Ages; Proceedings of the International Symposium, Beirut 2008* (BAAL Supplement 6), ed. F. Husseini and A. Maila-Afeiche (Beirut: Ministry of Culture, Directorate General of Antiquities, 2009), 361–74, esp. 363–64, fig. 2.

43. See Papadopoulos (chapter 7 in this volume), figure 7.2.

44. Dimitris G. Basakos, "Warriors in Movement: Warrior Burials in Eastern Crete during Late Minoan IIIC," in *Achaios: Studies Presented to Professor Thanassis I. Papadopoulos*, ed. Evangelia Papadopoulou-Chrysikopoulou, Vassilis Chrysikopoulos, and Guilika Christakopoulou (Oxford: Archaeopress, 2016), 23–32.

45. Hector Catling, "Heroes Returned? Subminoan Burials in Crete," in *The Ages of Homer: A Tribute to Emily Townsend Vermeule*, ed. Jane B. Carter and Sarah P. Morris (Austin: University of Texas, 1995), 123–36; and James Whitley, "Objects with Attitude: Biographical Facts and Fallacies in the Study of Late Bronze Age and Early Iron Age Warrior Graves," *Cambridge Archaeological Journal* 12, no. 3 (2002): 217–32. These events may be reflected in the Homeric adventures (especially the "false tales") of Odysseus: Sarah Morris, "Homer and the Near East," in *A New Companion to Homer*, ed. Ian Morris and Barry Powell (Leiden: Brill, 1997), 614–15.

46. For abundant evidence for such warrior burials in Late Helladic IIIC Achaea but also in Eastern Crete, see Vangelis Samaras, "Piracy in the Aegean during the Postpalatial Period and the Early Iron Age," in *The Mediterranean Mirror: Cultural Contacts in the Mediterranean Sea between 1200 and 750 BC*, ed. Andrea Babbi et al. (Mainz: RGZM Tagungen 20, 2015), 189–204. See Sherratt, chapter 6 in this volume, for related circulation of metals and materials, many associated with military use, in the same period.

47. Emily Vermeule, "The Mycenaeans in Achaea," *American Journal of Archaeology* 64 (1960): 1–21; and B. F. Steinmann, *Die Waffengräber der ägäischen Bronzezeit: Waffenbeigaben, soziale Selbstdarstellung und Adelsethos in der minoisch-mykenischen Kultur* (Wiesbaden: Harrassowitz Verlag, 2012), 222–54.

48. Reinhard Jung, "Pirates of the Aegean: Italy—East Aegean—Cyprus at the End of the Second Millennium BCE," in *Cyprus and the East Aegean: Intercultural Contacts from 3000 to 500 BC: Proceedings of an International Archaeological Symposium held at Pythagoreion, Samos, October 17th–18th 2008*, ed. Vassos Karageorghis and Ourania Kouka (Nicosia: A. G. Leventis Foundation, 2009), 72–93; Thomas Tartaron, *Maritime Networks in the Mycenaean World* (Cambridge: Cambridge University Press, 2013), 59–71; Margaretha Kramer-Hajos, "Sailor-Warriors and the End of the Bronze Age along the Euboean Gulf," in *Αρχαιολογικό Έργο Θεσσαλίας και Στέρεας Ελλάδας 3. Τόμος 2. Στέρεα Ελλάδα*, ed. Alexander Mazarakis-Ainian and Argyroula Doulgeri-Intzesiloglou (Volos: Ministry of Culture and Tourism and University of Thessaly, 2009), 811–20; and Samaras, "Piracy." See also A. Bernard Knapp, "Piracy in the Late Bronze Age Eastern Mediterranean? A Cautionary Tale," in *Nomads of the Mediterranean: Trade and Contact in the Bronze and Iron*

Ages; Studies in Honor of Michal Artzy, ed. Ayelet Gilboa and Assaf Yassur-Landau (Leiden: Brill, 2020), 142–60.

49. Nino Luraghi, "Traders, Pirates, Warriors: The Protohistory of Greek Mercenary Soldiers in the Eastern Mediterranean," *Phoenix* 60, no. 1–2 (2006): 21–47; Robert Rollinger, "Assyria and the Far West: The Aegean World," in *A Companion to Assyria*, ed. Eckart Frahm (Chichester: Wiley, 2017), 275–85; Sandra Blakely, "Images, Merchants, and Mercenaries: Aegeans and Southern Judah in the Eighth Century BC," in *Archaeology and History of Eighth-Century Judah*, ed. Zev I. Faber and Jacob L. Wright (Atlanta: Lockwood Press, 2018), 35–55. Ian S. Moyer, "Golden Fetters and Economies of Cultural Exchange," *Journal of Ancient Near Eastern Religions* 6 (2006): 225–56, explores the ties that bind, literally and figuratively, Greek soldiers in foreign service; see also Marcus Ziemann, "Mercenary Communities in the Near East and Their Contribution to an East Mediterranean Literary Koine," *Aula Orientalis* 37, no. 1 (2019): 173–96.

50. Alexander Fantalkin and E. Lytle, "Alcaeus and Antimenidas: Reassessing the Evidence for Greek Mercenaries in the Neo-Babylonian Army," *Klio* 98, no. 1 (2016): 90–117; Fantalkin, "Did Ionian or Other Greek or Carian Mercenaries Serve in the Neo-Assyrian Army?," in *Ionians in the West and East*, Proceedings of the International Conference "Ionians in East and West," Museu d'Arqueologia di Catalunya-Empuries, Empuries L'Escala, Spain, 26–29 October 2015, ed. Gocha Tsetskhladze (Leuven: Peeters, forthcoming); and David Mouritz, "East Greek Pottery and Graeco-Anatolian Mercenaries in the Southern Levant in Iron Age IIC (ca. 600 BCE)" (PhD diss., University of Melbourne, 2018).

51. Woodard, "*Phoinikeia Grammata*," 42–45, argues that literate Cypriots, still using an Aegean syllabary and already exposed to Phoenician letters on Cyprus, shared their learning to co-adopt an alphabet with other, illiterate "Ionian" soldiers serving in the Near East; cf. Rollinger, *Assyria*, 280; and Ziemann, "Mercenary Communities."

52. Alan Johnston, "Writing in and around Archaic Crete," in Niemeier, Pilz, and Kaiser, *Kreta*, 427–35, table 1, fig. 4-b; and inscriptions on bronze mitrae from Aphrati commemorate seizure or capture of the armor.

53. Martin, *Art of Contact*, 58, revives an argument by John Kenfield, "The Sculptural Significance of Early Greek Armor," *Opuscula Romana* 9 (1973): 149–56; cf. Dyfri Williams, "A Special Dedication to Aphrodite and Some Thoughts on the Early Years of the Greek Sanctuaries at Naukratis," *Kölner und Bonner Archaeologica* 2 (2015): 177–98, on the cultural role of settled mercenaries in Egypt; and Ziemann, "Mercenary Communities." Thomas Boyd and Michael Jameson suggest that Greek and Carian mercenaries in Egypt gained practical experience in Egyptian land division (and Babylonian mathematics) that inspired Greek orthogonal town planning: "Urban and Rural Land Division in Ancient, Greece," *Hesperia* 50 (1981): 335. On paying mercenaries as an incentive for the invention of coinage, see R. M. Cook, "Speculations on the Origins of Coinage," *Historia* 7 (1958): 257–62.

54. Coldstream, "Mixed Marriages," 98–99, does not see intermarriage on Cyprus, and Woodard, "*Phoinikeia Grammata*," does not mention it; see also Ziemann, "Mercenary Communities."

55. Joseph Shaw, "Phoenicians in Southern Crete," *American Journal of Archaeology* 93 (1989): 165–83; Shaw, "The Phoenician Shrine, ca. 800 B.C, at Kommos in Crete," in *Actas del IV Congreso*, 1107–19; Shaw, *Kommos: A Minoan Harbor Town and Greek Sanctuary in Southern Crete* (Princeton, NJ: American School of Classical

Studies at Athens, 2006), 40–45; and Joseph Shaw and Maria Shaw, *Kommos: The Greek Sanctuary* (Princeton, NJ: American School of Classical Studies, 2000). Johnston, "Writing," 433, calls Kommos "an equivocal location, in Crete but not wholly of Crete." For doubts on the Kommos shrine as "Phoenician," see E. Pappalardo, "Il 'tripillar shrine' di Kommos: alcune considerazioni," *Creta Antica* 3 (2002): 263–74 (thanks to Antonis Kotsonas for this reference).

56. Pratt, "Minor Transnationalism," 317; and Gunnel Ekroth, "Bare Bones: Zooarchaeology and Greek Sacrifice," in *Animal Sacrifice in the Ancient World*, ed. Sarah Hitch and Ian Rutherford (Cambridge: Cambridge University Press, 2017), 28–29.

57. Megan Daniels, "The Gods of Kommos: Reconsidering the Deities of the Tripillar Shrine and Their Cross-Cultural Meanings in the Iron Age," in *119th Annual Meeting Abstracts: Volume 41, January 4–7, 2018, AIA* (Boston, 2018), 31. Later Greek graffiti indicate traders, perhaps from central Greece: Eric Csapo, "An International Community of Traders in Late 8th–7th c. B.C. Kommos in Southern Crete," *Zeitschrift für Papyrologie und Epigraphik* 99 (1991): 211–16.

58. Maria Shaw, "Two Cups with Incised Decoration from Kommos, Crete," *American Journal of Archaeology* 87 (1983): 443–52; Oliver Pilz, "Narrative Art in Archaic Crete," in Pilz and Seelentag, *Cultural Practices*, 248–49, fig. 1; and Kotsonas, "Drinking Habits in Iron Age Crete."

59. Antonios Kotsonas, "The Iconography of a Protoarchaic Cup from Kommos: Myth and Ritual in Early Cretan Art," *Hesperia* 88, no. 4 (2019), 595–624; and Megan Daniels, "Death and Divinity at Kommos: Reinterpreting a Prothesis Scene on an Incised Cup from the Iron Age Sanctuary," in *120th Annual Meeting Abstracts: Volume 42, January 3–6, 2019, AIA* (San Diego, 2019), 269–70.

60. Harrison Lewis, "Warrior's Banquet"; and Whitley, "Citizenship and Commensality." At Eleutherna, an early *megaron* (hearth-temple) could anticipate an *andreion*: Petros Themelis, "The Polis: East Excavation Sector I," in Stampolidis, *Eleutherna*, 48–49, fig. 3.

61. Nijboer, "Banquet," 98; Solez, "Multicultural Banqueting": Martin, "Eastern Mediterranean Feasts"; Anna Lucia D'Agata, "Guerra, guerrieri e protopoleis a Creta tra la fine dell'èta del Bronzo e gli inizi dell'èta del Ferro," in *Guerra e memoria nel mondo antico*, ed. Elena Franchi and. Giorgia Proietti (Trento: Università degli Studi di Trento, 2014), 127–52.

62. Solez, "Multicultural Banqueting," 112–18. Finds such as the Egyptian/izing figurines found at Kommos, Eleutherna, and the Idaean Cave link these locales in a similar network of Orientalizing connections.

63. Hans Lohmann, "Ionians and Carians in the Mykale: The Discovery of Carian Melia and the Archaic Panionion," in *Landscape, Ethnicity and Identity in the Archaic Mediterranean Area*, ed. Gabriele Cifani and Simon Stoddart (Oxford: Oxbow Books, 2012), 32–50. For a different candidate for the Panionion, see Alexander Herda, "Panionion-Melie, Mykalessos-Mykale, Perseus und Medusa: Überlegungen zur Besiedlungsgeschichte der Mykale in der frühen Eisenzeit," *Istanbuler Mittheilungen* 56 (2006): 43–102.

64. Wolf-Dietrich Niemeier, "The Oracle Sanctuary of Apollo at Abai/Kalapodi from the Bronze to the Iron Age," in *Regional Stories towards a New Perception of the Early Greek World: Acts of an International Symposium in Honour of Professor Jan Bouzek, Volos, 18–21 June 2015*, ed. Alexander Mazarakis-Ainian, Alexandra Alexandridou, and Xenia Charalambidou (Volos: University of Thessaly, 2017),

323–42; Plakari (Karystos) in southern Euboea reconnects Archaic conviviality and military trophies in the fourth century: Jan Paul Crielaard and Filiz Songu, "Connectivity and Insularity in 1st-Millennium Southern Euboea: The Evidence from the Sanctuary of Karystos-Plakari," in *An Island between Two Worlds: The Archaeology of Euboea from Prehistoric to Byzantine Times: Proceedings of International Conference, Eretria, 12–14 July 2013*, ed. Žarko Tankosic, Fanis Mavridis, and Maria Kosma (Athens: Norwegian Institute at Athens, 2017), 275–90.

65. Carlo Tronchetti and Peter van Dommelen, "Entangled Objects and Hybrid Practices: Colonial Contacts and Elite Connections at Monte Prama, Sardinia," *Journal of Mediterranean Archaeology* 18, no. 2 (2005): 183–208. A new reading of the Nora Stone reveals intense militarism behind Phoenician settlement on Sardinia: Nathan Pilkington, "A Note on Nora and the Nora Stone," *Bulletin of the American Schools of Oriental Research* 365 (2012): 45–51.

66. See Papadopoulos, chapter 7 in this volume.

67. Richard Fletcher, "Fragments of Levantine Iron Age Pottery in Chalkidike," *MeditArch* 21 (2008): 3–7; Daniel Vainstub, "A Phoenician Votive Inscription on a Figurine from Stageira and the Root *TN*," *Cahiers de l'Institut du Proche-Orient Ancien du Collège de France* 2 (2014): 343–50; M. Tiverios, "The Phoenician Presence in the Northern Aegean," in *Greeks and Phoenicians at the Mediterranean Crossroads*, ed. Polyxeni Adam-Veleni and Evangelia Stefani (Thessaloniki: Archaeological Museum of Thessaloniki, 2011), 65–72, and 161–62 for Phoenician amphoras from Methone; Alexandra Kasseri, "Φοινικικοί εμπορικοί αμφορείς από τη Μεθώνη Πιερίας," in *Κεραμέως Παίδες: Αντίδωρο στον Καθηγητή Μιχάλη Τιβέριο από τους μαθητές του*, ed. Eurydike Kephalidou and Despoina Tsiafaki (Thessaloniki: Εταιρεία Ανδρίων Επιστημόνων, 2012), 299–308; and Petya Ilieva, "Phoenicians, Cypriotes, and Euboeans in the Northern Aegean: A Re-appraisal," *Aura* 2 (2019): 65–102. Phoenician amphorae may have held "Byblite" wine (Hesiod, *Works and Days*, 589), linked in Greek sources to Oisyme (or Antisara) on the Thracian coast (Athenaeus, *Deipnosophistae*, 31a).

68. Antonios Kotsonas et al., "Transport Amphorae from Methone: An Interdisciplinary Study of Production and Trade ca. 700 BCE," in Strauss Clay, Malkin, and Tzifopoulos, *Panhellenes at Methone*, 9–19; and Alexandra Kasseri, "Archaic Trade in the Northern Aegean: The Case of Methone in Pieria, Greece" (PhD diss., University of Oxford, 2015), https://ora.ox.ac.uk/objects/uuid:48f2cf91-f266-4d32-9521-680da39f0acd.

69. Manthos Bessios, *Πιερίδων Στέφανος* (Katerini: Mati Press, 2010), 89, 104–9; Manthos Bessios, Yiannis Tzifopoulos, and Antonis Kotsonas, *Μεθώνη Πιερίας 1: Επιγραφές, χαράγματα και εμπορικά σύμβολα στη γεωμετρική και αρχαϊκή κεραμική από το Υπόγειο της Μεθώνης Πιερίας στη Μακεδονία* (Thessaloniki: Ministry of Education, Instruction, and Religion: Center for the Greek Language, 2012); Yannis Z. Tzifopoulos, *"Letters from the Underground": Writing in Methone, Pieria Late 8th–Early 7th Century BC* (Thessaloniki: Center for Interdisciplinary Research and Innovation, Aristotle University of Thessaloniki, 2013).

70. Sarah Morris, John Papadopoulos, Manthos Bessios, Athena Athanassiadou, and Konstantinos Noulas, "The Ancient Methone Archaeological Project: A Preliminary Report on Fieldwork, 2014–2017," *Hesperia* 89, no. 4 (2020): 702–7, 712–13, figs. 58c, 65c–d.

71. Bessios, Tzifopoulos, and Kotsonas, *Μεθώνη Πιερίας 1*, 365–66, no. 22 (ΜΕΘ 2247); Węcowski, "Wine," 318–19, fig. 1. See Phoenician letters and Greek inscribed

cups in the Chalkidike: Kostas Sismanidis, *Ancient Stageira: Birthplace of Aristotle* (Athens: Ministry of Culture, Archaeological Receipts Fund, 2003), 90, figs. 98–99; and Vainstub, "Phoenician Votive Inscription."

72. David Hill, "Conceptualising Interregional Relations in Ionia and Central-West Anatolia from the Archaic to the Hellenistic Period," in *Bordered Places—Bounded Times: Cross-Disciplinary Perspectives on Turkey*, ed. Emma Baysal and Leonidas Karakatsanis (Ankara: British Institute, 2017), 89–90, citing Robert Revere, "'No Man's Coast': Ports of Trade in the Eastern Mediterranean," in *Trade and Market in Early Empires*, ed. Karl Polanyi, Conrad M. Arensberg, and Harry W. Pearson (Glencoe, IL: Free Press, 1957) 38–64. My model applies Susan Sherratt's use of Hill's research (chapter 6 in this volume) to East Greek activity in the North Aegean, as in Frankenstein's Phoenicians in service to Assyria (cf. Ionians and Carians in Egypt under Lydian aegis: Alexander Fantalkin, "Naukratis as a Contact Zone: Revealing the Lydian Connection," in *Kulturkontakte in Antiken Welten: Vom Denkmodell bis zum Fallbeispiel, Proceedings des Kolloquiums aus Ansicht des 90. Geburtstag von Christoph Ulf, Innsbruck, 26–30 January 2009*, ed. Robert Röllinger and Kordula Schnegg (Leuven: Peeters, 2014), 27–50.

73. Fantalkin, "Naukratis as a Contact Zone." Naucratis also has Phoenician inscriptions, attributed by some to mercenaries (Hodos, *Archaeology of the Mediterranean Iron Age*, 187, citing Herodotus 4.42).

74. Morris, "View from East Greece," 78–79; Michalis Tiverios, "Κάρες στο μυχό του Θερμαϊκού κόλπου," in *Ancient Macedonia VI: Papers Read at the Sixth International Symposium Held in Thessaloniki, October 15–19, 1996*, ed. Ioulia Votokopoulou (Thessaloniki: Institute for Balkan Studies, 1999), 1175–81; and Katerina Tzanavari and Anastasios-Phoebus Christidis, "A Carian Graffito from the Levet Table, Thessaloniki," *Kadmos* 34 (1995): 13–16.

75. Stavros Paspalas, "The Achaemenid Empire and the North-Western Aegean," *Ancient West and East* 1 (2006): 90–120; Eurydice Kefalidou and Ioannis Xydopoulos, "Strangers in a Strange Land: Two Soldiers' Graffiti from Ancient Thermi," in *Archaeology across Frontiers and Borderlands: Fragmentation and Connectivity in the North Aegean and the Central Balkans from the Bronze Age to the Iron Age*, ed. Stephanos Gimatzidis, Magda Pieniazek, and Sila Mangaloğlu-Votruba (Vienna: Austrian Academy of Sciences, 2018), 203–18; and Josef Wiesehöfer, "The Persian Impact on Macedonia: Three Case Studies," in *The History of the Argeads: New Perspectives*, ed. Sabine Müller et al. (Wiesbaden: Harrassowitz, 2017), 57–64.

76. Selene Psoma, "Did the So-Called Thraco-Macedonian Standard Exist?," in *ΚΑΙΡΟΣ: Contributions to Numismatics in Honor of Basil Demetriadi*, ed. Ute Wartenberg and Michel Amandry (New York: American Numismatic Society, 2015), 167–90; Peter van Alfen, "The Chalkid(ik)an Beginnings of Euboian Coinage," in Wartenberg and Amandry, *ΚΑΙΡΟΣ*, 255–83. East Greek coinage could have spread with mercenaries as well as merchants in northern Greece, as in one theory of its origins: Cook, "Origins of Coinage"; R. C. Knapp, "Greek Coinage, Mercenaries, and Ideology," *Eulimene* 3 (2002): 183–96.

77. See Osborne and Hall, chapter 1 in this volume, and especially Ian Morris, "Mediterraneanization," *Mediterranean Historical Review* 18 (2003): 13–55; and Fantalkin, "Identity in the Making," 199–200.

78. Knodell, *Societies in Transition*.

✷ CHAPTER 6 ✷

The Mediterranean and the Black Sea in the Early First Millennium BCE

Greeks, Phoenicians, Phrygians, and Lydians

SUSAN SHERRATT

This chapter arises from a couple of questions that have been on my mind for a few years. The first question is: Why, despite some of the earlier dates suggested by very late sources, such as Eusebius and pseudo-Scymnus,[1] does the earliest Greek material found around the shores of the Black Sea date to no earlier than the late seventh century BCE, well over a century later than documented Greek activity in the central Mediterranean?[2] The second question is: Why did Phoenicians, who in the ninth century were active over the entire length of the Mediterranean, not seem to have shown any interest in the Black Sea in the early first millennium? This is particularly surprising in view of the plentiful resources of silver along its southeastern shores,[3] as well as the fact that silver was the magnet that drew Phoenicians into the Aegean from the later eleventh century onward and to southwestern Iberia and Sardinia in the ninth.[4] Added to these is a subsidiary question whose relevance, I admit, might not seem immediately obvious at first: Why is Homer's war a specifically Trojan war, and not a war fought over some other city?

My goal in this chapter is to consider these questions and attempt some tentative answers. The results will inevitably be highly speculative, for the most part an exercise in informed imagination, which, if nothing else, has a part to play in raising questions and stimulating reactions and a search for counteracting evidence. The intention is to aim for an account that is characterized by some internal coherence rather than one based simply on detailed correspondence to a compilation of archaeological information, not least since archaeological information is often difficult to interpret and is, in any case, somewhat thin on the ground in the regions and periods in question. Moreover, straightforward compilations of archaeological data on their own are usually incapable of addressing these kinds of "why" questions.

Maritime Links at the End of the Second Millennium BCE?

It is necessary to provide some earlier background before tackling the above questions. Despite the fact that it has often in the past been taken for granted that Aegean ships regularly sailed into the Black Sea during the Late Bronze Age,[5] for a number of reasons that there is no space to go into here, I find it very difficult to believe that this was actually the case.[6] However, if we move on to the final two centuries of the second millennium BCE, by the end of which—almost certainly significantly—Troy seems to have lost much of its earlier importance, there are some reasons for suggesting, at least speculatively, that there may now have been a direct link by sea between the Mediterranean and the Black Sea. As a background to this is evidence of what must be maritime contacts around and across the Black Sea, including the maritime distribution of a type of handmade pottery decorated with finger-impressed cordons around the Black Sea and in Troy VIIB, and a number of oxhide ingots found without datable contexts around the Black Sea, either in the sea or in mixed hoards, which include some that are definitely not canonical Late Bronze Age copper ingots but rather of alloyed mixtures of metals including copper, tin, gold, and silver.[7]

Most spectacularly, we have the hoard from Şarköy, near Tekirdağ, on the northern shore of the Marmara, which seems of particular interest because of its very suggestive geographical location.[8] It, too, has no context, having been collected by villagers. But what is particularly interesting about it is the curious geographical implications of the objects it contains, which include among other things: swords of both Aegean and Syro-Anatolian forms; a series of sickles common in Anatolia and the Pontic region; spearheads, including part of one similar to a type known from the Trialeti culture of the early second millennium in Georgia; two cauldron handles; three shafthole double axes that have been claimed, like others from the northwest Black Sea, to be of Aegean type, together with a shafthole axe of Balkan type and a couple of typically Caucasian or East Anatolian trunnion axes; some of the heavy arm rings found in Caucasian graves; and an oxhide ingot fragment.[9] On the basis of what are estimated to be the latest items in it—fragments of a couple of fluted omphalos bowls—the hoard has been dated tentatively to the eleventh century at the earliest, though other pieces are more likely to date to the thirteenth or twelfth century and in some cases probably even earlier.[10]

Again, what is remarkable, but in tune with other hoards of this general period from various parts of the Mediterranean, is the wide geographical spread it represents—in this case from the Aegean in the west to the eastern Black Sea in the east.

In short, for a variety of reasons, it looks as though the Black Sea, which clearly had renewed maritime networks of its own at the end of the second millennium, had now become part of the greater Mediterranean, and was participating in—and contributing to—the long-distance multidirectional flows of bronze and other metals that also characterized the Mediterranean in the centuries following the end of the thirteenth century.[11] In broad agreement with James Osborne and Jonathan Hall's characterization (in chapter 1 of this volume) of the eastern Mediterranean during the early first millennium as "a highly decentralized socioeconomic environment populated by agents who were largely autonomous and able to travel and trade freely only in the most general sense," I would suggest that these multidirectional flows were in the hands of independent maritime traders and entrepreneurs from a wide range of different regions, including probably the Black Sea itself. I would further suggest that they were characterized by informal exchanges in ready-made bronze objects (acquired from over a wide area, sometimes probably by unconventional means) and commoditized bronze scrap, and also by widespread bronze recycling, sometimes in the hands of itinerant bronzeworkers, as seen, for example, on the late thirteenth-century Gelidonya wreck.

Greeks and the Black Sea in the Archaic Period: Phrygians, Lydians, and Milesians

I can now return to the first of my original questions. If the Mediterranean and Black Sea had direct maritime links as early as the twelfth–eleventh centuries, why did it take another 300 years or so for Archaic Greeks to penetrate into the Pontus? And why is it so consistently Miletus that is associated in later literary accounts with the start of this movement and the foundation of Black Sea settlements?

Miletus in the second and first millennia was almost entirely maritime, cut off from the inland routes by the very large bay at the mouth of the Maeander, which has since been filled in by alluviation.[12] Its reason for being there were the sea routes running north and south along the western Anatolian coast, as well as those westward to the Aegean islands. One of the earliest Milesian Black Sea landfalls—at least according to pseudo-Scymnus and also according to the limited amount we know about the

FIGURE 6.1 The topography of Sinope on the southern Black Sea coast. Google Earth image, modified by the author.

archaeology of its earliest Greek settlement—is Sinope, perched on the narrow neck of a small isthmus that protrudes at the northeast end of the larger Sinop promontory in the middle of the southern Pontic coast. There is also absolutely no doubt about the purely maritime focus of this position, with its double harbors, the southern one sheltered from the northwest winds—in many ways similar to a classical Phoenician site (figure 6.1). And in this it mirrors the maritime focus of Miletus itself. Moreover, as Owen Doonan and the Sinop Regional Archaeological Project have established, the colony at Sinope had very little interaction with the inhabitants of the Sinop hinterland until the Hellenistic period, when a Black Sea economic boom, which was to reach much greater intensity in the Roman and Byzantine periods, began to get underway.[13] Instead, if the later Greek literary sources are right, the Milesians of Sinope founded a daughter settlement (or *polis barbaron*) further along the coast at Trapezus (Trabzon) within a very short time of its own foundation, and were later, according to Strabo, possibly involved in foundations at Amisus at modern Samsun, and further west at Heraclea Pontica.[14] It is hard to escape the notion that the main purpose of Sinope was provisioning and supervising coastal traffic. It also sits at the point where the north–south crossing of the Black Sea from the Crimea to the Turkish coast is at its shortest.[15]

Both northeast Turkey and the Caucasus are rich in polymetallic ores, which include silver as well as gold,[16] while places such as Istros and Olbia/Berezan give easy access to the equally polymetallic resources of the eastern Carpathians and western Ukraine, including the Apuseni range which is particularly rich in gold and silver.[17] The Sea of Azov and the Don, on the other hand, allowed access to the mineral resources of the Urals, where silver occurs widely and was exploited from the earlier Late Bronze Age.[18]

Although the idea has often been dismissed,[19] I have absolutely no doubt that Greek—and particularly Milesian—interest in the Black Sea was motivated initially by a desire to secure, by means of way stations, the maritime routes along which metals, especially silver, could flow from the Black Sea to the east Mediterranean via Miletus.[20] By the seventh century, the Near East and the Levant were regularly using silver, not just as a standard of exchange by which prices were fixed but for actual payments of many sorts, including those of relatively small value, as is implied by the hack-silver hoards dating from the twelfth–seventh centuries found, for instance, in the Levant.[21] The result was that, by this time, the east could never have too much silver, despite the existence of plentiful resources in southern and western Anatolia and the Aegean, which had already long been exploited, and despite the fact that Phoenicians had been drawing directly on silver from sources in the Aegean from probably as early as the late eleventh century,[22] and in the West Mediterranean from around 900 BCE onward.[23] Not only, therefore, was demand for silver limitless, but we can observe a recurrent pattern in the long history of acquisition of silver from the fourth–third millennia BCE to the sixteenth century CE, which reflects the fact that the more distant the sources, in general the smaller the costs of exchange with indigenous peoples who had perhaps never been fully integrated into the economic system of the eastern Mediterranean and the Near East—particularly if the silver (or other metals) could be carried relatively directly by sea rather than pass overland through any number of intermediaries.[24] This in itself would provide an incentive even to regions themselves relatively rich in silver (like the Aegean and western Anatolia) from and through which silver flowed eastward. Though I certainly would not want to use Homer's *Iliad* as in any way a remotely historical document, the reference to faraway Alybe, which lay beyond Paphlagonia and "whence silver was brought to birth" (*ὅθεν ἀργύρου ἐστὶ γενέθλη*),[25] may well indicate that silver and the southeastern Black Sea were associated in the minds of Greek epic audiences by whatever date Homer's catalog of Trojan allies reached the form in which we have inherited it (see further below).

As for the timing of seventh-century Milesian interest in the Black Sea, this may have something to do with the increasing exchange costs involved in bringing silver from the western Mediterranean, where by now savvy locals were demanding much more in exchange, and where, despite the Samian Colaeus's venture to Tartessus recorded by Herodotus,[26] Phoenicians arguably had a monopoly. On the other hand, while we shall see that there were incentives by the late seventh century, there were probably also deterrents prior to this. It seems likely that some preexisting knowledge—and probably exploration—of the Black Sea preceded the establishment of Milesian settlements from around the end of the seventh century onward. However, the often emphasized—but perhaps unnecessarily exaggerated—difficulties of voyaging up through the Bosphorus against a strong current and, even more crucially, the possibility that the approaches to the Bosphorus were surrounded by potentially hostile inhabitants may well have presented something of a deterrent that required a fairly powerful motive to overcome.

We know very little about the political configuration of northern Anatolia in the early centuries of the first millennium, but who dominated the Bosphorus before the foundations of Chalcedon (by Megara in the earlier seventh century, according to Eusebius) and Byzantium (also by Megara, but seventeen years later according to Herodotus) seems to me an absolutely crucial question—particularly since one cannot imagine any major power in northwest Anatolia neglecting this crucial crossroad.[27] There are two possible contenders: Phrygians and Lydians at various times, who were clearly in strong competition with each other. From the early seventh century BCE, in the reigns of the Mermnad dynasty kings from Gyges onward, the Lydians gradually expanded as far east as the southern Black Sea shores, where, according to Herodotus, they subdued the Halybes in the reign of Croesus.[28] This is almost certainly too late, however, to have had any *deterrent* effect on Milesian activity in the Black Sea before the seventh century; indeed, it is much more likely to have helped facilitate it around the end of that century. On the other hand, the Phrygians a century or two earlier, particularly if they are the same as the Mushki of Assyrian texts, were clearly a force to be reckoned with; their access to wealth in the form of metals is perhaps reflected in later legends of Midas's golden touch. Although we do not know the limits of their political influence, Old Phrygian inscriptions of the ninth or eighth to early seventh centuries are found in Bithynia, on the Asiatic

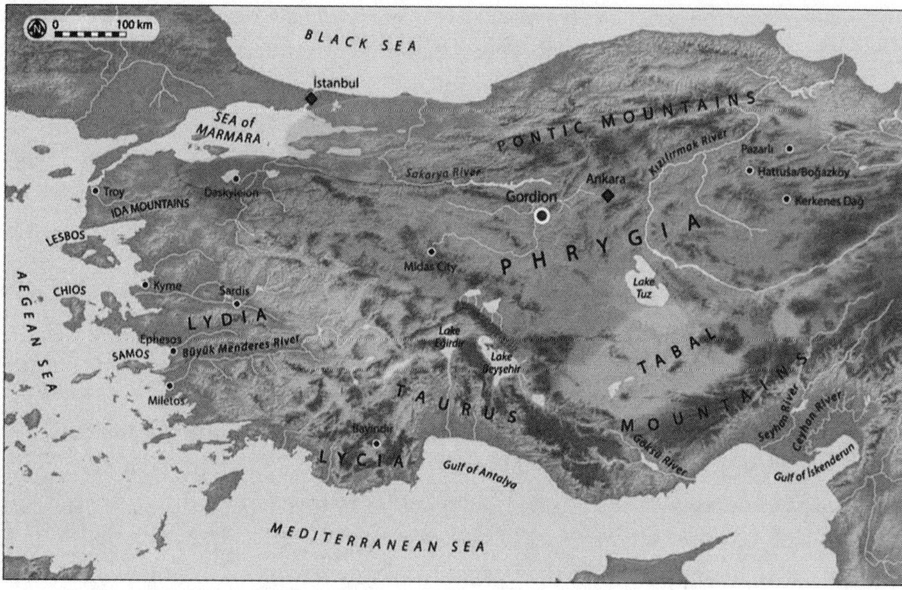

FIGURE 6.2 Reconstruction of area under Phrygian control during the eighth century BCE. Adapted by the author from map by Gareth Darbyshire, Gabriel H. Pizzorno, and Ardeth Anderson, https://www.penn.museum/sites/expedition/gordion-and-the-penn-museum/.

side of the Bosphorus,[29] and at Dascylium (Ergili), just to the south of the Sea of Marmara. Here there is also what appears to be a Phrygian settlement with evidence of Phrygian language in the form of graffiti on pottery and continuing evidence of Phrygian graffiti and inscriptions well down into the period of the Persian satrapy (figure 6.2).[30] If an evidently expansive power like Phrygia had an interest in controlling the Bosphorus and its western approaches, then they may not have been too happy about Greeks regularly entering the Black Sea in search of what it could offer, and may well have regarded them with active hostility. The Black Sea was perhaps thought of by Greeks as Πόντος Ἄξεινος (the inhospitable sea) with good reason.[31]

On the other side of the coin, we can probably count the increasingly expanding Lydia of the later seventh century as providing more in the nature of a positive incentive. Lydia's love affair with silver is clear from the quantities of silver that its king, Gyges, sent as offerings to Delphi around the beginning of the seventh century and probably also from the fabled wealth of his later descendant Croesus.[32] Significantly, shortly before the end of the seventh century, Lydia was to produce the first electrum and subsequently silver coinage.[33] It was one state that, by the later seventh and early sixth centuries, might be thought of as in need of as much cheap silver as possible for various reasons: in the interests of state capital accumulation, probably in part for passing on directly or indirectly to allies in the east,[34] or (as silver coins began to be produced perhaps from around the end of the seventh century) for coinage, not least as stocks of small state-guaranteed units of precious metal in order to pay for Greek and Carian mercenaries. Some of these mercenaries fought in the armies that the Mermnad kings of Lydia sent to the aid of Egyptians in the later seventh century,[35] and they may have found Lydia's electrum coins, designed primarily for use within the Lydian economy, of more limited use outside Lydia.

Miletus, whose early silver coinage shared a weight standard with that of Lydia, had long made a living from maritime activities and was particularly well placed to act as an effective outlet to the sea for Lydia. Perhaps this is why, as Herodotus tells us, Lydia made repeated attempts to conquer and dominate Miletus and other Ionian cities. Yet, as David Hill has recently argued, the fragmented coastal area in which Miletus acted out its important maritime role was actually treated by Lydian rulers, who had no independent access to the Aegean sea, in a much more ambivalent manner—as a fuzzy borderland or buffer zone that served their own economic interests in much the same way as the Hittites used Ugarit or the Assyrians the Phoenician cities.[36] The Lydian king Alyattes concluded a peace treaty with Miletus in the late seventh century and later, in the early sixth century (also according to Herodotus), Croesus entered a treaty of friendship with the Ionians before going on to expand his empire as far as the Halybes of the Black Sea coast.[37] If this were merely an explicit confirmation of an existing situation, as Hill suggests, rather than a volte-face, as Herodotus might have us believe, then it seems possible that from the start Miletus had active Lydian encouragement to embark on its Black Sea ventures.[38]

Why Not Phoenicians, and Why a Trojan War?

I finally come to my last two questions: Why were Phoenicians not apparently interested in making direct contact with the Black Sea; and why was Homer's war specifically a Trojan war? As for the Phoenicians, they were almost certainly subject to the same set of disincentives as Greeks until the later part of the seventh century and—perhaps more important—already had direct access to distant and prolific, and therefore relatively cheap, sources of silver from the western and probably northern Aegean, southwest Spain, and Sardinia during the four centuries preceding this. It is a curious thing, too, that, although Phoenician or Phoenician-carried material can be found on Rhodes and Cos from the later eleventh century onward, before the seventh century there is a surprising lack of Oriental artifacts at sites on the East Aegean islands north of Cos or on the west coast of Anatolia.[39] This lack includes the glass and faience objects otherwise common in the later eleventh and succeeding centuries in southern or eastern-facing areas of the Aegean, suggesting that Phoenician ships were not voyaging up the Anatolian west coast in these earlier centuries. A find at Methone on the Thermaic Gulf of six Phoenician transport amphorae of torpedo jar type in a context dating to around 700 BCE,[40] a time when eastern material begins to be found in several of the major east coast sanctuaries,[41] suggests that by this time they may have been using this route. At any rate and despite this, there is no sign of Phoenician activity in the Black Sea or its approaches.

Finally, Homer's Trojan War, and the question of why it is specifically a Trojan war and not some other war in some other place, may have something to contribute to the problems surrounding Greek involvement with the Black Sea by providing insights into Greek perceptions of the southern Black Sea coast and attitudes to Phrygians around 700 BCE. For many, the answer to why it is a Trojan war would lie simply in the traditional notion that Homer was an Ionian or Aeolian, and that the Trojan War was the most famous war that had ever taken place in or near his part of the world.[42] I have to confess, however, that I find this explanation rather unsatisfactory. In my view, there is much in Homer's epics that is ideological and designed to fit into ideological preoccupations of the period, in the decades around 700 BCE, when the epics probably emerged in a form that we might more or less recognize. These include the first stirrings of a collective Greek consciousness. In particular, the notion of a combined war against Troy under the leadership of a primus inter pares, something that one cannot imagine ever really happening at any point in Greek history, can be seen as a fiction with an ideological purpose, underlining an ideal of collective, collaborative endeavor; and this, at least, was certainly well embedded in Greek notions of their past by the time of Hesiod in the early Archaic period.[43] It is bolstered by the semblance of comprehensiveness in the Greek Catalogue in the *Iliad*, in which—curiously—only the Cycladic islands are missing altogether and only seven of the 100 cities of Crete take part.[44]

Is there anything in the late eighth or early seventh century that might explain why the epics center around a war at Troy, and not a war anywhere

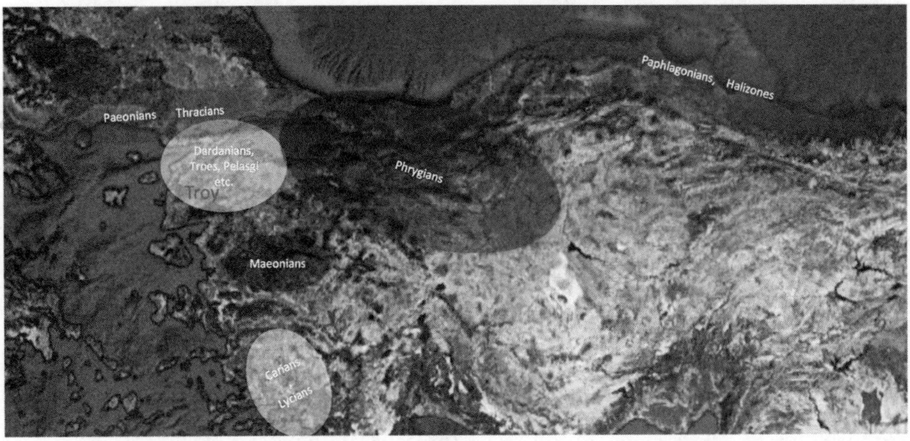

FIGURE 6.3 Map of the Trojan Catalogue (*Iliad* 2.815–877). Google Earth image, modified by the author.

else? Many have argued that Homer's Trojan War is not a historical war that actually took place in the Late Bronze Age but one formed for the purpose of the epics in bricolage fashion out of various ideological elements. This would include the very long-lived elite ideal of the successful siege of a city (some elements to do with Greeks but not with Troy, others perhaps to do with Troy but nothing to do with Greeks).[45] If so, then some explanation is needed as to why a war at Troy and not a war against some other city, of which there were plenty to choose from, might make ideological sense. Here it is perhaps worth looking more closely at the Catalogue of Trojan allies in the *Iliad*,[46] which to a large extent completes the circuit of the Aegean Sea begun by the Greek Catalogue. This starts with Troy and the region immediately surrounding it on both sides of the Hellespont, then moves to Macedonia and Thrace, then a diversion into the southern Pontic region, followed by Mysians (who are not associated with any place-names), then Phrygians, and Maeonians (associated with the Gygaean lake and Mount Tmolus); finally, it travels farther down the coast of Asia Minor, via the barbarophone Carians of Miletus, as far as Lycia (figure 6.3). Thus, the Phrygians—among others—are lined up as Greek opponents. It is also worth noting not only that, elsewhere in the *Iliad*, Phrygia is placed in the area of the Sangarios River in Bithynia,[47] but also that, in the Trojan Catalogue, the Phrygian allies of the Trojans are said to come from around Ascania—probably to be identified with the region surrounding the lake of that name (now Lake Iznik), a few miles south of the eastern end of the Sea of Marmara.[48] Both of these are in just the right places to defend against maritime access to and from the Black Sea. Moreover, since Priam's wife, Hecuba, was the daughter of the Phrygian king Dymas and sister of the Phrygian leader Asios, who lived on the Sangarios, Phrygia was particularly intimately allied to Troy.[49] The Lydians, meanwhile, who were also Trojan allies under the name of Maeonians, are confined in the Trojan Catalogue—as they actually appear to have been in the eighth century—strictly to the region around their historical capital, Sardis (which is not, however, mentioned).[50]

Trojan allies in the Pontic region include the Paphlagones from the land of the Enetoi, from Kytoros and around Sesamos and the Parthenios River,[51] which we might reasonably associate with the later coastal region of Paphlagonia, bounded by Bithynia to the west and centered on the modern Bartın Çay (ancient Parthenios). Another group is the Halizones, described as from faraway Alybe (whence silver was brought to birth),[52] whom one must presume are to be found further to the east, perhaps extending toward the rich metal—including silver—resources of the eastern Pontic mountains close to the Black Sea. It has been suggested that these enigmatic Pontic entries should be taken as an example of deliberate archaizing, inserted long after the Greek colonization of the Black Sea but specifically designed to reflect the lack of knowledge that preceded this.[53] However, even if this were the case, one might expect it to reflect epic audiences' or readers' traditional "memories" of what their forefathers believed about the Pontus in precolonial times; it is, therefore, unlikely to have been entirely invented out of nothing purely for the sake of an archaizing effect. In any case, the leaders of both the Paphlagones and Halizones appear elsewhere in the *Iliad*,[54] which suggests that they and their contingents were slightly more embedded than one might expect if they were simply archaizing interpolations into the Trojan Catalogue of a significantly later period. In short, the Catalogue of Trojan allies, insofar as the Pontic contingents are concerned, seems plausibly to reflect some (tantalizingly vague) Greek knowledge of the southern Black Sea coast and its promising metal potential in a period before regular access through the Bosphorus was able to become an actuality. Indeed, the Phrygian contingent equally plausibly reflects a political reality on the southern shores of the Bosphorus in the eighth–seventh century. The Trojan Catalogue might, then, be seen as providing a coherent background against which a war against Troy would make perfect sense—that is, within a context of Greek aspirations to penetrate the Bosphorus in the face of Phrygian hostility at the end of the eighth or in the early seventh century.

Conclusion

To sum up, I am suggesting that Archaic Greeks appear to have been aware that the Black Sea probably had something worthwhile to offer them but that in the eighth century, at a time when they were venturing westward, their way into the Pontus may well have been barred. This was due not simply to the difficulties of negotiating the Hellespont, the Marmara, and the Bosphorus, but probably more crucially to the presence of potentially hostile Phrygians (enemies of the Greeks in the *Iliad*) who, at that time, controlled the approaches to the Bosphorus. During the course of the seventh century, under the Mermnad dynasty, Lydians steadily expanded out from their eighth-century core around Sardis to drive back Phrygia—among other opponents—and eventually, by the early sixth century, to extend their empire as far eastward as the southern Black Sea shore.[55] This, and the Lydians' ever growing need for silver for various purposes, as well as their effectively symbiotic relationship with Miletus as the most maritime-focused of Ionian cities, provided the conditions and incentive for Miletus in particular to establish way stations and settlements in the Black Sea toward the end of the seventh century. Finally, Phoenicians, whom one might otherwise have expected to explore the mineral potential of the Black Sea as they did virtually all other mineral rich areas of the Mediterranean, by about 900 BCE had already found their El Dorado in the far west. In the ninth–eighth century, they too might have encountered Phrygian hostility had they tried to enter the Black Sea—although it does not look as though they ever did—and, by around 600, they were otherwise preoccupied, under pressure from, and eventually succumbing to, the Babylonians. As a result of a combination of timing and history, they had no need and little incentive or opportunity to access the resources of the Black Sea in any direct manner.

Speculative though this chapter may be, it is an attempt of the kind that Osborne and Hall encourage us to undertake in chapter 1 of this volume—namely, to make some sense out of the complicated, ambiguous, often contradictory and very partial nature of the archaeological and textual data that touch upon the questions I originally set out to address. It seems clear to me that what was involved in the beginning of the process of the integration of the Black Sea and the Mediterranean in the early first millennium BCE, starting in the late seventh century, were the priorities of seaborne communications and topography, essentially driven by economics and facilitated—as they had previously been hindered—by the vagaries of regional politics in particular historical contexts.[56] Wider interregional economic considerations provided the macro-context against which this transformative process took place,[57] in particular the ever-increasing significance of silver in Mediterranean maritime linkage, which was probably the single most important factor in drawing the Black Sea firmly into the Mediterranean ambit.[58]

Notes

1. See Robin Osborne, *Greece in the Making, 1200–479 BC* (London: Routledge, 1996), 121–25. Pseudo-Scymnus (ca. 90 BCE), for example, gives a date of before 757 for the foundation of Sinope by Miletus, while Eusebius (fourth century CE) gives a date of 757 for the foundation of Trapezus by Sinope.

2. John Boardman, "Early Greek Pottery on Black Sea Sites?," *Oxford Journal of Archaeology* 10, no. 3 (1991): 387–90; Gocha R. Tsetskhladze, "Greek Penetration of the Black Sea," in *The Archaeology of Greek Colonisation*, ed. Gocha R. Tsetskhladze and Franco De Angelis (Oxford: Oxford University Committee for Archaeology, 1994), 111–35; and Sergei L. Solovyov, "Ancient Greek Pioneering in the Northern Black Sea Coastal Area in the Seventh Century BC," in *The Black Sea: Past, Present and Future*, ed. Gülden Erkut and Stephen Mitchell (London: British Institute at Ankara, 2007), 37–43.

3. Joseph W. Lehner and K. Aslihan Yener, "Organization and Specialization of Early Mining and Metal Technologies in Anatolia," in *Archaeometallurgy in Global Perspective: Methods and Syntheses*, ed. Benjamin W. Roberts and Christopher Thornton (Berlin: Springer Verlag, 2014), 529–57, fig. 21.

4. Susan Sherratt, "Phoenicians in the Aegean and Aegean Silver, 11th–9th Centuries BC," in *Les Phéniciens, les Puniques et les autres: Échanges et identités en Mediterranée ancienne*, ed. Luisa Bonadies, Iva Chirpanlieva, and Elodie Guillon (Paris: de Boccard, 2019), 129–58; and Francisco González de Canales, Leonardo Serrano, and Jorge Llompart, "The Pre-Colonial Phoenician Emporium of Huelva ca 900–770 BC," *BABESCH* 81 (2006): 13–29.

5. E.g., Arthur Evans, *The Palace of Minos at Knossos*, vol. 4 (London: Macmillan, 1935), 766–69; Stefan Hiller, "The Mycenaeans and the Black Sea," in *THALASSA: L'Egée Préhistorique et la Mer*, ed. Robert Laffineur and Lucien Basch (Liège: Université de Liège, Histoire de l'art et archéologie de la Grèce antique, 1991), 207–16; and Marianna Koromila, *The Greeks in the Black Sea: From the Bronze Age to the Early Twentieth Century* (Athens: Panorama, 1991), 32; cf. David H. French, "Mycenaeans in the Black Sea," *Thracia Pontica* 1 (1982): 19–28.

6. See also Jan G. de Boer, "Phantom-Mycenaeans in the Black Sea," *Talanta* 38–39 (2006–7): 277–302.

7. Details will be found in Susan Sherratt, "Questions Concerning the Black Sea during the Late Bronze/Early Iron Age Transition Late 13th to 7th Centuries BC)," in *Archaeology of the Early Black Sea Region: Connectivity and Remoteness*, ed. Claudia Glatz, Alexander Bauer, and Susan Sherratt (London: Routledge, forthcoming); see also Göksel Sazcı and Meral Başaran Mutlu, "Maydos-Kilisetepe: A Bronze Age Settlement on the Border between Asia and Europe," in *Archaeology across Frontiers and Borderlands: Fragmentation and Connectivity in the North Aegean and the Central Balkans from the Bronze Age to the Iron Age*, ed. Stefanos Gimatzidis, Magda Pieniążek, and Sila Mangaloğlu Votruba (Vienna: Österreichische Akademie

der Wissenschaften), 139–58, esp. 150, where it is argued that the site of Maydos-Kilisitepe on the southern coast of the Gallipoli peninsula and contemporary with Troy VIIB was a significant maritime interstation between the Aegean, the Marmara, and the Black Sea.

8. N. Savaş Harmankaya, "Kozman Deresi Mevkii (Şarköy, Tekirdağ) Maden Buluntuları," in *Readings in Prehistory: Studies Presented to Halet Çambel* (Istanbul: Grafis, 1995), 217–54; cf. Krassimir Leshtakov, "The Eastern Balkans in the Aegean Economic System during the LBA: Ox-hide and Bun Ingots in Bulgarian Lands," in *Between the Aegean and Baltic Seas: Prehistory across Borders*, ed. Ioanna Galanaki et al. (Liège: Université de Liège, Histoire de l'art et archéologie de la Grèce antique, 2007), 447–58, esp. 450; Anthony F. Harding, "Interconnections between the Aegean and Continental Europe in the Bronze and Early Iron Ages: Moving beyond Scepticism," in Galanaki et al., *Between the Aegean and Baltic Seas*, 47–55, esp. 51; Constantinos Paschalidis, "Euboea at the Crossroads of the Metal Trade: The Aegean and the Black Sea in the Late Bronze Age," in Galanaki et al., *Between the Aegean and Baltic Seas*, 433–34, esp. 442; and Diana Doncheva, "The Northern 'Journey' of Late Bronze Age Copper Ingots," in *ΗΡΑΚΛΕΟΥΣ ΣΩΤΗΡΟΣ ΘΑΣΙΩΝ: Studia in honorem Iliae Prokopov sexagenario ab amicis et discipulis dedicate*, ed. Evgeni Paunov and Svetoslav Filipova (Veliko Turnovo: Faber, 2012), 671–714, esp. 677, 686–87. For the northern shores of the Marmara as particularly pertinent to ships traveling from northeast to southwest from the Bosphorus toward the Hellespont and the Aegean rather than vice versa, see Irad Malkin and Nino Shmueli, "The 'City of the Blind' and the Founding of Byzantium," *Mediterranean Historical Review* 3, no. 1 (1988): 21–36.

9. Harmankaya, "Kozman Deresi Mevkii."

10. For a recent suggestion, based on parallels for most of the objects, including the omphalos bowl, that the hoard dates to the fourteenth–thirteenth centuries, see Bogdan Athanassov, Dimitar Chernakov, Kalin Dimitrov, Ranko Krauss, Hristo Popov, Roland Schwab, Vladimir Slavchev, and Ernst Pernicka, "A New Look at the Late Bronze Age Oxhide Ingots from the Eastern Balkans," in *Objects, Ideas and Travelers: Contacts between the Balkans, the Aegean and Western Anatolia during the Bronze and Early Iron Age; Volume to the Memory of Alexandru Vulpe*, ed. Joseph Maran, Radu Băjenaru, Sorin-Cristian Ailincăi, Anca-Diana Popescu, and Svend Hansen (Bonn: Rudolf Habelt, 2020), 299–356, esp. 302–3. However, this takes little account of the extended date range attributed to many of the objects found in it and, indeed, of the probability that the hoard was collected and deposited sometime after the latest date of the latest of these objects. In any case, a date at the end of the thirteenth or in the early twelfth century would still accord well with other hoards of a mixed geographical nature found in various parts of the Mediterranean. See, e.g., Susan Sherratt, "The Intercultural Transformative Capacities of Irregularly Appropriated Goods," in *Materiality and Social Practice: Transformative Capacities of Intercultural Encounters*, ed. Joseph Maran and Philipp W. Stockhammer (Oxford: Oxbow Books, 2012), 152–72.

11. Sherratt, "Intercultural Transformative Capacities."

12. Michael Denis Higgins and Reynold A. Higgins, *A Geological Companion to Greece and the Aegean* (London: Duckworth, 1996), 149, fig. 13.14.

13. Owen Doonan, *Sinop Landscapes: Exploring Connections in a Black Sea Hinterland* (Philadelphia: University of Pennsylvania Museum, 2004), 93; see

also Doonan, "Exploring Community in the Hinterland of a Black Sea Port," in *Surveying the Greek Chora: The Black Sea Region in a Comparative Perspective*, ed. Pia Guldager Bilde and Vladimir Stolba (Aarhus: Aarhus University Press, 2006), 47–58; Doonan, "Colony and Conjuncture: The Early Greek Colony at Sinope," in *Frühes Ionien: Eine Bestandsaufnahme*, ed. Justus Cobet et al. (Mainz am Rhein: von Zabern, 2007), 613–20, esp. 616; and Doonan, "The Corrupting Sea and the Hospitable Sea: Some Early Thoughts toward a Regional History of the Black Sea," in *KOINE: Mediterranean Studies in Honor of R. Ross Holloway*, ed. Derek Counts and Anthony Tuck (Oxford: Oxbow Books, 2010), 68–74, esp. 72–73.

14. Milesians of Sinope: see Jan G. de Boer, "Sinope and Colchis: Colonisation, or a Greek Population in 'Poleis Barbaron'?," in *The Danubian Landsbetween the Black, Aegean and Adriatic Seas*, ed. Gocha R. Tsetskhladze, Alexandru Avram, and James Hargrave (Oxford: Archaeopress, 2013), 73–80, Strabo 12.3.

15. It is perhaps worth pointing out in this context that handmade pottery with finger-impressed cordons similar to that found in the northern Black Sea and in Troy VIIB also occurs at Sinope. See Sergei L. Solovyov, *Ancient Berezan: The Architecture, History and Culture of the First Greek Colony in the Northern Black Sea* (Leiden: Brill, 1999), figs. 20–22; Doonan, "Colony and Conjuncture," 614–16, pl. 77:3–4; and Alexander A. Bauer and Susan Sherratt, "The Handmade, Pre-Colonial and Para-Colonial Ceramics from the Citadel of Sinop, Turkey: Some Preliminary Observations," in *Sinop Kale Excavations 2015–2017*, ed. Owen Doonan, A. Bauer, and E. Sökmen (İstanbul: Ege Yayınları, forthcoming).

16. Jak Yakar, "Hittite Involvement in Western Anatolia," *Anatolian Studies* 26 (1976): 117–28, esp. 121; Prentiss S. de Jesus, "Metal Resources in Ancient Anatolia," *Anatolian Studies* 28 (1978): 97–102, esp. 100n13; and Lehner and Yener, "Organization and Specialization," fig. 4.

17. Evgenil N. Chernykh, *Ancient Metallurgy in the USSR: The Early Metal Age* (Cambridge: Cambridge University Press, 1992), fig. 3; Horia Ciugudean, "Ancient Goldmining in Transylvania: The Roşia Montană-Bucium Area," *Caiete ARA* 3 (2012): 219–32; and Attila Tóth, Aurélie Quiquerez, and István Márton, "Past and Present Mining in the Apuseni Mountains," *Romania Field Trip SEG Student Chapters Uni Geneva—ETH Zürich—Uni Budapest—Uni Cluj 05.09-14.09.2006*, VII-1-8 (2006). For metal resources in the Carpathians being exploited for a trade in metals by northwest Black Sea populations as early as the later fifth millennium, see Blagoje Govaderica, "Conflict or Coexistence: Steppe and Agricultural Societies in the Early Copper Age of the Northwest Black Sea area," in Glatz, Bauer, and Sherratt, *Archaeology of the Early Black Sea Region*.

18. Chernykh, *Ancient Metallurgy*, 202.

19. See, e.g., Aubrey Gwynn, "The Character of Greek Colonisation," *Journal of Hellenic Studies* 38 (1919): 88–123, esp. 95–96; Gocha R. Tsetskhladze, "Did Greeks Go to Colchis for Metals?," *Oxford Journal of Archaeology* 14, no. 3 (1995): 307–31; Tsetskhladze, "Greek Penetration," 123–26 with further references; and Alan Greaves, "Milesians in the Black Sea: Trade, Settlement and Religion," in *The Black Sea in Antiquity: Regional and Interregional Economic Exchanges*, ed. Vincent Gabrielsen and John Lund (Aarhus: Aarhus University Press, 2007), 9–21.

20. As pointed out by Gocha R. Tsetskhladze, "The Black Sea," in *A Companion to Archaic Greece*, ed. Kurt A. Raaflaub and Hans van Wees (Chichester: Wiley-Blackwell, 2009), 330–46, esp. 335, it seems thoroughly anachronistic to suppose

that the attraction of the Black Sea was primarily as a source of grain as early as the seventh to sixth centuries.

21. Christine M. Thompson, "Sealed Silver in Iron Age Cisjordan and the Invention of Coinage," *Oxford Journal of Archaeology* 22, no. 1 (2003): 67–107; see also Alain Bresson, "The Origin of Lydian and Greek Coinage: Cost and Quantity," *Historical Research* 5 (2006): 149–65.

22. Seymour Gitin and Amir Golani, "A Silver-Based Monetary Economy in the Seventh Century BCE: A Response to Raz Kletter," *Levant* 36 (2004): 203–5; and Sherratt, "Phoenicians in the Aegean and Aegean Silver."

23. González de Canales, Serrano, and Llompart, "Pre-Colonial Phoenician Emporium"; and Mark E. Polzer, "Excavating a Phoenician Shipwreck at Bajo de la Campana, Spain," *Center for Maritime Archaeology and Conservation News and Reports* 2, no. 2 (2010): 23–25.

24. See Brian Muhs, chapter 9 in this volume, for what he terms arbitrage: the practice of buying commodities like silver in places where they are more common and less valuable, and then selling them in places where they are less common and more valuable, in order to profit from the difference in prices; for further examples, see Susan Sherratt, "Why Was (and Is) Silver Sexy? Silver during the 4th–3rd Millennia in the Near East and Mesopotamia," in *Metals, Minds and Mobility: Integrating Scientific Data with Archaeological Theory*, ed. Xosé-Lois Armada, Mercedes Murillo-Barroso, and Mike Charlton (Oxford: Oxbow Books, 2018), 97–106, esp. 100–101.

25. *Iliad* 2.851–7.

26. Herodotus 4.152.

27. Herodotus 4.144.

28. Herodotus 1.28.

29. Claude Brixhe and Michel Lejeune, *Corpus des inscriptions paléo-phrygiennes* (Paris: Editions Recherches sur les civilisations, 1984), 57–71.

30. Tomris Bakır and Roberto Gusmani, "Eine neue phrygische Inschrift aus Daskyleion," *Epigraphica Anatolica* 18 (1991): 157–64, esp. 159; Tomris Bakır-Akbaşoğlu, "Phryger in Daskyleion," in *Frigi e Frigio*, ed. Roberto Gusmani, Mirjo Salvini, and Pietro Vannicelli (Rome: Consiglio Nazionale delle Ricerche, 1997), 229–38, esp. 233, 235–36; Machteld Mellink, "The Native Kingdoms of Anatolia," in *The Cambridge Ancient History*, vol. 3, part 2, *The Assyrian and Babylonian Empires and Other States of the Near East, from the Eighth to the Sixth Centuries BC*, 2nd ed. (Cambridge: Cambridge University Press, 1992), 619–65, esp. 624; and Garance Fiedler and Mehmet Taşlıalan, "Un monument rupestre phrygien au bord du lac de Hoyran," *Anatolia Antiqua* 10 (2002): 97–112, esp. 108. The dating of Old Phrygian inscriptions is very imprecise. The earliest (at Gordion) go back to the late ninth century, according to the recent Gordion chronology, but they are possibly particularly common in the eighth–seventh centuries, continuing into the early fifth century (Brixhe and Lejeune, *Corpus*, IX). For Old Phrygian inscriptions from the region considerably inland of Sinope, see David H. French, "The Iron Age on the Southern Black Sea Coast," *Thracia Pontica* 4 (1991): 237–40, esp. 239.

31. Pindar, *Pythian* 4, 203. This is not to suggest that hostility to Greeks was necessarily directed or encouraged by a Phrygian state with its center at Gordion, but more likely by Phrygian-speaking groups living close to the Bosphorus on both its east and west sides. Given the need for frequent landfalls and provisioning, it is

not difficult to imagine that hostile groups could have successfully deterred ships from approaching the Bosphorus. For a series of natural reasons why ships sailing through the Sea of Marmara toward the Hellespont would have wanted to stick close to the Asiatic shore, see Malkin and Shmueli, "'City of the Blind.'"

32. Herodotus 1.14.

33. See Edward S. G. Robinson, "The Coins from the Ephesian Artemision Reconsidered," *Journal of Hellenic Studies* 71 (1951): 156–67, esp. 157, for a number of silver dumps in the same contexts as the early electrum coins at Ephesus; cf. John Boardman, *The Greeks Overseas*, 2nd ed. (London: Thames and Hudson, 1980), 101. For the date of Alyattes, see Robert W. Wallace, "Redating Croesus: Herodotean Chronologies, and the Dates of the Earliest Coinages," *Journal of Hellenic Studies* 136 (2016), 168–81, esp. 175–78; and Dyfri Williams, "The 'Pot Hoard' from the Archaic Artemision at Ephesus," *Bulletin of the Institute of Classical Studies* 38 (1991–93): 98–103.

34. Perhaps particularly significant in view of an alliance made by Gyges with Assyria, which lasted for at least two generations and opened up a direct route of communication between Sardis and Nineveh: Walter Burkert, *The Orientalizing Revolution: Near Eastern Influence on Greek Culture in the Early Archaic Age* (Cambridge, MA: Harvard University Press, 1992), 14; and Simo Parpola, "Assyria's Expansion in the 8th and 7th Centuries and Its Long-Term Repercussions in the West," in *Symbiosis, Symbolism, and the Power of the Past*, ed. William G. Dever and Seymour Gitin (Winona Lake, IN: Eisenbrauns), 99–111, esp. 102.

35. Herodotus 2.152.4–5; and Alexander Fantalkin, "Naukratis as a Contact Zone: Revealing the Lydian Connection," in *Kulturkontakte in Antike Welten: Vom Denkmodell zum Fall Beispiel*, ed. Robert Rollinger and Kordula Schnegg (Leuven: Peeters, 2014), 27–51, esp. 35.

36. David Hill, "Conceptualising Interregional Relations in Ionia and Central-West Anatolia from the Archaic to the Hellenistic Period," in *Bordered Places/Bounded Times: Cross-Disciplinary Perspectives on Turkey*, ed. Emma L. Boysal and Leonidas Karakatsanis (London: British Institute at Ankara, 2017), 85–95; cf. Fantalkin, "Naukratis as a Contact Zone," 38.

37. Herodotus 1.22, 1.27–28. On the presence of the philosopher Thales of Miletus at the Battle of Halys between Lydians under Croesus and Medes inside the Halys bend in about 585 BCE, see Herodotus 1.74.

38. In a similar vein, Alexander Fantalkin, "Naukratis as a Contact Zone" argues that relations between Lydia and the Ionians, and particularly Alyattes's treaty with Miletus, were responsible for the foundation of Naucratis in the late seventh century. Like others, he also points out that it is perhaps no coincidence that the establishment of Naucratis and the beginning of Milesian activity in the Black Sea happened at roughly the same time, and suggests that both can be put down to the aspirations of the Lydian kingdom.

39. Rik Vaessen, "An Ionian Perspective on Aegeo-Levantine Interactions at the End of the Second Millennium BCE" (paper presented at the conference *The Aegean and the Levant at the Turn of the Bronze and Iron Ages*, Warsaw, September 27–28, 2016). I am grateful to Rik Vaessen for a copy of this as yet unpublished paper.

40. Alexandra Kasseri, "Φοινικικοί εμπορικοί αμφορείς από τη Μεθώνη Πιερίας," in *Κεραμέως Παίδες*, ed. Eurydike Kephalidou and Despoina Tsiafaki (Θεσσαλονίκη: Εταιρεία Ανδρίων Επιστημόνων, 2012), 299–308, esp. 300–303; see also 304 for other

contemporary Phoenician and/or Cypriot material in the North Aegean. For additional discussion of Methone and its Phoenician amphorae, see Papadopoulos, chapter 7 in this volume, including figure 7.7.

41. For Samos, see, e.g., Imma Kilian-Dirlmeier, "Fremde Weihungen in griechischen Heiligtümern vom 8. bis zum Beginn des 7. Jahrhunderts v. Chr.," *Jahrbuch des Römisch-Germanischen Zentralmuseums* 32 (1985): 215–54, esp. 249–53, fig. 20.

42. Malcolm M. Willcock, "Homer," in *The Oxford Classical Dictionary*, 3rd ed., ed. Simon Hornblower and Anthony Spawforth (Oxford: Oxford University Press, 1996), 718.

43. Hesiod, *Works and Days*, 652–53.

44. *Iliad* 2.484–759.

45. See, e.g., Susan Sherratt, "The Trojan War: History or Bricolage?," *Bulletin of the Institute of Classical Studies* 53, no. 2 (2010): 1–18.

46. *Iliad* 2.816–77.

47. *Iliad* 3.184–90; 16.717.

48. *Iliad* 2.862–63; cf. Geoffrey S. Kirk, *The Iliad: A Commentary*, vol. 1, books 1–4 (Cambridge: Cambridge University Press, 1985), 259–60, esp. 249, fig. 2.

49. *Iliad* 16.717–19.

50. See Christina Luke and Christoper H. Roosevelt, "Central Lydia Archaeological Survey: Documenting the Prehistoric through Iron Age Periods," in *Tree-Rings, Kings, and Old World Archaeology and Environment: Papers Presented in Honor of Peter Ian Kuniholm*, ed. Sturt W. Manning and Mary Jaye Bruce (Oxford: Oxbow Books, 2009), 199–217, esp. 209–10.

51. *Iliad* 2.851–55.

52. *Iliad* 2.856–57.

53. Denys L. Page, *History and the Homeric Iliad* (Berkeley: University of California Press, 1963), 147; see also Kirk, *Iliad*, 248; and for further discussion of the place-names Kytoros, Kromna, and Aigialos, see Askold I. Ivantchik, "Die Gründung von Sinope und die Probleme der Anfangsphase der griechischen Kolonisation des Schwarzmeergebietes," in *The Greek Colonisation of the Black Sea Area: Historical Interpretation of Archaeology*, ed. Gocha R. Tsetskhladze (Stuttgart: Steiner, 1998), 297–330, esp. 318–20.

54. *Iliad* 5.39, 576; 13.640; see also Kirk, *Iliad*, 258–59.

55. Hill, "Conceptualising Interregional Relations," fig. 7.1 inset.

56. Peregrine Horden and Nicholas Purcell, *The Corrupting Sea: A Study of Mediterranean History* (Oxford: Blackwell, 2000), 5, 45–49, 124, 130; cf. Osborne and Hall, chapter 1 in this volume.

57. Cyprian Broodbank, *The Making of the Middle Sea: A History of the Mediterranean from the Beginning to the Emergence of the Classical World* (London: Thames and Hudson, 2013); cf. Osborne and Hall, chapter 1 in this volume.

58. Broodbank, *Making of the Middle Sea*, 515, 556, 575–76.

✷ CHAPTER 7 ✷

Greeks, Phoenicians, Phrygians, Trojans, and Other Creatures in the Aegean

Connections, Interactions, Misconceptions

JOHN K. PAPADOPOULOS

Living in the Aegean "was rather like living in one of the more flamboyant and slapstick comic operas."

—GERALD DURRELL, *My Family and Other Animals* (1956)[1]

This chapter begins in the familiar landscape of the southern and central Aegean in the Early Iron Age, with iconic sites that have determined and defined the period: Athens, Lefkandi, and Knossos. From there it moves to the less familiar landscape of the north Aegean. The interactions of the Greeks and Phoenicians in the southern and central Aegean have been well mapped, discussed, and sometimes disputed, but it has been only recently that the Levantine—Phoenician, Cypriot, north Syrian—complexities of the north Aegean have received any close scrutiny. More consistently overlooked in this story are the Trojans and Phrygians—not Homer's mythical Trojans but the actual human communities living in Ilion. Incorporating the overlooked into the landscape of the north Aegean allows more complex and nuanced processes of interaction to emerge. These processes involved many stakeholders from across the Aegean, the Mediterranean, and the Black Sea. Moreover, if we ignore modern national borders, we can view the north Aegean in a new light, one where connectivity took place in a specific geographical/ecological context that provides all sorts of new interpretive opportunities.

By Early Iron Age I mean the period that extends from the collapse of the Mycenaean way of life to about 700 BCE.[2] It ends more or less at the same time that Peregrine Horden and Nicholas Purcell's *The Corrupting Sea* begins. This is a liminal, "protohistoric," period that the gaze of historians rarely penetrates, but one that overlaps nicely with Cyprian

Broodbank's chapter 9 ("From Sea to Shining Sea") in *The Making of the Middle Sea*.[3] These two important studies, building on the seminal work of Fernand Braudel, do much more than bookend my Early Iron Age: they provide a framework for, and articulate, many of the developments faced by all of us dealing with the period.[4]

Patterns of Connectivity in the Aegean: Knossos, Lefkandi, Athens

I begin with the best-known Early Iron Age Aegean sites, by way of introduction and to serve as a point of departure, comparison, and contrast with the north Aegean. More particularly, I look at imports, especially what have come to be known collectively as Orientalia, but also pottery imports and exports—Greek and non-Greek—to and from these sites. By looking at the exchange of commodities of value, such as silver and bronze vessels, ivory, and textiles, as opposed to those of less value like pottery, we begin to see different types of interaction that involve both elite (top-down) and non-elite (bottom-up) interactions. This material has been taken as a proxy for the movement of people, commodities, and ideas, but often overlooked are the underlying patterns in the movement of these commodities. The patterns we see in the distribution of nonceramic materials sometimes mirror, but sometimes do not, the patterns in the pottery. Moreover, these three settlements tell very different stories in terms of the quantities of imported Eastern material, as well as the quantities of imported pottery, and their own ceramic exports. The patterns that emerge are based on "hard things," breakable, but at the same time indestructible, things that often skew the archaeological record. "Soft things," as Robin Osborne calls them—including textiles, human bodies, and other organic commodities—that often defy the archaeological record, are more difficult to trace, particularly in the Aegean and much of the northern Mediterranean.[5] Part of the story is by necessity based on pottery and the vicissitudes of its survival and preservation. By looking also at materials other than pots I try to avoid a construct with feet of clay.

KNOSSOS

Knossos in the Early Iron Age was a vast landscape of death, and from the numerous tombs from the various cemeteries of the site, there is no shortage of imported Orientalia, among which is a bronze bowl with a Phoenician inscription from Tekke considered by Hector Catling a probable import from the Levant (figure 7.1).[6] Of all the Eastern material at

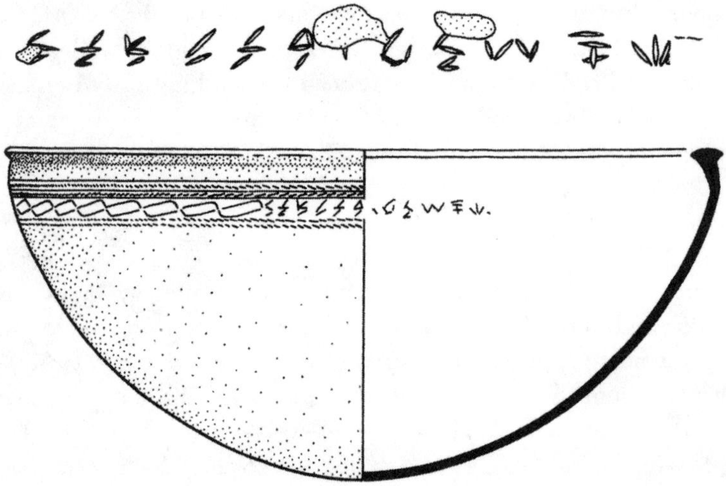

FIGURE 7.1 Bronze bowl with Phoenician inscription, Knossos, Tekke, Chamber Tomb J. Courtesy British School at Athens.

Knossos, I choose this one piece because, although the bowl could have been made anywhere, the inscription could not have been written by anyone. It was written by someone with a knowledge of the Phoenician language and script.

Gail Hoffman enumerates all manner of Eastern imports to Crete: bronzes, faience, glass, gold, ivory, lead, scarabs, stone, and pottery.[7] She also reconsiders the following: (1) evidence of Eastern ivory craftspeople living on Crete; (2) the possibility of north Syrian metalworkers; (3) nonspecialist immigrants at Arkades (Afrati); and (4) the unguent factory "manned by foreigners near Knossos."[8] There is also the Phoenician tri-pillar shrine at Kommos.[9] More recent work on Crete has now multiplied the known quantity of imported nonceramic Orientalia on the island (see Sarah Morris, chapter 5 in this volume). If we look at just the ceramic imports at Knossos they are plentiful, deriving from all over the Aegean and beyond.[10] From the North Cemetery alone, there are well over 100 imports, of which the Athenian are the most prolific: Attica (99), Corinth (4 or 5), Argos (1), Thessaly (1), Euboea (7), the Cyclades (15), east Greece (3), Cyprus (29), and Phoenicia (5).[11] The Fortetsa tombs published by James King Brock only bolster the pattern seen in the North Cemetery, as does the material from other contexts at Knossos.[12]

Interestingly, there are more Attic imports at Knossos than all other ceramic imports combined. Moreover, the range of Athenian shapes is impressive. In contrast, Cretan Early Iron Age pottery is rare during this period outside of Crete; there are no contemporary Cretan imports to my knowledge in Athens or Attica, Lefkandi or Euboea. Moreover, Early Iron Age Cretan material is not far-flung in the eastern or central Mediterranean, unlike Euboean and Athenian exports.

LEFKANDI

The wealth of Early Iron Age nonceramic Eastern imports at Lefkandi is impressive, and it begins relatively early in the Iron Age sequence, with the spectacular bronze amphora of Cypriot manufacture that served as the cinerary urn for the Middle Protogeometric (MPG) burial in the Toumba Building, itself an heirloom at least fifty years old at the time of deposition (figure 7.2).[13] The Toumba Building also brought to light gold jewelry associated with the inhumed female interred with the male.[14] Other tombs at Lefkandi yielded more imports, ranging in date from Late Protogeometric (LPG) through Subprotogeometric (SPG) II, at first largely faience and glass, but later including gold, bronze, stone, and other materials.[15] Among this wealth of Orientalia, I illustrate only an engraved Near Eastern bronze bowl (figure 7.3), one of several, together with a selection of small finds (figure 7.4).[16]

As for the imported pottery published in *Lefkandi* I, Vincent Desborough presented the material diachronically. In the earlier stages of Protogeometric he noted one Syro-Palestinian dipper juglet and one unidentified imported vessel.[17] These are now joined by numerous MPG imports from the Toumba Building, including seventeen Athenian pots, among which is the largest known Athenian amphora of the period.[18] Of the uncertain imports from the Toumba Building, two fragments may be Argive, and a number of suspected imports are also listed.[19] By LPG there is something of an explosion in imported pottery, including a dozen Athenian pots, and several more that are probably Attic.[20] Other LPG imports include a Cypriot Bichrome jug and an amphora of uncertain manufacture. The Geometric imports include an additional fourteen Athenian imports, two open vessels of uncertain origin, and a lentoid flask from the coastal Levant.[21] The pattern from the more recent excavations in the Toumba cemetery at Lefkandi confirms the conclusions from the earlier excavations, and adds considerably to the quantity of Athenian imports. Other new finds include a Phoenician Bichrome jug, a Cypriot Black-on-Red jug, and a small bowl of uncertain provenance.[22] What is telling is that some of the finest and most idiosyncratic Athenian vessels are found not in Athens, but at Knossos and Lefkandi.

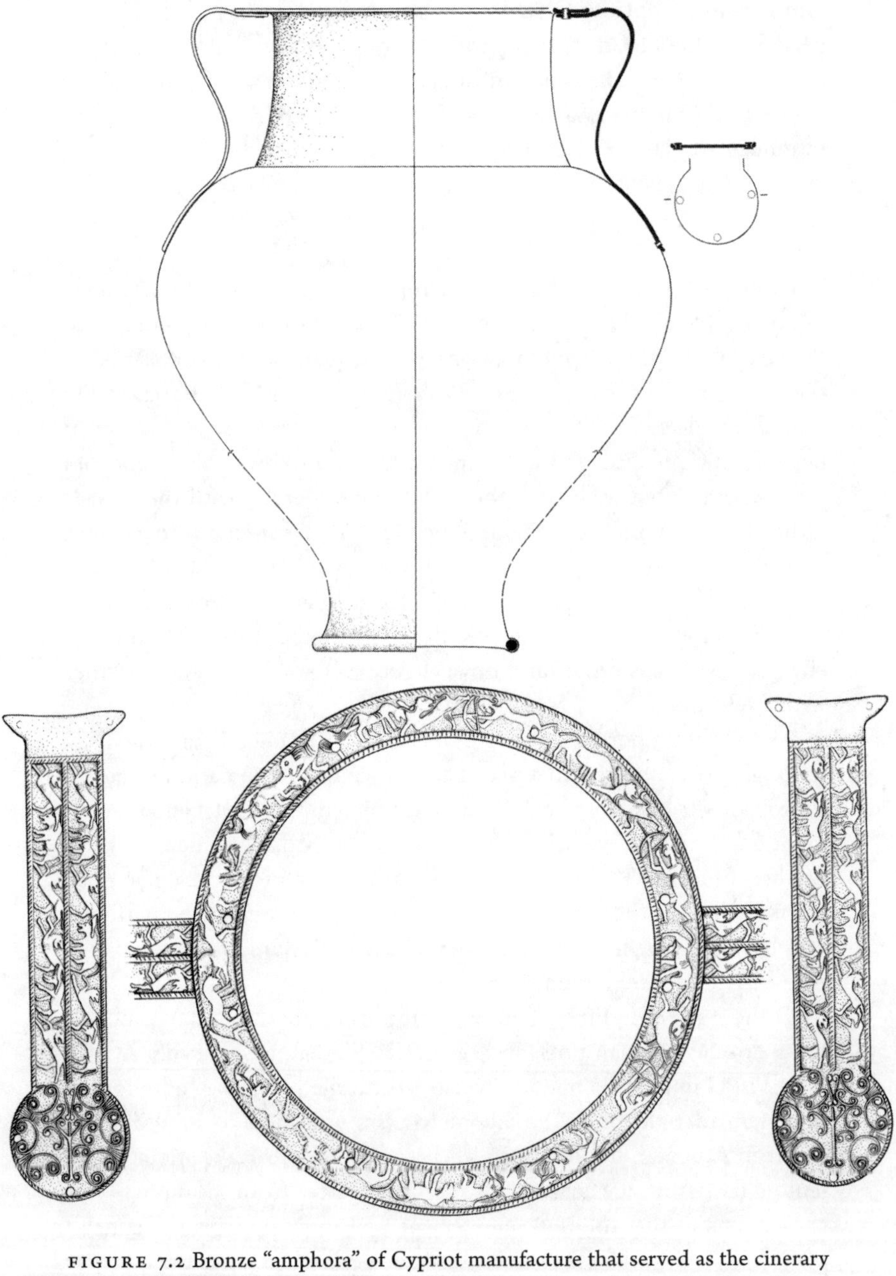

FIGURE 7.2 Bronze "amphora" of Cypriot manufacture that served as the cinerary urn of the Middle Protogeometric burial in the Toumba Building dubbed the "Hero of Lefkandi." Courtesy British School at Athens.

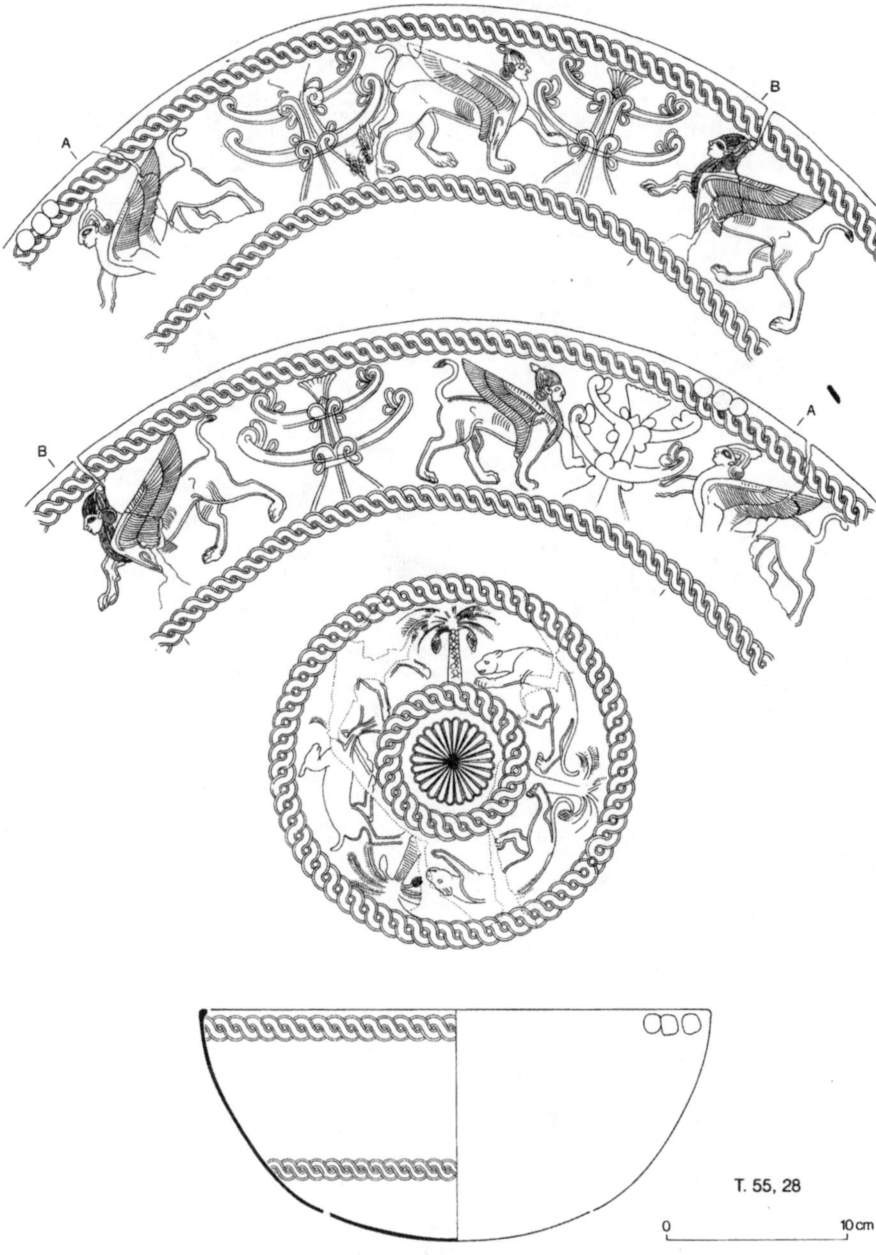

FIGURE 7.3 Engraved Near Eastern bronze bowl, Lefkandi, Toumba cemetery, Tomb 55, no. 28 (LPG/SPG I). Courtesy British School at Athens.

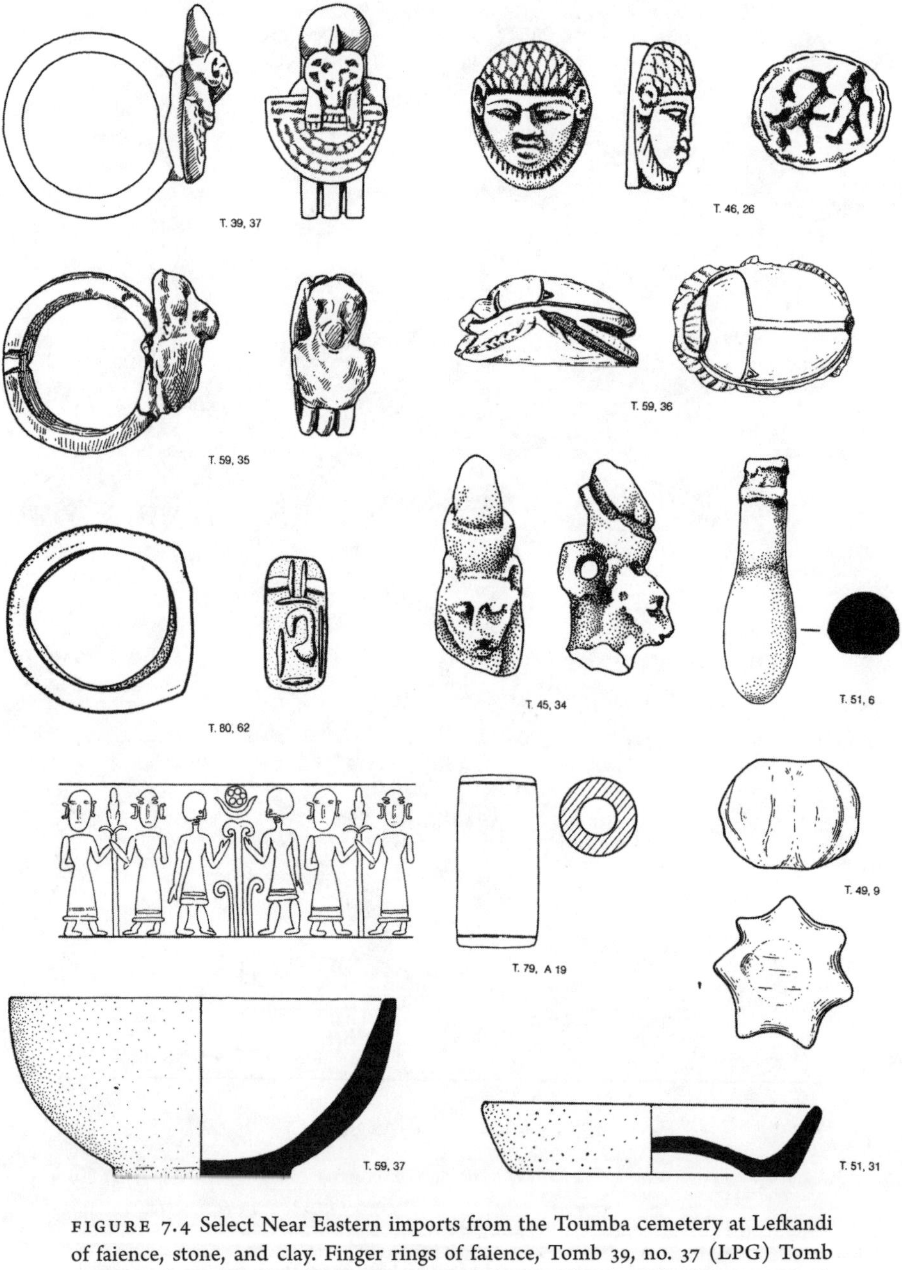

FIGURE 7.4 Select Near Eastern imports from the Toumba cemetery at Lefkandi of faience, stone, and clay. Finger rings of faience, Tomb 39, no. 37 (LPG) Tomb 59, no. 35 (LPG/SPG), and Tomb 80, no. 62 (SPG II/IIIa). Seal of faience, Tomb 46, no. 26 (LPG). Scarab of faience, Tomb 59, no. 36 (LPG/SPG I). Pendants of faience, Tomb 45, no. 34 (SPG I) and Tomb 51, no. 6 (SPG I). Near Eastern seal of haemetite, Tomb 79A, no. 20 (SPG II). Clay object, Tomb 49, no. 9 (MPG-LPG). Faience bowls, Tomb 59, no. 37 (LPG/SPG) and Tomb 51, no. 31 (SPG I). Courtesy British School at Athens.

Unlike Cretan pottery, which is rarely, if ever, found outside of Crete during the Protogeometric and Geometric periods, Euboean pottery traveled widely, both in the Aegean—though not as extensively as Athenian pottery—as well as the eastern and central Mediterranean.

Lefkandi has also produced a remarkable tomb—Toumba Tomb 79—that may represent the burial of a Phoenician who died and was buried at the site.[23] Richly furnished with weapons, including a sword, spearhead, and iron arrowheads, the tomb was interpreted by the excavators as a male, and a warrior. (The human remains were never analyzed.) The other tomb offerings, including a series of stone weights, a north Syrian cylinder seal, and pottery from Cyprus and Phoenicia, "indicate that he was a trader as well."[24] Further bedecked with bronze earrings, he was considered a Euboean trader by the excavators, while others have preferred to see him as a *proxenos*—a notable responsible for assisting the interests of Eastern merchants—or even as a pirate trader.[25] In all these scenarios, the individual in Tomb 79 is Greek, not Eastern. In the interests of calling a spade a spade, I asked the question: What would the burial of an Easterner who died in the Aegean look like? And I went on to refer to this individual, twenty years ago, as Phoenician—a conclusion reiterated here, with the caveat that the deceased may have been Phoenician, North Syrian, or Cypriot.[26]

ATHENS

I begin with those objects that have long been known, especially the Levantine bronze bowl from Kerameikos Geometric Grave 42, often considered Syrian; the date of the vessel and tomb—third quarter of the ninth century BCE—and its Near Eastern complexities were fully discussed by Karl Kübler in 1954 (figure 7.5).[27] The other well-known Eastern finds from Athens are the ivory stamp seals from the Tomb of the Rich Athenian Lady in the Classical Agora, found together with a fragmentary ivory plaque, the necklace of about 1,100 faience beads (figure 7.6), and a few other finds.[28]

In comparison to Knossos and Lefkandi, known Eastern imports to Athens are not numerous. As for imported pottery in Athens, the Athenian trajectory was unique and different from that of Knossos, Lefkandi, and most other sites. Crete took in a great deal of pottery, but exported little (I stress ceramics, as the island was replete with commodities of real value, primarily those of metal). Euboea, especially Lefkandi, was a two-way street, taking in much and exporting a good deal. In contrast, Athens stands alone: its pottery is far-flung, but it has few imports, both in terms

FIGURE 7.5 Levantine bronze bowl from Athens, Kerameikos Geometric Grave 42, often considered Syrian; third quarter of the ninth century BCE. Courtesy DAI Athen.

of ceramics and Eastern goods. What is perhaps most interesting about the few imported pots that have been found—the wheelmade cooking pot from the Booties Grave (Agora Tomb 11), the handmade burnished *kanoun* (Agora Tomb 45), and the Argive skyphos from Kerameikos Grave 51—is that they are not the standard wares that were commercially exchanged.[29] They were not part of a set, like the later symposion pottery, and they are hardly elite exchange items. They are small pots that accompany people. In such a scenario, Phoenician or Eastern intermediaries would make little sense. But if we focus on the distribution of Orientalia, especially in the tenth and ninth centuries BCE, then Phoenician merchants in the Aegean—well-known to Homer—make a lot of sense.[30] Whoever carried pottery in the Aegean, the Athenian pattern that was repeated at Knossos, Lefkandi, and sites like Asine, Aegina, and Torone often included the special Athenian pots found abroad, though smaller vessels—drinking cups, jugs, lekythoi—were also exported.[31] In contrast, I know of no Euboean or Cretan pot found in Athens. Moreover, the distribution of Athenian and Euboean pottery to Crete, the Cyclades,

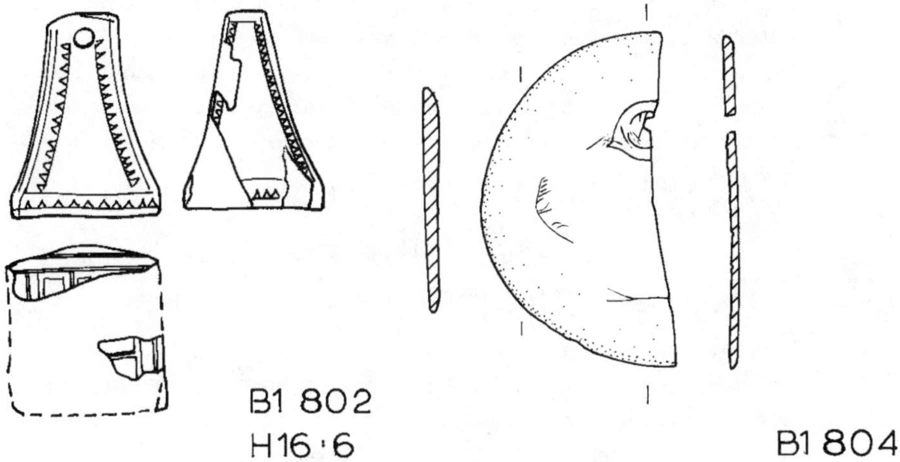

FIGURE 7.6 Athenian Agora, Grave 15, Tomb of the "Rich Athenian Lady": (a) one of two ivory stamp seals; (b) ivory plaque; (c) necklace of faience and glass beads. Courtesy American School of Classical Studies at Athens, Agora Excavations.

the north Aegean, and the Argolid, together with sites in the eastern and central Mediterranean, involved maritime trade. This was not an incidental pattern of a few pots making their way overseas. It was a full-fledged commercial industry, a profitable one for the carriers of these commodities. In such a scenario, both Greek and Eastern traders could well have been the instigators.

Greeks, Phoenicians, Phrygians, Trojans, and Other Creatures in the North Aegean

Before turning to the north Aegean, I wish to emphasize several points. First, by the time we reach the Early Iron Age in the north, it has already been inhabited for millennia, enjoying all manner of contacts with central and southern Greece, and the Mediterranean beyond. Imported materials—and peoples—are present in the Early, Middle, and Late Bronze Ages and continue into the Early Iron Age and later.[32] What I am suggesting is not new. It was well articulated by Alexander John Graham in 1990: "It is obvious that any serious colonization requires previous knowledge, both of the land to be settled and of the people who inhabit it."[33] The problem in part lies with the very reach of historical inquiry. Indeed, ancient historians have been deft in producing nuanced readings of the literary testimonia, challenging the underpinnings of that evidence and often coming up with novel and adroit perspectives,[34] but their gaze does not—cannot, or has not—penetrate(d) the era before about 700 BCE. Consequently, we resort to all sorts of proxies in the absence of literary evidence. Once again, the problem was well framed by Graham: "The centuries before the Greeks began to write history are of the greatest interest and significance, but they are also for the historian full of uncertainty, obscurity and dispute."[35] The north Aegean, like so much of the coastal Mediterranean, was a highly networked and connected place, seeing the movements of people, commodities, and ideas over a long time span, and this was a pattern that does not begin in the Early Iron Age.

The second basic point is that, by the onset of the historic period, there are various different types of settlements in the north Aegean. I have recently argued that there are at least four different types of site in this region: (1) colonies boasting a *metropolis-apoikia* relationship; (2) assumed "colonies" that were never referred to as an *apoikia* (e.g., Torone, see below); (3) noncolonies, like Olynthus, which was a Bottiaean city all along; and (4) all the rest, some named in our literary sources, others unnamed.[36] All this is to say that by the time we reach the Early

Iron Age, the north Aegean had been home to all sorts of settlements and urban experiments, many of which did not follow the trajectories of those farther south.

A third point is that the 800-pound gorilla in the north Aegean, the most important topos of the northeast Aegean both philologically and in terms of settlement size—Troy—is all but overlooked by Aegean archaeologists.[37] Because Troy is located in Turkey, its archaeology—as opposed to its Homeric reality—features surprisingly little in overviews of the Greek Iron Age and of connectivity in this region. The time is ripe to bring Troy back to where it belongs: the north Aegean. Before turning to the Phoenicians, Phrygians, Trojans, and others in the north, I begin with the most fully published Early Iron Age cemetery in the north, Torone.

TORONE

Torone was never a true colony—that is, a settlement that could boast (and in some cases it was little more than a boast) a *metropolis-apoikia* relationship. When the Greeks wanted to say "colony," the word they would use was *apoikia* (ἀποικία), and the north Aegean was no stranger to these.[38] In contrast, Torone, in Thucydides (4.110.1), is simply referred to as "Chalcidic Torone" (Τορώνην τὴν Χαλκιδικήν).[39] Similarly, Herodotus (7.185; 8.127) refers to a Χαλκιδικὸν γένος.[40] Neither Thucydides nor Herodotus refers to Torone as an *apoikia*.

The Early Iron Age cemetery at Torone has produced no shortage of imported pottery: nineteen wheelmade and painted vessels, as well as eight handmade pots considered imports, probably from elsewhere in central Macedonia or Chalcidice, four examples of black-slip pottery, and one example of red-slip.[41] Among the wheelmade and painted imports there are two from Athens, including the earliest of all the imported pots (Submycenaean and Protogeometric), ten from Euboea, ranging in date from Protogeometric to SPG I. Four other vessels are classified as Thessalo-Euboean, one Cycladic, and two of uncertain provenance. The fact that the two earliest imported vessels at Torone are Athenian, and one is of singular shape, mirrors the pattern seen at Knossos and Lefkandi, where the Athenian imports are among the earliest and most idiosyncratic.

More importantly, north Aegean handmade pottery, including examples stylistically close to pottery from Torone, was finding its way south at the same time, including a handmade jug with cutaway neck from Scyrus and several handmade jugs at Lefkandi, some perhaps Thessalian.

Lefkandi has also produced two wheelmade and painted vessels that are possibly north Aegean.[42] The other category of north Aegean ceramics making its way over a remarkably broad area are the neck-handled amphorae, first tracked by Richard Catling at Troy. These were distributed throughout various parts of the Greek world (Euboea, Phocis, Thessaly, Scyrus, Macedonia, Chalcidice, and the Troad), and as far afield as north Syria.[43] The growing quantities of this category of commodity container, and its relationship to other wine and oil containers, not least Attic and Euboean SOS amphorae, are further evidence of the significant movement of commodities—ceramic and nonceramic—from the north Aegean toward the south, east, and west.[44]

Thus far I have focused on the Greek pottery imported to Torone, and north Aegean ceramics exported to other parts of Greece and beyond, but Torone was no stranger to Eastern ceramic imports. Fragments of two Levantine juglets dating to the later eighth through earlier seventh century BCE were identified from topsoil on Terrace IV at Torone, just below the Early Iron Age cemetery.[45]

PHOENICIAN AND OTHER LEVANTINE COMMODITIES IN THE NORTH AEGEAN

In dealing with material from sites other than Torone, I begin with pottery and other objects, and then move to the kind of spectacular Eastern commodities mentioned in our literary testimonia. When dealing with Eastern ceramic imports, the issue of provenance, has led both Giorgos Bourogiannis and Antonis Kotsonas to introduce the term "Phoenician-type."[46] The pieces discussed below should largely be viewed as belonging to this type—except, perhaps, for the amphorae from Methone, which are probably from the Phoenician homeland.[47]

There are two inscriptions on pottery from Chalcidice. The first is a Cypriot graffito on an Athenian SOS amphora from Mende.[48] Inscribed on the shoulder of the vessel in the Cypriot syllabary, the graffito was interpreted as a personal name (of the owner of the amphora:]la-si), together with a patronym (Θεμι-[te-mi]), followed by the beginning of a place-name: "se," for Σελαμίνιος, that is, Salamis on Cyprus.[49] If the reading is correct, it might suggest that at least part of the trade of Aegean wine/oil containers within the Aegean was in the hands of Easterners.

Elsewhere in Chalcidice, there is the "Archaic" figurine—described as "an eastern deity wearing a polos"—with a Phoenician inscription from Stageira, in eastern Chalcidice, facing Thasos.[50] Fully published by Daniel Vainstub, the surviving inscription reads:

1. Z MṬ*N*'
2. [.]Š[..]' Ṭ[..]

1. This (is) the offering (of)
2. [.]š[..'ṭ[..][51]

The graffito, in two rows of letters, was interpreted as a dedication by a Phoenician to the deity of one of the two Archaic temples at the site. Vainstub noted the possibility that the inscription may have been Aramaic, but concluded that "the linguistic, philological and cultural criteria, definitely tilt the balance to the conclusion that it is Phoenician."[52] As with the bronze bowl with Phoenician inscription from Knossos (figure 7.1), the figurine could have been made in any number of places, but the dedication could not have been inscribed by just anyone. Farther east, beyond Chalcidice, the cemetery of Abdera has brought to light a distinctive basket-handled amphora dating to the second half of the seventh century BCE of Cypriot or Levantine manufacture.[53]

The northern locale that has most recently yielded no shortage of Eastern material is the Thermaic Gulf, with the finds from Karabournaki and Methone. A summary of the Phoenician and Phoenician-type pottery at Karabournaki would include fragments of the rim and neck of a red-slip trefoil jug. Originally published as Phoenician by the excavators, the fabric of the vessel was considered by Bourogiannis and Kotsonas as a southeast Aegean version of a diagnostic Phoenician shape.[54] The site also yielded body fragments of a characteristic Cypriot Black-on-Red jug, and a fragment of a Cypriot painted open vessel.[55]

On the opposite, western, shore of the Thermaic Gulf, Methone has brought to light a plethora of material, including Eastern imports, together with locally produced Eastern-inspired commodities. First and foremost are the amphorae from the so-called Hypogeion, from the lower fill dating to the late eighth and early seventh century BCE, among which only two are illustrated (figure 7.7a–b). Although such amphorae are found all over the Mediterranean, from the Phoenician homeland and Cyprus, where the majority occur, to Pithecussae (Ischia) and Carthage, and on to coastal Iberia, their features are such that their origin must be Phoenicia.[56] Another Phoenician amphora from Methone was found in the destruction level of the city associated with Philip II's campaigns in 354 BCE (figure 7.7c). In addition to the amphorae, other "hard things" found at Methone include clear evidence for the local working of glass and ivory. Although various glass objects were produced at Methone, including vessels, the bulk of the material from the eighth and seventh

FIGURE 7.7 Three Phoenician amphorae from Methone: (a–b) from the *Hypogeion*, late eighth to early seventh century BCE; (c) from the destruction deposit of Philip II in 354 BCE, (a) ΜΕΘ 2033; (b) ΜΕΘ 2034; (c) ΜΕΘ 3878 (photographs by Ian Coyle).

centuries BCE involves the characteristic three-eyed, triangular beads, many of them production discards, as well as glass rods for the manufacture of glass objects.[57] It was perhaps from Methone that similar beads, found elsewhere in the north—at Anchialos, Sedes, and Kastoria—originated.[58] The ivory, which derives from both elephant and hippopotamus tusk, includes items of personal ornament, appliqués, and the like that were locally made at Methone, with evidence of ivory debitage of the Late Geometric and early seventh century BCE (figure 7.8).[59] The identity of the glass and ivory workers at Methone is not known, but both industries have a long and venerable history in the Levant and Egypt. Whoever worked the ivory, the material was imported from the east—either northern Syria or Egypt—while a similar provenance is assured for the technology, if not the material itself, in the case of glass.

What is interesting about most of these Eastern finds from Methone, Karabournaki, and Torone, are their dates—late eighth or early seventh century, with some of the material extending into the sixth century BCE. The precise date of the figurine from Stageira is difficult to determine, and the basket-handled amphora from Abdera is dated to the second half

FIGURE 7.8 Elephant ivory debitage or manufacturing discard from the West Hill of Methone, showing that imported ivory was worked at the site (photograph by Jeff Vanderpool).

of the seventh century BCE. It would appear, then, that this was the time that Easterners were attracted to the north.

Thus far I have focused on the actual archaeological objects of the north. The growing number of such finds may suggest that they represent the tip of the proverbial iceberg. But the north Aegean has yielded spectacular Eastern commodities in our literary sources, both soft and hard things. In *Iliad* (6.286–96), Hecuba offered to Athena the finest of the Phoenician garments, produced by Sidonian women, which Paris/

Alexandros brought from Sidon to Troy. By offering the most prized of these to the goddess, Hecuba elevated the garment to the ranks of an inalienable possession.[60] In *Iliad* (23.740–45), highly skilled Sidonian men (πολυδαίδαλοι),[61] in the well-known passage of Achilles assembling prizes for the games in honor of Patroclus:

> Then the son of Peleus straightway set forth other prizes for fleetness of foot: a mixing-bowl of silver, richly-wrought; six measures it held, and in beauty it was far the goodliest in all the earth, seeing that Sidonians, well skilled in deft handiwork, had wrought it cunningly, and men of the Phoenicians brought it over the murky deep, and landed it in the harbor, and gave it as a gift to Thoas; and as a ransom for Lycaon, son of Priam, Jason's son Euneos gave it to the warrior Patroclus.[62]

Perhaps the most-discussed of all our sources dealing with the Phoenicians in the north Aegean, is the passage in Herodotus (6.47) that describes Phoenician mines on Thasos. Herodotus saw the mines, of which the most remarkable were those discovered by the Phoenicians. According to his account, the Phoenicians came with Thasos, the son of Phoenix, to colonize the island. The Phoenician mines lie between Koinyra and Ainyra, on the southeast side of the island, facing Samothrace. The place-names framing these mines have often been connected to the Semitic roots for silver and gold (or to the Cypriot king Kinyras).[63] But these are not the only Phoenician mines in the north Aegean. Strabo (14.5.28) credits the earliest exploitation of the gold mines of Mount Pangaion, opposite Thasos, to Cadmus. Elsewhere, Herodotus (2.44) speaks of the cult of Heracles on Thasos, and he even traveled to Tyre, where he visited two temples of Heracles, one dedicated to Thasian Heracles. Pausanias (5.25.12) records a related story: "The Thasians, who were originally Phoenicians and sailed from Tyre in Phoenicia with Agenor's son, Thasos, in search of Europa, dedicated a Heracles at Olympia. . . . I heard in Thasos that they worshipped the same Heracles as the Tyrians."[64] Beyond the cult of Heracles, and even beyond the quest for metals, it has also been suggested that the wine from Oisyme (*Byblinos oinos*), on the mainland opposite Thasos, was introduced by the Phoenicians.[65] Consequently, two of the most lucrative industries of the north, mining and viticulture, were linked to Phoenicians.

The association of Cadmus and Pangaion takes us into a mythical realm, but this is not the only north Aegean myth with a Phoenician pedigree. When discussing the namesake of Torone, both Lycophron (*Alexandra* 115–16) and Nonnus (*Dionysiaca* 21.289) state that Torone was the wife of Proteus, but Stephanus of Byzantium (629.10–13) gives a variant in which Torone was either the daughter—not wife—of Proteus, or else the daughter of Poseidon by Phoinice.[66] Similarly, Stephanus (s.v. Galepsos), when dealing with Galepsos in Chalcidice, also has Phoenician mythical figures for the name of the site, and Graham has suggested that the name of Abdera had a Phoenician origin.[67]

THE PHRYGIANS AND TROJANS OF THE NORTH AEGEAN

Greeks, from various parts of the Aegean, and Phoenicians, together with Cypriots and North Syrians, were not the only traders, prospectors, and inhabitants of the north. Herodotus (7.73) gives us the north Aegean ancestry of the Phrygians: "This people, according to the Macedonian account, were known as Briges during the period when they were Europeans and lived in Macedonia, and changed their name at the same time as, by migrating to Asia, they changed their country." What is interesting about Herodotus's testimony is that Phrygian, although an Indo-European language and in spite of its geographic location, does not belong with the Anatolian subgroup of Indo-European languages, like Hittite or Lycian, but is much more closely connected with Greek.[68] In a show of erudition, Plato (*Cratylus* 410–14) has Socrates cite several words that are common in both Greek and Phrygian, not least some of the most basic words of any core vocabulary: fire (*pyr*), water (*hydōr*), dog (*kyōn*). More recently, Sandra Blakely has collected material related to Phrygians and Phoenicians on the north Aegean island of Samothrace.[69] Her arguments revolve around several points. The first is the possibility that the toponym Dindymene, inscribed on a sherd from Samothrace, may refer to an Anatolian—Phrygian—mountain.[70] The second is that the Cabiri, who number among the gods of the rites of Samothrace, are Phrygians according to a variety of ancient sources.[71] Finally, a number of Byzantine lexicographers derive the name of the Cabiri from Mount Kabeiros in Phrygia.[72]

A connected issue is the relationship of the Phrygian language to that of the Thracians living along the north coast of the Aegean. As Roger Woodard has noted, "the Phrygian language does show certain similarities to Thracian, and some linguists have argued for linking the two in a single linguistic unit (Thraco-Phrygian)."[73] The appropriateness of such a subgrouping remains uncertain, largely on account of the dearth of conclusive evidence,[74] but it is in keeping with the testimony of Herodotus. More to the point, whatever language the Trojans actually spoke, the Greeks of the Classical era certainly believed that they spoke Phrygian.

Greek mythology has Troy as a locale where Greek and Phrygian letters (Φρύγια γράμματα) comingled. The dramatis personae are none other than Odysseus and Palamedes. Although the latter figured prominently in the *Cypria,* there is little in that epic about him and letters.[75] The evidence is in Apollodorus's *Bibliotheca* (Vatican Epitome 3.8), where "Odysseus 'planted' in the Greek camp a letter (δέλτος) written in Phrygian, as though to Palamedes from Priam." The letter fell into the hands of Agamemnon, and the fate of Palamedes was sealed.[76] It is telling that "Phrygian" in ancient sources often means "Trojan."

The close connection between Greek and Phrygian to which I alluded goes deeper still, especially in the close similarity of their vowels, as I have argued elsewhere.[77] Indeed, as a number of scholars have noted, the overlap of the shared vowel letters in both Phrygian and Greek seems to rule out an adoption of the vowels independently from one another: "Either the Phrygian script was adopted from the Phoenician and subsequently the Greek from the Phrygian, or vice versa."[78] There is thus a confluence of evidence—the growing number of early alphabetic inscriptions at Methone,[79] the similarity of Phrygian and Greek vowels, the testimony of Herodotus—that places the adoption and adaptation of the alphabet squarely in the Aegean. Any number of places in the Aegean thus emerge as contenders, but the players involved point to the north Aegean, where Greeks and Phrygians and Phoenicians and Trojans were in close contact. Whatever their precise relationships, here was a locale where Semitic, Greek, and Phrygian letters may have coalesced.

Beyond the myths and the letters, the connections between Phrygia and Troy and Greece take on an important material dimension. There are, first of all, those things that Keith DeVries noted, such as Herodotus's (1.14) claim that the splendid wooden throne at Delphi was a gift of Midas, the Phrygian king of the late eighth–seventh centuries BCE, and stories traceable to the fourth century BCE had Midas taking a wife from the East Greek city of Cyme. Phrygian fibulae and bronze bowls of the eighth–seventh centuries BCE have been recovered from Greek sanctuaries in eastern and mainland Greece, and at Gordion, the Phrygian capital, fragmentary Greek pottery dating to the decades before and after 700 BCE is abundant.[80] As for Trojans and Greeks, there is a considerable quantity of Greek pottery in various contexts of Troy Settlement VIII, including East Greek—broadly defined, especially Aeolian and related Gray Wares—Attic, Corinthian, and various other wares, such as G 2–3 ware, and Greek inscriptions on pottery.[81] Neutron activation analysis has shown G 2–3 ware to be made in the Troad, and it has been found in early habitation levels at Thasos, Samothrace, Lesbos, Tenedos, and

Lemnos,[82] and in Chalcidice and elsewhere in the north Aegean. What also links Early Iron Age Troy with the Aegean, both north and south, are the paved stone circles, no fewer than twenty-eight in Troy Settlement VIII,[83] which are similar to those in the Argolid (Mycenae, Asine, Prosymna, Argos), Grotta and Tsikalario on Naxos, and Mende in Chalcidice.[84]

Conclusion

The in-betweeness of the early first millennium—so nicely framed by Broodbank's *The Making of the Middle Sea*—coupled with the fact that part of this period in the Aegean has been considered a "Dark Age," has obscured a complex, but at the same time, nuanced story. The north Aegean in particular, often viewed as a topos somehow beyond the domain of Greece proper, emerges as a place as intimately connected as any region of the central and southern Aegean, a place without Mycenaean palaces and one where the idea of a Dark Age borders on the jejune. By incorporating the cultural powerhouses that were Troy and Phrygia into the story of the north Aegean, we not only see a more complex set of understudied connections, but also that this connectivity did not end at the Aegean shoreline or at modern political borders. One primary difference of the north Aegean from central and southern Greece is its entanglement with an entire mainland—and the many different peoples, ideas, and ways of doing things that it contained—an entanglement extending through a series of navigable rivers (the Haliacmon, Loudias, Axios, Strymon, and Nestos) throughout the Balkans and well into central Europe, an expanse traversing even more modern borders. The incorporation of Troy and Phrygia as major north Aegean nodes brings not only Anatolia into play and the resources of the land beyond the coast of Asia Minor, but those of the Black Sea, another corrupting sea often overlooked.

To be sure, the north Aegean is a specific geographical and ecological context, one that fueled its own entanglements between cultures in the region, and with the greater Mediterranean. Moreover, the growing numbers of high-value Levantine imports, together with low-value commodities like pottery from all over the Aegean and beyond, points to connections that are both elite and non-elite—processes that are both top-down and bottom-up. More to the point, the interactions were never one-way, for the north Aegean was replete with commodities of real value—timber, textiles, and above all, metals; those from central and southern Greece and those from the eastern Mediterranean who ventured into this realm returned home richer for their efforts. Whereas the Athenians, Euboeans, and Easterners peddled their pottery and trinkets (*athyrmata*), the northerners dealt with commodities of much higher value and fungibility. The north Aegean was not a passive landscape to be exploited by enterprising southerners or Phoenicians or others, but an active player in cultural contacts across many periods. The north Aegean was thus a veritable middle ground where Greeks, from all over the Greek world, Phoenicians, North Syrians, Cypriots, Phrygians, and Trojans, together with numerous local tribes or groups like the Macedonians, Thessalians, Epirotes, Illyrians, Briges, Bottiaei, and many others, interacted and did business together in myriad ways—a small world that was part of a much larger Mediterranean world.

Notes

1. Paraphrased from the original, which begins: "*Living in Corfu . . .*" The passage is taken from the end of the opening section of the book, "The Speech for the Defense." Emphasis added. I am grateful to James Osborne and Jonathan Hall for inviting me to contribute to the conference and this publication.

2. For overviews and periodization, see, most recently, Sarah C. Murray, *The Collapse of the Mycenaean Economy: Imports, Trade, and Institutions, 1300–700 BCE* (Cambridge: Cambridge University Press, 2017); John K. Papadopoulos and Evelyn Lord Smithson, *The Early Iron Age: The Cemeteries (The Athenian Agora XXXVI)* (Princeton, NJ: American School of Classical Studies at Athens, 2017), 18–34; Antonis Kotsonas, "The Politics of Periodization and the Archaeology of Early Greece," *American Journal of Archaeology* 120 (2016): 239–70.

3. Peregrine Horden and Nicholas Purcell, *The Corrupting Sea: A Study of Mediterranean History* (Malden, MA: Blackwell, 2000); and Cyprian Broodbank, *The Making of the Middle Sea: A History of the Mediterranean from the Beginning to the Emergence of the Classical World* (Oxford: Oxford University Press, 2013), 445–505. For the problematic nature of the term "protohistoric," see John K. Papadopoulos, "Greek Protohistories," *World Archaeology* 50, no. 5 (2018): 690–705, doi: 10.1080/004338243.2015.1568294.

4. Fernand Braudel, *The Mediterranean and the Mediterranean World in the Age of Philip II*, trans. Siân Reynolds, 3 vols. (New York: Harper and Row, 1972 [1966]).

5. Robin Osborne, "Early Greek Colonization? The Nature of Greek Settlement in the West," in *Ancient Greece: New Approaches and New Evidence*, ed. Nick Fisher and Hans van Wees (London: Duckworth, 1998), 251–69; John K. Papadopoulos, *The Early Iron Age Cemetery at Torone* (Los Angeles: Cotsen Institute of Archaeology at UCLA, 2005), 571–80.

6. J. Nicolas Coldstream and Hector W. Catling, eds., *Knossos North Cemetery: Early Greek Tombs* (London: British School at Athens, 1996), 30, 563–64, fig. 157 (Tomb J f1).

7. Gail L. Hoffman, *Imports and Immigrants: Near Eastern Contacts with Iron Age Crete* (Ann Arbor: University of Michigan Press, 1997).

8. Hoffman, *Imports and Immigrants*, 153–72, 176–89; John Boardman, "The Khaniale Tekke Tombs, II," *Annual of the British School at Athens* 62 (1967): 57–75 (for the Eastern goldsmith at Knossos).

9. Joseph W. Shaw, "Phoenicians in Southern Crete," *American Journal of Archaeology* 93 (1989): 165–83; Hoffman, *Imports and Immigrants*, 172–76.

10. John K. Papadopoulos, "Owls to Athens: Imported Pottery in Early Iron Age Athens," in *Pots, Workshops and Early Iron Age Society: Function and Role of Ceramics in Early Greece*, ed. Vicky Vlachou (Brussels: CReA-Patrimoine, 2015), 201–15.

11. Coldstream and Catling, *Knossos North Cemetery*, 393–409.

12. James K. Brock, *Fortetsa: Early Greek Tombs near Knossos* (Cambridge: Cambridge University Press, 1957); Papadopoulos, "Owls to Athens," 201–3.

13. Mervyn R. Popham, Evi Touloupa, and L. Hugh Sackett, "The Hero of Lefandi," *Antiquity* 56 (1982): 169–74; Mervyn R. Popham, Petros G. Calligas, and L. Hugh Sackett, eds., *Lefkandi II: The Protogeometric Building at Toumba*, part 2, *The Excavation, Architecture and Finds* (Oxford: British School at Athens, 1993), 81–96.

14. See Joan Aruz, Sarah B. Graff, and Yelena Rakic, *Assyria to Iberia at the Dawn of the Classical Age* (New York: Metropolitan Museum of Art, 2014), 32–37.

15. See Mervyn R. Popham, L. Hugh Sackett, and Petros G. Themelis, eds., *Lefkandi I: The Iron Age Settlement and the Cemeteries* (Oxford: British School at Athens, 1979–1980), 218, pls. 233–35; Mervyn R. Popham and Irene S. Lemos, *Lefkandi III: The Toumba Cemetery; The Excavations of 1981, 1984, 1986, and 1992–4; The Plates* (Oxford: British School at Athens, 1996), pls. 132–35.

16. Popham and Lemos, *Lefkandi III*, pls. 133, 135. For engraved bowls, see Glenn Markoe, *Phoenician Bronze and Silver Bowls from Cyprus and the Mediterranean* (Berkeley: University of California Press, 1985).

17. Popham, Sackett, and Themelis, *Lefkandi I*, 347–48.

18. Richard W. V. Catling and Irene S. Lemos, *Lefkandi II: The Protogeometric Building at Toumba*, part 1, *The Pottery* (Oxford: British School at Athens, 1990), 86–90; for the amphora, see pls. 44, 80.

19. Catling and Lemos, *Lefkandi II*, part 1, 89–90.

20. Popham, Sackett, and Themelis, *Lefkandi I*, 348–50.

21. Popham, Sackett, and Themelis, *Lefkandi I*, 350–53.

22. Mervyn R. Popham, Evi Touloupa, L. Hugh Sackett, "Further Excavation of the Toumba Cemetery at Lefkandi, 1982," *Annual of the British School at Athens* 77 (1982): 213–48; Popham and Lemos, *Lefkandi III*; see also Polyxeni Adam-Veleni and Evangelia Stefani, eds., *Greeks and Phoenicians at the Mediterranean Crossroads* (Thessaloniki: Hellenic Ministry of Culture, 2012), 119–20, figs. 29–33.

23. Mervyn R. Popham and Irene S. Lemos, "A Euboean Warrior Trader," *Oxford Journal of Archaeology* 14 (1995): 151–57; Popham and Lemos, *Lefkandi III*, pls. 26, 74–79.

24. Popham and Lemos, "Euboean Warrior Trader," 151.

25. Carla M. Antonaccio, "Warriors, Traders, Ancestors: The 'Heroes' of Lefkandi," in *Images of Ancestors*, ed. Jakob Munk Højte (Aarhus: Aarhus University Press, 2002), 13–42, esp. 28–29 (*proxenos*); Nino Luraghi, "Traders, Pirates, Warriors: The Protohistory of Greek Mercenary Soldiers in the Eastern Mediterranean," *Phoenix* 60 (2006): 21–47, esp. 34 (pirate trader); see also John H. Kroll, "Early Iron Age Balance Weights at Lefkandi, Euboea," *Oxford Journal of Archaeology* 27 (2008): 37–48.

26. John K. Papadopoulos, "Phantom Euboians," *Journal of Mediterranean Archaeology* 10, no. 2 (1997): 191–219; Papadopoulos, "'Phantom Euboians': A Decade On," in *Euboea and Athens: Proceedings of a Conference in Memory of Malcolm B.*

Wallace, Athens 26–27 June 2009, ed. David W. Rupp and Jonathan E. Tomlinson (Athens: Canadian Institute in Greece, 2011), 113–33.

27. Karl Kübler, *Kerameikos*, vol. V, part 1, *Die Nekropole des 10. bis 8. Jahrhunderts* (Berlin: Walter de Gruyter, 1954), 201–3, fig. 5.

28. Evelyn Lord Smithson, "The Tomb of a Rich Athenian Lady, ca. 850 B.C.," *Hesperia* 37 (1968): 77–116; Papadopoulos and Smithson, *Early Iron Age (Athenian Agora XXXVI)*, 171–76, figs. 2.98–2.100; J. Nicolas Coldstream, "The Rich Lady of the Areiopagos and Her Contemporaries: A Tribute in Memory of Evelyn Lord Smithson," *Hesperia* 64 (1995): 391–403, esp. 397; for the ivory "beinplätchen" from Grave 41, see Kübler, *Kerameikos*, vol. V, part 1, 236, pl. 161. I do not include here the five remarkable ivory statuettes dating to ca. 730 BCE depicting women wearing a *polos*, referred to as the Dipylon ivories, because general consensus has them as belonging to a Greek Geometric idiom. This said, the material itself is certainly an import; see, among others, J. Nicolas Coldstream, *Geometric Greece: 900–700 BC* (London: Routledge, 2004), 110.

29. Fully discussed in Papadopoulos, "Owls to Athens," 208–13.

30. Irene J. Winter, "Homer's Phoenicians: History, Ethnography, or Literary Trope? [A Perspective on Early Orientalism]," in *The Ages of Homer: A Tribute to Emily Townsend Vermeule*, ed. Jane. B. Carter and Sarah. P. Morris (Austin: University of Texas Press, 1995), 247–71.

31. Papadopoulos, "Owls to Athens," 208 (Asine and Aegina); for the rich Eastern material from Rhodes and Cos, see J. Nicolas Coldstream, "The Phoenicians of Ialysos," *Bulletin of the Institute of Classical Studies* 16 (1969): 1–8, and Giorgos Bourogiannis, "The Black-on-Red Pottery Found in Cos: From Pots to Trade or Immigrants," *Annali dell'Istituto Universitario Orientali di Napoli* 7 (2000): 9–23; Bourogiannis, "Cypriot and Phoenician Pottery in the Aegean in the Early Historic Period: Commercial Networks and the Problem of the Black-on-Red Ware" (PhD diss., University of Athens, 2007, in Greek); Bourogiannis, "Eastern Influence on Rhodian Geometric Pottery: Foreign Elements and Local Receptiveness," in *Cyprus and the East Aegean: Intercultural Contacts from 3000 to 500 BC; An International Archaeological Symposium held at Pythagoreion, Samos, October 17th–18th 2008*, ed. Vassos Karageorghis and Ourania Kouka (Nicosia: A. G. Leventis Foundation, 2009), 114–30; and Bourogiannis, "Instances of Semitic Writing from Geometric and Archaic Greek Contexts: An Unintelligible Way to Literacy?," in *Transformation and Crisis in the Mediterranean: "Identity" and Interculturality in the Levant and Phoenician West during the 12th–8th Centuries BCE*, ed. G. Garbati and T. Pedrizzi (Pisa: Fabrizio Serra Editore, 2015), 159–70.

32. John K. Papadopoulos, "Torone and Its Colonial Experiences: Thoughts on the Early History of the North Aegean," in *Argilos, 25 Années de Recherches: Organisation de la Ville et de la Campagne dans les colonies du Nord de l'Égée. VIIIe–IIIe siècles av. n.è, (Argilos 3). Actes du colloque de Thessalonique, 25-27 mai 2017*, ed. Zisis Bonias and Jacques Perreault (Athens: The Canadian Institute in Athens, 2021).

33. Alexander John Graham, "Pre-colonial Contacts: Questions and Problems," in *Greek Colonists and Native Populations: Proceedings of the First Australian Congress of Classical Archaeology Held in Honour of Emeritus Professor A. D. Trendall, Sydney 9–14 July 1985*, ed. Jean-Paul Descoeudres (Oxford: Oxford University Press, 1990), 45–60, quote on 45.

34. Among others, see Osborne, "Early Greek Colonization?"; Nicholas Purcell, "Review of *The Archaeology of Greek Colonization*, edited by Gocha Tsetskhladze and Francesco de Angelis," *Antiquity* 71 (1997): 500–502; and Nino Luraghi, "Partage du sol et occupation du territoire dans les colonies grecques d'Occident au VIIIe siècle," in *Les moyens d'expression du pouvoir dans les sociétés anciennes*, ed. M. Broze, P.-J. Dehon, P. Talon, T. Van Compernolle, and E. Warenbol (Louvain: Peeters, 1996), 213–19.

35. Alexander Graham, "Patterns in Early Greek Colonisation," *Journal of Hellenic Studies* 91 (1971): 35–47, quote on 35.

36. Papadopoulos, "Torone and Its Colonial Experiences." An interesting type specimen is the mound at Sindos/Anchialos on the Thermaic Gulf coast, excavated by Michalis Tiverios, "The Ancient Settlement in the Anchialos-Sindos Double Trapeza: Seven Years (1990–1996) of Archaeological Work," in *Euboica: L'Eubea e la presenza euboica in Calcidica e in Occidente*, ed. Michel Bats and Bruno d'Agostino (Naples: Centre Jean Bérard Istituto Universitario orientale, 1998), 243–53, and fully published by Stephanos Gimatzidis, *Die Stadt Sindos: Eine Siedlung von der späten Bronze- bis zur klassischen Zeit am Thermaischen Golf in Makedonien* (Rahden: Verlag Marie Leidorf, 2010). The site has produced veritable mother lodes of Euboean pottery, yet there is no literary reference that it was ever a colony or in any way connected to Euboea.

37. For Troy/Ilion in the Early Iron Age, see, most recently, C. Aslan, M. Lawall, and K. Lynch, *Troy Excavation Project Final Reports: The West Sanctuary at Troy: Iron Age through Classical* (Bonn: Rudolf Habelt, 2019).

38. Alexander Graham, *Colony and Mother City in Ancient Greece* (Manchester: Manchester University Press, 1964).

39. See Nicholas G. L. Hammond, "The Chalcidians and 'Apollonia of the Thraceward Ionians,'" *Annual of the British School at Athens* 90 (1995): 307–15; John K. Papadopoulos, "Euboians in Macedonia? A Closer Look," *Oxford Journal of Archaeology* 15 (1996): 151–81.

40. Papadopoulos, *Early Iron Age Cemetery at Torone*, 584; Simon Hornblower, "Thucydides and 'Chalkidic' Torone (IV.110.1)," *Oxford Journal of Archaeology* 16 (1997): 177–86; and John K. Papadopoulos, "Archaeology, Myth-History and the Tyranny of the Text: Chalkidike, Torone and Thucydides," *Oxford Journal of Archaeology* 18 (1999): 377–94, esp. 379.

41. Papadopoulos, *Early Iron Age Cemetery at Torone*, 482–93.

42. See Papadopoulos, "Owls to Athens," 206–8 for references. For possible northern and Cypriot pottery from Naxos, see Xenia Charalambidou, "Ceramics, Cultural Interactions and Influences on Naxos," in *ΤΕΡΨΙΣ: Studies in Mediterranean Archaeology in Honour of Nota Kourou*, ed. Vicky Vlachou and Anastasia Gadolou (Brussels: CReA-Patrimoine, 2017), 375–92, esp. 381–82, figs. 7–8.

43. Richard W. V. Catling, "A Typology of the Protogeometric and Subprotogeometric Pottery from Troia and Its Aegean Context," *Studia Troica* 8 (1998): 151–87; and for north Syria, see Paul Courbin, "Fragments d'amphores protogéométriques grecques à Bassit (Syrie)," *Hesperia* 62 (1993): 95–113. For recent overviews, see Manthos Bessios, Yiannis Tzifopoulos, and Antonis Kotsonas, *Μεθώνη Πιερίας 1: Επιγραφές, χαράγματα και εμπορικά σύμβολα στη γεωμετρική και αρχαϊκή κεραμική από το Υπόγειο της Μεθώνης Πιερίας στη Μακεδονία* (Thessaloniki: Ministry of Education, Instruction, and Religion: Center for the Greek Language, 2012), 150–62; Gimatzidis, *Die Stadt Sindos*, 252–74.

44. Most recently, see Catherine E. Pratt, *Oil, Wine, and the Cultural Economy of Ancient Greece: From the Bronze Age to the Archaic Era* (New York: Cambridge University Press, 2021). See also Pratt, "The SOS Amphora: An Update," *Annual of the British School at Athens* 110 (2015): 213–45.

45. Richard Fletcher, "Fragments of Levantine Iron Age Pottery in Chalcidice," *Mediterranean Archaeology* 21 (2008): 3–7. Fletcher considers one of the fragments Cypriot, the origin of the other less certain.

46. These are Phoenician, Cypriot, or Levantine versions of shapes produced in the southeast Aegean, in Rhodes or Cos; see Bourogiannis, "Cypriot and Phoenician Pottery in the Aegean," esp. 344, 430, 433, and 438; Antonis Kotsonas, "Η ενεπίγραφη κεραμική του 'Υπογείου': Προέλευση, τυπολογεία, χρονολόγηση και ερμενεία," in Bessios, Tzifopoulos, and Kotsonas, *Μεθώνη Πιερίας 1*, 238, 303n1620; and Fletcher, "Fragments of Levantine Iron Age Pottery," 7n29.

47. Athena Athanassiadou, entries on Phoenician amphoras from Methone, in Adam-Veleni and Stefani, *Greeks and Phoenicians*, 161–62, and see further below.

48. Ioulia Vokotopoulou and Anastasios-Phoivos Christides, "A Cypriot Graffito on an SOS Amphora from Mende, Chalcidice," *Kadmos* 34 (1995): 5–12.

49. Vokotopoulou and Christides, "Cypriot Graffito."

50. Konstantinos Sismanidis, *Ancient Stageira: Birthplace of Aristotle* (Athens: Ministry of Culture, 2003), 27, 90.

51. Daniel Vainstub, "A Phoenician Votive Inscription on a Figurine from Stageira and the Root *ṬN*," in *Phéniciens d'Orient et d'Occidente: Mélanges Josette Elayi*, ed. André Lemair et al. (Paris: Jean Maisonneuvre, 2014), 345–50, esp. 345.

52. Vainstub, "Phoenician Votive Inscription," 349.

53. Eudokia Skarlatidou, *Το αρχαϊκό νεκροταφείο των Αβδήρων* (Thessaloniki: Ziti, 2010), 173–75, fig. 269; Pierre Dupont and Eudokia Skarlatidou, "Archaic Transport Amphora from the First Necropolis of Clazomenian Abdera," in *Archaic Pottery of the Northern Aegean and its Periphery (700–480 B.C.)*, ed. Michalis A. Tiverios et al. (Thessaloniki: Ziti, 2012), 260, 263, fig. 31.

54. Michalis A. Tiverios, Eleni Manakidou, and Despoina Tsiafaki, "Ανασκαφικές έρευνες στο Καραμπουνάκι το 2001," *To Archaiologiko Ergo sti Makedonia kai Thrake* 15 (2001): 255–62, esp. 259, 262, fig. 8; Michalis A. Tiverios, "Οι πανεπιστημιακές ανασκαφές στο Καραμπουρνάκι Θεσσαλονίκης και η παρουσία των Φοινίκων στο βόρειο Αιγαίο," in *Το Αιγαίο στην Πρώιμη Εποχή του Σιδήρου*, ed. N.C. Stampolidis and A. Giannikouri (Athens: University of Crete and Ministry of Culture, 2004), 295–306, esp. 297, fig. 4; Bourogiannis, "Cypriot and Phoenician Pottery in the Aegean," 344; and Kotsonas, "Η ενεπίγραφη κεραμική του 'Υπογείου,'" 303n1620.

55. Michalis A. Tiverios, Eleni Manakidou, and Despoina Tsiafaki, "Ανασκαφικές έρευνες στο Καραμπουνάκι κατά το 2004: Ο αρχαίος οικισμός," *To Archaiologiko Ergo sti Makedonia kai Thrake* 18 (2004): 337–44, esp. 341, 344, fig. 8; Michalis A. Tiverios, "Εισαγμένη κεραμική στο Θερμαϊκό κόλπο και την Ιβηρική χερσόνησο-αργανθώνιος (παρατηρήσεις στο πρώιμό εμπόριο κεραμικής)," in Vlachou and Gadolou, *ΤΕΡΨΙΣ*, 419–34, esp. 422, fig. 5β.

56. Athanassiadou, entries on Phoenician amphoras from Methone, 161–62; and Alexandra Kasseri, "Phoenician Trade Amphorae from Methone, Pieria," in *Κεραμέως παῖδες: Αντίδωρο στον Καθηγητή Μιχάλη Τιβέριο από τους μαθητές του*, ed. Eurydike Kephalidou and Despoina Tsiafaki (Thessaloniki: Etaireia Andrion Epistimonon, 2012), 299–308, esp. 307, fig. 3 for their distribution.

57. Despoina Ignatiadou, "Early Glass in Methone," in *Annales du 19e Congrès de l'Association Internationale pour l'Histoire du Verrem Piran 2012*, ed. Irena Lazar (Piran: Koper, 2015), 81–88.

58. Gimatzidis, *Die Stadt Sindos*, 298–99 (Anchialos-Sindos); Despoina Ignatiadou and Kalliopi Chatzinikolaou, "Γυάλινες χάντρες από το αρχαίο νεκροταφείο Θέρμης (Σέδες), Θεσσαλονίκης," in *Το γυαλί από την αρχαιότητα ως σήμερα*, ed. Petros Themelis (Athens: Etaireia Messeniakon Spoudon, 2002), 57–72; and Ignatiadou, "Early Glass in Methone," 82.

59. Adam DiBattista, "The Production of Worked Animal Objects at Ancient Methone (Late Geometric and Archaic)" (MA thesis, University of California, Los Angeles, 2016); and DiBattista, "Transformations of Animal Materials in Early Greece" (PhD thesis, University of California, Los Angeles, 2021).

60. In the terms of Annette B. Weiner, *Inalienable Possessions: The Paradox of Keeping-while-Giving* (Berkeley: University of California Press, 1992).

61. Sarah P. Morris, *Daidalos and the Origins of Greek Art* (Princeton, NJ: Princeton University Press, 1992).

62. Homer, *Iliad*, trans. A. T. Murray, Loeb Classical Library (Cambridge, MA: Harvard University Press, 1957).

63. For discussion and references, see Morris, *Daidalos*, 143–46.

64. Pausanias, *Guide to Greece*, trans. Peter Levi (Harmondsworth: Penguin, 1979).

65. François Salviat, "Vignes et vins de Maronée à Mendé," in *Μνήμη Δ. Λαζαρίδη: Πόλις και χώρα στην αρχαία Μακεδονία και Θράκη*, ed. Ch. Koukouli-Chrysanthaki and O. Picard (Thessaloniki: Ministry of Culture, 1990), 457–76.

66. Alexander Cambitoglou, John K. Papadopoulos, and Olwen Tudor Jones, eds., *Torone I: The Excavations of 1975, 1976, and 1978* (Athens: Athens Archaeological Society, 2001), 41, with references.

67. Alexander Graham, "Abdera and Teos," *Journal of Hellenic Studies* 112 (1992): 44–73.

68. Claude Brixhe and M. Lejeune, *Corpus des inscriptions paléophrygiennes* (Paris: Éditions recherches sur les civilisations, 1984); Claude Brixhe, "Phrygian," in *The Cambridge Encyclopedia of the World's Ancient Languages* (Cambridge: Cambridge University Press, 2004), 777–78.

69. Sandra Blakely, "Daimones in the Thracian Sea," *Archive für Religionsgeschichte* 14, no. 1 (2012): 155–82, esp. 163–64.

70. Sandra Blakely (personal communication). Cf. Claude Brixhe, "Zone et Samothrace: Lueurs sur la langue thrace et nouveau chapitre de la grammaire compare?," *Comptes rendus de l'Academie des inscription et Belles-Lettres* 150 (2006): 121–46.

71. The *scholia* to Aristophanes, *Peace*, 177–78; the *scholia* to Apollonios of Rhodes 1.197; Nonnos 3.7, 3.194, 43.307–313; and the *scholia* to Libanius, *Oratio* 14.64.

72. Cf. Robert S. P. Beekes "The Origin of the Kabeiroi," *Mnemosyne* 157 (2004): 465–77; Chryssa Karadima and Nora Dimitrova, "An Epitaph for an Initiate at Samothrace and Eleusis," *Chiron* 33 (2003): 335–45 (Kabeiroi in Samothrace); and Blakely, "Daimones," 163–64 (for Phoenicians on Samothrace).

73. Roger D. Woodard, ed., *The Cambridge Encyclopedia of the World's Ancient Languages* (Cambridge: Cambridge University Press, 2004), 12.

74. Brixhe, "Phrygian," 777–88.

75. *Cypria* 5, 12, and cf. fragment 27; *Returns* (Νόστοι), 11; see also Lilian Hamilton Jeffery, "ΑΡΧΑΙΑ ΓΡΑΜΜΑΤΑ: Some Ancient Greek Views," in *Europa: Studien zur Geschichte und Epigraphik der frühen Aegaeis; Festschrift für Ernst Grumach*, ed. William C. Brice (Berlin: De Gruyter, 1967), 152–66.

76. Jeffery, "ΑΡΧΑΙΑ ΓΡΑΜΜΑΤΑ," 152; the relevant passage in Apollodorus, reads: "Having taken a Phrygian prisoner, Odysseus compelled him to write a letter of treasonable purport ostensibly sent by Priam to Palamedes; having buried gold in the quarters of Palamedes, he dropped the letter in the camp. Agamemnon read the letter, found the gold, and delivered up Palamedes to the allies to be stoned as a traitor" (translated by James Frazer).

77. John K. Papadopoulos, "The Early History of the Greek Alphabet: New Evidence from Eretria and Methone," *Antiquity* 90 (2016): 1238–45; Papadopoulos, "To Write and to Paint: More Early Iron Age Potters' Marks in the Aegean," in *Graphê in Late Geometric and Protoarchaic Methone, Macedonia (ca. 700 BCE)*, ed. Jenny Strauss Clay, Irad Malkin, and Yannis Z. Tzifopoulos (Berlin: De Gruyter, 2017), 36–104.

78. Benjamin Sass, *The Alphabet at the Turn of the Millennium: The West Semitic Alphabet ca. 1150–850 BCE; The Antiquity of the Arabian, Greek and Phrygian Alphabets* (Tel Aviv: Emery and Claire Yass Publications, 2005), 147.

79. Bessios, Tzifopoulos, and Kotsonas, *Μεθώνη Πιερίας 1*.

80. Keith DeVries, "Greeks and Phrygians in the Early Iron Age," in *From Athens to Gordion: The Papers of a Memorial Symposium for Rodney S. Young*, ed. Keith DeVries (Philadelphia: University of Pennsylvania Museum of Archaeology and Anthropology, 1980), 33–49; for an earlier, 800 BCE date, for Phrygian letters, see C. Brian Rose and G. Darbyshire, eds., *The New Chronology of Iron Age Gordion* (Philadelphia: University of Pennsylvania Museum, 2011).

81. Carl W. Blegen et al., *Troy: Excavations Conducted by the University of Cincinnati, 1932–1938*, vol. 4, *Settlements VIIa, VIIb, and VIII* (Princeton, NJ: Princeton University Press, 1958), 251–58, pls. 293–316. For G 2–3 Ware, see Petya Ilieva, "G 2–3 Ware: The Sub(proto)geometric Tradition of the Northeastern Aegean," in *Pottery Workshops in the Northeastern Aegean (8th–early 5th c. BC)*, ed. Polyxeni Adam-Veleni, Eurydike Kephalidou, and Despoina Tsiafaki (Thessaloniki: Archaeological Museum, 2013), 123–31; and Petya Ilieva, "Regional Standardization and Local Variation: The Case of the North Aegean G 2–3 Ware," in *Understanding Standardization and Variation in Mediterranean Ceramics, Mid 2nd to Late 1st Millennium BC* (Leuven: Peeters, 2014), 85–96.

82. Charles Brian Rose, *The Archaeology of Greek and Roman Troy* (Cambridge: Cambridge University Press, 2014), 53.

83. Blegen et al., *Troy*, 274–75, figs. 156–59, 161–67, 369, 370; Rose, *Greek and Roman Troy*, 50–51, fig. 2.4.

84. Carla M. Antonaccio, *An Archaeology of Ancestors: Tomb Cult and Hero Cult in Early Greece* (Boston: Rowman and Littlefield, 1995), 199–207; Papadopoulos and Smithson, *Early Iron Age (Athenian Agora XXXVI)*, 634–35.

✷ CHAPTER 8 ✷

Anatolia, the Aegean, and the Neo-Assyrian Empire

Material Connections

ANN C. GUNTER

Since the late nineteenth century, Phoenicians have been widely viewed as the chief intermediaries between the Iron Age Aegean and the Neo-Assyrian Empire.[1] An ever-expanding wealth of archaeological evidence surely affirms the significant role they played in cultural interaction between Greece and both the coastal and interior Near East, along with the objects in multiple styles they transported over vast distances (see Marian Feldman, chapter 4, and Carolina López-Ruiz, chapter 2 in this volume). Yet scholars have also long been aware of an independent, non-Levantine historical figure who was clearly tied in the late eighth century both to Greek and Neo-Assyrian political and cultural spheres. For more than a century, the Mita named in several inscriptions of Sargon II (721–705 BCE) has been identified with the Midas of Phrygia known from classical sources, including Herodotus and Strabo.[2] In his Greek persona, Midas dedicated a throne to the Apollo sanctuary at Delphi, married an Aeolian princess, and accumulated legendary wealth, among other notable accomplishments.[3] Assyrian royal inscriptions and correspondence dating to a decade within Sargon's reign, between 718 and 709 BCE, attest a Mita, king of Mushki, reportedly allied with rulers of the central Anatolian kingdom of Tabal, north Syria, and Urartu. During this period, according to Assyrian sources, Mita emerged as a determined and pivotal player in anti-Assyrian coalition efforts over a wide geographical region. Assyria eventually blocked his attempt to expand Phrygian power into southern Anatolia and defeated his allies, although Mita himself remained beyond its reach. In 709 BCE, Mita sent an envoy to the Assyrian governor in Que (Cilicia), as acknowledged in an enthusiastic response from Sargon: "Without a battle or anything, the Phrygian has given us his word and become our ally!"[4]

Phrygia's material interaction with the Aegean and Neo-Assyrian spheres engages with issues of Iron Age connectivity in two principal ways. First, the presence of Phrygian-style objects in Archaic Greek sanctuaries has generally been examined in conjunction with the broader "Orientalizing" phenomenon (see James Osborne and Jonathan Hall, chapter 1 in this volume), whereby objects fashioned in Egyptian and various regionally defined Near Eastern styles reached the eastern Aegean and the Greek mainland—and the central and western Mediterranean—through commercial exchange, elite social networks, and the long-distance travels of merchants and soldiers. Both in the Aegean world and farther west, artisans responded by imitating and adapting these imports and introducing their forms and decoration to different media, producing Orientalizing styles in ceramics, metalwork, and ivory. The Orientalizing movement has been understood primarily as a maritime affair dependent on Greek and Phoenician actors, with a separate (and less significant) overland component that drew in Urartu and Phrygia, and perhaps also northwestern Iran.[5] Moreover, the classical tradition concerning gifts to Delphi by Midas of Phrygia, and later by Lydian kings, has tended to reinforce a reconstruction of special relationships between these Anatolian rulers and Greek sanctuaries, bolstering the notion that ties with the Phrygian kingdom operated independently from other networks linking the Aegean with the Near East. Second, from Assyria's perspective, Phrygia lay on the empire's northwestern frontier and effectively evaded sustained military or political control. Yet Neo-Assyrian records indicating a friendly conclusion to hostilities between these states toward the end of Sargon's reign have likewise encouraged anticipation that such an alliance would be materially manifested, and potentially recognizable, in the archaeological record.[6]

Here I consider from the perspective of connectivity selected results from studies of Phrygian material culture in the Aegean region and the Neo-Assyrian world, emphasizing recent work at the Phrygian capital of Gordion and in the Assyrian heartland. Shared material cultural practices within a restricted social stratum indicate an awareness of Phrygian craft traditions at exalted levels of Assyrian society, introduced during the decades preceding Mita's reign. I then briefly discuss the Phrygian-style metalwork from Archaic Greek sanctuaries, drawing on recent studies reinvestigating this group of artifacts both to include new discoveries, especially in Ionia, and to address the consequences of Gordion's revised chronology. The restricted repertoire of these objects—bronze fibulae and belts (perhaps accompanied by elaborate textiles or garments), and two types of bowls—might point to a comparable uniformity in the means by which they reached the eastern Aegean or mainland Greece.[7] Yet their contexts attest multiple mechanisms of transfer and replication, in which intersanctuary connections and local workshops played a major role.

Redefining the "Age of Mita/Midas"

The Phrygian kingdom and its interaction with "eastern" and "western" neighbors have generated renewed interest in recent decades, for several reasons. A dramatic redating of Gordion's Iron Age settlement and related tumulus burials has prompted significant revision to the archaeological remains identified as comprising the "age of Midas," with repercussions far beyond the internal sequence of political or material developments in the west-central Anatolian homeland.[8] At the same time, new editions of Neo-Assyrian texts have allowed a more detailed picture of Assyria's interactions with Phrygia, Tabal, and other kingdoms on the empire's northwestern frontier. This new picture also embraces the figure of Mita/Midas.

The independent yet converging traditions concerning the Phrygian ruler were recognized at almost precisely the same moment, in an early phase in the modern history of both Assyriology and Anatolian archaeology. In 1898 the Assyriologist Hugo Winckler proposed that the Mita of the Assyrian inscriptions was Midas of Phrygia.[9] Prompt publication of explorations at Gordion (modern Yassıhöyük), which had begun in 1900 by Alfred and Gustav Körte and had unearthed well-preserved artifacts from trenches in the main settlement and five nearby burial tumuli, ensured that the Phrygian finds would be cited as parallels for closely related metalwork recovered in subsequent decades from votive deposits at Archaic Greek sanctuaries. They also provided crucial evidence for regionally defined typologies of fibulae, or metal dress fasteners.[10] The Phrygian-style artifacts at these sanctuaries could in turn be understood in light of the classical tradition regarding Midas and his gift to Delphi, as Herodotus (1.14) reported. The University of Pennsylvania's initial expedition to Gordion (1950–73) extensively explored the City Mound and thirty-one tumuli, yielding abundant material for elaborating artifact typologies and their chronological development, as well as new sources for exploring Mita's activities as documented in Neo-Assyrian texts.[11] One figure in a procession of tribute bearers depicted in a relief at Sargon's palace at Khorsabad (Dur-Šarrukin) wears a Phrygian-type

FIGURE 8.1 Tribute bearer wearing bow fibula. Drawing of relief from Khorsabad (Dur-Šarrukin), Palace of Sargon. From P. É. Botta and E. Flandin, *Monument de Ninive* (Paris: Imprimerie nationale, 1849–50), 2: pl. 106 *bis*. New York Public Library Digital Collections; public domain.

fibula, characterized by a semicircular arch or bow with heavy moldings (figure 8.1). Its distinctive form has been interpreted as an "ethnic signifier" identifying a Phrygian delegation sent to Assyria around 709 BCE, when Mita offered his allegiance.[12]

The dates for Mita/Midas's activities afforded by cuneiform records, and the assumption that Gordion's massive Destruction Level correlated with the Cimmerian invasion (and Midas's death) around 700 BCE, provided a historical and chronological framework that persisted until reexamination of artifact sequences and newly available radiocarbon dates prompted significant alterations. The revised chronology, along with new studies of excavated material in preparation for final publication, has established that Gordion was culturally more connected with the North Syrian/Neo-Hittite realm than previously understood and that these connections began at an early date, in the ninth century.[13] The Early Phrygian Destruction Level (ca. 800 BCE) and Tumulus MM (ca. 740 BCE), with their associated finds, are now dated significantly earlier than the late eighth century.

Reappraisal of references to Yaman/Yamanaia ("Ionians") in late eighth-century Neo-Assyrian records has likewise suggested a reorientation of the geopolitical framework within which the ruler of an interior Anatolian kingdom interacted with the Aegean world.[14] Assyria's confrontation with "Ionians," as asserted in Sargon's texts, hints that the empire's westward expansion profoundly affected not only local polities but also Greek traders along the Cilician and northern Levantine coasts, together with their elite sponsors. As a result, central and southern Anatolian kingdoms were likely drawn into new relationships with Greeks. Giovanni B. Lanfranchi has proposed repositioning Midas's overture to Delphi as an effort to gain support for his anti-Assyrian coalition in the face of the growing threat to north Syria and southern and central Anatolia.[15] Recent excavations at Greek sanctuaries in the eastern Aegean have both increased the quantity of Phrygian-style objects known from votive deposits and complicated their chronology, prompting reconsideration of workshops of origin and mechanisms of replication.[16] Finally, the recent suggestion that an ivory figure found at Delphi belongs to furniture decoration of Phrygian workmanship, perhaps part of Midas's famous throne, has refreshed interest in the tradition of royal patronage at mainland sanctuaries.[17]

Assyria, Phrygia, and Tabal: Material Interaction

Neo-Assyrian royal inscriptions and correspondence furnish a historical framework for Assyrian activity in the south-central Anatolian plateau in the late eighth century, and they also affirm the material dimensions of diplomatic marriages and alliances with client kingdoms. Political and military interests centered on "Tabal," a term that designates both the interior Anatolian zone of modern Kayseri and Niğde and one of the multiple kingdoms in its vicinity (known during Sargon's reign as Bīt-Purutaš).[18] An administrative record dating to the reign of

Tiglath-pileser III (744–727 BCE) lists tribute, including horses, mules, and alabaster, delivered by nine kings of Tabal.[19] Another text itemizes gifts of gold rings from Assyria to foreign envoys, including one from Tabal, and their servants.[20] Ambaris, king of Tabal, who joined Mita's coalition (with Pisiri, king of Carchemish, and Tarhunazi, king of Melid/Malatya), married Sargon's daughter Ahat-abisha and resided with her in Tabal. Following the discovery of Ambaris's treacherous alliance with Rusa of Urartu, Ambaris was removed and deported with his wife to Assur in 713 BCE, along with his nobles; deportees were sent to Parsua, in western Iran.[21] Assyria annexed Tabal in 713 but lost it again in 711, and never recovered control. Sargon's renewed campaign there a few years later, where he died in action in 705 BCE, indicates that Mita's overture did not terminate local resistance to Assyrian rule.[22] The shared cultural traditions of this multistate region were manifested in Hieroglyphic Luwian inscriptions and rock reliefs, but perhaps also in crafting practices that are poorly known archaeologically. Sargon's letter to Assur reporting on his Eighth Campaign against Rusa made special mention of Tabalian-style silver cups and censers with gold handles, found in the palace of Urzana during the destruction of Musasir—implying a highly distinctive (and widely recognized) regional metalworking technique.[23]

While texts thus suggest high-level interaction between Phrygia, Tabal, and Assyria in the realm of material culture, archaeological testimony is scarce. The rock relief depicting King Warpalawa (Assyrian Urpallâ) of Tuhana and the storm god Tarhunzas at Ivriz, near Ereğli in south-central Turkey, is often cited as testimony that Phrygian textiles and dress accessories were presented as gifts to neighboring rulers (figure 8.2). The king's outer garment is fastened with a bow fibula, his belt decorated with a geometric pattern. Yet his dress, hair, and beard are in Assyrian style, and he is shown in the Assyrian prayer gesture (*ubāna tarāṣu*).[24] Fibulae, among other artifact types, were introduced to the Assyrian realm in the eighth century as a consequence of westward expansion, and the earliest examples are western imports, with a semicircular arch. Most Assyrian examples are triangular in form, disseminated over a wide region and distributed among a broad social range, as numerous bronze specimens found in Neo-Assyrian burials of men, women, and occasionally children attest.[25] An administrative text from Nineveh recording two "Phrygian" (*mu-us-ku*) undergarments as the gift of Abdi-milki, the chief tailor, furnishes rare testimony for Phrygian-style artifacts in official Assyrian contexts.[26] What constituted their "Phrygianness," however—shape, style, material(s), method of manufacture or decoration, or another feature—remains unknown.[27]

FIGURE 8.2 Rock relief depicting Warpalawa of Tuhana and Tarhunzas, Ivriz, south-central Turkey, ca. 730–710 BCE. Author's photograph.

The redating of Gordion's Early Phrygian Destruction Level and several tumuli (including W, K-III, P, and MM) has also modified, or mooted, earlier inferences about material connections between Phrygia and Assyria. The ram- and lion-headed bronze beakers from Tumulus MM have long been associated with representations of lion-headed examples among Sargon's reliefs at Khorsabad (Dur-Šarrukin). They appear in the hands of Assyrian courtiers and are also presented by foreign tributaries, who perhaps hailed from the empire's client states in southern Anatolia or north Syria.[28] Susanne Ebbinghaus has suggested that the wide distribution of animal-headed bronze beakers resulted at least in part from their status as appropriate gifts to the Assyrian court. Consequently, they circulated in elite exchange networks and have survived in archaeological contexts, including the Hera sanctuary on Samos and a tomb in Etruscan Veii.[29]

Reanalysis of specific architectural contexts on Gordion's City Mound provides new evidence for buildings and their contents dating from the late eighth to early seventh century. The South Cellar, a structure of the Middle Phrygian period (ca. 800–550 BCE), preserved an important stratified deposit closely datable through associated Greek ceramics (including a Corinthian Late Geometric *kotyle* fragment) and other chronological indicators. The deposit also yielded a serpentine seal of the Lyre Player group, a distinctive category probably of Cilician origin and dated to the late eighth century; numerous examples have been recovered from sanctuaries, and also burials, throughout the Mediterranean.[30] Additional South Cellar deposit finds were carved ivory artifacts, including works in local style—a remarkable female figurine and a stamp seal—along with fragments of decorated plaques perhaps with Levantine affiliation.[31] Reinvestigation of another structure on the City Mound, Building A, of late eighth-century date, produced a carved ivory fragment with date palm decoration.[32] Late eighth-century Gordion was thus in contact with sources of ivory and carved ivories in Levantine styles.

Gordion's new chronology also recalibrates Phrygian craft innovations with respect to Assyrian royal centers. Tumulus P, a richly furnished child's burial previously assigned to the late eighth century, offers an example. Its new date (around 770 BCE) alters earlier inferences about the origins of a molded, colorless glass phiale found inside a bronze bowl, decorated on both interior and exterior with radiating petals (figure 8.3a). Since its initial publication in 1959, the phiale has been compared with a group of glass vessels employing a new technology invented to imitate rock crystal: cups, hemispherical bowls, and small handled jars, ranging in color from almost clear to pale green, with cut or ground decoration. Multiple examples were recovered from Nimrud and dated to the late eighth and seventh centuries; a glass alabastron inscribed for Sargon II further implied both an Assyrian court workshop and a link with this particular king.[33] The only close parallel for the Tumulus P bowl, however, is a fragment of a molded, colorless petaled phiale, reportedly from Mesopotamia but lacking specific provenance.[34] A second specimen from Gordion, from a mid-eighth-century context on the City Mound, is a fragmentary molded, colorless glass bowl whose petal design echoes, in a distinctively Phrygian style, that of a group of bronze relief bowls found in Tumulus MM (figure 8.3b).[35] Given the early dates now assigned to the Gordion molded colorless glass, Janet Jones has suggested that this technology originated locally; she rightly draws attention to the explicit interplay between bronze and glass exhibited in shape, petal

FIGURE 8.3 (a) Molded colorless glass phiale; diameter 15.4 cm. Gordion, Tumulus P (ca. 770 BCE). Gordion inv. no. 4000 (G206). Photograph courtesy of Janet Duncan Jones. Penn Museum Gordion Archive; (b) Petaled bronze phiale with decorated omphalos; diameter 17.8. Gordion, Tumulus MM (ca. 740 BCE). Gordion inv. no. B881 (MM 73). Courtesy of the Penn Museum Gordion Archive, image #103049.

decoration, and reflective surfaces. Rather than probable Assyrian imports, these examples point instead to an innovation in glass technology used to fashion luxury drinking vessels that was developed in Phrygia in close association with a sophisticated local bronzeworking industry, and subsequently introduced to the Neo-Assyrian courtly sphere.[36]

Recent discoveries in the Assyrian heartland strengthen the impression that artistic interaction with western regions took place at exalted levels of court society several decades prior to Sargon's reign. Between 1988 and 1992, Iraqi archaeologists at Nimrud unearthed several mostly undisturbed tombs dating to the ninth and eighth centuries in the Northwest Palace built by King Ashurnasirpal II (883–859 BCE). A few of their lavish furnishings suggest Phrygian, or perhaps central and south-central Anatolian, affiliations in type or decoration. The nearly complete skeleton in Coffin 2, in Tomb III, has been identified as Hama, queen of Shalmaneser IV (782–773 BCE). Associated artifacts from the tomb's antechamber included a fragmentary imported gold bow fibula and a small gold strainer-spouted jug decorated with repoussé ornamental and figural friezes; its handle terminates in a dragon's head at the top and a lion's head at the bottom (figure 8.4).[37] Its closest similarities in shape are with Type 3 ceramic side-spouted sieve jugs recovered chiefly from Gordion's Early Phrygian Destruction Level and Tumulus K-III (now dated around 780 BCE), whose design is convincingly linked to the consumption of grainy beverages such as beer.

The gold jug's figural friezes depict hunts of exotic animals, including lions, ostriches, and wild donkeys, and a battle scene of chariot warfare and archers defending a fortified city. Their subjects and style indicate multiple sources, but exhibit most similarities with the repoussé bronze bands from the Balawat Gates commissioned by Shalmaneser III (859–824 BCE). The decorative themes suggest an original male owner; Queen Hama may have received the jug as a dowry item, diplomatic gift, or heirloom.[38] The queen wore an elaborate headdress made of gold and lapis lazuli, incorporating tiny four-winged female figures. Citing parallels for the figures and their dress among carved figures on orthostat reliefs from Karatepe, Tell Halaf, and Carchemish, R. M. Boehmer proposed an origin in Cilicia or the Neo-Hittite/North Syrian sphere.[39] Other scholars have argued that the headdress, along with other objects of dress or personal ornament from the tombs, evince a deliberately cosmopolitan and intercultural style that drew on multiple foreign sources especially from western or Levantine regions.[40] Vessels and other objects made in—or reflecting—"western" or "Levantine" styles or elements, such as the elaborately decorated gold bowl in Tomb II inscribed for

FIGURE 8.4 Decorated gold juglet; H. 13 cm. Nimrud, Northwest Palace, Tomb III, Coffin 2 (ca. 830–760 BCE). Iraq Museum 115618 (ND 1989.308). Courtesy of the Nimrud Photo Archive.

Queen Yabâ, have been similarly interpreted along personal biographical lines: they are thought to reflect the "Levantine" (or "western") origins of several Assyrian queens, as their names indicate.[41]

Finally, the gold or gold-colored garments, dress ornaments, and headgear that adorned the bodies of royal personages may represent a shared aesthetic modality. Neo-Assyrian written sources document elaborate gold decoration for garments and other textiles used to clothe royalty and divine images. Although they do not specifically mention clothing for the dead, Assyrian texts make clear that luxury textiles consonant with the status of the deceased, including garments, were presented during burial rituals for the royal family (both kings and queens).[42] The finds from the

Queens' Tombs have dramatically expanded the archaeological evidence for gold textile ornaments, along with gold jewelry and other personal adornment.[43] At Gordion, analysis of the textile fibers from fabrics found on the bier of the male in Tumulus MM revealed a film of goethite, an inorganic mineral of golden yellow color. Unlike yellow hues made from natural dyes, the goethite film is permanent and does not fade.[44]

More broadly, ninth- and eighth-century elite Phrygian burials and the Queens' Tombs preserve numerous objects fashioned from valuable and highly reflective materials, many of them clearly aiming to transfer distinctive visual qualities or surface patterning across media. Tumulus D at Bayındır near Elmalı, in southwestern Turkey, yielded spectacular objects in Phrygian style, including silver vessels, fibulae, belts, appliqués, and equestrian equipment.[45] The rock crystal cup inscribed for Atalia, wife of Sargon II, found in Tomb II at Nimrud, points to the close relationship in the late eighth century between this prized material and emerging colorless glass technology.[46] Royal burials and their furnishings are too rare to permit general inferences or support direct connections across these cultural spheres. But similarities hint at common practices involving the covering of the deceased in royal or elite contexts, or perhaps shared notions about the materiality of light.[47] The wide range of materials exceptionally well preserved at Gordion, including wood, ceramic, stone, ivory, and metal, document the highly transmedial character of Phrygian art across multiple scales—of crucial significance in understanding the complex craft interaction exhibited here.[48]

Phrygian Imports and Phrygian-Style Material Culture in Archaic Greek Sanctuaries

Phrygian-style bronze dress ornaments (fibulae and belts) and shallow vessels (omphalos bowls and bowls with bolster and swiveling ring handles) have been recovered in the Aegean world chiefly in the sanctuaries of a small group of deities (Artemis, Aphrodite, Athena, and Hera), over a wide geographical range: from Olympia in western Greece to Ephesus and Miletus in Ionia, with largest concentrations primarily in the eastern Aegean (Chios, Samos, and Lindus) and Ionia.[49] As with most votives fashioned in foreign styles, scholars have sought to distinguish genuine imports from local imitations or adaptations, as clues both to the identity of the donor and to the means by which these objects reached the sanctuary. Specialists generally agree that most of these Phrygian-style bronzes are local versions, either inspired by a small number of actual imports or perhaps acquired from Ionian sanctuary workshops; molds for casting fibulae, found at Smyrna and Miletus, for example, document local production. Phrygian-style metalwork appears primarily in votive deposits datable to the seventh or early sixth century, although some specimens are typologically earlier. Recent excavations especially at Ephesus and Miletus have contributed significantly to this corpus and permitted new inferences about their quantity, origin, and chronology; these studies have also benefited from fresh analyses of the abundant material from Gordion. Current interpretations tend to emphasize the cult-related function and knowledgeable acquisition of Phrygian-style bronzes to explain their local meaning and means of transmission. Yet these investigations have also brought into relief significant differences among the sanctuaries in the consumption of Phrygian-style metalwork, despite the overall consistency in its circumscribed repertoire throughout the Aegean sphere.

In their study of Near Eastern imports in Greek sanctuaries, Eva Braun-Holzinger and Ellen Rehm argued that the objects' different contexts or functions in their regions of origin suggested that in most cases Greeks, not foreigners, presented them as sanctuary offerings.[50] Their conclusion extended to at least some of the Phrygian-style finds, although they did not examine this material in detail. At Gordion, for example, bronze omphalos bowls found in large quantities in Tumulus MM were used as drinking vessels in funeral feasting, while in Greek sanctuaries they were generally used for libations.[51] Braun-Holzinger and Rehm noted that the large number of Phrygian-style fibulae at certain sanctuaries suggests a local demand and a period of use before they were deposited as sanctuary offerings. The fibulae thus may have influenced Greek clothing practices. Whether the typologically early Phrygian-style objects (including genuine imports) arrived in Greek sanctuaries only in the seventh or sixth century, or were deposited there long after their manufacture, remains an open question.

An important reassessment of Phrygian metalwork in Greek sanctuaries appeared well before the redating of Gordion's Iron Age settlement and associated tumuli. Reexamining foreign-style votives at the Argive Heraion and other sanctuaries, Ingrid Strøm observed key differences among the quantities and functions of their Phrygian artifacts. While both Phrygian-type bronze bowls in Greek sanctuaries were apparently used for cult-related libations, Strøm suggested that the exceptionally large numbers of petaled omphalos bowls found at the Argive Heraion and the Hera sanctuary at Perachora argued for their function as parts of drinking sets. These sanctuaries also yielded bronze cauldrons equipped with bull attachments in so-called North Syrian styles. Multiple examples of these types of vessels had been recovered from Tumulus MM at Gordion—then identified by some as the tomb of Midas—where they were certainly used for banqueting. Strøm suggested that this combination of vessels, found at two sanctuaries of Hera that were not far distant from one another, pointed to the introduction of new drinking or banqueting practices and a special relationship between these sanctuaries and Phrygian aristocracy.[52] She argued that sanctuary officials had played a crucial role in the knowledgeable acquisition of cult-related drinking equipment through cultural ties to Phrygian elites. These ties could also account for the Phrygian-style fibulae, which perhaps represented dress offerings presented to major sanctuaries. Strøm's interpretation raised the possibility of multiple, overlapping mechanisms to explain the transfer or local imitation of Phrygian-style objects in Archaic Greek sanctuaries, including organized import, even given the highly restricted repertoire represented by the bronze dress ornaments and shallow vessels.

A more recent contribution also emphasizes religious meaning in explaining the nature and distribution of Phrygian-style votives, building on close analysis of Gordion's numerous bronze fibulae and belts and a new understanding of their late eighth-century contexts. Maya Vassileva suggests that the presence of Phrygian-style fibulae and belts in Greek sanctuaries, broadly speaking, reflects the influence of the Phrygian goddess Matar and her cult. In Phrygia, belts are almost exclusively associated with royal or elite male burials, and their geometric ornament has been plausibly interpreted as symbolic of this important female deity. Vassileva postulates that Phrygian aristocrats initially introduced these dress ornaments to Ionia either as high-level gifts or as votive offerings, where they prompted a local industry at sanctuaries of Artemis, Hera, and Athena (figures 8.5a and 8.5b). In the process of their transfer from Phrygian contexts to numerous sanctuaries of female deities in the eastern Aegean, she argues, these objects acquired new social and religious associations. As their original meaning was lost within the communities of ritual practice into which they were being incorporated, Phrygian-style belts and fibulae (as shorthand for belts) also appeared in the sanctuaries of male deities on mainland Greece, such as Olympia (Zeus) and Isthmia (Poseidon).[53]

Phrygian influence in the realm of Greek cult practices has been well demonstrated by finds at several locations in Ionia, especially in and near Ephesus. Cult sites for the Phrygian goddess Matar have been found at several Ionian cities and on the island of Chios, and in the vicinity of Ephesus; a sanctuary with rock-cut features similar to those known from Phrygian cult sites is located near Roman Ephesus.[54] Close ties are also

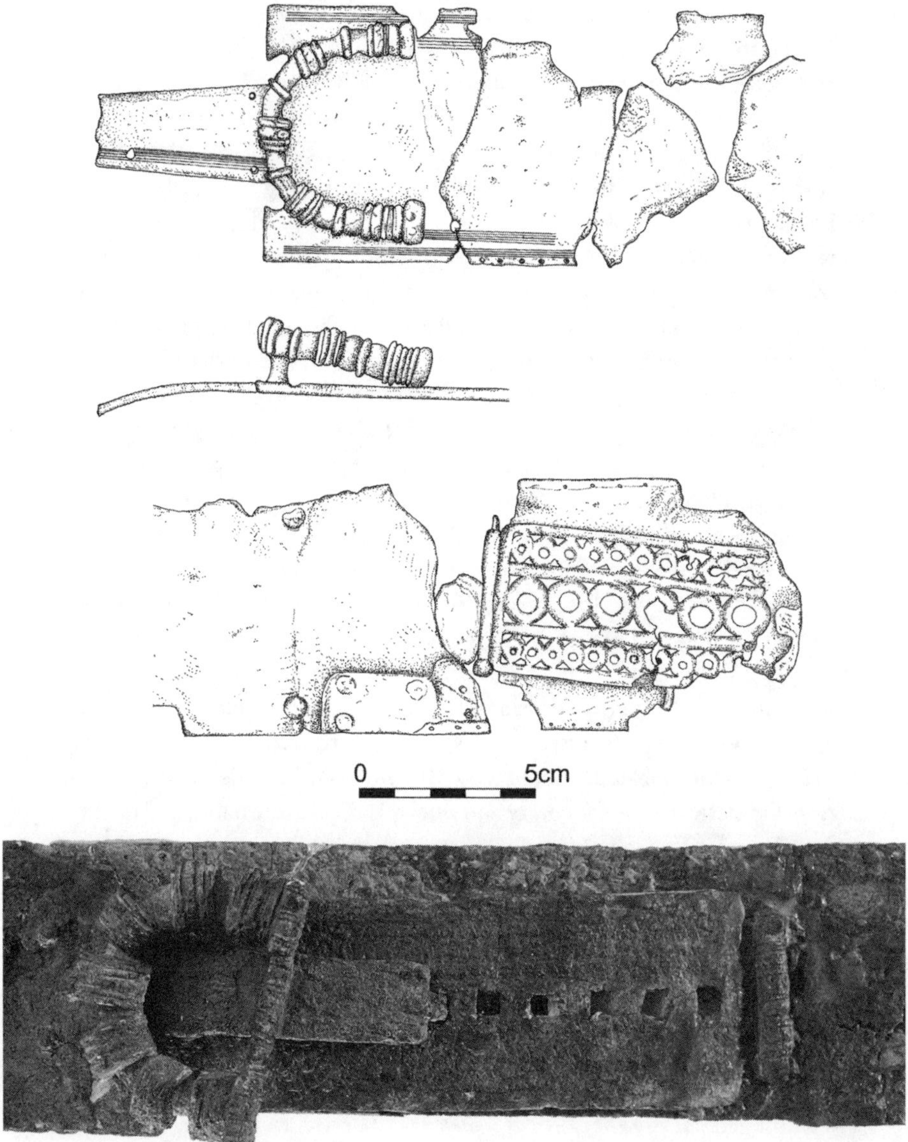

FIGURE 8.5 (a) Detailed views of the two ends of bronze belt B-1605 (max. pres. l. 82 cm), from Gordion City Mound, South Cellar deposit (ca. 720–690 BCE). Drawing courtesy of Maya Vassileva. Penn Museum Gordion Archive; (b) Detail, bronze belt, pres. l. 24.9 cm. From the Artemision, Ephesus, second half of the seventh century. Efes Arkeoloji Müzesi 93/51/91 (Art. 900795). Photo courtesy of Österreichische Akademie der Wissenschaften–Österreichisches Archäologisches Institut / Niki Gail.

manifested in the garments and dress ornaments shown on ivory figurines from Ephesus, one of which also holds a distinctive Phrygian-style bowl and trefoil-mouth jug.[55] The rich evidence for bronzeworking at Ephesus has enabled Gudrun Klebinder-Gauß to reconstruct the local development of this industry and further elaborate the sanctuary's special relationship with Phrygia. The large assemblage, comprising fibulae, belts, and bowls, included a few genuine Phrygian imports; local products closely replicating them; and more fluid interpretations perhaps better characterized as Phrygian-inspired, indicating that local bronzeworkers invented their own versions of Phrygian styles. Although evidence for manufacturing at the sanctuary has not yet come to light, Klebinder-Gauß suggests that Phrygian artisans migrated to Ionia in search of employment, perhaps following a decline in patronage at Gordion and its vicinity after the eighth century.[56] Whether exercised by Phrygian artisans or imports, however, Phrygian bronzeworking traditions had a considerable impact on the local industry.[57] By contrast, Phrygian imports to the region in other media, such as monochrome pottery, were scarce.[58]

In addition to its close ties to Phrygia, the bronze assemblage from Ephesus also revealed that the Artemision was involved in networks that diverged from those of other eastern Aegean or Ionian sanctuaries. Unlike Samos and Miletus, for example, the Artemision yielded no bronze artifacts from Cyprus, Egypt, or Assyria.[59] With respect to nonwestern Anatolian and non-Ionian contacts, Klebinder-Gauß finds a special relationship between the sanctuary and Phrygia, on the one hand, and northern Greece (Thessaly, Macedonia, and southern Thrace) on the other. Variations in the number and types of Near Eastern imports in sanctuary votive deposits could result, at least in part, from location along Mediterranean seafaring routes, as has often been proposed. More significant than established patterns of maritime or overland traffic, however, seem to have been the human interactions shaped by linked religious institutions and their shared forms of material expression. "Die Nähe zum Phrygerreich war offenkundig nicht entscheidend für die Frequenz der Weihungen phrygischer Bronze," observes Michael Kerschner.[60]

Conclusion

The figure of Mita/Midas has loomed large in investigations of Phrygian material connections with both the Greek and the Assyrian worlds—an importance perhaps magnified by the precise dates for his activities available from cuneiform records and the broad geographical reach of his putative personal influence. Yet archaeological evidence now suggests that important moments of contact or interaction between Phrygia and both "eastern" and "western" spheres preceded or followed Midas's reign, and emphasizes various forms of human agency: the transfer of manufacturing practices or craft technologies, the relocation of artisans, the acquisition of cult-related equipment by sanctuary officials, and perhaps the adoption of new customs involving foreign styles of banqueting and dress or personal ornament.

The redating of archaeological contexts at Gordion long associated with Midas makes plausible an acquaintance with Phrygian artifact types and craft traditions over a wide area of the Near East in the ninth and eighth centuries BCE. Royal burials at Gordion and Nimrud suggest a shared elite preference for intercultural styles of vessels associated with drinking customs and fashioned from valuable materials (including gold, glass, and bronze); new materials or technologies for luxury items, such as molded colorless glass; and perhaps also practices governing the dress and adornment of deceased royal personages that drew on special materials and aesthetic modalities. Their contexts predate the late eighth century, indicating geographically extensive interaction rather than exclusive or direct transfer resulting from specific diplomatic circumstances. The artistic traditions of Phrygia, or of west-central and southeastern Anatolia—themselves partly shaped by contacts with ninth-century developments in the North Syrian/Neo-Hittite realm—were among the regional sources that informed the intercultural styles of objects and personal adornment manifested in the Queens' Tombs.

Phrygian-style finds at Archaic Greek sanctuaries in the eastern Aegean and on mainland Greece, often understood to corroborate a literary tradition of Phrygian royal patronage, now seem in many cases to reflect intersanctuary activity, dating primarily to the seventh century BCE and later. Although the Phrygian-style sanctuary votives comprise a highly circumscribed group of bronze artifacts—fibulae and belts, omphalos bowls, and bowls with ring handles—they apparently had different functions or significance at different sanctuaries, and underwent changes in meaning over time. Thus, at Perachora and the Argive Heraion, large quantities of shallow bowls suggest their use in drinking sets. The connection linking fibulae and belts, elite Phrygian males, and the goddess Matar may have been recognized in the Ionian sanctuaries where they were introduced, yet these objects came to be considered appropriate gifts to female, then also to male, Greek deities.

Further probing the transfer and reception of Phrygian-style metalwork over long distances in western Anatolia, the eastern Aegean, and mainland Greece could yield valuable insights into the "etic" and "emic" approaches discussed in the introduction to this volume. The distribution and chronology of these objects also shed light on Phrygia's role in the broader Orientalizing movement, suggesting networks diverging from those engaged with acquiring or circulating works in Egyptian, Levantine, Cypriot, and Assyrian styles. These artifacts and their circumscribed repertoire challenge a common assumption about "Eastern" votives as a disparate array of objects from geographically diverse regions of origin, transported by foreign donors themselves or by Greek (or Levantine) intermediaries or sanctuary visitors. They also call into question widely accepted (if often implicit) notions about imports and local adaptations, in which we draw a firm distinction between genuine imports and imitations as crucially indicative of common source and perhaps also local meaning or owner's identity.

Notes

1. I am grateful to Jonathan Hall and James Osborne for including me in their productive workshop on Iron Age connectivity and for their patience and helpful advice on my written contribution. I also benefited from comments and editorial suggestions by the reviewers for the press. My thanks also to Jean M. Evans and Carolina López-Ruiz for quickly and generously answering requests for library materials.

2. Andreas Fuchs, "Mita," in *The Prosopography of the Neo-Assyrian Empire*, vol. 2, part 2 (Helsinki: The Neo-Assyrian Text Corpus Project, 2001), 755–56; and Robert Rollinger, "Mita," in *The Encyclopedia of Ancient History*, ed. Roger Bagnall et al. (Malden, MA: Wiley-Blackwell, 2013), 4543–44, both with bibliography.

3. Lynn E. Roller, "The Legend of Midas," *Classical Antiquity* 2 (1983): 299–313; Susanne Berndt-Ersöz, "The Chronology and Historical Context of Midas," *Historia* 57 (2008): 1–37; Rollinger, "Mita," 4543–44.

4. *The Correspondence of Sargon II, Part I: Letters from Assyria and the West*, ed. Simo Parpola (Helsinki: Helsinki University Press, 1987), no. 1; Cecily Grace, "King Midas: Evidence from Assyria," in *Pessinus and Its Regional Setting*, vol. 1, ed. Gocha R. Tsetskhladze (Leuven: Peeters, 2018), 25–63, reexamines references to Mita in royal inscriptions and correspondence. For the Khorsabad inscriptions, see Andreas Fuchs, *Die Inschriften Sargons II. aus Khorsabad* (Göttingen: Cuvillier, 1994). A new edition of Sargon's royal inscriptions has just appeared: Grant Frame, *The Royal Inscriptions of Sargon II, King of Assyria (721–705 BC)* (University Park, PA: Eisenbrauns, 2021). On the Mushki-Phrygian question, see Karen Radner, review of Anne-Maria Wittke, *Mušker und Phryger: Ein Beitrag zur Geschichte Anatoliens vom 12. bis zum 7. Jh. v. Chr.*, in *Zeitschrift für Assyriologie* 96 (2006): 144–49; and Cecily Grace, "Muški Revisited," *Ancient West and East* 14 (2015): 23–49, both with bibliography.

5. Ann C. Gunter, *Greek Art and the Orient* (Cambridge: Cambridge University Press, 2009), esp. 117–19, with further references.

6. Oscar White Muscarella, "Relations between Phrygia and Assyria in the 8th Century BC," in *XXIV. Uluslararası Assiriyoloji Kongresi, 6–19/VII/1987, Istanbul*

(Ankara: Türk Tarih Kurumu Basımevi, 1998), 149–57, first assembled the evidence for this interaction.

7. R. M. Boehmer, "Phrygische Prunkgewänder des 8. Jahrhunderts v. Chr. Herkunft und Export," *Archäologischer Anzeiger* 1973: 149–72.

8. Keith DeVries, "The Age of Midas at Gordion and Beyond," *Ancient Near Eastern Studies* 43 (2007): 30–64; C. Brian Rose and Gareth Darbyshire, eds., *The New Chronology of Iron Age Gordion* (Philadelphia: University of Pennsylvania Museum of Archaeology and Anthropology, 2011); G. Kenneth Sams, "Artifacts," in Rose and Darbyshire, *New Chronology of Iron Age Gordion*, 59–78; and C. Brian Rose, ed., *The Archaeology of Phrygian Gordion, Royal City of Midas* (Philadelphia: University of Pennsylvania Museum of Archaeology and Anthropology, 2012).

9. J. D. Hawkins, "Mita," *Reallexikon der Assyriologie und Vorderasiatischen Archäologie* 8 (1993): 272, with bibliography.

10. Gustav Körte and Alfred Körte, *Gordion: Ergebnisse der Ausgrabung im Jahre 1900* (Berlin: G. Reimer, 1904); David G. Hogarth, *Excavations at Ephesus: The Archaic Artemisia* (London: Trustees of the British Museum, 1908), 244; Christian Blinkenberg, *Lindiaka V: Fibules grecques et orientales* (Copenhagen: Andr. Fred. Høst & Søn, 1926), 204–30. Catherine Saint-Pierre, "La notion d' 'offrande orientale' en archéologie grecque," *European Review of History—Revue européenne d'histoire* 13 (2007): 589–605 offers important historiographic observations on the publication of Phrygian and Phrygian-style votives at Greek sanctuaries and the evolution of the category "Oriental offering."

11. For the history of research at the site, see Mary M. Voigt, "Gordion: The Changing Political and Economic Roles of a First Millennium B.C.E. City," in *The Oxford Handbook of Ancient Anatolia, 10,000–323 B.C.E.*, ed. Sharon R. Steadman and Gregory McMahon (Oxford: Oxford University Press, 2011), 1069–75; and Oscar White Muscarella, "King Midas of Phrygia and the Greeks," in *Anatolia and the Ancient Near East: Studies in Honor of Tahsin Özgüç*, ed. Kutlu Emre, Barthel Hrouda, Machteld Mellink, and Nimet Özgüç (Ankara: Türk Tarih Kurumu Basımevi, 1989), 333–44. For a different perspective, see Philip Kaplan, "Foreign Rulers and Greek Sanctuaries," *Historia* 55 (2006): 129–52.

12. Oscar White Muscarella, "Fibulae Represented on Sculpture," *Journal of Near Eastern Studies* 26 (1967): 82. Muscarella, "Relations between Phrygia and Assyria," assembles archaeological and representational evidence, with bibliography.

13. These links are evident in architectural decoration, for example, and they have also prompted reconsideration of when and how the Phrygian alphabet was adopted. See Lynn E. Roller, *The Incised Drawings from Early Phrygian Gordion* (Philadelphia: University of Pennsylvania Museum of Archaeology and Anthropology, 2009); and Sams, "Artifacts," 59–60, with further references. Recent surveys, with rich bibliography include Erik van Dongen, "The Overland Route: Intra-Anatolia Interaction ca. 1000–540 BCE and the Transmission of the Alphabet," *Ancient West and East* 12 (2013): esp. 60–65; and van Dongen, "The Extent and Interactions of the Phrygian Kingdoms," in *From Source to History: Studies on Ancient Near Eastern Worlds and Beyond, Dedicated to Giovanni Battista Lanfranchi on the Occasion of his 65th Birthday on June 23, 2014* (Münster: Ugarit-Verlag, 2014), 697–711.

14. Robert Rollinger, "Der Blick aus dem Osten: 'Griechen' in Vorderasiatischen Quellen des 8. und 7. Jahrhunderts V. Chr.—Eine Zusammenschau," in *Der Orient und die Anfänge Europas: Kulturelle Beziehungen von der Späten Bronzezeit bis zur Frühen*

Eisenzeit, ed. Hartmut Matthäus, Norbert Oettinger, and Stephan Schröder (Wiesbaden: Harrassowitz Verlag, 2011), 267–82, with bibliography. See also Giovanni B. Lanfranchi, "The Ideological and Political Impact of the Assyrian Expansion on the Greek World," in *The Heirs of Assyria*, ed. Sanna Aro and R. M. Whiting (Helsinki: The Neo-Assyrian Text Corpus Project 2000), 7–34.

15. Giovanni B. Lanfranchi, "The Expansion of the Neo-Assyrian Empire and Its Peripheries: Military, Political and Ideological Resistance," in *Lag Troia in Kilikien? Der aktuelle Streit um Homers Ilias*, ed. Christoph Ulf and Robert Rollinger (Darmstadt: Wissenschaftliche Buchgesellschaft, 2011), 225–39, citing an earlier suggestion by Hartmut Matthäus. Cf. van Dongen, "Extent and Interaction of the Phrygian Kingdom," 703–4n30.

16. Gudrun Klebinder-Gauß, "Ephesos und seine Beziehungen zur phrygischen Bronzekunst," in *Die Archäologie der ephesischen Artemis: Gestalt und Ritual eines Heiligtums*, ed. Ulrike Muss (Vienna: Phoibos Verlag, 2008), 235–40; Gudrun Klebinder-Gauß, *Bronzefunde aus dem Artemision von Ephesos* (Vienna: Verlag der Österreichischen Akademie der Wissenschaften, 2007), esp. 208–10. See also the important discussion in Michael Kerschner, "Die Ionier und ihr Verhältnis zu den Phrygern und Lydern: Analyse der literarischen, epigraphischen und numismatischen Zeugnisse," in *Neue Forschungen zu Ionien: Fahri Işık zum 60. Geburtstag gewidmet*, ed. Elmar Schwertheim and Engelberg Winter (Bonn: Rudolf Habelt, 2005), 113–46. See also Lynn E. Roller, "Phrygia and Hellenism: Phrygian Interaction with Asia Minor Greeks, 8th–6th Centuries BC," in *Phrygia in Antiquity: From the Bronze Age to the Byzantine Period*, ed. Gocha R. Tsetskhladze (Leuven: Peeters, 2019), 37–55, for a thoughtful and up-to-date review of archaeological and textual sources, with extensive bibliography.

17. Keith DeVries and C. Brian Rose, "The Throne of Midas? Delphi and the Power Politics of Phrygia, Lydia, and Greece," in *The Archaeology of Phrygian Gordion, Royal City of Midas*, ed. C. Brian Rose (Philadelphia: University of Pennsylvania Museum of Archaeology and Anthropology, 2012), 189–200, referring to the carved ivory lion tamer found at Delphi. For a critical response, see Oscar White Muscarella, "An Ivory Statuette from Delphi—Not from King Midas's Throne," *Source: Notes in the History of Art* (2016): 182–93.

18. Tabal appears in Assyrian sources with the campaigns of Shalmaneser III (853–824 BCE) in the Taurus region west of the Euphrates River. Sanna Aro, "Tabal," *Reallexikon der Assyriologie und Vorderasiatischen Archäologie* 13 (2012): 388–91, with bibliography. On Neo-Assyrian sources, and for different views on Assyrian strategy toward Tabal, see Trevor Bryce, *The World of the Neo-Hittite Kingdoms* (Oxford: Oxford University Press, 2012), esp. 39–43, 278–89; Sarah C. Melville, "Kings of Tabal: Politics, Competition, and Conflict in a Contested Periphery," in *Rebellions and Peripheries in the Mesopotamian World*, ed. Seth F. C. Richardson (Winona Lake, IN: Eisenbrauns, 2010), 85–107; Melville, *The Campaigns of Sargon II* (Norman: University of Oklahoma Press, 2016), esp. 77–89, 143–45, 172–74; and Mark Weeden, "Tabal and the Limits of Assyrian Imperialism," in *At the Dawn of History: Ancient Near Eastern Studies in Honour of J. N. Postgate*, ed. Yağmur Heffron, Adam Stone, and Martin Worthington (Winona Lake, IN: Eisenbrauns, 2017), 721–36, with further references.

19. J. D. Hawkins and J. N. Postgate, "Tribute from Tabal," *State Archives of Assyria Bulletin* 2 (1988): 31–40; and Karen Radner, "Urpallâ," in *The Prosopography*

of the Neo-Assyrian Empire, vol. 3, part 2 (Helsinki: The Neo-Assyrian Text Corpus Project, 2011), 1417–18. Weeden, "Tabal and the Limits of Assyrian Imperialism," 726, cites Sanna Aro's proposed redating of the record to Sargon's reign.

20. F. M. Fales and J. N. Postgate, *Imperial Administrative Records, Part I: Palace and Temple Administration* (Helsinki: Neo-Assyrian Text Corpus Project, 1992), no. 58. From the late eighth century onward, Tabalians are attested in other regions of the empire, often as deportees. For Tabal in seventh-century Neo-Assyrian sources, see Aro, "Tabal," 390; and Rollinger, "Mita," 4543–44, both with further references. Tabalians were particularly numerous in western Iran and Babylonia.

21. Fuchs, *Die Inschriften Sargons II. aus Khorsabad*. For the Letter to Assur recounting the Eighth Campaign, see Walter Mayer, *Assyrien und Urarṭu: Der Achte Feldzug Sargons II. im Jahr 714 v. Chr.* (Münster: Ugarit-Verlag, 2013). See also Karen Radner, "Assyrians and Urartians," in Steadman and McMahon, *Oxford Handbook of Ancient Anatolia*, esp. 740–41, 746–48.

22. Melville, *Campaigns of Sargon II*, 187–88; and Weeden, "Tabal and the Limits of Assyrian Imperialism," 731–32; both with bibiliography.

23. Mayer, *Assyrien und Urarṭu*, 132–33 (ll. 358–61). Melville, *Campaigns of Sargon II*, 138, suggests that the presence of this unique metalwork style among the inventory seized from Urzana's palace provided Sargon's officers with indisputable evidence of Ambaris's treachery: vessels in this style, in other words, should not have been where they were found in Musasir. Anne-Sophie Crespin, "Between Phrygia and Cilicia: The Porsuk Area at the Beginning of the Iron Age," *Anatolian Studies* 49 (1999): 69, also observes that the text identifies only the Tabalian vessels by geographical region.

24. Mirko Novák, "Akkulturation der Aramäern und Luwiern und der Austausch der ikonographischen Konzepten in der späthethitischen Kunst," in *Brückenland Anatolien? Ursachen, Extensität und Modi des Kulturaustausches zwischen Anatolien und seinen Nachbarn*, ed. Hartmut Blum, Betina Faist, Peter Pfälzner, and Anne-Maria Wittke (Tübingen: Attempto Verlag, 2002), 152; and Eleanor Guralnick, "Neo-Assyrian Patterned Fabrics," *Iraq* 66 (2004): esp. 226–27. Sanna Aro, "Art and Architecture," in *The Luwians*, ed. H. Craig Melchert (Leiden: Brill, 2003), 336, doubts that the dress of Warpalawa is Phrygian, as often asserted, but "probably indigenous Tabalian."

25. Friedhelm Pedde, "Fibulae in Neo-Assyrian Burials," in *The Adventure of the Illustrious Scholar: Papers Presented to Oscar White Muscarella*, ed. Elizabeth Simpson (Leiden: Brill, 2018), 354–55, with further references.

26. Fales and Postgate, *Imperial Administrative Records, Part I*, no. 126.

27. Salvatore Gaspa, *Textiles in the Neo-Assyrian Empire: A Study of Terminology* (Boston: DeGruyter, 2018), 272–73 for the garment type (*šupālītu ḫalluptu*).

28. Muscarella, "Relations between Phrygia and Assyria," 152–55; see also J. E. Curtis, "Animal-Headed Drinking Cups in the Late Assyrian Period," in *Variatio delectat. Iran und der Westen: Gedenkschrift für Peter Calmeyer*, ed. R. Dittman et al. (Münster: Ugarit-Verlag, 2000), 193–213; and Javier Álvarez-Mon, "'Give to Drink, O Cup-Bearer!' The Arjan Beaker in the Context of Lion-headed Drinking Vessels in the Ancient Near East," *Iranica Antiqua* 43 (2008): 127–52.

29. Susanne Ebbinghaus, "Patterns of Elite Interaction: Animal-Headed Vessels in Anatolia in the Eighth and Seventh Centuries BC," in *Anatolian Interfaces: Hittites, Greeks and Their Neighbours*, ed. Billie Jean Collins, Mary R. Bachvarova, and Ian

C. Rutherford (Oxford: Oxbow Books, 2008), 184–86, with bibliography; Ann C. Gunter, "Contemplating an Empire: Artistic Responses to the Neo-Assyrian World," in *Assyria to Iberia: Art and Culture in the Iron Age*, ed. Joan Aruz and Michael Seymour (New York and New Haven, CT: Metropolitan Museum of Art and Yale University Press, 2016), 222–23; and Eva A. Braun-Holzinger and Ellen Rehm, *Orientalischer Import in Griechenland im frühen 1. Jahrtausend v. Chr.* (Münster: Ugarit-Verlag, 2005), 102–4, pl. 23.

30. Elspeth R. M. Dusinberre, *Gordion Seals and Sealings: Individuals and Society* (Philadelphia: University of Pennsylvania Museum of Archaeology and Anthropology, 2005), 43–44, cat. no. 19. For the Lyre Player group, see Yelena Rakic, in *Assyria to Iberia at the Dawn of the Classical Age*, ed. Joan Aruz, Sarah B. Graff, and Yelena Rakic (New York: Metropolitan Museum of Art, 2014), 254, nos. 134a–b; and John C. Franklin, "Theios Aoidos: A New Reading of the Lyre-Player Group of Seals," *Gaia* 18 (2015): 405–18, with bibliography.

31. DeVries, "Age of Midas," 41, 60, fig. 34, for the female figurine, with bibliography; see also DeVries and Rose, "Throne of Midas," 193, 198, fig. 13.15. For the seal: Dusinberre, *Gordion Seals and Sealings*, 44–45, cat. no. 20. The carved ivory plaques, which do not seem to me to represent a coherent or readily identifiable stylistic group, have not yet been fully published. Sams, "Artifacts," 62, cites preliminary reports that include a few illustrations.

32. Brendan Burke, "The Rebuilt Citadel at Gordion: Building A and the Mosaic Building Complex," in Rose, *Archaeology of Phrygian Gordion*, 205–11, 217–18; "When trying to place the initial construction of Middle Phrygian Building A in historical context, one's thoughts turn to Midas" (217).

33. Rodney S. Young, *The Gordion Excavations Final Reports*, vol. 1, *Three Great Early Tumuli* (Philadelphia: University of Pennsylvania Museum of Archaeology and Anthropology, 1981), 32, with bibliography. For the technology and opinions on its region of origin, see P. R. S. Moorey, *Ancient Mesopotamian Materials and Industries: The Archaeological Evidence* (Oxford: Oxford University Press, 1994), 199.

34. Dan Barag, *Catalogue of Western Asiatic Glass in the British Museum*, vol. 1 (London: British Museum Publications, 1985), 66–67, no. 42 (ME 127342), "from British Museum excavations in Mesopotamia during the second half of the nineteenth century."

35. Young, *Three Great Early Tumuli*, 131–41 (MM 70–123), 233–35.

36. Janet Duncan Jones, "Glass Vessels from Gordion: Trade and Influence along the Royal Road," in *The Archaeology of Midas and the Phrygians: Recent Work at Gordion*, ed. Lisa Kealhofter (Philadelphia: University of Pennsylvania Museum of Archaeology and Anthropology, 2005), 104–8; Sams, "Artifacts," 66.

37. Muzahim Mahmoud Hussein with Mark Altaweel and McGuire Gibson, *Nimrud: The Queens' Tombs* (Baghdad and Chicago: State Board of Antiquities and Heritage and the Oriental Institute of the University of Chicago, 2016), 34–36, pls. 134–37; Tracy L. Spurrier, "Finding Hama: On the Identification of a Forgotten Queen Buried in the Nimrud Tombs," *Journal of Near Eastern Studies* 76 (2017): 149–74.

38. Alessandra Cellerino, ed., *La brocca d'oro dalla Tomba Reale III a Nimrud: Un caso di studio* (Oxford: BAR Publishing, 2016); see also A. Cellerino, E. Foietta, and E. Quirico, "A Decorated Gold Jug from Nimrud Royal Tomb III," in *Proceedings of the 9th International Congress on the Archaeology of the Ancient Near East*,

vol. 1, *Dealing with the Past: Finds, Booty, Gifts, Spoils, Heirlooms*, ed. Rolf Stucky (Wiesbaden: Harrassowitz, 2016), 33–47, both with literature.

39. Hussein, *Nimrud Queens' Tombs*, 32–33, pls. 129–32; R. M. Boehmer, "Das Herkunftsgebiet der Goldene Krone aus Gruft III des Nordwest-Palastes zu Nimrud," *Baghdader Mitteilungen* 37 (2006): 213–19.

40. Amy Rebecca Gansell, "Imperial Fashion Networks: Royal Assyrian, Near Eastern Intercultural, and Composite Style Adornment from the Neo-Assyrian Royal Women's Tombs from Nimrud," in Aruz and Seymour, *Assyria to Iberia*, 54–64. Spurrier, "Finding Hama," 164–65, sees Assyrian workmanship.

41. The Egyptian-style gold bowl from Tomb II inscribed for Queen Yabâ, perhaps made in the tenth century in a workshop in the southern Levant, has been identified as a dowry item or diplomatic gift from her homeland. See Dirk Wicke with Erika Fischer and Angela Busch, "Die Goldschale der Iabâ—eine levantinische Antiquität," *Zeitschrift für Assyriologie* 100 (2010): 109–41, for a detailed analysis.

42. Gaspa, *Textiles in the Neo-Assyrian Empire*, 166–67.

43. Gaspa, *Textiles in the Neo-Assyrian Empire*, 164–82; Amy Rebecca Gansell, "Dressing the Neo-Assyrian Queen in Identity and Ideology: Elements and Ensembles from the Royal Tombs at Nimrud," *American Journal of Archaeology* 122 (2018): 65–100.

44. Mary W. Ballard, "King Midas' Textiles and His Golden Touch," in Rose, *Archaeology of Phrygian Gordion*, 165–70.

45. For Bayındır Tumulus D, see Engin Özgen and Ilknur Özgen, *Antalya Museum* (Ankara: Turkish Republic Ministry of Culture, General Directorate of Antiquities and Museums, 1992), 187–94; and Ilknur Özgen and Jean Öztürk, *Heritage Recovered: The Lydian Treasure* (Ankara: Republic of Turkey Ministry of Culture, General Directorate of Monuments and Museums, 1996), 27 (ivory figurine). See DeVries, "Age of Midas," 42, for a date in the late eighth century; cf. Kerschner, "Die Ionier," 115, with further references, on differing opinions about the date and style of the Bayındır finds. More recent discussions include Tuna Şare, "An Archaic Ivory Figurine from a Tumulus Near Elmalı: Cultural Hybridization and A New Anatolian Style," *Hesperia* 79 (2010): 53–78; and Roller, "Phrygia and Hellenism," esp. 48–50.

46. Hussein, *Nimrud Queens' Tombs*, 16, pl. 42.

47. A cross-cultural exploration of this phenomenon might prove fruitful, perhaps also in relation to cultural notions about materiality and light. See Mary Helms, *Ancient Panama: Chiefs in Search of Power* (Austin: University of Texas Press, 1979), 87; Nicholas J. Saunders, "'Catching the Light': Technologies of Power and Enchantment in Pre-Columbian Goldworking," in *Gold and Power in Ancient Costa Rica, Panama, and Colombia: A Symposium at Dumbarton Oaks, 9 and 10 October 1999*, ed. Jeffrey Quilter and John W. Hoopes (Washington, DC: Dumbarton Oaks Research Library and Collection, 2003), 15–47.

48. DeVries, "Age of Midas," 41, notes the diamond-pattern faceting on fine lustrous Phrygian black pottery, imitating earlier decoration preserved on wooden vessels. Elizabeth Simpson, *The Wooden Furniture from Tumulus MM* (Leiden: Brill, 2011), 93–99, compares ornament on wooden furniture with carved designs on rock-cut shrines, offering a thoughtful discussion of cross-media interaction involving geometric ornament and its evocation of Phrygian Matar.

49. Surveys based on the initial detailed analysis of material from Gordion and Boğazköy include Oscar White Muscarella, *Phrygian Fibulae from Gordion*

(London: Quaritch, 1967); Rainer Michael Boehmer, *Die Kleinfunde von Boğazköy: Aus den Grabungskampagnen 1931–1939 und 1952–1969* (Berlin: Gebr. Mann Verlag, 1972), esp. 46–66; Rainer Michael Boehmer, *Die Kleinfunde aus der Unterstadt von Boğazköy: Grabungskampagnen, 1970–1978* (Berlin: Gebr. Mann Verlag, 1979); and Muscarella, "King Midas and the Greeks," 333–44. For the cauldron with bull's head attachment, see Muscarella, "King Midas and the Greeks," 341, who recognizes as "genuine" Phrygian work only an example from Samos; and Ulf Jantzen, *Ägyptische und Orientalische Bronzen aus dem Heraion von Samos* (Bonn: Rudolf Habelt Verlag, 1972), pl. 76 (B1266). More recent overviews with extensive bibliography are found in Klebinder-Gauß, *Bronzefunde aus dem Artemision von Ephesos*, 208–15; and Maya Vassileva, "Phrygian Bronzes in the Greek World: Globalization through Cult?," in *The Ancient World in an Age of Globalization*, ed. Markham J. Geller (Berlin: Max Planck Institute for the History and Development of Knowledge, 2014), http://edition-open-access.de/proceedings/7/. See also Maya Vassileva, "Early Bronze Fibulae and Belts from the Gordion City Mound," in Rose, *Archaeology of Phrygian Gordion*, 111–26.

50. Braun-Holzinger and Rehm, *Orientalischer Import in Griechenland*, 168–76.

51. Young, *Three Great Early Tumuli*, 235–36, section contributed by Machteld J. Mellink.

52. Ingrid Strøm, "Evidence from the Sanctuaries," in *Greece between East and West: 10th–8th Centuries BC*, ed. Günter Kopcke and Isabelle Tokumaru (Mainz: von Zabern, 1992), 46–60; and Strøm, "The Early Sanctuary of the Argive Heraion and Its External Relations (8th–Early 6th Century B.C.): Bronze Imports and Archaic Greek Bronzes," *Proceedings of the Danish Institute at Athens* 2 (1998): 46–58.

53. Vassileva, "Phrygian Bronzes in the Greek World."

54. Roller, "Phrygia and Hellenism," 42–44, provides a recent discussion and further references.

55. Roller, "Phrygia and Hellenism," 42–50, with bibliography.

56. Klebinder-Gauß, "Ephesos und seine Beziehungen zur phrygischen Bronzekunst," 235–40; and Klebinder-Gauß, *Bronzefunde aus dem Artemision von Ephesos*, 208–15. Kerschner, "Die Ionier," 128–29, also suggests that Phrygian artisans sought work in Ionia and Lydia.

57. In a pioneering study, Arthur Steinberg, "Technology and Culture: Technological Styles in the Bronzes of Shang China, Phrygia and Urnfield Central Europe," in *Material Culture: Styles, Organization, and Dynamics of Technology*, ed. Heather Lechtman and Robert Merrill (St. Paul: West, 1977), 62–70, elaborated a distinctive "technological style" of Phrygian metalworking documented at Gordion, for example, in the forming and finishing of bronze trefoil-mouth jugs. Yet it was almost exclusively the moldmade fibulae and bowls that were replicated or refashioned in Archaic Greek sanctuaries. Culturally specific (or ritually authorized) ways of making things seem not consistently to have traveled with the notion of Phrygian artistic style in material, shape, or decoration.

58. Michael Kerschner, "Phrygischer Keramik in griechischem Kontext: Eine Omphalosschale der schwartz glänzenden Ware aus der so genannten Zentralbasis im Artemision von Ephesos und weitere phrygische Keramikfunde in der Ostägäis," *Jahreshefte der Österreichischen Archäogischen Institutes in Wien* 74 (2005): 147, has identified a single example of Phrygian black glazed ware in Ionia: a petaled bowl found in the so-called cult basis of the Artemision at Ephesus. He suggests it

resulted from the action of a single individual—either a Phrygian traveling to Ephesus or an Ionian who visited Phrygia and returned with the object.

59. Klebinder-Gauß, *Bronzefunde aus dem Artemision von Ephesos*, 206–7, 214.

60. Kerschner, "Die Ionier," 126: "Proximity to the Phrygian kingdom was evidently not a determining factor in the frequent occurrence of Phrygian bronze dedications."

✷ CHAPTER 9 ✷

Egypt and the Mediterranean in the Early Iron Age

BRIAN MUHS

This chapter reevaluates Egyptian connectivity with the Mediterranean basin and its hinterland in the Early Iron Age, in light of the new approaches to Mediterranean connectivity described by the editors of the volume, James Osborne and Jonathan Hall, in chapter 1.[1] It responds to Osborne and Hall's call for expanding the discussion of Mediterranean connectivity beyond the usual suspects, because scholars have rarely treated Egypt as an active participant in such connectivity, despite the region's prominent role in the historical record of this period. The chapter also takes up the editors' warning against projecting ethnicities or cultures on objects and styles, by pushing back against the proposal that the Egyptian-style luxury goods frequently found outside of Egypt in Early Iron Age contexts represent Phoenician rather than Egyptian material culture. Osborne and Hall suggest that simple overarching explanations for Mediterranean connectivity are unlikely to account for what was probably a complex phenomenon. The present chapter supports this suggestion by examining some Egyptian artifacts found outside of Egypt, whose inscriptions suggest a wide variety of object biographies, from royal and private gifts and booty to exchanges mediated by both Egyptians and non-Egyptians. The editors also hypothesize that frequent local trade in quotidian goods may have generated at least as much connectivity as less frequent long-distance trade in finished luxury goods. The chapter explores this hypothesis by examining indirect archaeological evidence for exchange of commodities between Egypt and the Mediterranean, which suggests intense economic connectivity between Egypt and the Levant.

Historical Record

The absence of Egypt from discussions of Mediterranean connectivity in the Early Iron Age is surprising, given Egypt's prominence in the historical record. The Egyptian kings of the Twenty-First Dynasty (ca. 1069–943 BCE) and of the Twenty-Second Dynasty (c. 943–733 BCE) ruled Egypt from the port of Tanis in the eastern Delta.[2] The Story of Wenamun depicts a lively trade between Tanis and the Levant,[3] ostensibly at the beginning of the Twenty-First Dynasty when the story is set, but possibly describing the Twenty-Second Dynasty when the sole manuscript of the story was written.[4] The first king of the Twenty-Second Dynasty, Shoshenq I, famously invaded the southern Levant, and he and his successors apparently sent dedications to sanctuaries at Byblos. Egypt may no longer have been an imperial power as it had been during the Late Bronze Age, but it was probably still the largest polity and market in the Eastern Mediterranean prior to the arrival of the Assyrian Empire on its shores, and as such Egyptian rather than Assyrian demand may have stimulated the early expansion of the Phoenicians westward.

Tanite royal authority over the rest of Egypt declined in the eighth century BCE, encouraging the kings of the Twenty-Fourth Dynasty (ca. 728–715 BCE), based at Sais in the western Delta, to try to assert their authority. The Kushite kings of the Twenty-Fifth Dynasty (ca. 747–656 BCE), based at Napata in Nubia, intervened in Egypt (ca. 727 BCE), however, and eventually suppressed the Twenty-Fourth Dynasty (ca. 715 BCE). The Kushite kings then intervened in the southern Levant, which supposedly motivated the Assyrians to invade Egypt (c. 672 BCE), to drive out the Kushite kings, to place their clients back on their thrones, and to deport Egyptian craftsmen to Assyria. The Saite kings of the Twenty-Sixth Dynasty (ca. 672–525 BCE), probably clients of the Assyrians, were subsequently able to reunite Egypt under their rule. They expanded into the Levant until they were driven out by the Neo-Babylonians, but they were also oriented toward the Aegean. In the seventh century BCE, they established a new Mediterranean port at Herakleion-Thonis to the west of Tanis,[5] they recruited Ionian and Carians to emigrate to Egypt to serve as soldiers,[6] they sent dedications to Greek sanctuaries, and they established a Greek entrepot in Egypt at Naucratis between Sais and Herakleion-Thonis.[7]

Style and Object Biographies

A large number of Egyptian-style luxury goods have been found outside of Egypt in Early Iron Age contexts.[8] Some scholars would attribute at least some of these ivories, metal vessels, scarabs, amulets, and statuettes to Egyptian manufacture.[9] Other scholars, however, such as Eric Gubal, have proposed that Egyptian iconography had become completely normalized in Phoenician culture during the Late Bronze Age and that most Egyptian-style artifacts found outside of Egypt in the Early Iron Age represent Phoenician rather than Egyptian material culture.[10] Marian Feldman has justifiably questioned whether the use of Egyptian iconography outside of Egypt can be attributed exclusively to Phoenician culture, and she suggests instead that it was common throughout the Levant, Syria, and Assyria.[11] Clearly, style is not a conclusive indicator of ethnic or cultural origin or use, as Osborne and Hall have noted in chapter 1. Consequently, the following two sections use object biographies of selected Egyptian-style statues and stone vessels to argue that at least some Egyptian material culture was exported from Egypt in the Early Iron Age. The evidence is extremely anecdotal, as it is limited to objects bearing inscriptions in Egyptian or other languages that hint at their object biographies, but nonetheless it provides a useful supplement to the traditional use of style as an indicator of connectivity.

Egyptian Statues

Inscribed Egyptian-style statues and monuments found outside of Egypt are good indicators of connectivity, due to the object biographies suggested by their inscriptions. Some probably commemorated victories, like the fragment of a stela of the Egyptian king Shoshenq I (ca. 943–923 BCE) found at Megiddo,[12] the statues of the Kushite king Taharqa (ca. 690–664 BCE) found at the entrance to the palace of the Assyrian king Esarhaddon (680–669 BCE) at Tell Nebi Yunus at Nineveh,[13] or the three fragments of an Egyptian granite obelisk found at Assur.[14] In many cases it is unclear how or even when they arrived abroad, like the statue of the Egyptian king Psammetichus I (664–610 BCE) found at Arwad or Aradus,[15] or the basalt tablet fragment mentioning the Egyptian king Necho II (610–595 BCE), supposedly found at Sidon.[16] A few Egyptian statues found abroad, however, bear secondary inscriptions that clarify they were sent abroad in the late tenth through the early sixth centuries BCE. These statues witness close ties between the kings of Egypt and those of the Phoenician city of Byblos in the late tenth and ninth centuries BCE, and then between the kings of Egypt and private individuals from the eastern Aegean in the late seventh and early sixth centuries BCE.

Three or four Egyptian royal statues of the late tenth and ninth centuries BCE have been found at Byblos. They bear hieroglyphic inscriptions identifying the kings that they represent, and at least two of the statues also bear Phoenician royal inscriptions whose paleography suggests that they are contemporary with the Egyptian kings represented, though this has been contested.[17] Consequently, the statues are usually assumed to have been diplomatic gifts from the kings of Egypt to the kings of Byblos.[18] There is one granite fragment from a throne base of a seated statue of the Egyptian king Shoshenq I (ca. 943–923 BCE) acquired at Byblos by a Danish consul. An added Phoenician inscription of Abiba'al, king of Byblos, states that he brought it from Egypt for the goddess Ba'alat Gebal.[19] There are eight sandstone fragments from one or two statues of Shoshenq I's successor, Osorkon I (ca. 923–890 BCE) also found at Byblos.[20] A Neapolitan banker acquired the first three fragments before 1882, including the upper body, belt, and statue base. The upper body has an added Phoenician inscription of Eliba'al, another king of Byblos, stating that he made it for the goddess Ba'alat Gebal.[21] Pierre Montet excavated three more fragments at Byblos in the Syrian Temple, including one of the kilt and two of the throne back,[22] and Maurice Dunand found two more fragments at Byblos, including an elbow and a shoulder and arm. The shoulder and arm possessed a portion of an added Phoenician inscription, possibly part of the text on the upper body.[23] There is also the lower portion of a grano-diorite seated statue of Osorkon I's grandson, Osorkon II (ca. 861–831 BCE), excavated at Byblos by Dunand, but if there was an added inscription it has not survived.[24] Another Egyptian statue fragment from Moab also has an added ninth century BCE Moabite royal inscription mentioning Kemoshyat, but too little is preserved to determine whether the Egyptian statue was royal or private, and contemporary or reused from an earlier period.[25]

In contrast, three smaller Egyptian statues of the late seventh or early sixth centuries BCE have been found near Priene and on Rhodes in the eastern Aegean. None of the statues is obviously royal or bears any hieroglyphic inscriptions, and their Greek dedicatory inscriptions name private individuals, though one also mentions an Egyptian king. Private individuals are therefore thought to have taken these statues out of Egypt. One of the three is an Egyptian block statue of the late seventh or early sixth centuries BCE found near Priene in the eastern Aegean.[26] It has an added Ionic Greek inscription reading "Pedon the son of Amphinnes dedicated me, having brought me from Egypt. The Egyptian king Psammetichus gave to him as a prize of valor a golden armlet and a city because of his virtue." Pedon was probably one of the Ionian soldiers who served under the kings of the Saite Twenty-Sixth Dynasty, but it is unclear whether the inscription refers to Psammetichus I (664–610

BCE) or Psammetichus II (595–589 BCE), and whether the statue was also a royal gift.[27] A fragment of a basalt Egyptian statuette of a kneeling man was found at the sanctuary of Athena at Camirus on Rhodes, with a fragmentary Greek inscription, possibly reading "[Smyr]des dedicated me."[28] Another fragmentary kneeling Egyptian statuette was found at the sanctuary of Zeus on Mount Atabyros on Rhodes, and has a similar but better-preserved Doric Greek inscription apparently naming the same man, "Smyrdes son of Syndos dedicated me." The paleography of both inscriptions appears to date to the late seventh or early sixth century BCE.[29] The inscriptions on the two statuettes found in Rhodes do not mention Egyptian kings, but there is evidence that they took an interest in Rhodes and the eastern Mediterranean. Inlays from a shrine of Necho II (610–595 BCE) were found at the sanctuary of Athena at Ialysus on Rhodes,[30] and Herodotus wrote that Necho II dedicated his armor to the sanctuary of Apollo at Branchidae near Miletus in the eastern Aegean.[31]

Egyptian Stone Vessels

Egyptian-style stone vessels found outside of Egypt are also good indicators of connectivity, because they sometimes bear Egyptian inscriptions that hint at their object biographies. Egyptian stone vessels of the ninth through seventh centuries BCE are usually but not exclusively made from calcite, a common Egyptian stone that Egyptologists call alabaster, and frequently are conical or cylindrical-ovoid in shape with lug handles, imitating the forms of ceramic Phoenician "bullet" or "torpedo" storage and transport jars used for wine and well known in Egypt (see below). They often bear Egyptian hieroglyphic inscriptions, with royal or divine names in cartouches and sometimes with sophisticated dedicatory inscriptions identifying the contents as wine from the Bahariya-Farafra and Dakhla-Kharga oases for the ka-spirits of officials or priests,[32] which helps explain why they imitate the forms of Phoenician wine jars. Egyptian stone vessels of this type have been found as funerary offerings in both Egyptian and Nubian royal tombs, reused as oil containers in palaces in the Levant and Assyria, and as cinerary urns in Phoenician cemeteries in southern Spain. From the seventh century BCE onward, larger inscribed alabaster vessels disappear and smaller more portable forms become common in Nubian royal tombs,[33] as well as throughout the Mediterranean. Many of the smaller vessels were produced in Naucratis, presumably for export, but they were also frequently imitated abroad, often in other media. Greek texts refer to them as alabastra, from which the term "alabaster" derives, and indicate that they contained unguents, perfumes, or spices.[34]

Curiously, some have suggested that many or all of the larger vessels are of Phoenician manufacture, and that the inscriptions are copies of original Egyptian texts because they are eccentric.[35] This seems improbable, however, given the presence of such vessels in royal Egyptian and Nubian tombs naming the tomb owners. One conical alabaster vessel with the cartouches of King Osorkon I (ca. 923–890 BCE) was found in the burial chamber of his son Takeloth I at Tanis in Egypt, in the tomb complex of his grandson Osorkon II.[36] Fragments of at least twenty large conical and cylindrical-ovoid alabaster vessels, one porphyry vessel, and one quartzite jug were found at the royal cemetery at el-Kurru in Nubia, in the tombs of Queen Khenisa,[37] Queen Nefrukekashta,[38] and Queen Tabiry,[39] all wives of King Piye (ca. 747–716 BCE); in the tomb of Queen Arty,[40] wife of King Shebitku (ca. 716–704 BCE); in the tomb of King Shabako (ca. 704–690 BCE);[41] in the tomb of King Tanwetamani (ca. 664–656 BCE);[42] and in two anonymous tombs.[43] Four alabaster vessels and one quartzite jug had hieroglyphic inscriptions for Queen Khenisa, but all the other examples were uninscribed. Presumably the Kushite kings of Nubia acquired the stone vessels and their contents from Egypt for the same reasons that Egyptian kings included them in their tombs, because wine from the Egyptian oases was a prestigious offering for gods and the ka-spirits of the dead,[44] and some funerary rituals specified that wine be offered in stone vessels.[45]

Egyptian stone vessels were also exported or carried off to the Levant and Assyria, where they were reused and perhaps imitated. A conical alabaster vase with cartouches of King Osorkon II (ca. 861–831 BCE) and a hieroglyphic Egyptian label reading "81 hin" (about 40 liters) was found in the courtyard of the Palace of Ahab at Samaria in Israel.[46] Nine conical and cylindrical-ovoid alabaster vessels were found in Rooms 1 and 2 of the Old Palace of Ashurnasirpal II at Assur in Iraq, of which six bore cuneiform inscriptions of the Assyrian kings Sennacherib (704–681 BCE), Esarhaddon (680–669 BCE), and Ashurbanipal (668–631 BCE).[47] One of these, a conical alabaster vessel, also had an older hieroglyphic text, with cartouches containing names of the god Herishef, and a dedicatory inscription mentioning wine for the future Egyptian king Takeloth III before his accession (ca. 765 BCE). The later cuneiform inscription described it as an oil jar (*naḫbaṣu*) and stated that the Assyrian king Esarhaddon (680–669 BCE) took it from the palace treasury of King Abdimilkuti of Sidon in 677 BCE.[48] Two fragments of a granite vase with a hieroglyphic inscription of the Kushite king Taharqa (ca. 690–664 BCE) were probably also found at Assur.[49] Two complete alabaster vessels with cuneiform inscriptions mentioning the palace of the Assyrian king Sargon II

(721–705 BCE) were found in the Northwest Palace at Nimrud.[50] They were found with fragments of other alabaster vessels, some with similar cuneiform inscriptions, and one with a fragmentary Egyptian hieroglyphic inscription. Ann Searight, Julian Reade, and Irving Finkel argued that they were all acquired in the Levant, and Kenneth Kitchen suggested that the hieroglyphic inscription was a Levantine copy, because the cartouche did not contain a royal name,[51] but there are clear Egyptian parallels such as the above-mentioned vase with names of the god Herishef in cartouches. A green glass cylindrical-ovoid vessel was also found there, again with a cuneiform inscription mentioning the palace of Sargon II.[52] Barag argued that it was manufactured in Phoenicia imitating Egyptian forms, because it is similar to a rock crystal vessel with a hieroglyphic inscription naming the Egyptian king Rudamun (ca. 753–747 BCE),[53] but Margaret O'Hea has suggested possible North Syrian or Mesopotamian manufacture.[54] Many more fragments of alabaster vessels with cuneiform inscriptions naming Sennacherib (704–681 BCE), Esarhaddon (680–669 BCE), and Ashurbanipal (668–631 BCE) have also been found, at least some of them at the Southwest Palace at Kuyunjik at Nineveh. Searight, Reade, and Finkel argued that these were manufactured locally in Assyria for court use,[55] but a diorite bowl with an Egyptian hieroglyphic inscription naming a prophet of Amun, Khamope, was also found at the Southwest Palace.[56] It is possible that Egyptians abroad manufactured some of these Egyptian-style stone vessels in the Levant and in Assyria. The Assyrians record that they deported many Egyptian craftsmen from Egypt after their defeat of the Kushites in 672 BCE, though they do not specify stonemasons.[57] Furthermore, Libyan Egyptians are already documented living and owning property in Assyria alongside Samarians by 700 BCE, suggesting that they could have been resident in Samaria and deported with the Samarians in 722 BCE.[58]

Egyptian stone vessels have also been found in Phoenician cemeteries in southern Spain, presumably brought from Egypt by Phoenician merchants and colonists.[59] Twenty-one conical and cylindrical-ovoid alabaster vessels were found reused as cinerary urns in the cemetery of Cerro de San Cristobal near the Phoenician site of Almuñécar in Spain, of which five cylindrical-ovoid vessels bore hieroglyphic inscriptions.[60] One vessel from Grave 17 was inscribed for King Osorkon II (ca. 875–840 BCE),[61] as was another vessel from Grave 20.[62] One from Grave 1 was inscribed with a dedicatory text for King Takeloth II (ca. 834–810 BCE),[63] and one from Grave 16 was inscribed for King Sheshonq III (ca. 831–788 BCE).[64] A fifth vessel from Grave 15 was inscribed with a dedicatory text for a nonroyal individual in Bubastis named Osorkon.[65] A similar conical alabaster vessel with a hieroglyphic dedicatory text for a priest named Djedhorefankh was part of an old Spanish private collection.[66] A glass jug with a hieroglyphic inscription was also found in southwest Spain as part of the Aliseda treasure.[67] The form resembles Phoenician biconical juglets,[68] and is also similar to the inscribed quartzite jug found in the tomb of Queen Khenisa at el-Kurru in Nubia. It has been claimed that the inscription is illegible and must therefore be a Phoenician copy,[69] but the name of the goddess Isis is clearly readable in the cartouche, which has parallels on other Egyptian stone vessels.

Commodities

Styles and object biographies are important indicators of connectivity in the Early Iron Age, but for later periods Peregrine Horden and Nicholas Purcell famously argued that trade in regionally specialized or environmentally specific commodities was the engine of Mediterranean connectivity, as the inhabitants of microecologies sought to diversify their economies and reduce their environmental risks.[70] Osborne and Hall have therefore suggested that local trade in commodities and quotidian goods may have also contributed to connectivity in the Early Iron Age, though perhaps not to the extent that it did in later periods. The ecological conditions that encouraged trade between Egypt and its neighbors in later periods certainly also existed in the Early Iron Age. For example, Phoenicia was the nearest region to Egypt with access to long timber, and the Story of Wenamun depicts Byblos in Phoenicia as a regular exporter of timber to Egypt. The following three sections explore evidence for trade in other environmentally or geologically restricted commodities in the Early Iron Age, namely, for the possible import of wine and silver to Egypt from its neighbors and for the possible export of papyrus, linen, and grain from Egypt to its neighbors.

Wine

Wine from the Egyptian oases was religiously significant for the Egyptians, but they also appear to have imported large quantities of wine from the Levant, and this trade may have been a source of connectivity in the Early Iron Age. This trade should be visible in the archaeological record, because ancient Mediterranean wine and oil were usually transported in distinctive ceramic storage jars whose forms were often characteristic of specific regions, and whose archaeological discovery beyond those regions can provide evidence for export of wine or oil or other bulky goods. In Egypt, however, Aegean vessel forms have historically received more archaeological attention than Levantine forms, obscuring this potential evidence for Egyptian connectivity with the Levant in the ninth through seventh centuries BCE.

Storage jars typical of Aegean regions found in Egypt,[71] as well as Greek drinking cups and vessels found there,[72] have been studied intensively but do not seem to appear in Egypt until the end of the seventh century BCE. Traditionally, Greek traders at Naucratis and Greek mercenaries at Tell Defenneh were thought to be the primary users of such Greek pottery in Egypt. More recently, however, it has become accepted that Greek pottery was an internationally traded commodity, and that Egyptians were also consumers of Greek pottery and products such as wine, as early as the seventh century BCE.[73]

Storage jars typical of the Levant found in Egypt have received much less attention than those of Greece. Nonetheless, torpedo-shaped storage jars, known to be produced in the Phoenician city-kingdoms,[74] have been found in Egypt in contexts dating between the ninth and seventh centuries BCE, and/or with forms assigned to those dates.[75] Furthermore, such Phoenician "torpedo" storage jars are often anecdotally said to be extremely common at Egyptian sites in the eighth and seventh centuries BCE,[76] and they even appear at the royal cemetery of el-Kurru in Nubia in the tomb of Queen Nefrukekashta, the wife of King Piye (ca. 747–716 BCE).[77] Phoenician "torpedo" storage jars have also been found in two shipwrecks in the Mediterranean Sea north of Egypt and west of Israel, dating to the eighth century BCE. The presence of an Egyptian bowl alongside several Phoenician cooking pots suggests that the ships had sailed between Phoenicia and Egypt previously, and the location of the shipwrecks and the presence of almost four hundred Phoenician "torpedo" storage jars on each ship suggests that they were traveling from Phoenicia to Egypt when wrecked. The jars were pitched with resin and thus were probably intended for wine transport.[78] Volumetric analysis of these vessels has suggested that the jars on the two shipwrecks were produced to contain a standard volume of about 19.2 liters, so that they would correspond to 4 hekats (each 4.8 liters) in the Egyptian system of weights and measures for the Egyptian market.[79] Actually, the hekat is a dry measure, so the jars were more likely intended to correspond to 40 hin (each 0.48 liters) in the Egyptian system. Furthermore, Egyptian-made alabaster vessels intended for Egyptian wine from the oases deliberately imitated the forms of Phoenician "torpedo" storage jars, suggesting that the Phoenician forms had become synonymous with wine in Egypt. It is perhaps also worth noting that the Egyptian hieroglyphic volume notation on a fragment of one of these alabaster vessels reads "81 hin," double the volume of a standard Phoenician "torpedo" jar.[80]

Silver

Egypt may have imported large quantities of silver in the Early Iron Age, in addition to wine, and this trade may also have been a source of connectivity. Silver became the primary form of money in the Eastern Mediterranean in the Early Iron Age, but it was also a commodity whose main Mediterranean sources were in Anatolia, the Aegean, Sardinia, and southern Iberia. The Phoenicians are usually thought to be responsible for bringing silver from western Mediterranean sources to the eastern Mediterranean in the ninth through seventh centuries BCE, primarily because of the Phoenician settlements in southern Iberia and their association with mining and smelting sites there.[81] Trace element analysis may also suggest Sardinian and Iberian origins for some silver in Levantine hoards.[82] Many scholars, including Cyprian Broodbank, have suggested that the Phoenicians were motivated to go west by Assyrian demands for silver as tribute,[83] or as payment of customs duties on other commodities passing through Phoenician harbors.[84] The Phoenician expansion began before the Assyrian Empire threatened the Phoenician city-kingdoms, however, and imperial domination was not a prerequisite for customs duties, since the Saite kings may have established customs posts on Egypt's borders by the beginning of the sixth century BCE.[85]

It seems more likely that the Phoenicians were motivated to go west to engage in arbitrage, the practice of buying commodities like silver in places where they are more common and less valuable, and then selling them in places where they are less common and more valuable, in order to profit from the difference in prices. Historically, silver arbitrage has been responsible for massive shifts in the global distribution of silver. For example, the switch from paper to silver currency in Ming China in the fifteenth century CE encouraged the Spanish to ship silver from the New World to Manila in the Philippines in the sixteenth century to purchase Chinese goods to import to Europe.[86] Ancient Near Eastern merchants certainly also engaged in silver arbitrage, because Assyrian merchants say they did so in letters from Anatolia from the early second millennium BCE.[87]

No letters testifying to silver arbitrage in the early first millennium BCE have yet been found, but changes in the relative values of gold and silver in Egypt and Mesopotamia from the Late Bronze Age to the Iron Age suggest that arbitrage may have occurred. Previously in the Late Bronze Age, Egypt used a variety of commodities as measures of value, media of exchange, and stores of wealth, including but not limited to gold, silver, copper, linen, and grain.[88] Silver had not yet become the primary form of money in Egypt, and Egypt controlled and exploited abundant local sources of gold in its Eastern Desert and in Nubia. The grave goods of King Tutankhamun contained far more gold than silver, for example, and silver hoards are rare.[89] One of them, the el-Till hoard from Tell el-Amarna, contained three times as much gold as silver by weight.[90] This archaeological abundance of gold and relative scarcity of silver parallels textual evidence that gold was only valued twice as much as silver by weight in Egypt at this time.[91] Egypt may have also supplied the Eastern Mediterranean with considerable amounts of gold through royal gift exchange. In Mesopotamia at this time, texts reveal that gold was valued eight times as much as silver by weight, compared to twelve times as much in the Early Iron Age.[92]

By the Early Iron Age, however, Egypt lost control of, and access to, Nubia so gold was probably no longer as available as it had been in the Late Bronze Age. Meanwhile, silver appears to have become more common. The grave goods of the Twenty-Second Dynasty kings buried at Tanis contained far more silver than that of Tutankhamun, though gold objects still outnumber silver ones,[93] and transactions in Egypt were increasingly valued in, and possibly also used, weights of silver rather than other commodities.[94] In addition, silver hoards may increase in number and size in this period, though they are difficult to date precisely prior to the appearance of coins in Egypt at the end of the sixth century BCE. The most securely dated silver hoard without coins was found at Elephantine. It consisted of a small pottery jar stylistically dated to the Twenty-Fifth or early Twenty-Sixth Dynasty (ca. 750–600 BCE), which contained three linen packets and 118 pieces of cut silver together weighing 39.45 grams.[95] Three other silver hoards without coins have been found in Egypt, but they could date as late as the sixth century BCE.[96] One of these was found at Tell el-Atrib (Athribis) in 1924 and contained fifty kilograms of silver.[97] Finally, textual sources confirm that by the late first millennium BCE, gold was valued in Egypt at ten to twelve times as much as silver by weight.[98] In Mesopotamia as well, gold was valued twelve times as much as silver by weight by the early first millennium BCE.[99]

Some of this change in the relative values of gold and silver was undoubtedly due to the increasing scarcity of gold, but some was certainly also driven by the increasing availability of silver. This increased availability of silver, in turn, was probably at least partially due to silver arbitrage, especially in Egypt, which was not in a position to demand silver as tribute or taxes for most of this period, except from merchants who chose to come to Egypt.

Papyrus, Linen, and Grain

Egypt is famous for its exports of papyrus, linen, and grain to the rest of the Mediterranean in later periods, so it is not unreasonable to inquire whether this trade existed and was a source of connectivity already in the Early Iron Age. However, these organic commodities neither preserve well nor require distinctive ceramic transport vessels, which makes them difficult to track archaeologically. Later textual sources make it clear that papyrus eventually became the preferred writing medium around the Mediterranean, though never the only one, but it is unknown when Egypt began to produce and export papyrus in large volumes.[100] Alphabetic scripts related to, or derived from, the Phoenician script began to appear around the Mediterranean by the ninth century BCE if not earlier,[101] but it is unknown whether their adoption was related to possible Phoenician distribution of Egyptian papyrus, since there were other media on which they could have been written. Later textual sources also suggest that Egypt eventually produced and exported large quantities of linen around the Mediterranean as well,[102] but unlike papyrus and alphabetic scripts there are no obvious proxies for linen.

Egyptian grain provides an illuminating comparison to highly portable papyrus and linen. Many scholars have suggested that Egypt regularly exported grain from a very early date, and Broodbank has even argued that texts from Ugarit referring to emergency shipments of grain from Egypt to Anatolia show that Egyptian grain was feeding the Eastern Mediterranean already in the Late Bronze Age.[103] Grain is an extremely bulky commodity, however, and consequently one of the most sensitive to transportation risks and costs. In northern Europe, the medieval Hanseatic League primarily transported rich cargoes of cloth and wine around the North and Baltic Seas, and the Dutch did not begin to transport bulk cargoes of grain until the fifteenth century.[104] Textual sources from the Roman period clearly indicate that the food supply of Rome was dependent in part on regular shipments of grain from Egypt,[105] but Mediterranean maritime connectivity was at its peak at that time according to shipwreck evidence.[106] In contrast, textual sources from the Classical period suggest that Athens regularly supplemented its local grain production with imports from elsewhere in the Aegean before the Peloponnesian War (431–404 BCE), and from the Black Sea afterward, but not from Egypt.[107] Indeed, prior to the Roman period, references to grain shipments from Egypt to the Aegean refer to royal gifts in response to local food shortages, such as the gift of Psammetichus V to Athens in 445–444 BCE,[108] or the gift of Ptolemy III to Rhodes in 227–226 BCE.[109] Food shortages, however, often lead to hoarding and speculation, which have a tendency to greatly increase margins and profits, so one cannot extrapolate regular long-distance bulk shipments of grain from emergency shipments.[110]

Based on these later textual sources, it seems unlikely that Egypt regularly exported grain in the ninth through seventh centuries BCE. Rather, the Egyptian kings and temples probably used their surplus grain to feed craftspeople, who produced elite artifacts like royal statues and stone vessels, or portable finished commodities like papyrus and linen, which could more easily be exported. The limited archaeological evidence for organic Egyptian commodities like papyrus, linen, and grain makes this hypothesis impossible to confirm at this time, however.

Conclusion

This chapter has presented evidence for connectivity between Egypt and the Mediterranean basin, and especially the Levant, in the ninth through seventh centuries BCE. Some of it is unambiguous, like the Egyptian royal statues in Byblos or the Phoenician storage jars in Egypt. Some of it is circumstantial, like the distribution of Egyptian stone vessels in the Mediterranean, their imitation of Phoenician forms, shifts in the distribution of silver to Egypt, and the possible relation of the spread of Phoenician-derived alphabets to the export of Egyptian papyrus. Taken together, however, the evidence for connectivity between Egypt and the Levant in the Early Iron Age is strong.

Notes

1. The author would like to acknowledge and thank the editors and anonymous reviewers of this volume for their comments and recommendations, and especially Tasha Vorderstrasse for carefully reviewing this chapter and making innumerable invaluable suggestions.

2. Dates are based on David A. Aston, "Takeloth II, A King of the Herakleopolitan/Theban Twenty-Third Dynasty Revisited: The Chronology of Dynasties 22 and 23," in *The Libyan Period in Egypt, Historical and Cultural Studies into the 21st–24th Dynasties: Proceedings of a Conference at Leiden University, 25–27 October 2007*, ed. G. P. F. Broekman, R. J. Demarée, and O. E. Kaper (Leuven: Peeters, 2009), 1–28.

3. Papyrus Moscow Pushkin 120, see Robert K. Ritner, *The Libyan Anarchy: Inscriptions from Egypt's Third Intermediate Period* (Atlanta: Society of Biblical Literature, 2009), 87–99, no. 18.

4. Ricardo A. Caminos, *A Tale of Woe, from a Hieratic Papyrus in the A. S. Pushkin Museum of Fine Arts in Moscow* (Oxford: Griffith Institute, Ashmolean Museum, 1977), 3; and Benjamin Sass, "Wenamun and His Levant: 1075 BC or 925 BC?," *Ägypten und Levante* 12 (2002): 247–55.

5. Catherine Grataloup, "12: Occupation and Trade at Heracleion-Thonis; The Evidence from the Pottery," in *Alexandria and the North-Western Delta*, ed. Damian Robinson and Andrew Wilson (Oxford: Centre for Maritime Archaeology, 2010), 151–59.

6. Herodotus 2.152–54, supported by numerous Greek and Carian graffiti and funerary inscriptions in Egypt, see Günter Vittmann, *Ägypten und die Fremden im ersten vorchristlichen Jahrtausend* (Mainz: Philipp von Zabern, 2003), 155–76 (Carians), 197–208 (Greeks).

7. Herodotus 2.178–79, attributed the establishment of Naucratis to the Saite king Amasis (570–526 BCE), but archaeological evidence dates it to the end of the seventh century BCE; see Astrid Möller, *Naukratis: Trade in Archaic Greece* (Oxford: Oxford University Press, 2000), 182–96; and Vittmann, *Ägypten und die Fremden*, 209–23.

8. For example, Ingrid Gamer-Wallert, *Ägyptische und ägyptisierende Funde von der Iberischen Halbinsel* (Wiesbaden: Reichert, 1978); Günther Hölbl, *Beziehungen der ägyptischen Kultur zu Altitalien*, 2 vols. (Leiden: Brill, 1979); Josep Padró I Parcerisa, *Egyptian-Type Documents from the Mediterranean Littoral of the Iberian Peninsula Before the Roman Conquest*, 3 vols. (Leiden: Brill, 1980–1985); Günther Hölbl, *Ägyptisches Kulturgut im phönikischen und punischen Sardinien*, 2 vols. (Leiden: Brill, 1986); Nancy Joan Skon-Jedele, "*Aigyptiaka*: A Catalogue of Egyptian and Egyptianizing Objects Excavated from Greek Archaeological Sites, ca. 1100–525 B.C., with Historical Commentary" (PhD diss., University of Pennsylvania, 1994); and Andrée Feghali Gorton, *Egyptian and Egyptianizing Scarabs: A Typology of Steatite, Faience and Paste Scarabs from Punic and other Mediterranean Sites* (Oxford: Oxbow Books, 1996).

9. For example, Günther Hölbl, "Appendix 3: Aegyptiaca from the Mound at Chatal Höyük," in *Excavations in the Plain of Antioch 3: Stratigraphy, Pottery, and Small Finds from Chatal Höyük in the Amuq Plain*, ed. Marina Pucci (Chicago: Oriental Institute, 2019), 305–18.

10. Eric Gubal, "Crossing Continents: Phoenician Art and How to Read it," in *Assyria to Iberia: Art and Culture in the Iron Age*, ed. Joan Aruz and Michael Seymour (New York: Metropolitan Museum of Art, 2016), 169–71, 175–79.

11. Marian Feldman, *Communities of Style: Portable Luxury Arts, Identity and Collective Memory in the Iron Age Levant* (Chicago: University of Chicago Press, 2014), 73–74, 179.

12. Jerusalem Rockefeller Museum I. 3554, see Clarence S. Fisher, *The Excavation of Armageddon* (Chicago: University of Chicago Press, 1929), 12–16; Ritner, *Libyan Anarchy*, 218–19, no. 51.

13. Naji al Asil, "Editorial Notes and Archaeological Events: The Assyrian Palace at Nebi Unis," *Sumer* 10 (1954): 110–11; William Kelly Simpson, "The Pharaoh Taharqa," *Sumer* 10 (1954): 193–94; Vladimir Vikentiev, "Quelques considerations à propos des statues de Taharqa trouvées dans les ruines du palais d'Esarhaddon," *Sumer* 11 (1955): 111–16; and John Malcolm Russell, *The Final Sack of Nineveh: The Discovery, Documentation and Destruction of King Sennacherib's Throne Room at Nineveh* (New Haven, CT: Yale University Press, 1988), 241, pl. 230.

14. Istanbul AOM/ES 9698–9700, see "Wissenschaftliche Berichte: Museen. Die Antiken-Museen in Istanbul," *Archiv für Orientforschung* 10 (1935–1936): 92–94.

15. Ernest Renan, *Mission de Phénicie* (Paris: Imprimerie impériale, 1864), 27.

16. Possibly now British Museum EA 65913, see Francis Llewellyn Griffith, "A Relic of Pharaoh Necho from Phoenicia," *Proceedings of the Society of Biblical Archaeology* 16 (1894): 90–91.

17. William F. Albright, "The Phoenician Inscriptions of the Tenth Century B.C. from Byblus," *Journal of the American Oriental Society* 67 (1947): 153–60; André Lemaire, "La datation des rois de Byblos Abibaal et Élibaal et les relations entre l'Égypte et le Levant au Xe siècle av. notre ère," *Comptes rendus des séances de l'Académie des Inscriptions et Belles-Lettres* 150, no. 4 (2006): 1697–716; and Christopher A. Rollston, "The Dating of the Early Royal Byblian Phoenician Inscriptions: A Response to Benjamin Sass," *MAARAV* 15 (2008): 57–93.

18. Ashley Fiutko Arico, "The Contexts of Ancient Egyptian Statuary in the Levant" (PhD diss., Johns Hopkins University, 2016), 423–33. I am grateful to the author for a copy of her dissertation, and for permission to cite it here.

19. Statue Berlin VA 3361, see Charles Clermont-Ganneau, "Inscription égypto-phénicienne de Byblos," *Comptes rendus des séances de l'Académie des Inscriptions et Belles-Lettres* 47, no. 4 (1903): 378–85; Charles Clermont-Ganneau, "Inscription égypto-phénicienne de Byblos," *Recueil d'Archéologie Orientale* 6 (1905): 74–78; Ritner, *Libyan Anarchy*, 219–20, no. 52; and Arico, "Ancient Egyptian Statuary," 263–65, no. 67.

20. Ritner, *Libyan Anarchy*, 233–34, no. 57; Arico, "Ancient Egyptian Statuary," 266–77, nos. 68–75.

21. Including statue fragments Louvre AO 9502/E 17451, and Louvre AO 9503, see Alfred Wiedemann, "Varia," *Recueil de travaux relatifs à la philologie et à archéologie égyptiennes et assyriennes* 17 (1895): 1–17, esp. 14 (no. 14); and Alfred Wiedemann, "Varia," *Sphinx* 16, no. 1 (1912): 11–22, esp. 14 (sec. X.A.).

22. Including statue fragment Louvre AO 31153; see Pierre Montet, *Byblos et l'Égypte: Quatre campagnes de fouilles à Gebeil; 1921–1922–1923–1924, Texte* (Paris: Librairie Orientaliste Paul Geuthner, 1928), 49–51, 53–54, and fig. 14 (nos. 26–28).

23. Maurice Dunand, *Fouilles de Byblos. Tome Ier: 1926–1932, Texte* (Paris: Librairie Orientaliste Paul Geuthner. 1939), 17–18, and fig. 7 (no. 1048).

24. Statue Beirut National Museum DGA 2050, see Dunand, *Fouilles de Byblos*, 115–17 (no. 1741); Ritner, *Libyan Anarchy*, 288, no. 75; and Arico, *Ancient Egyptian Statuary*, 278–81, no. 76.

25. Jordan Kerak Museum No. 6807, see Heather Dana Davis Parker and Ashley Fiutko Arico, "A Moabite-Inscribed Statue Fragment from Kerak: Egyptian Parallels," *Bulletin of the American Schools of Oriental Research* 373 (2015): 105–20; and Arico, *Ancient Egyptian Statuary*, 124–26, no. 20.

26. Now in the Pamukkale Hieropolis Archaeology Museum; see Mehmet Çetin Şahin, "Zwei Inschriften aus dem südwestlichen Kleinasien, 1. Archaische Inschrift aus Priene, aus der Zeit des Psammetichos," *Epigraphica Anatolica* 10 (1987): 1–2 and plate 25; and Olivier Masson and Jean Yoyotte, "Une inscription ionienne mentionnant Psammétique Ier," *Epigraphica Anatolica* 11 (1988): 171–80.

27. Damien Agut-Labordère, "Plus que des mercenaires! L'intégration des hommes de guerre grecs au service de la monarchie saïte," *Pallas* 89 (2012): 293–306.

28. Rhodes Archaeological Museum inv. 14341, see Skon-Jedele, "*Aigyptiaka*," 1989–90 (no. 3011).

29. Rhodes Archaeological Museum E. 7020, Γ 2649, see Vassiliki Patsiada, in *Beyond the Nile: Egypt and the Classical World*, ed. Jeffrey Spier, Timothy Potts, and Sara E. Cole (Los Angeles: J. Paul Getty Museum, 2018), 103 (no. 73).

30. Rhodes Archaeological Museum inv. nos. 7683, 9799–9800, 9804–18, 9821, and SNO 27–31 and 27–32, see Skon-Jedele, *"Aigyptiaka,"* 2355–73 (nos. 4354–4374); Panagiotis Kouzoulis and Ludwig D. Morenz, "Ecumene and Economy in the Horizon of Religion: Egyptian Donations to Rhodian Sanctuaries," in *Das Heilige und die Ware: Zum Spannungsfeld von Religon und Ökonomie*, ed. M. Fitzenreiter (London: Golden House Publications, 2007), 184–88.

31. Herodotus 2.159; and Kouzoulis and Morenz, "Ecumene and Economy," 187.

32. Karl Jansen-Winkeln, "Zu einigen 'Trinksprüchen' auf ägyptischen Gefaßen," *Zeitschrift für Ägyptische Sprache und Altertumskunde* 116 (1989): 143–53.

33. Susanne Gänsicke, "King Aspelta's Vessel Hoard from Nuri in the Sudan," *Journal of the Museum of Fine Arts, Boston* 6 (1994): 14–40.

34. Aurélia Masson, "Stone Vessels," in *Naukratis: Greeks in Egypt*, ed. Alexandra Villing, Marianne Bergeron, Giorgos Bourogiannis, Alan Johnston, François Leclére, Aurélia Masson, and Ross Thomas, 3–8, http://www.britishmuseum.org/naukratis, accessed February 23, 2019.

35. Luisa Bonadies, "Stone Jars in the Mediterranean of the First Millennium BCE," in *There and Back Again: The Crossroads II, Proceedings of an International Conference Held in Prague, September 15–18, 2014*, ed. Jana Mynářová, Pavel Onderka, and Peter Pavúk (Prague: Charles University, 2015), 529–48; and Luisa Bonadies, "Cultural Exchange in the Stone Vessels Production of the First Millennium BCE," in *Cultural and Material Contacts in the Ancient Near East, Proceedings of the International Workshop 1–2 December 2014*, ed. E. Foietta, C. Ferrandi, E. Quirico, F. Giusto, M. Mortarini, J. Bruno, and L. Somma (Sesto Fiorentino: Apice libri, 2016), 73–82.

36. Pierre Montet, *Le nécropole royal de Tanis I: Les constructions et le tombeau d'Osorkon II à Tanis* (Paris: CNRS, 1947), 82 and fig. 46.

37. Dows Dunham, *The Royal Cemeteries of Kush, 1: El Kurru* (Cambridge, MA: Harvard University Press, 1950), 30–37 (Ku4), nos. 19-3-560, 562–65.

38. Dunham, *Royal Cemeteries 1*, 81–85 (Ku52), nos. 19-3-1032, 1033, 1055, 1083.

39. Dunham, *Royal Cemeteries 1*, 86–90 (Ku53), nos. 19-3-1223, 1359, 1363, 1365.

40. Dunham, *Royal Cemeteries 1*, 42–43 (Ku6), no. 19-2-513.

41. Dunham, *Royal Cemeteries 1*, 55–59 (Ku15), nos. 19-2-489, 490, 19-3-217.

42. Dunham, *Royal Cemeteries 1*, 60–63 (Ku16), no. 19-2-346 + 19-3-323.

43. Dunham, *Royal Cemeteries 1*, 93–97 (Ku55), nos. 19-3-240, 1447; and 103–8 (Ku72), nos. 19-3-1525, 1539.

44. Mu-Chou Poo, *Wine and Wine Offering in the Religion of Ancient Egypt* (London: Kegan Paul International, 1995), 11–12, 19–21, 89–98, 117, 126–30.

45. Poo, *Wine Offering*, 71–74.

46. George Andrew Reisner, *Harvard Excavations in Samaria, 1908–1910*, vol. 1 (Cambridge, MA: Harvard University Press, 1924), 247 figs. A–c, 334 fig. 205.

47. Vessels Berlin VA Ass. 2254–58, and Istanbul AOM/ES 4620–22, see Melanie Wasmuth and Georg Brein, "Das Alabastergefäß VA Ass. 2258 aus Assur," in *Florilegium Aegyptiacum: Einewissenschaftliche Blütenlese von Schülern und Freunden für Helmut Satzinger zum 75.Geburtstag am 21. Jänner 2013*, ed. Julia Budka, Roman Gundacker, and Gabriele Pieke (Göttingen: Seminar für Ägyptologie und Koptologie, 2013), 343–48.

48. Vessel Berlin VA Ass. 2258, see Wasmuth and Brein, "Alabastergefäß," 349–65.

49. Istanbul AOM/ES 9583–9584, see Ernst F. Weidner, "Wissenschaftliche Berichte: Museen. Die Antiken-Museen in Istanbul," *Archiv für Orientforschung* 10

(1935–36): 92–94, esp. 94; Ann Searight, Julian Reade, and Irving Finkel (with contributions by Kenneth Kitchen, Marcel Marée, and Shahrokh Rasmjou), *Assyrian Stone Vessels and Related Material in the British Museum* (Oxford: Oxbow Books, 2008), 100.

50. Vessels BM 91639 and 91595, see Searight, Reade, and Finkel, *Assyrian Stone Vessels*, 16–18 (nos. 51–52).

51. Searight, Reade, and Finkel, *Assyrian Stone Vessels*, 16–21 (nos. 53–60).

52. Vessel BM 90952, the Sargon Vase, see Dan Barag, *Catalogue of Western Asiatic Glass in the British Museum*, vol. 1 (London: British Museum, 1985), 60–61 (cat. 26), fig. 2, pl. 3, col. pl. B.

53. Vessel Louvre E. 23325, see Barag, *Western Asiatic Glass*, 60–61.

54. Margaret O'Hea, "Another Look at the Origins of Iron Age II Cast Glass Vessels in the Levant," *Levant* 43, no. 2 (2011): 153–72, esp. 156–57.

55. Searight, Reade, and Finkel, *Assyrian Stone Vessels*, 21–30 (nos. 61–253).

56. Searight, Reade, and Finkel, *Assyrian Stone Vessels*, 100–101 (no. 619).

57. Karen Radner, "The 'Lost Tribes of Israel' in the Context of the Resettlement Programme of the Assyrian Empire," in *The Last Days of the Kingdom of Israel*, ed. Shuichi Hasegawa, Christoph Levin, and Karen Radner (Berlin: Walter de Gruyter, 2019), 103–4.

58. Charles Draper, "Two Libyan Names in a Seventh Century Sale Document from Assur," *Journal of Ancient Egyptian Interconnections* 7, no. 2 (2015): 4–5.

59. William Culican, "Almuñecar, Assur and Phoenician Penetration of the Western Mediterranean," *Levant* 2 (1970): 28–36; José Luis López Castro, "Colonials, Merchants and Alabaster Vases: The Western Phoenician Aristocracy," *Antiquity* 80 (2006): 74–88.

60. Gamer-Wallert, *Ägyptische und ägyptisierende Funde*, 20–39; Josep Padró, "Las inscripciones egipcias de la Dinastia XXII procedentes de Almunecar (Provencia de Granada)," *Aula Orientalis: Revista de estudios del Proximo Oriente Antiguo* 1 (1983): 215–25; Josep Padró I Parcerisa, *Egyptian-Type Documents from the Mediterranean Littoral of the Iberian Peninsula before the Roman Conquest, III: Study of the Material* (Leiden: Brill, 1985), 49–101; and Ann Neville, *Mountains of Silver and Rivers of Gold: The Phoenicians in Iberia* (Oxford: Oxbow Books, 2007), 47–56.

61. Vessel G41/MAPG 8332, see Gamer-Wallert, *Ägyptische und ägyptisierende Funde*, 38–39; Padró I Parcerisa, *Egyptian-Type Documents*, 94–97.

62. Vessel G44/MAPG 8335, see Gamer-Wallert, *Ägyptische und ägyptisierende Funde*, 38–39; Padró I Parcerisa, *Egyptian-Type Documents*, 100–101.

63. Vessel G29/MAPG 8319, see Gamer-Wallert, *Ägyptische und ägyptisierende Funde*, 24–30; Padró, "Las inscripciones egipcias," 217–20; Padró I Parcerisa, *Egyptian-Type Documents*, 64–70; and Jansen-Winkeln, "Zu einigen 'Trinksprüchen,'" 143–46.

64. Vessel G40/MAPG 8331, see Gamer-Wallert, *Ägyptische und ägyptisierende Funde*, 34–38; Padró I Parcerisa, *Egyptian-Type Documents*, 91–94.

65. Vessel G39/MAPG 8329, see Gamer-Wallert, *Ägyptische und ägyptisierende Funde*, 30–34; Padró, "Las inscripciones egipcias," 220–23; Padró I Parcerisa, *Egyptian-Type Documents*, 84–90; and Jansen-Winkeln, "Zu einigen 'Trinksprüchen,'" 147–49.

66. Ingrid Gamer-Wallert, "Die hieroglypheninschrift auf dem Alabastergefass in Puerto de Santa Maria," *Habis* 7 (1976): 223–28, pls. I–II; Gamer-Wallert, *Ägyptische und ägyptisierende Funde*, 81–85; and Jansen-Winkeln, "'Trinksprüchen,'" 146–47.

67. José Ramón Mélida y Alinari, *Tesoro de Aliseda: noticia y descripción de la joyas que le componen* (Madrid: Museo Arqueológico Nacional, 1921), 30–32 (no. 24).

68. O'Hea, "Cast Glass Vessels," 156–57.

69. Ingrid Gamer-Wallert, "Die hieroglyphen der Glaskanne von La Aliseda (Cáceres)," *Revista de la Universidad Complutense* 25, no. 101 (1976): 127–31; and Gamer-Wallert, *Ägyptische und ägyptisierende Funde*, 116–20, pls. 31–32.

70. Peregrine Horden and Nicholas Purcell, *The Corrupting Sea: A Study of Mediterranean History* (Malden, MA: Blackwell, 2000), 53–88.

71. Janine Bourriau and Peter French, "Imported Amphorae from Buto Dating from ca. 750 BC to the Early 6th Century AD," in *Amphores d'Égypte de la Basse Époque à l'Époque arabe*, vol. 1, ed. Sylvie Marchand and Antigone Marangou (Cairo: IFAO, 2007), 119–20; Lucien-François Gantès, "Les amphores commerciales grecques, levantines et égyptiennes découvertes à Naucratis: une révision récente," in Marchand and Marangou, *Amphores d'Égypte*, 144–45; and David Aston, "Amphorae, Storage Jars and Kegs from Elephantine: A Brief Survey of Vessels from the Eight–Seventh Centuries BC to the Seventh–Eighth Centuries AD," in *Amphores d'Égypte de la Basse Époque à l'Époque arabe*, vol. 2, ed. Sylvie Marchand and Antigone Marangou (Cairo: IFAO, 2007), 438–41.

72. Květa Smoláriková, *Greek Imports in Egypt: Graeco-Egyptian Relations during the First Millennium B.C.* (Prague: Czech Institute of Egyptology, 2002), 23–46; and Sabine Weber, "Greek Painted Pottery in Egypt: Evidence of Contacts in the Seventh and Sixth Centuries B.C.," in *Moving across Borders: Foreign Relations, Religion, and Cultural Interactions in the Ancient Mediterranean*, ed. P. Kousoulis and K. Magliveras (Leuven: Peeters, 2007), 299–316.

73. Alexandra Villing, "Egypt as a 'Market' for Greek Pottery: Some Thoughts on Production, Consumption and Distribution in an Intercultural Environment," in *Pottery Markets in Ancient Greek World (8th–1st c. B.C.), Proceedings of the International Symposion held at the Université libre de Bruxelles 19–21 June 2008*, ed. Athena Tsingarida and Didier Viviers (Brussels: Centre de Recherches en Archéologie et Patrimoine, 2013), 73–101.

74. Carolina A. Aznar, "Exchange Networks in the Southern Levant during the Iron Age II: A Study of Pottery Origin and Distribution" (PhD diss., Harvard University, 2005), 56–70, 156–61.

75. Josep Padró, "La présence des Phéniciens en Égypte à l'époque libyenne," in *La vallée du Nil et la Méditerranée. Voies de communications et vecteurs culturels, Actes du colloque des 5 et 6 juin 1998, université Paul-Valéry, Montpellier*, ed. S. H. Aufrère (Montpellier: Université Paul Valery-Montpellier 3, 2001), 127–50; Josep Padró and Joan Ramón, "Les amphores phéniciennes en Égypte et le commerce du vin," in *La dépendance rurale dans l'Antiquité égyptienne et proche-orientale*, ed. Bernadette Menu (Cairo: IFAO, 2004), 77–102.

76. Bourriau and French, "Imported Amphorae," 117–18; Aston, "Amphorae, Storage Jars and Kegs," 433–38; and Paula Waiman-Barak, "Circulation of Early Iron Age Goods: Phoenician and Egyptian Ceramics in the Early Iron Age: An Optical Mineralogy Perspective" (PhD diss., University of Haifa, 2015), 197–98.

77. Dunham, *Royal Cemeteries 1*, 81–85 (Ku19), no. 19-3-1158. I thank Lisa A. Heidorn for identifying this vessel as an import.

78. Robert D. Ballard, Lawrence E. Stager, Daniel Master, Dana Yoerger, David Mindell, Louis L. Whitcomb, Hanumant Singh, and Dennis Piechota, "Iron Age

Shipwrecks in Deep Water off Ashkelon, Israel," *American Journal of Archaeology* 106 (2002): 151–68. The authors hesitated between Egypt and Carthage as the intended destination of the ships because they were unaware of the presence of any Phoenician "torpedo" storage jars in Egypt, but see notes 75–77.

79. Israel Finkelstein, Elena Zapassky, Yuval Gadot, Daniel M. Master, Lawrence E. Stager, and Itzhak Benenson, "Phoenician 'Torpedo' Amphoras and Egypt: Standardization of Volume Based on Linear Dimensions," *Ägypten und Levante* 21 (2011): 249–59.

80. Reisner, *Harvard Excavations in Samaria,* 247, figs. a–c, and 334, fig. 205.

81. Neville, *Mountains of Silver,* 108–9, and 135–58.

82. Christine M. Thompson and Sheldon Skaggs, "King Solomon's Silver? Southern Phoenician Hacksilber Hoards and the Location of Tarshish," *Internet Archaeology* 35 (2013), http://intarch.ac.uk/journal/issue35/thompson_index.html.

83. Susan Frankenstein, "The Phoenicians in the Far West: A Function of Neo-Assyrian Imperialism," in *Power and Propaganda: A Symposium on Ancient Empires,* ed. Mogens Trolle Larsen (Copenhagen: Akademisk Forlag, 1979), 263–94; Maria Eugenia Aubet, *The Phoenicians and the West: Politics, Colonies and Trade,* 2nd ed. (Cambridge: University Press, 2001), 54–60, 80–84; Neville, *Mountains of Silver,* 163; and Cyprian Broodbank, *Making of the Middle Sea: A History of the Mediterranean from the Beginning to the Emergence of the Classical World* (Oxford: Thames and Hudson, 2013), 491.

84. Frankenstein, "Phoenicians in the Far West"; Aubet, *Phoenicians and the West,* 88–95; Seymour Gitin and Amir Golani, "The Tel Miqne-Ekron Silver Hoards: The Assyrian and Phoenician Connections," in *Hacksilber to Coinage: New Insights into the Monetary History of the Near East and Greece,* ed. Miriam S. Balmuth (New York: American Numismatic Society, 2001), 27–48; and Broodbank, *Making of the Middle Sea,* 511.

85. Georges Posener, "Les douanes de la Méditerranée dans l'Égypte saïte," *Revue de philologie de littérature et d'histoire anciennes* 21 (1947): 117–31.

86. Robertus J. van der Spek, "The 'Silverization' of the Economy of the Achaemenid and Seleukid Empires and Early Modern China," in *The Economies of Hellenistic Societies, Third to First Centuries BC,* ed. Zosia H. Archibald, John K. Davies, and Vincent Gabrielsen (Oxford: Oxford University Press, 2011), 408–10; Bas van Leeuwen and Yi Xu, "Silverization of China during the Ming-Qing Transition (ca. 1550–1770) and the Consequences for Research into the Babylonian Economy," in *Silver, Money and Credit: A Tribute to Robartus J. van der Spek on the Occasion of His 65th Birthday,* ed. Kristin Kleber and Reinhard Pirngruber (Leiden: Netherlands Institute for the Near East, 2016), 129.

87. K. R. Veenhof, *Aspects of Old Assyrian Trade and Its Terminology* (Leiden: Brill, 1972), 87–88, 140–43, 349–51; and Jan Gerrit Dercksen, *The Old Assyrian Copper Trade in Anatolia* (Leiden: Netherlands Institute for the Near East, 1996), 149–53, 157–61.

88. Jac J. Janssen, *Commodity Prices from the Ramessid Period: An Economic Study of the Village of the Necropolis Workmen at Thebes* (Leiden: Brill, 1975), 514–23, 545–50.

89. Claus Jurman, "'Silver of the Treasury of Herishef': Considering the Origin and Economic Significance of Silver in Egypt during the Third Intermediate Period," in *The Mediterranean Mirror: Cultural Contacts in the Mediterranean Sea*

between 1200 and 750 B.C., ed. Andrea Babbi, Friederike Bubenheimer-Erhart, Beatriz Marín-Aguilara, and Simone Mühl (Mainz: Verlag des Römisch-Germanischen Zentralmuseums, 2015), 51, 56–57.

90. Barry Kemp, *Ancient Egypt: Anatomy of a Civilization* (London: Routledge, 1989), 242–46; Graciela Gestoso Singer, "The Gold and Silver Hoard from Tell el-Amarna," *Aula Orientalis* 31, no. 2 (2013): 249–59, esp. 254–59.

91. Jaroslav Černý, "Prices and Wages in Egypt in the Ramesside Period," *Cahiers d'histoire mondiale* 1 (1954): 903–21, esp. 904–906.

92. Kristin Kleber, "The Kassite Gold and the Post-Kassite Silver Standards Revisited," in Kelber and Pirngruber, *Silver, Money and Credit*, 39–60.

93. Pierre Montet, *La nécropole royal de Tanis*, 3 vols. (Paris: CNRS, 1947–1960), summarized in David A. Aston, *Burial Assemblages of Dynasty 21–25, Chronology—Typology—Developments* (Vienna: Österreichische Akademie der Wissenschaften, 2009), 39–61; and Jurman, "'Treasury of Herishef,'" 51–56.

94. Brian Muhs, *The Ancient Egyptian Economy, 3000–30 BCE* (Cambridge: Cambridge University Press, 2016), 159–62.

95. Hans-Christoph Noeske, "Ein Hackstilberfund aus Elephantine," in *Die Münze: Bild, Botschaft, Bedeutung: Festschrift für Maria R.-Alföldi*, ed. Hans-Christoph Noeske and Helmut Schubert (Frankfurt: Peter Lang, 1991), 342–51; and Noeske, "Prämonetäre Wertmesser und Münzfunde aus Elephantine," *Mitteilungen des Deutschen Archäologischen Instituts Abteilung Kairo* 49 (1993): 203–9, esp. 204–5.

96. John H. Kroll, "A Small Bullion Find from Egypt," *American Journal of Numismatics* 13 (2001): 1–20, esp. 3–4.

97. Reginald Engelbach, "The Treasure of Athribis (Benha)," *Annales du Service des antiquités de l'Egypte* 24 (1924): 178–85, esp. 181–85.

98. Brian Muhs, *Tax Receipts, Taxpayers, and Taxes in Early Ptolemaic Thebes* (Chicago: Oriental Institute Press, 2005), 11–12.

99. Kleber, "Kassite Gold," 56.

100. Richard Parkinson and Stephen Quirke, *Papyrus* (London: British Museum Press, 1995), 65–68.

101. Willemijn Waal, "On the 'Phoenician Letters': The Case for an Early Transmission of the Greek Alphabet from an Archaeological, Epigraphic and Linguistic Perspective," *Aegean Studies* 1 (2018): 83–125.

102. Horden and Purcell, *Corrupting Sea*, 359–63.

103. Broodbank, *Making of the Middle Sea*, 460–61.

104. Jonathan I. Israel, *The Dutch Republic: Its Rise, Greatness, and Fall, 1477–1806* (Oxford: Oxford University Press, 1995), 16–25, 111–19.

105. Peter Garnsey, *Famine and Food Supply in the Graeco-Roman World, Responses to Risk and Crisis* (Cambridge: Cambridge University Press, 1988), 182–243.

106. Horden and Purcell, *Corrupting Sea*, 371, table 5.

107. Alfonso Moreno, *Feeding the Democracy: The Athenian Grain Supply in the Fifth and Fourth Centuries BC* (Oxford: Oxford University Press, 2007), 323–24.

108. Philochorus, FGrHist 328 F119 = Felix Jacoby, *Fragmente der griechischen Historiker, Dritter Teil: Geschichte von Staeden und Voelkern (Horographie und Ethnographie), B. Autoren ueber einzelne Staedte (Laender), Nr. 297–607* (Leiden: Brill, 1950), 133 (no. 119).

109. Polybius 5.89.1.

110. Garnsey, *Famine and Food Supply*, 69–86.

✷ CHAPTER 10 ✷

Globalizing the Mediterranean's Iron Age

TAMAR HODOS

The Mediterranean's Iron Age—roughly 1200–600 BCE—may be regarded as one of its most dynamic periods. Although it is not the first era in which people across the sea exchanged goods, ideas, values, customs, practices, and technologies, the difference is the scale at which this occurred. The interactions that resurged from the tenth century onward came to eclipse their Bronze Age antecedents in geographical, material, and ideological scope. The period is characterized perhaps most of all by the movement of peoples from their homeland to areas far away on a geographically unprecedented scale, notably the settlement of Greeks and Phoenicians in the central and western Mediterranean, which began largely in the ninth and eighth centuries. The long-term impact of this extensive interaction was the creation of what may be regarded as the Mediterranean's first globally connected period.

Scholarship has not always presented the narrative of this era as a globalizing one, however. Initially, the evidence for increased communication and exchange between Mediterranean communities and cultures, in the form of the widespread adoption of primarily Greek material culture and facilitated by the Greek and Phoenician overseas settlements, was regarded from purely colonial perspectives. Under the influence of postmodern cultural critiques of the 1980s, scholarship began to examine material culture patterns from postcolonial perspectives to highlight evidence of cultural hybridization and acts of indigenous agency. At times, however, such interpretations were criticized for writing out of the narrative any influence foreign populations might have had on local cultural developments. Contemporary perspectives on globalization provide a means of rehabilitating these different, and sometimes competing, perspectives. This chapter outlines interpretations surrounding connectivity during the Mediterranean Iron Age from its colonialist origins through postcolonial perspectives to explore how contemporary globalization theories are transforming our understandings of this culturally complex and socially vibrant era.

The Mediterranean Iron Age

Despite its moniker, the Mediterranean's Iron Age era is not strictly correlated to the development of ironworking, since iron was already known in the fifth and fourth millennia BCE in Iran (Sialk), Iraq (Samarra), and Egypt (Gerzeh), and in third millennium Mesopotamia and Anatolia (Tilmen Höyük; Alaca Höyük).[1] Over the second millennium BCE, iron remained rare in the eastern Mediterranean and was reserved for ornamental and ceremonial/ritual objects. At the very end of the second millennium, iron began to be used for weapons and tools, and by the tenth and ninth centuries BCE, the metal was used more regularly for a range of ornamental, utilitarian, and military objects in diverse form, and iron similarly became more popular in other regions of the Mediterranean.[2] This development appears alongside a range of other changes evidenced widely around the Mediterranean in material remains—for example, new ceramic shapes and styles, architectural forms, and burial practices—which collectively suggest evolution in social practices. Such changes did not occur in a single instance but developed over time, while the rate of change within any material category was not uniform from site to site or region to region. Furthermore, for other areas of the Mediterranean, the Iron Age begins not at the end of the second millennium, as in the eastern Mediterranean, but well into the first millennium BCE.[3] The term "Iron Age" therefore is best regarded as a means to mark changes in the traditions and practices associated with its temporal antecedents: the concept of an Iron Age is as much one of temporal as it is of material and social relations, but it is not one of absolute chronology.

What characterizes the Mediterranean's Iron Age most is the movement of people, distinguished by numbers and nature. From before the end of the second millennium BCE, individuals and small groups were moving around the Mediterranean, following a number of Bronze Age networks and establishing new ones. Some of these were itinerant traders and craftsmen, but we also see the movement of larger groups of people who took up residence on foreign shores. The two with the greatest influence in terms of geographic reach and cultural developments are the Phoenicians and the Greeks.

Despite the fact that both Greeks and Phoenicians founded overseas settlements across the Mediterranean, and sometimes in the same geographical territory (e.g., Sicily), study of their expansion has been divided between disciplines.[4] Near Eastern scholars traditionally have focused on the Phoenician colonization process while classical scholars examined the Greek movement. This disciplinary division may be traced to nineteenth-century western European scholarship and the respective primacy of biblical and ancient classical literary sources accorded by archaeological research in that era. This is often expressed as a competition for primacy in colonial innovation. Symptomatic of this rivalry are questions over the foundation dates of the earliest colonies, framed as if a supremacy of innovation depended upon it. Most ancient literary sources tell us that Phoenician expansion in the Mediterranean began in the twelfth century BCE, while concurring that Greek colonization started only in the eighth century.[5] For well over a century, however, Greek scholarship argued that Phoenician expansion could not have begun before the eighth century,[6] on the grounds that material evidence could not be identified to support such early foundations in places where the Phoenicians were supposed to have colonized.[7] For example, John Boardman maintained that

> it is only after the Greeks establish themselves on the Syrian coast that Greece begins to receive and appreciate eastern products; and there is no clear evidence for Phoenician trading colonies overseas earlier than the Greeks ones. For all that, they may have been the carriers of what little did travel into the Greek world from the east before the eighth century. The nature of this trade did not require the establishment of regular trading posts or colonies until Greek example and competition led them to similar undertakings.[8]

More recently, Gocha Tsetskhladze noted:

> In the eighth century BC Greeks were moving into the relatively close territories of central and southern Italy, whilst the Phoenicians established small settlements in Sardinia and further to the west and south. The Greek settlements were designed for permanence; those of the Phoenicians disappeared over time, probably absorbed by the locals.[9]

This statement is factually problematic, for it overlooks the enduring, substantial Phoenician settlements of Sicily, Spain, and North Africa, as well as contemporary Greek communities that failed to survive. Phoenician foundations were no less "permanent" than Greek ones. In fact, discussion of a particular territory is often framed in terms of Greek or Phoenician priority; scholarship has tended to lend little consideration to the possibility that a landscape may have been shared between both groups, or anyone else, despite the fact that others were already established in territories at which the Greeks and Phoenicians arrived.[10]

Phoenician scholarship has done much the same. For example, Sabatino Moscati argued in his seminal work on the Phoenicians that the lack of Phoenician material evidence in the wider Mediterranean prior to the eighth century (as was the case until recently) was no reason to doubt the Greek and biblical texts and Phoenician records that attest Phoenician activity far earlier.[11] The difficulty arises from the fact that pottery is our primary means of dating sites and contexts during this period. The problem with evidence for Phoenician settlement, however, is that Phoenician pottery changes little in style over the late second and first millennia, and lacks the fine chronological precision of Greek pottery. So when Phoenician ceramic material is found, it can be very difficult to determine a precise date for it. By contrast, almost everywhere Greeks settled, their wine and associated drinking wares—which are very closely dated—quickly became integrated with local tastes and customs, and their ceramic assemblages influenced regional indigenous outputs. In addition, many settlements adopted Greek-derived architectural forms. The Greek alphabet was sometimes adapted to express local languages (even though it originally derived from the Phoenician alphabet while the Greek language itself displays features of other influences: see John Papadopoulos, chapter 7 in this volume), and many communities eventually borrowed the Greek system of coinage. While the Phoenicians were just as prevalent in the Mediterranean, their material culture was not widely adopted by others. In fact, Greek ceramic use and architectural ideas were also incorporated by the Phoenicians into their practices and urban constructions.

Initially, this prevalence of Greek cultural forms was interpreted as a craving for cultural enlightenment and sophistication by indigenous communities (and the Phoenicians, to a certain extent, who were largely ignored as they were part of Near Eastern studies). This is best summed up by Boardman's description of Greek interaction with the nonforeign populations of Sicily and Italy, when he says, "In the west, the Greeks had nothing to learn, much to teach."[12] In this "Hellenization" model, the Greeks maintain cultural, social, political, and economic superiority. They remain immune from any such influence by those who were Hellenized and, in becoming so, adopted Hellenic culture wholesale and unquestioningly. There is little consideration of agency or reciprocity. Hellenization is therefore a binary, unidirectional process. This interpretation dominated our views for much of the twentieth century—especially from the interwar period, when Greek colonies were considered glorious counterparts to Europe's own colonial holdings.

By the early 1990s, however, archaeology began to be influenced by the postmodern deconstruction that commenced in wider western intellectual discourse during the 1980s, especially the emergence of postcolonialism through work by Edward Said and Gayatri Spivak.[13] In particular, such counternarratives, as deconstructions of the metanarratives of colonial discourse, inspired archaeological scholarship to reconsider its interpretations of Greek and Roman colonizations by exploring their impact from the perspective of the colonized.[14] Detailed examinations of material culture use and practice among indigenous peoples revealed that wholesale adoption of foreign goods and practices was not taking place. For instance, it was observed in a number of arenas, such as Sicily, North Africa, and France, that indigenous communities were very selective in what they chose to acquire from their foreign neighbors, notably with regard to particular ceramic forms or architectural features. Furthermore, the rate of take-up could be decades or even centuries after the arrival of the Greeks in a region.[15] Hellenization did not fit with such evidence. Instead, these examples fit better within a hybridization model. When connected to cultural practice, hybridization may be regarded as the cultural mixture that arises when practices of diverse origins are blended.[16] People in such situations create new social and material practices that often combine both colonial and traditional ways; the mixture is unique to the group in question. In short, hybridization is an active process related to social agents and their negotiations and interactions in culture contact situations; it is also a locally contextualized, temporally specific process.

Postcolonially inspired interpretations of the Iron Age Mediterranean that focus upon the experiences of the colonized have sometimes been accused of being nothing more than examples of political correctness. Thus, in the 1999 edition of *The Greeks Overseas*, Boardman wonders if the recent emphasis on the experiences of the colonized is merely part of a "thrusting [of] the desired modern standards on to antiquity and making assumptions about the prejudices of recent generations of scholars."[17] He is not alone.[18] These criticisms reflect a dissatisfaction with the change of emphasis because the result appears to remove the colonizer from the narrative, especially when the adaptation takes place over the long term. In reality, however, postcolonial works have never denied that colonial cultures had a profound impact upon the so-called colonized. Rather, postcolonial discourse has sought explicitly to emphasize the acts of agency on the part of the colonized, and to highlight that the changes that ensued in local populations were more nuanced than simply an adoption of colonial ways of life. Furthermore, in some instances the temporal scale of adaptation suggests that the explicitly Greek origin of forms or practices had been lost in time, such that the use of certain styles or customs may no longer have held any meaningful association with Hellenic traditions.

By the late 1990s and early 2000s, reactions to the Hellenization framework of interpretation had taken two distinct trajectories.[19] The first was an emphasis on the diversities of "being Greek." This saw the deconstruction of the notion that Greek colonies were replicas of their mother-cities, with scholars instead emphasizing their diversities.[20] It also led to challenges to a unified concept of "the Greeks" as a cultural entity.[21] The second emphasis drew out the role of the indigenous populations in the Greek–non-Greek relationship. Studies have demonstrated that the use of any Greek features, whether pottery, architecture, burial forms, writing, or other, was gradual and selective in a manner appropriate to the local circumstances.[22]

The best Phoenician example of this paradigm shift is seen in interpretations of the role of the *tophet*, open-air ritual precincts where child sacrifice and infant burial took place as part of Phoenician religious practices. *Tophets* have been found mostly in the central Mediterranean settlements, although examples from the Near East beyond Phoenician territories have also been identified (e.g., Tell Sukas). Despite this, it has nevertheless been assumed that the *tophet* reflects homeland practices. Moscati was certain of this when he noted, "There is no evidence of these sacred places actually in Phoenicia, but there is no doubt that they existed, if we add to the biblical evidence the ample proof provided by excavations in the western colonies,"[23] thereby adhering to the notion of a colony as the replica of the mother-city in the wider Phoenician world. Today, however, more nuanced approaches recognize diversity with regard to the function of the *tophet*, and the variabilities are regarded as significant for local circumstances, rather than reflective of determinative "Phoenician" practice.[24] The word never appears in Phoenician or Punic textual evidence, so our understanding of the function and significance of what we call *tophets* in Phoenician/Punic contexts is entirely etic. It was a sanctuary like others, where people could have transactions with the gods. But there was tremendous variability in burial and commemoration methods in *tophet* contexts. Recent analysis reveals that social prestige is emphasized in the placement of stelae. The presence of a *tophet* itself is also associated with other characteristics of urbanization to the extent that it may be regarded as the first expression of the urban character of the settlement, where it served both the civic and territorial communities.[25] In sum, current thinking is that the *tophet* is a general label for different archaeological and conceptual realities across the Phoenician world, rather than a distinctly Phoenicio-Punic element. As Jo Crawley Quinn pithily observes, "if there was a corporate Western Phoenician or Punic diaspora culture, the *tophet* sanctuaries weren't part of it."[26]

We now find ourselves with various sets of evidence that have created polarizing perspectives: the shared practices that gave rise to notions like Hellenization in the first place, the variability in practice of being Greek and Phoenician, and the resurgence of local practices in the face of the spread and impact of Hellenic and Phoenician cultures. Each, on its own, has merit, as generations of scholars past and present have demonstrated. On the one hand, there is still the overwhelming adoption of, particularly, Greek material culture across a wide area. On the other hand, when considered from a bottom-up perspective, the uses of such objects are variable, and locally significant. Therefore, is it appropriate to reject one interpretation in favor of another? To rehabilitate these seemingly contrasting perspectives into an accommodating narrative, scholars are increasingly turning to globalization theories.[27] This is because globalization emphasizes both shared sets of practices on a cross-cultural level and variability in such practices between engaged groups, as well as variable degrees of engagement between groups. As a framework of interpretation, therefore, it can accommodate the various material culture patterns scholars have identified in the ancient Mediterranean to support their respective interpretational perspectives. To understand how this can be, it is worth further exploring globalization itself.

Defining Globalization

Globalization is one of the most important processes of economic, social, and cultural integration in the world today, involving trade, capital and investment, labor migration, and knowledge dissemination. Many would say that it is realized through free trade and capitalism.[28] Yet globalization is more than just another way to describe contemporary neoliberalism. Although there is no consensus on the definition of globalization, increasing connectivity is its most widely agreed upon trait.[29] This connectivity is specifically of a type that encompasses a wide-scale flow of ideas and knowledge alongside the sharing of cultural customs and civil society practices. These flows and connections may be manifested through closer economic integration via increased movement of goods and services, capital and labor, or they may be shaped by politics.[30]

Scholars debate globalization's features, however, such as whether it is informed by technological changes, involves the reconfiguration of states, goes together with regionalization, or includes a sense of time-space compression.[31] Usually globalization is described and discussed within a particular disciplinary context, so that we hear of different kinds of globalization, such as financial, commercial, economic, or political globalization. Most will at least agree that globalization is uneven and asymmetric in pace, scope, and impact. Scholars understand these developments either as a process (e.g., Robbie Robertson; Jan Nederveen Pieterse), as a system (e.g., Jonathan Friedman; Immanuel Wallerstein), or as a discourse (e.g., Manfred Steger).[32]

John Tomlinson defines globalization simply as complex connectivities.[33] Roland Robertson, on the other hand, defines globalization as the process by which the world increasingly becomes seen as one place and the ways in which we are made conscious of that process,[34] although, as Mike Featherstone has noted, this should not be taken to imply that there is a unified world culture.[35] For this reason, Jan Nederveen Pieterse defines globalization as "a process of hybridization that gives rise to a global mélange,"[36] and he argues that globalization can be understood as an open-ended synthesis of a number of disciplinary approaches to such developments, in which there are as many globalization modes as there are agents, dynamics, and impulses.[37]

I have elsewhere defined globalization as "processes of increasing connectivities that unfold and manifest as social awareness of those connectivities."[38] Because globalization is about the processes themselves, it is an active concept rather than a descriptive one. I have also noted that the idea suggests a world-scale, and that this is why some insist it is a phenomenon that begins only with the onset of global circumnavigation.[39] It is used more frequently, however, to reflect wider changes within a conceptual or experienced world. Most often, it involves increasing integration and cooperation derived from evolving common practices that facilitate such integration and cooperation.[40] This is not to suggest that connectivity and awareness of such connections alone render a period or place globalized. Contributions to the recent *Routledge Handbook of Archaeology and Globalization* demonstrate that the nature of the complex connections, and how social awareness of them is manifested, are what determine whether an era in the past may be considered globalized or not.[41]

An important corollary to the rising sense of similarity, accessibility, and commonality we associate with globalization is the awareness, and even increase, of more pronounced differences and inequalities with those not so closely integrated into the experiential sphere, or those not involved at all. This indicates that there are two primary aspects of globalization processes: (1) the development of shared practices and values that contribute to the sense of one-placeness and (2) increased awareness of and sensitivity to differences, especially cultural ones. Both derive from a variety of increasing connectivities, although it is usually the former that receives more attention. Nevertheless, growing awareness of cultural difference is a function of globalization, not merely a feature of it. This manifests usually as a resurgence of local identity practices in explicit contrast to the increasingly shared practices of the globally connected level. These local expressions of identity are also commonly linked to widely divergent levels of wealth, health, and political power. As a result, such developments often heighten the contrasts between the parties involved in the global system and the degree of social investment in maintaining cultural difference. Globalization thus maintains a balance between shared, binding practices and diversities that distinguish participants. Not only are the two in tension with one another, but they are also interdependent, and together they create the paradox of globalization.[42] Globalization cannot be conceptualized or adequately discussed without consideration of both aspects. However, many academic and popular discussions of globalization acknowledge only the former and overlook the latter.

Identifying Globalization

Justin Jennings identifies eight trends that occur in contemporary globalization.[43] They are overlapping and spurred by complex connectivity to create a global culture. He argues that all should be present for any period to be considered an era of globalization.

1. *Time-space compression.* Identified by the geographer David Harvey,[44] this is the experience of having one's world shrunk through the acceleration of long-distance economic, political, and social processes, such that changes in one place can have ramifications across a broad region. While speed of communication is often cited as the main reason for this acceleration, it can also be achieved through frequency of interaction.[45]
2. *Deterritorialization.* This is the sense that a place seems less exclusively connected to its local, geographically fixed context. It occurs both through the stretching of social networks and the incorporation of foreign people, goods, ideas, or practices into a local setting.
3. *Standardization.* This develops as people navigate means to overcome geographic and sociocultural divides. It relates to social-cultural

interaction arenas in which cultural meanings are evolved to create shared understanding.

4. *Unevenness*. Not everyone is globally engaged to the same extent. Furthermore, even among those engaged at a more global level, not all will benefit from participation in the same way or to the same degree. This is because processes that foster movement and connectivity often do so among some, but not all. Furthermore, efforts to connect may also result in exclusion and disconnections for others. Participation levels and degrees will remain diverse and fluctuate over time.
5. *Homogenization*. A degree of cultural homogenization occurs as people come to share a similar suite of practices and products to manage an increasing traffic of ideas, objects, and people. This is not so much about a single way of life, however. Rather, it pertains to how we come into contact with widely shared ideas and goods, and how we make them our own within our local contexts. Homogenization is seen in the shared aspects of practice, which are often most easily regarded from the level of interconnectivity, or broad-level (global) connectedness.
6. *Cultural heterogeneity*. This occurs because, alongside increasing homogenization, cultural variation often increases at the same time, especially as practices get reinterpreted locally, and these blendings of outside influences with local practices vary from place to place. Heterogeneity is visible in the diversities within shared practices; it is part of the paradox of globalization noted above. Consideration of this aspect often requires a more bottom-up perspective.
7. *Re-embedding of local culture*. This might be seen as a resurgence, or even invention, of local practices and forms in explicit reaction to the homogenization promoted by increasing globalization. This is because one of the outcomes of increased connections is awareness of similarities with and differences from others. It is another counterpart to processes that increase connectivity, in fact.
8. *Vulnerability*. The numerous, deeply embedded connections between various groups that create a circumstance of complex connectivity also leads to interdependence, and thus risk. Awareness of the risks of globalization becomes acute when an event reverberates across the network.

A Globalizing Mediterranean Iron Age?

Many of the case studies in the present volume illustrate features of Jennings's eight criteria of globalization. For example, Catherine Kearns (chapter 3) uses a bottom-up approach to examine the connectivity of rural groups in Cyprus. In so doing, she highlights social and economic diversities that enrich prevailing narratives of urban connectivity. The relative lack of imports in rural settlements along the Vasilikos and Maroni Rivers illustrates the agency of the residents of these valleys: direct access to foreign goods existed, but the residents here chose not necessarily to use them (or at least not those that required transportation in ceramic containers). In contrast, the elites of Amathus and other major contemporary Cypriot sites, such as Salamis, not only engaged substantially in offerings from the wider Mediterranean but also participated in more pan-Mediterranean expressions of elite status during the Iron Age, using Near Eastern and Greek goods and styles in common with other Levantine and Aegean elites. Despite direct coastal access and sporadic use of Greek and Levantine imports, those of elevated status in the valleys inland from Amathus appear to have chosen to be less directly connected with this more pan-Mediterranean world, at least as derived predominantly from ceramic assemblage survey data. Although their products could reach both regional and foreign destinations, these communities seem to have focused on building stronger regional connections. Kearns's emphasis on the *heterogeneity* of cultural practice among these rural Cypriot settlements—in terms of the connective properties of their consumption practices during the Iron Age in comparison with contemporary Cypriot centers—exemplifies not only the unevenness of connectivity but also that such unevenness could be determined by choice of the actors themselves.

Marian Feldman's practice-oriented concept of style (chapter 4), which defines style as the physical and visual results of acquired ways of doing, highlights how styles speak to social groups both horizontally and vertically, while accommodating variability in presentation and reception. Her case study of metal bowl production exemplifies this complex scenario. While the vessels are often collectivized as "Phoenician," Feldman notes that manufacturing practices support evidence of diverse production centers. She identifies, for example, a Cypriot network of metal bowl production whose products reached Greece. Similarly, an assemblage from Nimrud blends features that link practices shared among several production centers. None can be explicitly or exclusively linked with the Phoenicians. Furthermore, the imagery itself on this corpus mediates between diversely spread populations. Feldman's Mediterraneanism with regard to the style-as-practice of this group thus unites the balance between *homogenization* and *deterritorialization* that features in broader globalization theory. Their technical production is a common aspect.

The Cypriot bowls maintain a cluster of features that link them together sufficiently to suggest a Cypriot-based network of shared practices. Concurrently, other technical and stylistic features link them to assemblages elsewhere, including Athens and Euboea.

Certain features link Feldman's bowls together across substantial geographical distances, and between cultural groups. These features contributed to a shared understanding between the elite consumers of these products by, as Nicholas Vella has noted, mediating divergent viewpoints among their disparate users.[46] At the same time, the features do not bundle together into clearly demarcated groups. In this sense, the objects are deterritorialized from a clearly identified production group of craftspeople. Feldman herself sees these vessels as quintessential objects of concurrent fragmentation and connectivity.

Carolina López-Ruiz's discussion (chapter 2) of the Phoenicians highlights globalization in action. She challenges the notion of the Phoenicians purely as the cultural constructs of others and instead emphasizes the widespread and strong commonly shared features that support the identification of a cultural group we call the Phoenicians—a *standardization* that allows us to discuss them collectively. Standardization is not the same as identical replication, however, and thus we should still accept a degree of variability even within a collectivized group. López-Ruiz furthermore highlights the cultural package of "Oriental" features that were marketed, sold, consumed, and customized on demand around the Mediterranean, arguing that the Phoenicians were the primary disseminators of this package. This, too, is another form of standardization. There were shared material, stylistic, architectural, and scribal features, and more, from which individuals and groups selected. Motifs and ideas were used by people in diverse ways, however. Some aspects were used to indicate awareness of and connectedness with the international, the prestigious, and the sophisticated. Others incorporated aspects that spoke directly to local needs, beliefs, practices, and characteristics. This "Oriental" package created the sense of one-placeness that we associate with globalization. As with the metal bowls of Feldman's study, these "Oriental" features created a sense of *homogenization* through their common nature, but the selective ways in which they were adopted and adapted by individual groups facilitated cultural *heterogeneity* between these groups in comparison with one another. The diversity in take-up reflects the degree of *unevenness* in globalizing environments.

Ann Gunter's study (chapter 8) of Phrygian material and stylistic interactions with the Aegean and Neo-Assyrian spheres focuses us to confront the messy use of "Orientalizing" to characterize a variety of processes of material, stylistic, and ideational appropriation. Phrygian textiles and metallic accessories were well-known and highly regarded by Assyrian and Greek elites, and their styles were incorporated into local outputs in both regions (at least as we can see in terms of metalwork since textiles are not widely or well preserved archaeologically). Items deposited in Greek sanctuary contexts may reflect the influence of Phrygian deities around the eastern Mediterranean, as well as the use of these sites by a wider array of people. These styles devolved from their culturally specific Phrygian origins to one more generally associated with the eastern Aegean, and gaining wider uses in the process. Thus, we have multiple, overlapping mechanisms for the transfer of objects in styles. In some cases, items themselves maintained explicit links with the Phrygian world, emphasizing the *re-embeddedness of local culture* in globalizing contexts. In other cases, they evolved into a vernacular, reinforcing *homogenization* aspects that concurrently exist.

Brian Muhs's exploration (in chapter 9) of connectivity between Egypt and the wider Mediterranean world (including Assyria) is particularly valuable for its focus on the role of the Phoenicians. Muhs argues that connections between Egypt and the Mediterranean were partially mediated by the Phoenicians in a practical sense, through direct distribution, but also an ideational one, in terms of the dissemination of styles that were adopted in diverse production contexts and evolved to meet the needs and interests of consumers and markets. He demonstrates this through distributional study of statues and ceramics. This body of evidence suggests more intensive Egyptian–Phoenician interactions than are usually recognized and has implications for our understandings of Egyptian-style artifacts found across the Mediterranean. These have often been regarded as derivative, and thus subsumed under the amorphous notion of "Orientalizing" to explain the adoption and adaptation of a range of eastern Mediterranean ways of making, doing, representing, and styling, as noted by others in this volume. Muhs's reassessment rehabilitates the idea of a more directly connected Egypt during the Iron Age. It also sheds additional light on the *unevenness* of globalization, in terms of place, groups, and materials over time.

Several chapters in the present volume draw out mechanisms in which the complex connections of globalization operated. For example, Sarah Morris (chapter 5) highlights the role of transnationalism, which emphasizes daily interaction and the rise of small-scale hybrid practices, in spreading knowledge and understanding. Using a series of case studies (drinking cups inscribed with owners' names on Crete and at Methone; Levantine features in a number of funerary contexts on Crete; and warrior dedications and representations on Crete), she illustrates the importance of practice, rather than just artifacts themselves. Alongside this, she explores the role of military personnel, who were part of the cross-cultural traffic around the Mediterranean during the first millennium BCE. These were individuals who moved within different cultures for extended periods of time, rather than just circulating between them. Their role in the dissemination of knowledge and practice is different from that played by contemporary merchants, for example, who migrated in different ways and shared other kinds of understandings and ways of doing. Recognition of these other groups active in this era adds to our awareness of the diverse types of connections at play in the Mediterranean during the Iron Age, another facet of which is illustrated by both Susan Sherratt (chapter 6) and Papadopoulos (chapter 7) with regard to the Phrygians and Lydians around the north Aegean. This diversity is another aspect of the complex connectivity that characterizes the period.

The nature of communication between groups also features in several chapters. This brings us to globalization's time-space compression quality. Our impression of it derives from the more rapid communication between groups, which creates the sense that the world is smaller, rather than any kind of physical shrinkage or contraction. Increased communication can be experienced in terms of immediacy or frequency. The ability of technology today to span time and space into a negligible moment enables us to hold a conversation with someone on the other side of the world in what feels like real time. Networks of long-distance shipping routes and roads compressed the sense of distance between places in the past by enabling increased frequency of communication. For example, it is well-known that in the Roman world, speed of travel and communication did not increase substantially across the Roman Empire when a region became incorporated into it, despite the construction of road networks, which improved speed time over a fixed distance, since the absolute distance increased as new areas were integrated. There was, however, increased frequency of communication along these avenues. This led to increased information about regions, routes, and prices, as well as more regular movement of shared items and services, resulting in widespread use of common goods and the development of shared practices.[47] These in turn helped bind together the Roman world and created a sense of one-placeness.[48] In other words, increased frequency of communication gave rise to distributional networks of materials, styles, and knowledge and it is through these that we trace the acceleration of shared social practices between connected communities. As many of the chapters in this volume demonstrate, similar processes can be identified in the

"Phoenician" (López-Ruiz; Feldman), Phrygian (Gunter), and Aegean (Morris; Papadopoulos) orbits.

Complex connectivity leads to interdependence because of the numerous, deeply embedded connections between various groups. In this lies vulnerability to others, particularly once complex connections are established. For example, Sherratt and Papadopoulos both demonstrate the *vulnerability* of the north Aegean and Black Sea zones to changes in regional power. In the long term, the globalized system created by the networks of Greek and Phoenician settlements caught up the local populations in their conflicts with one another. By the sixth century, with the destruction of Tyre in the eastern Mediterranean, Carthage took a more overtly active political role in the central Mediterranean, emerging as the focal point for Phoenician civilization, and substantially changing power dynamics in the central and western Mediterranean. Persian expansion during the sixth century across the Levant and into western Anatolia brought this eastern power into direct conflict with those living around not only the eastern Mediterranean littoral but also the Aegean. This ultimately engaged mainland Greece and heralded the rise of Athens as a major power player. This is the coda to this particular globalizing era of Mediterranean history.[49] Exposure to vulnerability is a feature of increasing connections and associated interdependence, but the impact of that vulnerability is recognized only after the risk has been realized.

Conclusion

Michael Dietler (chapter 11) balances "big history" perspectives against locally focused studies. He notes that the distinctiveness of bottom-up studies often does not fit well within overarching narratives in six specific arenas: scale; connectivity; networks; network analysis; boundaries and borders; and colonialism. He observes that controversies about connectedness are really about scalar issues. Broad perspectives do not always apply at a local or lived experience level, given diversities in such practices. In turn, the diversities sometimes make it difficult to generalize more broadly. In other words, he argues that one size does not fit all and advocates looking at multiple scales concurrently. Globalization, for all that it is an overarching framework, provides a heuristic means to consider different scales alongside one another. Its consideration of the practices shared—rather than identically replicated—between groups stands alongside variability in the performance of those practices when those groups are compared with one another. Furthermore, agency, which plays an important role in how messages are communicated by an object or style to a particular audience, given that object and style use/meaning are driven by habitus, is central to discussions of globalization in action.

Even just from consideration of the examples presented throughout this volume, it can be seen that Iron Age complex connectivities took place in specific geographic and ecological contexts. The bottom-up case studies also highlight the fact that connectivities did not develop in a linear manner, or at an even pace, and nor were they stable, while their extent reached considerably beyond the Mediterranean's littoral zones. Given these variabilities, we should not necessarily expect a bottom-up example to show all eight characteristics Jennings calls for. It may be more beneficial instead to consider globalization in such contexts from the combined dimensions of place, medium, time, and rate.[50] Globalization has a spatial component, but its boundaries are contextualized by medium and time and thus are fuzzy geospatially. Furthermore, experiences of globalization may be direct or indirect, and its media varies between groups (and even individuals). Finally, complex connections take time to establish, with uneven, variable rates of evolution and maturity, fluctuating even once established. Collectively, this suggests that globalization is best explored concurrently from both the bottom-up approach of individual, localized case studies, and the top-down level of shared practices.[51] What links the two are the networks of connectivity through which goods and ideas move. The networks facilitate the development of shared practices. Those engaged within these networks will respond individually to their participation, with some engaging more closely (in certain arenas of connectivity), and others less closely, and each will respond to their interactions in the globalized network in a manner that addresses the needs and demands of their own sociocultural system. As a result, a globalization approach creates a far richer understanding of the social complexities that evolved during the Mediterranean's Iron Age than previous interpretative models have facilitated.

Notes

1. Jane Waldbaum, *From Bronze to Iron: The Transition from the Bronze Age to the Iron Age in the Eastern Mediterranean* (Gothenburg: Paul Aström, 1978); Waldbaum, "The Coming of Iron in the Eastern Mediterranean," in *The Archaeometallurgy of the Asian Old World*, ed. Vincent C. Piggot (Philadelphia: University of Pennsylvania Museum, 1999), 27–57; and Ünsal Yalçın, "Early Iron Metallurgy in Anatolia," *Anatolian Studies* 49 (1999): 177–87.

2. Tamar Hodos, *The Archaeology of the Mediterranean Iron Age* (Cambridge: Cambridge University Press, 2020), 37 with references.

3. See Hodos, *Archaeology of the Mediterranean Iron Age*, 38–48.

4. Tamar Hodos, "Colonial Engagements in the Global Mediterranean Iron Age," *Cambridge Archaeological Journal* 19, no. 2 (2009): 221–41.

5. See Hodos, "Colonial Engagements," 235n4 for details.

6. Karl Julius Beloch, *Griechische Geschichte*, vol. 1, part 1 (Strassburg: K. J. Trübner, 1913), 229–32.

7. Although no longer the case: Fernando González de Canales, Leonardo Serrano Pichardo, Jorge Llompart Gómez, Marcos García Fernández, Juan Ramon Torres, Adolfo Domínguez Monedero, and Aurelio Montaño Justo, "Archaeological Finds in the Deepest Anthropogenic Stratum at 3 Concepción Street in the City of Huelva, Spain," *Ancient West and East* 16 (2017): 1–61.

8. John Boardman, *The Greeks Overseas* (London: Thames and Hudson, 1999), 38.

9. Gocha Tsetskhladze, "Introduction: Revising Ancient Greek Colonisation," in *Greek Colonisation: An Account of Greek Colonies and Other Overseas Settlements*, ed. Gocha Tsetskhladze (Leiden: Brill, 2006), xxiii–lxxxiii, xlix.

10. E.g., Boardman, *Greeks Overseas*, 213, with regard to Spain.

11. Sabatino Moscati, *Il Mondo dei Fenici* (Milan: Il Saggiatore, 1966).

12. Boardman, *Greeks Overseas*, 190.

13. E.g., Edward Said, *Orientalism* (New York: Pantheon Books, 1978); Gayatri Spivak, "Can the Subaltern Speak?," in *Marxism and the Interpretation of Culture*, ed. Cary Nelson and Lawrence Grossberg (Urbana: University of Illinois Press, 1988), 271–313.

14. Discussed in Tamar Hodos, "Stage Settings for a Connected Scene: Globalization and Material Culture Studies in the Early First Millennium B.C.E. Mediterranean," *Archaeological Dialogues* 21, no. 1 (2014): 24–30.

15. E.g., Michael Dietler, *Archaeologies of Colonialism: Consumption, Entanglement and Violence in Ancient Mediterranean France* (Berkeley: University of California Press, 2010); and Tamar Hodos, *Local Responses to Colonisation in the Iron Age Mediterranean* (London: Routledge, 2006).

16. Jonathan Friedman, "Global Crises, the Struggle for Cultural Identity and Intellectual Pork Barrelling: Cosmopolitans versus Locals, Ethnics and Nationals in an Era of Dehegemonisation," in *Debating Cultural Hybridity: Multi-Cultural Identities and the Politics of Anti-Racism*, ed. Pnina Werbner and Tariq Modood (London: Zed Books, 1997), 70–89, 88; Peter Burke, *Cultural Hybridity* (Cambridge: Polity Press, 2009), 34.

17. Boardman, *Greeks Overseas*, 268.

18. E.g., Adolfo Domínguez, "Local Responses to Colonisation: Some Additional Perspectives," *Ancient West and East* 11 (2012): 205–18.

19. Hodos, "Stage Settings," 27.

20. E.g., Carol Dougherty and Leslie Kurke, eds., *The Cultures within Greek Culture: Contact, Conflict, Collaboration* (Cambridge: Cambridge University Press, 2003); Katheryn Lomas, ed., *Greek Identity in the Western Mediterranean* (Leiden: Brill, 2004); and Tsetskhladze, *Greek Colonisation*.

21. Jonathan Hall, *Hellenicity* (Chicago: University of Chicago Press, 2002).

22. E.g., Dietler, *Archaeologies of Colonialism*; Hodos, *Local Responses*.

23. Sabatino Moscati, *The World of the Phoenicians* (London: Cardinal, 1968), 77.

24. Marie Eugenia Aubet, *The Phoenicians and the West: Politics, Colonies and Trade* (Cambridge: Cambridge University Press, 2001), 250–56; Jo Crawley Quinn,

In Search of the Phoenicians (Princeton, NJ: Princeton University Press, 2018), 91–112; and Hodos, *Archaeology of the Mediterranean Iron Age*, 161–62.

25. Jo Crawley Quinn, "Tophets in the Punic World," in *The "Tophet" in the Phoenician Mediterranean: Studi Epigrafici e Linguistici 29–30 (2012–13)*, ed. Paolo Xella (Verona: Essedue, 2013), 23–48.

26. Quinn, "Tophets in the Punic World," 40.

27. In addition to works by Hodos, see also Kostas Vlassopoulos, *Greeks and Barbarians* (Cambridge: Cambridge University Press, 2013); Susan Sherratt, "A Globalizing Bronze and Iron Age Mediterranean," in *The Routledge Handbook of Archaeology and Globalization*, ed. Tamar Hodos (London: Routledge, 2017), 602–17; Peter van Dommelen, "Classical Connections and Mediterranean Practices," in Hodos, *Routledge Handbook of Archaeology and Globalization*, 618–33; and Christel Müller, "Globalization, Transnationalism, and the Local in Ancient Greece," *Oxford Handbooks Online*, http://www.oxfordhandbooks.com/view/10.1093/oxfordhb/9780199935390.001.0001/oxfordhb-9780199935390-e-42.

28. Joseph Stiglitz, *Making Globalization Work* (London: Penguin, 2006), 3–24; Kevin Ward and Kim England, "Introduction: Reading Neoliberalization," in *Neoliberalization: States, Networks, Peoples*, ed. Kevin Ward and Kim England (Oxford: Blackwell, 2007), 1–22; and Jan Nederveen Pieterse, "Rethinking Modernity and Capitalism: Add Context and Stir," *Sociopedia Colloquium* 1 (2014): 1–11.

29. E.g., Anthony Giddens, *The Consequences of Modernity* (Cambridge: Polity Press, 1990); Roland Robertson, *Globalizaton, Social Theory and Global Culture* (London: Sage, 1992); and Karl Moore and David Lewis, *The Origins of Globalization* (New York: Routledge, 2009).

30. Stiglitz, *Making Globalization Work*, 5.

31. See discussion and references in Jan Nederveen Pieterse, *Globalization and Culture* (Malden, MA: Rowman and Littlefield, 2015), 7–25.

32. Nederveen Pieterse, *Globalization and Culture*, tables 1.6 and 1.7, 19–20, with references, 183–210.

33. John Tomlinson, *Globalization and Culture* (Chicago: University of Chicago Press, 1992), 2.

34. Robertson, *Globalization*, 8.

35. Mike Featherstone, *Undoing Culture: Globalization, Postmodernism and Identity* (London: Sage, 1995), 114.

36. Nederveen Pieterse, *Globalization and Culture*, 67.

37. Nederveen Pieterse, *Globalization and Culture*, 68.

38. Tamar Hodos, "Globalization: Some Basics," in Hodos, *Routledge Handbook of Archaeology and Globalization*, 3–11, 4.

39. Giddens, *Consequences of Modernity*; Immanuel Wallerstein, *Geopolitics and Geoculture* (Cambridge: Cambridge University Press, 1991); Robbie Robertson, *Three Waves of Globalisation: A History of a Development Global Consciousness* (London: Zed Books, 2003); and Robertson, "Globalization Thinking and the Past," in Hodos, *Routledge Handbook of Archaeology and Globalization*, 54–65.

40. Hodos, "Globalization," 4.

41. Hodos, *Routledge Handbook of Archaeology and Globalization*.

42. Hodos, "Globalization," 5.

43. Justin Jennings, *Globalizations and the Ancient World* (Cambridge: Cambridge University Press, 2011), 123–41; Jennings, "Distinguishing Past

Globalizations," in Hodos, *Routledge Handbook of Archaeology and Globalization*, 12–28, at 14–16.

44. David Harvey, *The Condition of Postmodernity* (Oxford: Blackwell, 1989).

45. Hodos, *Archaeology of the Mediterranean Iron Age*, 29–32.

46. Nicholas Vella, "'Phoenician' Metal Bowls: Boundary Objects in the Archaic Period," *Bollettino di Archeologia On Line* 1 (2010): 22–37.

47. Morley, "Globalisation and the Roman Economy," in *Globalisation and the Roman World*, ed. Martin Pitts and Miguel John Versluys (Cambridge: Cambridge University Press, 2014), 49–68.

48. Martin Pitts and Miguel John Versluys, eds., *Globalisation and the Roman World: World History, Connectivity and Material Culture* (New York: Cambridge University Press, 2014).

49. On the end of the Iron Age in the Levant, Egypt and Greece, and elsewhere, see Hodos, *Archaeology of the Mediterranean Iron Age*, 48–49.

50. Hodos, *Archaeology of the Mediterranean Iron Age*, 217–20.

51. As advocated explicitly by van Dommelen, "Classical Connections," 628–29.

CHAPTER 11

Six Provocations in Search of a Pretext

MICHAEL DIETLER

The chapters of *The Connected Iron Age* offer a timely and important contribution to debates among historians, archaeologists, and cultural anthropologists about the nature and definition of the Mediterranean as a region and as a concept. Timely because they arrive at a moment when the future direction of the field of Classics, and Mediterranean studies in general, is in flux; and important because they provide a set of critically thoughtful and productively diverse reflections on key problems, methods, and stakes of the field. As James Osborne and Jonathan Hall (chapter 1) point out, the idea of the Mediterranean as an interconnected world or a coherent "culture area" has generated a great deal of controversy over the years. Occupying one end of the spectrum are approaches favoring sweeping "big history" narratives of the kind espoused by Fernand Braudel, Peregrine Horden, Nicholas Purcell, Cyprian Broodbank, and others, which have naturalized purported pan-Mediterranean characteristics and connections in a set of geographical imperatives or evolutionary forces. At the other end are more locally focused ethnographic, historical, and archaeological studies that often argue forcefully against the existence of pan-Mediterranean processes or cultural homologies.[1]

To a certain extent, these recurring disputes may be seen as a reflection of differences in scholarly dispositions laid out in Isaiah Berlin's famous allegorical dichotomy between the hedgehog, who knows one big thing, and the fox, who knows many things.[2] However, the argument is not only about the conflicting ontological premises of "monist" hedgehogs and "pluralist" foxes. As several critics have pointed out, claims about the connectedness or unity of the Mediterranean have ideological underpinnings and political stakes. Critiques of Mediterranean connectedness have argued that such models risk being an intellectual product of asymmetrical North–South geopolitical relations: an imposition by Northern scholars (especially Anglophone and Germanic) of cultural homogeneity on a region that has been constructed as part of a Romantic imaginary. It has also been noted that visions of Mediterranean regional connectedness often bear an uncanny resemblance to the dominating gaze of past colonial and imperial projects, a perspective that was not necessarily shared by those enduring or resisting such efforts.[3] Whatever the case, it is clear that the connectedness of the ancient or modern Mediterranean is no longer a subject that can be approached naively. That is precisely what gives this volume import and urgency, as the authors strive to critically reassess the empirical evidence for connections and interactions in a particular historical period and region, with a sober evaluation of methods and more self-reflexive awareness of the sociohistorical context of research.

Following the lively discussions at the conference that gave rise to this publication, the editors asked me to write a few concluding reflections. In the event, it has proved a difficult task to find a way to add something of potential value and relevance to the conversation, given the high quality, eloquence, and diversity of the chapters and the fact that I have no expertise at all in the archaeology and history of the Eastern Mediterranean. In full recognition of the inadequacy of multiple abandoned false starts, I decided in the end to eschew any attempt at synthesis or even at commenting on the chapters directly. Instead I resolved to modestly paddle my canoe up a few of the tributaries leading off from the main course of the river explored by the volume as a way of providing some context for it. Hence, I offer a few scattered observations and questions, without claiming any coherent theme or thesis. Claims of relevance might also be difficult to defend. Productive provocation is perhaps the best I can aspire to here, which may excuse the unconventional form of this intervention. In what follows, prompted by the spirit of Pirandello's famous absurdist play, *Six Characters in Search of an Author*, invoked in the title of this piece, I put forward six brief and rather inchoate polemical observations and questions that are loosely linked by a desire to test the fabric of some approaches currently circulating widely in the field by pulling at a few loose threads. This includes devoting discussion to some approaches that the authors of this volume have chosen not to pursue, on the premise that such an exercise provides useful context for choices made. The exercise is intended to be constructively complementary rather than simply cranky or contrarian. At least that is my cover story.

Provocation 1. Scale: Epistemological Problem and Methodological Opportunity

To proclaim the obvious, scale is a centrally important concern in understanding Mediterranean connectedness. Indeed, many of the controversies about connectedness can be traced to scalar issues. I would suggest that the importance of scale is actually twofold, in that it both poses an epistemological problem and presents a methodological opportunity. It is no secret that sociohistorical explanations in general tend to be scale dependent: what looks like a convincing interpretation on a broad regional or global scale usually falls apart or seems like banal reductionism when scrutinized on a local micro level. And purely local explanations, no matter how richly textured, tend to suffer from myopic limitations that render them unable to account for broader structural forces, relations, and homologies. The same is true on a temporal axis, with long-, medium-, and short-term histories telling different stories—a conundrum that especially preoccupied Braudel and the *Annaliste* historians.[4] The upshot of the epistemological enigma of scale is that it usually tends to be invoked as a spoiler argument of the "yes, but your model can't explain *this* situation" or "your situation can't explain *this* pattern" variety.

In the Mediterranean case, at the most basic level, scholarly dispositions of the hedgehog versus fox variety have led analysts to approach the phenomenon of interaction and its consequences from broad macro-scale, local micro-scale, and sometimes intermediary meso-scale perspectives, often yielding incommensurable results. For example, viewing the Mediterranean from the standpoint of world-systems analysis, the Braudelian *longue durée*, or other such programs requires a level of schematic abstraction and data selectivity (based on assumptions about criteria for separating pattern from "noise") that severely limit the ability to offer much interpretive power for specific local sites or histories or to explain variation at the local level of lived experience. Similarly, studies at the household or village level can be challenged as powerless to explain broader homologies or patterns and blind to larger historical forces and structures: as not being able to see the forest for the trees.

But scale can serve a much more positive role than this. I would suggest that we need first to acknowledge that scale is not a Goldilocks phenomenon where some intermediary level between extremes can be found that is "just right." Social life is simply too complex to be understood from a single vantage point and any explanation or model that operates entirely on a single scale (temporal or spatial) is inherently flawed. Realistic explanations must mobilize multiple scales on multiple axes simultaneously. Indeed, constantly shifting scales and perspectives (*both* spatially and temporally) is something I have found to be an extremely revealing methodological strategy and it should be a necessary part of any approach to understanding the nature and significance of Mediterranean connections.[5] This means not simply finding ways to reconcile different scalar levels of analysis, but constantly moving back and forth among different scales to reveal contradictions and confront different forms, loci, and logics of agency. It means simultaneously taking forests, trees, and even leaves seriously as equally powerful perspectives that are best studied as a dynamic relational complex.

In practical terms for archaeologists studying ancient Mediterranean connectedness, this would mean doing such things as examining comparatively the histories of individual households and neighborhoods within settlements while simultaneously comparing the histories of settlements within a region and the histories of regions across the Mediterranean and beyond for evidence of different kinds of interactions and their consequences. Constantly shifting spatial and temporal perspective by moving back and forth among these levels of analysis can reveal new kinds of relational insights about patterns of historical transformation and their trajectories and meaning. Of course, this is a lot of work and it complicates our picture of the messy webs of connective acts and relations and their consequences. It risks yielding explanations and models that are less elegant and less immediately gratifying to some scholars than those that emerge from single-scale analyses, but also, I would aver, far richer and more realistic.[6] This approach might also be better accomplished by reorienting research practices toward teams of scholars working together in multisited projects with collaborative strategies and publications.

Provocation 2. Connectivity: An "Ityology"

"Connectivity" is a term that has become increasingly fashionable in recent years as a way to describe linkages in the Mediterranean and elsewhere, but I want to raise a red flag of caveat on this issue. This concern is not motivated by a desire to instigate petty semantic battles, nor by a curmudgeonly annoyance at what might be interpreted as peddling old wine in new bottles. There are, in fact, many reasons for my skepticism, but let me begin with a mildly sardonic exercise in what I will call "ityology": that is, an analysis of the practice of attaching the suffix "-ity" to words in an effort to give the impression of theoretical novelty and heft (in less charitable moments, I have been known to call this practice "ityocy"). Examples are ubiquitous throughout the social sciences and humanities, extending back to the seminal "modernity" and "identity," which everyone seems to find problematic and *dépassé* nowadays. In fact, ity-talk is flourishing as never before in theory land, including such popular terms as "materiality," "hybridity," "postcoloniality," "intersubjectivity," "intertextuality," "spatiality," "rurality," "governmentality," "historicity," "connectivity," and so forth. One recent article surely merits the grand prize for ityolatry (or, perhaps, itymania) for embarking on a discussion of "intertheoricity" that also manages to work in the terms "intertextuality," "intermediality," "interartiality," "elasticity," "plasticity," "hybridity," "pluridisciplinarity," "interdisciplinarity," and "transdisciplinarity." And, of course, Bruno Latour has given us the delightful tongue-twister "actantiality."[7] All signs suggest that our accelerating theory gyrator is in the midst of a full blown "ity-turn," with an endless supply of adjectives and nouns just waiting to be ityized.

My wariness of the discourse of connectivity stems in part from the fact that it shares an emulative abstract vagueness with its ity-brethren. Such gestures of mimetic indexical mistiness give rise to suspicions of a kind of cargo-cult approach to theory, in which the deployment of semantic forms associated with other bodies of theory is expected to magically deliver meaning in a new context. One might also see this as an example of a phenomenon described by Yves Gingras in which "some scholars have the curious habit of thinking that giving a name, a label, to a practice is sufficient to transform it into a concept and serves an important analytical purpose or even 'explain[s]' the practice itself."[8] But what kind of theoretical work is actually performed by transforming connections, interactions, and relations of extremely diverse kinds and scales into "connectivity?" I would suggest that it is more than a benign act of rebranding, but rather a form of reductionism that diverts attention away from active processes and agents of interaction toward a vague, reified, transhistorically homogenized, flattened, and passive state or quality of "being connected." It masks a host of crucial *qualitative* differences under an abstract term that is so general that it covers virtually any form of movement, contact, or relationship.

For some fans, the attraction of connectivity is also that it seems to imply that this state or quality is in some way measurable (at least aspirationally), that there is a quantifiable amount or degree of connectivity, and that this has some explanatory power. I will have more to say about this in a later discussion of network analysis, but let me here simply state that, when pursued, this often leads down the same garden paths and pathologies that characterize the field of economics and its manic devotion to quantification. The attraction to connectivity also, I suspect, has something to do with the way that "social networks" of the cyberspace kind have come to dominate the recent postmodern popular imaginary in a way that genetics did a decade or so ago, as a central organizing metaphor for envisioning society. But it is well to remember that prior forms and structures of interaction did not all articulate through a single homogenizing medium that enables handy measurement by numbers of clicks or "friends." Even today, this presents a grossly distorted and highly superficial picture of social worlds and their complex linkages.

Enthusiasts of connectivity would do well to heed the warnings that have emerged from critiques of earlier ity-ized concepts. For example, Rogers Brubaker and Frederick Cooper pointed out two decades ago that "identity" had come to signify "too much, too little, or nothing at all."[9] When applied in a hard sense, it risked becoming reified as a stable "thing" that all people or groups possess and thereby falling prey to the problem of essentialism. When applied in the more fluid, fractured, contingent, interactional sense that became popular in the postmodern and postcolonial literature, it often became so expansively flexible that it ceased to have much analytical force as a concept. They advocated that, when trying to understand the ways in which people locate their place in society through intersecting relational and categorical understandings of social space, it is less useful to turn to "identity" as a reified thing or state than to think about the quite different kinds of emotionally charged attachments—which they called "commonality, connectedness, and groupness"—that emerge from these relational and categorical perceptions.[10] Similarly, the transhistorical, homogenizing implications of "modernity" have given rise to such strong critiques that most anthropologists who still use this term do so only in the plural, as in "multiple modernities," or "alternative modernities." I'm not sure that this pluralization gambit actually solves many problems, any more than does a shift from connectivity to "connectivities" that one sees in some recent literature. Contrary to a suggestion that was made at the conference, I do not see these as corresponding to, respectively, etic and emic perspectives on the phenomenon of connections. In practice, both tend to be quite resolutely etic analytical conceptions—unless one stands this on its head by interpreting "connectivity" as the emic worldview of a community of young twenty-first-century Western middle-class academics who have been socialized on Facebook and Twitter. In any case, I am skeptical that plotting the distribution of Iron Age objects or architectural styles really yields emic understandings of ancient social worlds. On the contrary, I think it suggests an approach toward what Pierre Bourdieu called "objectivist" knowledge in his analysis of "the three forms of theoretical knowledge" (the others being "phenomenological" and "praxeological").[11]

In summary, I am not advocating a complete ban on connectivity and other ity-talk, if people feel a need for it. There are undoubtedly contexts where such concepts may be made heuristically (or pragmatically) useful. But this requires us, at the least, to be self-consciously clear about precisely what we mean by these terms and what analytical work they are actually doing, so that we are not simply consuming new jargon without reflecting on the questions that remain unasked and the pitfalls that remain unexamined. If anthropology teaches us anything, it is that the *nature and logic* of interaction (or the processes that create "connectivity") are all important, not simply its relative intensity. For example, in early colonial situations, the specific nature of agents of contact (missionaries, traders, soldiers, settlers, etc.), the precise kinds of goods and services that were exchanged, the nature of consumption patterns, the social and cultural logic of demand for exotic goods, practices, and relationships, and the relations of power that structured exchanges are crucial in determining the consequences of interactions. Warfare and marriage are, after all, both instances of connectivity, but they have rather different repercussions.

Provocation 3. Networks, Maslow's Hammer, Zombie Resurrections, and Killing Flies with Dynamite

The growing popularity of connectivity as a concept in Mediterranean studies has been accompanied by an increasing attraction to networks as a methodological framework for envisioning and measuring connections. This has involved primarily several versions of standard network analysis, and to a much lesser extent the adoption of the quite different actor- network theory (ANT) developed by Bruno Latour and others.[12] Among many differences, unlike standard network analysis, the concept of "network" operates entirely at the level of inspirational metaphor in ANT. The approach is based on the conceit that agency is dispersed in complex networks of "human and nonhuman actants," but it has no actual method for empirically mapping networks of interaction and no interest in doing so: network is valued as a literary device rather than a scientific method. Moreover, as Yves Gingras has noted, ANT is actually "not a *theory* in any standard epistemological sense, but simply a descriptive *language*. It would thus be more precise to call it 'actor-network language' or, to use an acronym, ANL."[13]

Given the currently limited impact of ANT (or ANL) in Mediterranean studies (at least beyond the Roman context), and the fact that I have already declaimed against its dangers elsewhere at some length, I will refrain from further maligning ANT here except to note that there is a significant problem in attributing agency to objects, as it does.[14] The danger is that this both trivializes the concept of agency and, most importantly, depoliticizes analysis by obscuring relations of power. I would suggest that the elevation of material objects to positions of agency creates an unduly myopic focus on the relationship between people and things in a way that replicates the kind of fetishization of the commodity that Marx was so concerned to explode in his analysis of capitalism.[15] In other words, it misidentifies and mystifies relations of power between people (which are mediated by objects) by representing them as if they were a symmetrical relationship between people and objects. Indeed, under a guise of radical theory, it ends up endorsing a fundamental fantasy of conservative neoliberal economic ideology and precludes an understanding of the way social power shapes networks.[16] And, do we really want to follow a path that, as Slavoj Žižek and Artur Ribeiro have pointed out, would compel us to envision the Holocaust as a diffuse network of agentive relations among symmetrical "actants" such as Nazis, trains, guns, barbed wire, gas, and victims?[17] What happens to the notion of responsibility, and the identification of power and violence? Moreover, beyond the intellectual frisson of the "radicality effect," one has to ask what ANT really has to offer in terms of novel theoretical insight.[18] I confess to being baffled by its appeal and alarmed by its ramifications.

But enough of Cassandraic caveats about ANT (and its even more extreme archaeological spawn, sometimes called "symmetrical archaeology"). Let me now turn to a few qualms concerning the more popular uses of orthodox network analysis. The recent growing popularity of network analysis in archaeology does not mean that this idea is new to the social sciences. In fact, I am old enough to remember that there was a period during the 1960s and 1970s when it enjoyed a wave of enthusiasm in anthropology as a technique for modeling social relations in a number of ethnographic studies, especially in those situations where kinship systems did not seem to be a very good guide to how social behavior was organized.[19] Among the primary sources of its attraction were, as one of its main proponents, Jeremy Boissevain, noted, that it seemed promising as a way of handling some of the issues of scale that I noted earlier, that it offered an approach to data "at a lower level of abstraction than the institutional complex," and that it also provided "apparently 'hard' data which could be plotted and even computerized."[20] The latter feature was something of a seductive novelty for anthropologists of the period. However, it became increasingly evident that the quantification demands and end products of such models were too complex to be very useful in providing significant representations of, or insights into, social life.

Even Boissevain was eventually forced to admit that network analysis had failed to reach its potential for a variety of reasons, including especially "an overelaboration of technique and data and an accumulation of trivial results." As he noted, "Networks are compared with regard to density, size, and even composition, much in the way that butterfly-collectors compare the coloring, wingspread, and number of spots of their favorite species. Trivial, but extremely costly results . . . are put forward with great solemnity." Moreover, "the battery of techniques with which social scientists have equipped themselves to answer the limited questions that network analysis can resolve produces overkill. Flies are killed with dynamite." And finally, "as enthusiastic network practitioners strive towards ever greater rigor, network analysis risks becoming further removed from human life and bogged down ever deeper in the swamp of methodological involution."[21] Tough love, to say the least! This heroically candid assessment by a leading advocate of the program, written over forty years ago, sounds uncannily prescient for the contemporary revival. In the event, by the 1980s network analysis had, as Boissevain feared, joined "the Dodo, Neanderthal man, and sociometry as an extinct species,"[22] at least as far as anthropology was concerned. It had passed out of fashion, except as a lingering metaphor. To be sure, some sociologists, who have always been more susceptible to the charms of quantification, continued to find it intriguing, as did geographers, and it has witnessed an explosion of renewed cross-disciplinary interest since the 1990s.[23] Hence, network analysis is now back from the dead and stalking the halls of archaeology programs looking for ever more powerful computers. What could go wrong?

"If a hammer is your only tool, everything begins to look like a nail." This useful piece of folk wisdom adapted to the practice of science is often referred to as "Maslow's hammer," after the psychologist Abraham Maslow who formulated a version of it. It is a problem common with many new techniques and theories that enjoy a wave of popularity in archaeology: seemingly powerful new analytical tools are rapidly applied in a range of situations to which they are often not really appropriate. In the current case, I am afraid that both the nature of the problem being addressed and the nature of archaeological data severely limit the utility of network analysis and related forms of formal quantified modeling as a means of helping us understand ancient processes of interaction and their consequences. This is not only because the complexity of this issue is enormous but also because not every type of socially organizing behavior takes the form of a network.[24] Indeed, a case could be made that, as was hinted at earlier, a dominance of networks as a mode of social organization is technology dependent: that is, it relies on the proliferation of certain forms of communication technology that are especially flexible, egalitarian, and capable of reciprocal flows of information. Moreover, many of the most important variables involved in processes of interaction are of a qualitative and historically contingent nature that staunchly resists quantification.

Of course, one solution to such problems is that adopted by economists, who cling to the disciplinary chimera that anything that cannot be quantified is inherently unimportant and must be excluded from the analysis. One might restate this strategy as "if a hammer is your only tool, anything that is not a nail is irrelevant." Making a virtue out of necessity, many economists simply ignore the inconvenient ambiguities, incongruities, and holes in their evidence and concentrate on the dazzling elegance of the mathematical models they devise—preferring a robust model ("my hammer is a beautiful hammer") to a realistic understanding of human behavior. This is what led the economist Yanis Varoufakis, in a moment of refreshing candor, to describe his own discipline as "a sinister priesthood purveying thinly disguised, heavily mathematized superstition as scientific economics."[25] I would hope that archaeologists can be trusted to resist the temptation to indulge in this kind of self-delusion, although the history of the field suggests that this is perhaps a misplaced hope.

It is important to remember that, for archaeologists, these issues of quantification are not trivial. We are never in a position to directly observe and measure actual instances of human interaction in a network. Rather, we must rely on extremely partial data as second-order proxies with many serious epistemological problems. Most significantly, there are well-recognized problems of preservation: we reconstruct models of the distribution of remnants of the most durable objects that have been preserved in the archaeological record (e.g., ceramics, metalwork, architecture) to make hypotheses about webs of connections among people. But we are completely ignorant about many other domains of perishable material culture (cloth, wood, foods, etc.) that may have circulated in other kinds of networks—and, of course, about nonmaterial practices, knowledge, and relationships. Moreover, evaluating the quantitative significance of even the durable categories of material culture is highly problematic, except in very broad terms, because of the way that such data are produced (different excavation and survey strategies yielding different degrees of representativeness of samples, divergent methods of counting and reporting ceramic sherds, etc.). To put it bluntly, archaeological data do not meet the minimum standards necessary to satisfy the requirements for the kinds of quantified network analyses that are performed by geographers and others who work on contemporary societies. Hence, no matter how impressive the quantitative calculations and three-dimensional network images that are derived from archaeological data, we must admit that the concept remains essentially at the level of suggestive metaphor. That is not to propose that such exercises in quantified mapping are useless—far from it. But we must not allow ourselves to be intoxicated by the glamour of the hammer into imagining that everything is a nail, or that we are even very good at hitting nails with it.

The risk of bedazzling and confusing ourselves with alluring three-dimensional sociograms and other network visualizations is a very real one. Aside from the issues outlined above, it is clear that network diagrams are most intuitively compelling when representing small quantities of data. As the data load grows, the diagrams usually descend into an escalating chaos of overlapping lines that can make patterns increasingly difficult to discern, until the entire visual surface may eventually be covered. At this point complex mathematical algorithms become the only viable form of representation and analysis. Hence, it is essential for archaeologists not to lose sight of what these visualizations are actually representing—which is decidedly not patterns of interaction in any direct sense—and what the purpose of constructing them is. Otherwise, it is easy to be sucked down the rabbit hole into the world of butterfly collecting and methodological involution that Boissevain warned against.

Provocation 4. Network Analysis and the Ghost of Functionalism

As with many techniques, several kinds of fetishization can arise in the pursuit of network analysis. One is the problem of methodological involution described above—a problem that was aptly articulated by Johnny Rotten singing "I don't know what I want, but I know how to get it."[26] Another lies in the danger of imbuing the form of networks with a kind of agency. This is something that one sees quite commonly in the use of network analysis by geographers, who expend a great deal of effort attempting to identify and classify different types of networks, under the assumption that networks of different forms and density characteristics will have predictable social and historical effects. These ideas have also been carried over into archaeology, where one sees, for example, the descriptive identification of "small-world networks" touted as having an explanatory value in terms of historical processes in the ancient Mediterranean.[27]

To me, however, this seems to be edging dangerously close to reviving the ghost of functionalism in the same way that we saw with "systems theory" and its "feedback loops" back in the 1970s. That is, it attributes agency to the form and needs of a system, while the behavior of individuals, groups, and institutions is explained by the structure of the system. In the case of the anthropological and sociological versions of functionalism, this meant that every behavior, cultural practice, and belief came to be interpreted as a function of the social system: they were ostensibly mechanisms for social cohesion. This left no place for potentially dysfunctional behaviors, practices, or institutions and the theory could not accommodate conflict or the agency of groups or individuals. This was not the only problem with functionalism, but it was a major one that, astonishingly, keeps reemerging from the grave in new zombie guises.

I fear this is the case with many iterations of network analysis in archaeology (and elsewhere). For example, mapping a regional exchange network in the Mediterranean and deciding that it resembles a "small-world network" does not provide an explanation of the demand for exotic goods, the diffusion of innovations, the logic of consumption practices, the politics of trade relations, or other such things. It provides, at best, a *description* of the general structure of certain connections that suggests the conditions of possibility for certain things to happen. But what actually happens depends upon the specific nature of the interactions at each particular node of the network. What is the social position of the agents who interact? What kinds of interchanges and relationships are involved? What are the cultural dispositions that structure the choices and interests of the agents? What is the broader political framework that establishes the spaces for interaction and organizes the relations of power for the actors? And finally, what is the local history of such interactions and of the social formations that underlie them? These are some key questions that must be addressed if we are to move beyond mere skeletal description and functionalist conjecture.

Let me make clear that I am not arguing against the practice of constructing network diagrams or using network analysis. These tools can be very useful for visualizing, and sometimes even discovering, patterns in data of various kinds. As one example of particular interest to graduate students who might be reading this, I would point to their role in the analysis of faculty hiring networks in American anthropology departments.[28] But network analysis is essentially a technique for identifying certain kinds of patterns, not for explaining them. We must be careful not to get carried away and lose sight of the limitations of network analysis, especially in the realm of archaeology. Boissevain was very clear-eyed in outlining what network analysis can and cannot do, and it is well to remember his admonition that it can only be "an adjunct or complement to other research techniques."[29] Using faster and more powerful computers than were available in the 1970s does not fundamentally alter that situation, although it may increase the dangers of self-mystification.

Provocation 5. Boundaries and Borders

Talking about boundaries and borders is currently rather unfashionable, but we still need to take them seriously. The increasing popularity of connectivity and networks in studies of the Mediterranean has, I think, served to obscure the importance of boundaries as a force in social life. It's all about flows and nodes now. But social and cultural boundaries do not necessarily involve spatial discreteness or segregation, and they do not necessarily correlate with the limits or shapes of networks. As Frederick Barth pointed out long ago, ethnic distinctions do not develop because of isolation, but rather as part of processes of frequent interaction.[30] They exist within networks and go hand in hand with "connectivity."

Another source for the neglect of boundaries has been a tendency to celebrate various kinds of cultural fusion, described alternatively as hybridity, creolization, and *métissage*, by archaeologists studying the ancient Mediterranean who have been influenced by postcolonial theory. To be sure, these can be useful concepts in contexts where they are appropriate and retain analytical specificity. But what has often been swept aside in the uncritical pursuit of theoretical fashion is an understanding of the very real significance of perceived boundaries and distinctive local identities in the daily lives of people. Not every consumption of an alien object or appropriation of an alien concept is an example of hybridity—at least if this term is to have some analytical utility in the sense that it was developed by Homi Bhabha, following Mikhail Bahktin.[31] Nor are they simply instances of connectivity. What is crucial to understanding the significance and consequences of such acts of consumption and appropriation is to realize that they are often accomplished across perceived social and cultural boundaries and are frequently even motivated by the symbolic demands of maintaining such boundaries. In the contemporary world, the Olympic Games are a prime example of a ritualized situation of intense interaction using a common set of implements and rules that is motivated precisely by highly charged sentiments of national cultural and political boundaries and that serves principally to reify those boundaries through competitions enveloped with flags, uniforms, and anthems. In the longer term, the Mediterranean has been crisscrossed by various kinds of shifting webs of interaction over the millennia, but this does not necessarily produce increasing cultural fusion or uniformity. Rather, social groups and individuals create and exploit these networks for highly ethnocentric reasons that have to do with local social and cultural logics. Those groups, logics, and boundaries are transformed by the process, but not necessarily in the direction of uniformity or hybridity.

Let me also offer a word of preemptive clarification in defending the significance of boundaries. In speaking of such things as cross-cultural consumption and the persistence of culture as it is constructed through consumption, let me state categorically that I am not invoking the old structural-functionalist organic model of culture as a homogeneous entity with rigid boundaries. Rather, I am assuming a more processual understanding of culture that implies a great deal of fluidity and socially differentiated embodiment of cultural categories, dispositions, and tastes. Moreover, it is clear that, from an analytical perspective, social and cultural boundaries do not necessarily involve spatial discreteness or segregation. Rather, they are symbolically constituted and contextually defined and invoked, often with variable indexical attributes. Yet, for individuals, such boundaries have great *affective* importance and are often seen as clear and distinct, and group identities are often perceived in ways that make them seem essentialized and stable, even as they are rapidly changing. Think, for example, about American conceptions of race and their consequences in social life, politics, health, education, music, and just about everything else. Perceived categorical boundaries have real motivational and structuring effects within networks of interacting people.

In colonial contexts, such boundaries may be more distinctly perceived (in either emic or etic terms) at certain periods in the history of an encounter than at others, they may be very differently perceived by different parties in the encounter, and they may undergo significant transformations. Hence, the term "cross-cultural," as used here, implies a sense of difference (in terms of categorical perceptions, dispositions to action, etc.) but not necessarily separation or discreteness. The boundaries in such processes are always subject to definition within specific contexts and they are always an evolving relational phenomenon. At the same time, colonialism in action transgresses boundaries and borders in complex ways. It produces alliances that traverse ethnic and political boundaries as it aligns structural oppositions within colonial and indigenous societies in new configurations of interest. But social and cultural boundaries remain affectively charged resources of the imaginary and sources of motivation for action.

The point is that even if social and cultural boundaries are not visible to our preferred analytical tools (such as network analysis), we cannot ignore their existence if we want to understand the motivations behind the choices people make and the consequences those choices have.

Provocation 6. Colonialism and Mediterranean Connectedness

To return to a theme broached at the beginning, two propositions have tended to orient debates about the Mediterranean as a region: (1) that there is some kind of enduring essential unity to the Mediterranean and (2) that this unity is somehow lodged in a particular geography or ecology that provokes a state of interconnection. Why do these assumptions raise red flags for me? In addition to the empirical challenges noted by others, I am vexed by the knowledge that pan-regional unity or identity of the kind proposed is a very common core motif of imperialist and nationalist discourse (if very rarely of on the ground fact)—and this is a vision that is not necessarily shared by all of those engaged in colonial situations. The very establishment of imperial boundaries, for example, is designed to assert, and symbolically construct, a kind of landscape of identitary unification within those borders. One is reminded immediately, for example, of the ideological project of Augustus with his res gestae and Agrippa's map designed to define the Mediterranean (mare nostrum) as a unitary region with its center at Rome.[32] Moreover, the implication that this purported integration might be lodged in a common geography or ecology raises the issue of the potential "naturalization" of what I would see as arbitrary, historically contingent human constructions and ideological projects.

I am not trying to deny, a priori, that either of these foundational propositions might, in some sense or in some period, be true. What I am saying is that because of their striking resemblance to the discursive products of colonialism, they necessitate an especially vigilant attention to the origin of the sources employed to support them, to the potential sources that were *not* brought into the narrative, to the relative standards of proof utilized in evaluating competing interpretations, and to the implicit landscape of the taken-for-granted on which the narrative is constructed.

All of this is to explain why, for example, in reading a book such as Horden and Purcell's *The Corrupting Sea*, with its championing of the idea of connectivity as a geographically mandated unifying force in Mediterranean history, my attention is immediately drawn to the silences and the silencing that the narrative produces. One obvious feature is that the book favors texts over the material record of archaeological evidence. Because Greeks and Romans were literate and most subjects of colonial domination were not (at least originally), the textual evidence for such encounters tends to be highly partial. We get the colonizers' view of the world and little else. When reference is made to archaeology it is almost entirely to the archaeology of Greeks and Romans. Hence, we get various descriptions of Greco-Roman ships, buildings, and practices, such as trade and cadastration, but virtually no discussion of the reactions of the colonized or of the lives of people outside the zones of colonial domination. Indeed, Celts and Iberians did not even make it into the index. To my mind, it is a very pregnant kind of silence when the two most populous peoples of the Western Mediterranean during the first millennium BCE pass virtually without mention. They provide simply a space on the map—a silent, passive backdrop for the "real" narrative of Mediterranean history, which is assumed to be one of "connectivity."

The point is that scholars who work on the ancient Mediterranean have a special weight of obligation to approach their studies with a critical self-reflexive awareness because of the role that the ancient Mediterranean colonial powers have played in the mythologies of cultural identity of modern European nations and their colonial projects. Studies of the past that do not challenge these ideological projections risk unwittingly naturalizing colonial models of essentializing continuity.

Conclusion (of Sorts)

Many other provocative points could (and possibly should) be raised, but I promised to limit myself to Pirandello's six. So, let me conclude by voicing the question most readers who have made it this far will be asking themselves: What is the objective of this meandering jeremiad, aside from stirring up trouble? Is it simply an exercise in intellectual vandalism? Could it be a diagnostic sign of the onset of creeping curmudgeonism? Or a Luddite tantrum? Epistemological dyspepsia, perhaps? I can't exclude any of these possibilities. But insofar as there is a guiding strategy (or pretext), it might be something like the desire for a minor academic prose equivalent to a Brechtian alienation effect. My comments were intended to complement the chapters in the volume, without naming names, by pointing to a few theoretical, epistemological, and methodological issues that seem important to explicitly address as scholars launch into the current reimagining of the Mediterranean and the forces that connect and divide it. Many of my observations simply emphasize furrows already being plowed in the chapters, while others are calls to push back harder against received notions and narratives, to be wary of hidden traps, to resist the sirens of scholarly fashion, and to avoid reinventing square wheels. Hopefully, everyone will find at least one thing in the text to annoy and agitate them. Agitation is not a bad outcome, if it leads to critical reflection and action.

Notes

1. For a range of conflicting perspectives, see Dionigi Albera, "Anthropology of the Mediterranean: Between Crisis and Renewal," *History and Anthropology* 17 (2006): 109–33; Fernand Braudel, *The Mediterranean and the Mediterranean World in the Age of Philip II*, trans. Siân Reynolds, 3 vols. (New York: Harper and Row, 1972); Cyprian Broodbank, *The Making of the Middle Sea: A History of the Mediterranean from the Beginning to the Emergence of the Classical World* (Oxford: Oxford University Press, 2013); João de Pina-Cabral, "The Mediterranean as a Category of Regional Comparison: A Critical View," *Current Anthropology* 30 (1989): 399–406; David D. Gilmore, ed., *Honor and Shame and the Unity of the Mediterranean* (Washington, DC: American Anthropological Association, 1987); Michael Herzfeld, "The Horns of the Mediterraneanist Dilemma," *American Ethnologist* 11 (1984): 439–54; and Peregrine Horden, and Nicholas Purcell, *The Corrupting Sea: A Study of Mediterranean History* (Malden, MA: Blackwell, 2000).

2. Isaiah Berlin, *The Hedgehog and the Fox: An Essay on Tolstoy's View of History* (New York: Simon and Schuster, 1953).

3. For example, see Michael Dietler, *Archaeologies of Colonialism: Consumption, Entanglement, and Violence in Ancient Mediterranean France* (Berkeley: University of California Press, 2010), 27–53.

4. Archaeologists and anthropologists have devoted too little explicit theoretical attention to the issue of scale, although they have frequently become aware of the problem, especially in the analysis of globalization or "glocalization." Geographers and, to a certain extent, sociologists have pursued the issue in much greater depth: see especially Clark C. Gibson, Elinor Strom, and T. K. Ahn, "The Concept of Scale and the Human Dimensions of Global Change: A Review," *Ecological Economics* 32, no. 2 (2000): 217–39; Sébastien Boulay and Sylvie Fanchette, eds., *La question des échelles en sciences humaines et sociales* (Versailles: Éditions Quæ, 2019); and Michel Grossetti, "L'espace à trois dimensions des phénomènes sociaux: Échelles d'action et d'analyse," *SociologieS, La recherche en actes* (2011), http://journals.openedition.org/sociologies/3466). For some examples of archaeological attempts to deal explicitly with scale, see Gary Lock and Brian L. Molyneaux, eds., *Confronting Scale in Archaeology: Issues of Theory and Practice* (New York: Springer, 2006); and John Robb and Timothy R. Pauketat, eds., *Big Histories, Human Lives* (Santa Fe, NM: SAR Press, 2013). Graduate students at UCLA also organized a conference on this theme at the Cotsen Institute in 2013.

5. Michael Dietler, "Scale and the Archaeology of Colonial Encounters: Reflections from the Western Mediterranean," The Pritchett Lecture, University of California, Berkeley, 2015; and Dietler, *Archaeologies of Colonialism.*

6. I am aware that the metaphor of scale is not without problems, and some scholars (such as actor-network theory [ANT] fans) prefer to think in terms of interlinked, or nested, or flattened networks. Alternative theoretical imaginaries are fine, but we are all still left with the same epistemological problems, however we choose to describe them. Moreover, in terms of the pragmatic methodological aspect I am targeting here, scale seems to me a more persuasive way of envisioning and describing the strategies that guide archaeological fieldwork and data analysis.

7. Astrid Guillaume, "The Intertheoricity: Plasticity, Elasticity and Hybridity of Theories," *Human and Social Studies* 4 (2015): 11–29; and Guillaume,

"Intertheoricity: Plasticity, Elasticity and Hybridity of Theories, Part II: Semiotics of Transferogenesis," *Human and Social Studies* 4 (2015): 59–77. Despite the vocabulary, the articles actually offer some interesting observations. Bruno Latour, "On Recalling ANT," *Sociological Review* 47, no. 1, Supplement (1999): 15–25.

8. Yves Gingras, "Naming without Necessity: On the Genealogy and Uses of the Label 'Historical Epistemology,'" *CIRST: Note de recherche* (2010): 1–17.

9. Rogers Brubaker and Frederick Cooper, "Beyond 'Identity,' " *Theory and Society* 29 (2000): 1–47, at 1.

10. Brubaker and Cooper,"Beyond 'Identity,'" 19.

11. Pierre Bourdieu, "The Three Forms of Theoretical Knowledge," *Social Science Information* 12, no. 1 (1973): 53–80.

12. Bruno Latour, *Reassembling the Social: An Introduction to Actor-Network-Theory* (Oxford: Oxford University Press, 2005); John Law and John Hassard, eds., *Actor Network Theory and After* (Oxford: Blackwell, 1999). Critiques of ANT have been wide ranging and withering: for a sample, see Yves Gingras, "'Please, Don't Let Me Be Misunderstood': The Role of Argumentation in a Sociology of Academic Misunderstandings," *Social Epistemology* 21 (2007): 369–89; Tim Ingold, "When ANT Meets SPIDER: Social Theory for Arthropods," in *Material Agency: Towards a Non-Anthropocentric Approach*, ed. Carl Knappett and Lambros Malafouris (New York: Springer, 2008), 209–15; David Bloor, "Anti-Latour," *Studies in the History and Philosophy of Science* 30, no. 1 (1999): 81–112; H. M. Collins and Steven Yearley, "Epistemological Chicken," in *Science as Practice and Culture*, ed. Andrew Pickering (Chicago: University of Chicago Press, 1992), 301–26; and Michel Dubois, "'Cela nous a échappé . . .': théorie de l'acteur-réseau et le problème des générations scientifiques," *Social Science Information* 56, no. 1 (2017): 107–41.

13. Gingras, "'Please, Don't Let Me Be Misunderstood,'" 385.

14. For my fuller critique of the use of ANT in archaeology, see Michael Dietler, "*Emporia*: Spaces of Encounter and Entanglement," in *The Emporion in the Ancient Western Mediterranean: Trade and Colonial Encounters from the Archaic to the Hellenistic Period*, ed. Eric Gailledrat, Michael Dietler, and Rosa Plana Mallart (Montpellier: Presses Universitaires de la Méditerranée, 2018), 231–42. Although not yet widely popular in Mediterranean archaeology, ANT has attracted some enthusiasts working in the region: for example, see Miguel John Versluys, "Understanding Objects in Motion: An Archaeological Dialogue on Romanization," *Archaeological Dialogues* 21, no. 1 (2014): 1–20; and Astrid Van Oyen, "Actor-Network Theory's Take on Archaeological Types: Becoming, Material Agency and Historical Explanation," *Cambridge Archaeological Journal* 25, no. 1 (2015): 63–78.

15. Karl Marx, *Capital: A Critique of Political Economy*, vol. 1, p. 1, c. 4. (London: Penguin Books, 1990), 163–77.

16. In addition to my critique in Dietler, "*Emporia*," see also Torill C. Lindstrøm, "Agency 'in Itself': A Discussion of Inanimate, Animal and Human Agency," *Archaeological Dialogues* 22, no. 2 (2015): 207–38; Artur Ribeiro, "Against Object Agency: A Counterreaction to Sørensen's 'Hammers and Nails,'" *Archaeological Dialogues* 23, no. 2 (2016): 229–35; and Tim Ingold, "Is There Life amidst the Ruins?," *Journal of Contemporary Archaeology* 1, no. 2 (2014): 29–33. The more extreme offspring of ANT in archaeology, which have become obsessively thing-centric, are often called "symmetrical archaeology": see, for example, the seminal article on this theme by

Bjørnar Olsen, "Material Culture after Text: Re-membering Things," *Norwegian Archaeological Review* 36, no. 2 (2003): 87–104.

17. The Holocaust example was raised in critiques by Ribeiro, "Against Object Agency," 232, and Slavoj Žižek, *Absolute Recoil: Towards a New Foundation of Dialectical Materialism* (London: Verso, 2014), 8. To use a current example, one might also ask: Does ANT help or hinder our understanding of the relationship among power, capitalist exploitation, institutional racism, and police violence in American society? That the increasing militarization of the police, including the use of military weaponry, body armor, armored vehicles, and so forth, has had effects on police behavior is hardly a novel insight for which ANT "actant" language is needed. Moreover, what would seem more important is analysis of the relations of power between people involved in police deployments (class positions, political actors, etc.), the legal and institutional frameworks that authorize and regulate the use of force, the social context of cultural dispositions regarding the exercise of violence, the social and economic frameworks of institutional racism, and so forth. These are precisely the kinds of factors that are obscured by flattening situations into metaphorical networks of "symmetrical" human and material actants.

18. See Gingras, "'Please, Don't Let Me Be Misunderstood,'" 378–81, on "radicality effects."

19. For example, see J. A. Barnes, "Networks and Political Process," in *Local Level Politics*, ed. Marc Swartz (Chicago: Aldine, 1968), 107–30; Barnes, *Social Networks* (Reading, MA: Addison-Wesley, 1972); Jeremy Boissevain, "Network Analysis: A Reappraisal," *Current Anthropology* 20 (1979): 392–94; and Jeremy Boissevain and J. Clyde Mitchell, eds., *Network Analysis: Studies in Human Interaction* (The Hague: Mouton, 1973).

20. Boissevain, "Network Analysis," 392.

21. Boissevain, "Network Analysis," 393.

22. Boissevain, "Network Analysis," 394.

23. For sociology and geography, see, for example, Peter J. Carrington, John Scott, and Stanley Wasserman, eds., *Models and Methods in Social Network Analysis* (Cambridge: Cambridge University Press, 2005); and Anne L. J. Ter Wal and Ron A. Boschma, "Applying Social Network Analysis in Economic Geography: Framing Some Key Analytic Issues," *Annals of Regional Science* 43 (2009): 739–56.

24. For example, nation-states and ethnic groups are not networks. See also Urry's conceptualization of the difference between global networks and "fluids" (the latter would include such things as international terrorism, various social movements, world money, etc.): John Urry, *Global Complexity* (Cambridge: Polity Press, 2003).

25. Yanis Varoufakis, "Being Greek and an Economist While Greece Burns: An Intimate Account of a Peculiar Tragedy," Modern Greek Studies Association keynote speech, November 16, 2013, 1, https://www.yanisvaroufakis.eu/2013/11/16/being-greek-and-an-economist-while-greece-burns-an-intimate-account-mgsa-keynote-2013/.

26. From the song "Anarchy in the UK" by the Sex Pistols.

27. Most prominently for the Mediterranean, see Irad Malkin, "Networks and the Emergence of Greek Identity," *Mediterranean Historical Review* 18, no. 2 (2003): 56–74; and Malkin, *A Small Greek World: Networks in the Ancient Mediterranean*

(Oxford: Oxford University Press, 2011). Among many other examples, see also Carl Knappett, ed., *Network Analysis in Archaeology: New Approaches to Regional Interaction* (Oxford: Oxford University Press, 2013).

28. Nicholas C. Kawa, José A. Clavijo Michelangeli, Jessica L. Clark, Daniel Ginsberg, and Christopher McCarty, "The Social Network of US Academic Anthropology and Its Inequalities," *American Anthropologist* 121 (2018): 14–29.

29. Boissevain, "Network Analysis," 392. Excellent sober assessments of both the promise and limitations of archaeological use of network analysis have been published by Tom Brughmans, "Thinking Through Networks: A Review of Formal Network Methods in Archaeology," *Journal of Archaeological Method and Theory* 20, no. 4 (2013): 623–62; and Anna Collar, Fiona Coward, Tom Brughmans, and Barbara J. Mills, "Networks in Archaeology: Phenomena, Abstraction, Representation," *Journal of Archaeological Method and Theory* 22, no. 1 (2015): 1–32.

30. Frederick Barth, "Introduction," in *Ethnic Groups and Boundaries*, ed. Frederick Barth (Boston: Little, Brown, 1969), 9–38.

31. See Homi K. Bhabha, *The Location of Culture* (London: Routledge, 1994); and Robert J. C. Young, *Colonial Desire: Hybridity in Theory, Culture and Race* (London: Routledge, 1995).

32. See Claude Nicolet, *Space, Geography, and Politics in the Early Roman Empire* (Ann Arbor: University of Michigan Press, 1991); see also J. K. Noyes, *Colonial Space: Spatiality in the Discourse of German South West Africa 1884–1915* (Philadelphia: Harwood Academic Publishers, 1992), on the production of colonial space.

Contributors

MICHAEL DIETLER is Professor of Anthropology at the University of Chicago. His research interests include ancient and modern colonialism, especially in the western Mediterranean, as well as archaeological history and theory.

MARIAN H. FELDMAN is the W. H. Collins Vickers Chair in Archaeology and Professor of History of Art and Near Eastern Studies at the Johns Hopkins University. Her scholarship focuses on the arts of Mesopotamia, the Levant, and the eastern Mediterranean from the end of the third through the first millennia BCE, with an interest in artistic interactions and questions of style, materiality, agency, and practice.

ANN C. GUNTER is Professor in Art History and the Humanities at Northwestern University. Her chief research interests are the artistic and cultural interaction between the Iron Age Aegean and Near East, and the history of its scholarship.

JONATHAN M. HALL is the Phyllis Fay Horton Distinguished Service Professor in the Humanities and Professor of History and Classics at the University of Chicago. His scholarship has focused on ancient ethnicities, historical method and its integration with material culture, and issues of archaeological heritage in modern Greece.

TAMAR HODOS is Reader in Mediterranean Archaeology in the Department of Anthropology and Archaeology at the University of Bristol and an expert on the archaeology of the Mediterranean's Iron Age. Her most recent book is *The Archaeology of the Mediterranean Iron Age* (Cambridge, 2020).

CATHERINE KEARNS is Assistant Professor in Classics and the College at the University of Chicago. Her research focuses on rural settlements and environmental change on Iron Age Cyprus and concepts of place and space in Mediterranean antiquity.

CAROLINA LÓPEZ-RUIZ is Professor of Classics at the Ohio State University. She works on cultural contact in the ancient Mediterranean and on comparative mythology, with special foci on early Greece and the Phoenician world, including the western Mediterranean.

SARAH P. MORRIS is the Steinmetz Professor of Classical Archaeology and Material Culture in the Department of Classics and the Cotsen Institute of Archaeology at the University of California at Los Angeles. Her research interests involve the interaction of early Greece with the Near East in art, literature, religion, and culture, with material specializations in ceramics and architecture from prehistoric through classical Greece.

BRIAN MUHS is Associate Professor of Egyptology at the University of Chicago and Oriental Institute. His major research interests include ancient Egyptian law, economy, society, and intercultural interactions in the first millennium BCE.

JAMES F. OSBORNE is Associate Professor of Anatolian Archaeology at the University of Chicago's Oriental Institute and Department of Near Eastern Languages and Civilizations. His research focus lies in the Bronze and Iron Ages of Anatolia and surrounding regions, and includes thematic interests in spatial analysis and the built environment, monumentality, and territoriality.

JOHN K. PAPADOPOULOS is Professor of Archaeology and Classics at the University of California at Los Angeles. His research and teaching interests include the Aegean, as well as the eastern and central Mediterranean from the Late Bronze and Early Iron Ages into the Classical and later periods, the archaeology of colonization, and the integration of literary evidence with the material record in the study of the past.

SUSAN SHERRATT is Emeritus Professor of East Mediterranean Archaeology in the Department of Archaeology at the University of Sheffield. Her research interests are in the Bronze and Early Iron Ages of the Aegean, Cyprus, and the wider eastern Mediterranean, particularly in all aspects of trade and interaction within and beyond these regions, and in exploring the ways in which the Homeric epics and the archaeological record can most usefully be combined.

Index

Page numbers in italics refer to figures.